JAPAN

Ryukyu Islands

Taipei

TAIWAN

LUZON

LIPPINES

nila

ORO

LEYTE

PANAY

NEGROS

ulu
ea

MINDANAO

D1307791

MAP OF MEMBER
COUNTRIES OF ASEAN

N

PACIFIC

OCEAN

Celebes
Sea

Molucca Sea

HALMAHERA

AWESI

BURU

SERAM

Banda
Sea

AMBON

PAPUA

PAPUA
NEW
GUINEA

FLORES

Dili

TIMOR LESTE

Arafura
Sea

AUSTRALIA

SOUTHEAST ASIAN AFFAIRS 2015

Introduction

Daljit Singh and Veena Nair

Southeast Asia in 2014 presented a very mixed picture. The economies on the whole were more sluggish; political uncertainty in two key countries, Thailand and Malaysia, was higher; Islamic conservatism appeared to on the rise in Malaysia and Brunei; the Islamic State of Iraq and Syria (ISIS) was a growing security concern, especially in Indonesia and Malaysia; geopolitical trends, particularly China's quest for leadership, were causing unease; and questions were raised about whether ASEAN would be able to rise up to the challenges it faced. On the other hand, more engagement with major powers also presented economic opportunities, foreign direct investment in Southeast Asia was increasing, Indonesia saw a successful transfer of power in democratic elections to a reformist President, and Myanmar continued on the path of reform and democratization, even though the rise of Buddhist nationalism and its implications for community relations was a matter of concern.

This Introduction highlights some of the salient themes in this volume.

Economic Trends

At an estimated aggregate growth rate of 4.6 per cent, Southeast Asia's economic performance was below the 5 per cent average of 2013, marking the second consecutive year of slowdown since 2012, though Malaysia and Myanmar had higher growth than in 2013. The sluggish recoveries in the advanced industrial countries, the slowdown in China and declines in growth of domestic consumption and investment contributed to the more anaemic growth. Arief Ramayandi and Megananda Suryana, in their economic survey of the region in

DALJIT SINGH is a Senior Research Fellow at the Institute of Southeast Asian Studies (ISEAS), Singapore.

VEENA NAIR is a Research Associate at the Institute of Southeast Asian Studies (ISEAS), Singapore.

this volume, argue that since these factors will not improve anytime soon, the short-term growth prospects for the Southeast Asian economies were not rosy. They also point to the risks of financial market volatilities when the U.S. Federal Reserve raises interest rates later in 2015 as asset prices in some of the large economies were inflated.

On the other hand, lower commodity prices were on balance positive for Southeast Asian economies and inward foreign direct investment (FDI) to the five largest regional economies had been increasing steadily. But to ensure that this trend continued, Southeast Asian countries needed to maintain their level of economic competitiveness. Ramayandi and Suryana note that while in China rising wages were accompanied by healthy growth in labour productivity, in three major Southeast Asian countries — Indonesia, Malaysia and Thailand — wages have been outstripping productivity, thereby reducing labour productivity substantially. They stress the necessity of continued investment in human capital and, over the longer term, a reorientation from the export-led model of growth to more reliance on domestic demand.

The Major Powers and Southeast Asia

See Seng Tan and Oleg Korovin observe in the opening chapter of this volume that judging by the high profile initiatives it undertook, 2014 was the year of China. President Xi Jinping floated his New Asian Security Concept at the summit of the Conference on Interactions and Cooperation (CICA) in Shanghai. It portrays cooperative Asian development as the core security mantra and calls for Asians to manage Asian security, meaning without the involvement of the United States. China signed an agreement to set up the China-led Asian Infrastructure Investment Bank (AIIB). It vigorously promoted its "one belt and one road" initiative, the Eurasian Silk Road and the Maritime Silk Road. All involve Southeast Asia, with the latter being announced in 2013 during President Xi's high profile visit to Indonesia. In November, China hosted an APEC summit with much fanfare, at which President Xi proposed another mega-project, the Free Trade Area of the Asia-Pacific.

On the other hand, while these developments possibly made more media headlines, other aspects of China's international and regional relations did not go unnoticed. In Southeast Asia, these centred on the South China Sea where China was carrying out massive reclamation projects. The deployment in May of a Chinese oil rig in waters disputed with Vietnam drew much international attention and criticism and damaged relations with Vietnam. There was no concession, even clarification, of the nine-dash line which encompasses much of the South China Sea. Meanwhile China's double digit increases in defence expenditure continued in 2014 and its navy continued to expand its capabilities.

David Arase, in his chapter on "China's Two Silk Roads Initiative: What It Means for Southeast Asia", argues that the Initiative is designed to promote China's great power status and bring the countries around China into its economic and geopolitical orbit. If successfully established, it would be a form of regional cooperation in which each country would have an asymmetrical economic and political bilateral relationship with China characterized by dependence on China and no recourse to international arbitration in the event of a dispute with China. Arase argues that while China faces many serious obstacles and uncertainties, "it is quickly advancing this agenda both across the (Eurasian) heartland and around the margins of the Eurasian land mass … the impact of its Eurasian strategy could be lasting, and is today certainly changing the existing Eurasian order."

The U.S. actions in the Asia-Pacific in 2014 were comparatively low profile. It was quietly strengthening its alliances and pushing for a successful conclusion of the high quality Trans-Pacific Partnership (TPP) trade deal. The latter, an important part of the U.S. pivot to Asia, remained an unfinished business at the end of the year. Meanwhile U.S. attention was increasingly focused on the various crises in the Middle East and on Ukraine. This, together with sharp cuts, even if sequestration was avoided, in the defence budget and an inward-looking mood in the country, reinforced some perceptions in the region of relative U.S. decline. While few doubted U.S. commitment to South Korea and Japan, many wondered to what extent the U.S. would be prepared to stand up to China in Southeast Asia to maintain a balance of power in this subregion.

Yet, China's rising power and its mega-initiatives were not creating any discernible bandwagoning effect though membership in the AIIB has expanded. Beijing had yet to win any loyal follower in the Indo-Pacific region, except Pakistan. Some countries are U.S. allies or security partners, while several others were hedging their bets by having closer security ties with the U.S. or with America's two most significant allies, Japan and Australia, even as they continue to have expanding economic relations with China. In much of Southeast Asia, suspicions of China still ran deep, especially over its actions and posture in the South China Sea. China's FDI flows into the region especially to the five major Southeast Asian countries were still far behind those of the U.S. and Japan.

The U.S. and its allies Japan and Australia, on their part, were expanding their own network of economic, political and security ties with Southeast Asian countries. Japan and Australia would be contributing more to share the military burden that the U.S. bears in preserving the Asia-Pacific security order. A major development of 2014 was the re-interpretation by the administration of Prime Minister Abe of Article 9 of Japan's 1947 constitution to enable the country to take part in collective security with the U.S. and with others important to the security of Japan. Japan was also moving to strengthen its armed forces and was proactive in enhancing security ties with key Southeast Asian states, at this stage mainly for capacity building. Likewise Australia, the southern anchor of the U.S. alliance system in the western Pacific, is providing more access and base facilities to U.S. forces, while significantly enhancing defence cooperation with Japan. Japan's air force and ground troops will soon be exercising with Australian and American counterparts on the ground and in the skies of Australia.

Further, India, under the Modi Government, has indicated more strategic interest in East and Southeast Asia under its new "Act East" policy. Although it is not expected to be a major strategic factor in Southeast Asia for some time to come, India's economic and security links with the region will continue to expand. And it too will be bolstering its security ties with America's two staunchest allies in the Western Pacific, Japan and Australia.

ASEAN in the Midst of Strategic Change

See Seng Tan and Oleg Korovin argue that Southeast Asia and ASEAN are trying to adjust and adapt to the "new normal" of a changing strategic environment in the broader Asia-Pacific characterized by keener big power competition and possibly increased pressures on ASEAN. ASEAN seemed slow in responding to the new strategic dynamics. At a time when its unity and cohesiveness were more needed than perhaps ever before, its pace of change appeared relatively glacial. Its Economic Community, due to be established at the end of 2015, would be incomplete because political leaders lack the political will to address thorny issues like non-tariff barriers to trade and impediments to investments. The organization is hobbled in dealing effectively with major power pressures because of different national interests and preoccupation with domestic problems.

Yet, without ASEAN, Southeast Asia would be much worse off in terms of its capacity to deal with major power pressures. The grouping is likely to face testy times in the next few years because China may strongly assert its interests in Southeast Asia before a new U.S. Administration takes over in Washington in 2017. Beijing feels entitled to paramount influence for reasons of history, geography and power. It is left to be seen how ASEAN's traditional strategy, which See Seng Tan and Oleg Korovin aptly describe as "strategic hedging, institutional engagement through the ASEAN-based regional architecture and maintaining a balance of major powers in the region" will fare under new pressures.

Domestic Political Stability and Change

Thailand and Malaysia

There was more uncertainty in the domestic politics of two major countries, Thailand and Malaysia, than has been the case for some time.

In Thailand the elected government of Prime Minister Yingluck Shinawatra was ousted by a military coup. It was not clear how long the military-installed government would stay in power or even what its longer term intentions were, though some analysts believed that the coup leaders would want to be in charge during the delicate transition period to the installation of a new monarch after King Bhumibol, eighty-seven, passes away, whenever that occurs. All supporters of the coup agreed though they wanted to ensure that no future government is led by a pro-Thaksin leader or political party (something that the 2006 coup had failed to achieve). They were planning to do this through new constitutional arrangements with more checks and balances to prevent abuse of power by top office holders.

Duncan McCargo, in his review chapter on Thailand, argues that the Thai traditional elite and its supporters are "structurally outnumbered" in a country where the rural masses have been politically awakened — as demonstrated by the fact that Thaksin or pro-Thaksin parties had won every election since 2001. Hence the goals of the military leaders would be difficult to achieve and efforts to do so are likely to cause significant instability. McCargo points to the possibility of an even darker scenario: that the military harbours a deep distrust of all elected politicians, whether pro-Thaksin or not, and wants to "depoliticize" the country.

A different perspective is offered by Suchit Bunbongkarn in his chapter "What Went Wrong with Thai Democracy?" His message is this: democratic consolidation takes a long time and it has not happened in Thailand yet for historical, cultural and other reasons. The experience of recent years has shown that the leaders of a democratically elected government too can abuse power in the absence of the sorts of checks and balances that exist in mature democracies, not just formal but also informal like an educated, informed and discerning public. Further, he argues, it was time to end the instability of the past decade and chart a new course. Suchit is aware of the risks but sees no other viable alternative. He does not think that the Yingluck government enjoyed legitimacy simply because it had won elections. To him, the fact that Yingluck incurred the wrath of a large and important part of the Thai electorate, the middle class, even if not its numerical majority, by seeking amnesty for Thaksin; and the fact that she could not maintain law and order in the months leading up to the coup, gravely compromised her legitimacy. Suchit advocates reforms, not just to the political system but also for "the strengthening of the people's sector and civil society", and hopes that the reforms undertaken would ensure that a more stable, effective and democratic government emerges in the not too distant future. But he thinks this is a "very formidable task ... which cannot be completed easily within a few years."

Malaysia seemed to be moving towards more fractured and more racialized politics — and a weakened Prime Minster.

In his review of Malaysia, Faisal S. Hazis argues that the Barisan National (BN) government's continued insecurity over its ability to hold on to power after the losses in the 2013 general election has led to an increase in racial politics and authoritarianism. Pressures from right-wing Malay groups linked to the main component party of the BN, the Malay-based United Malay National Organisation (UMNO), forced Prime Minister Najib Razak to backtrack on his relatively liberal and inclusive agenda before the 2013 general election. Inflammatory racial and religious rhetoric by Malay right wing groups continued in 2014. Meanwhile moves in the Islamic party, Parti Islam SeMalaysia (PAS), to introduce *hudud* laws in the state of Kelantan, where the party has a large majority in the State Assembly, received encouragement from some officials in UMNO as a tactic to break up the opposition PR coalition before the next general election — given the fact that the mainly Chinese-based Democratic Action Party will not accept the implementation of *hudud* by its PR coalition partner. These developments were causing anxiety, especially among non-Muslims in peninsular Malaysia and strengthening centrifugal tendencies in the East Malaysian states of Sabah and Sarawak where non-Muslims, especially Christians, who constitute a significant part of the population, feel these trends violate the letter and spirit of the agreement in 1963 on the basis of which they joined Malaysia.

While there was no immediate threat to Najib's premiership, his position had weakened since the 2013 elections and could be further undermined, depending on how the scandal involving government investment agency 1 Malaysia Development Berhad (IMDB) develops.

Indonesia

In Indonesia, the largest and most populous country of Southeast Asia, the change of political leadership through keenly contested but peaceful elections was certainly a big plus for the young democracy. Yet the strong support for the losing presidential candidate Prabowo Subianto also revealed that there is still substantial constituency for rolling back democratic reforms in favour of a "strong" central government. The uncertainties confronting Indonesia were of a different kind from those in Thailand and Malaysia as they revolved more around the kind of policies newly-elected President Joko Widodo, a leader of a different mould from the old elite from which Indonesian leaders had traditionally been drawn, would adopt and how effective he would be in implementing his reform agenda. The President was hobbled by a lack of majority of his Indonesian Democratic Party-Struggle (PDI-P) in parliament and pressures to make compromises with established elites, especially from the PDI-P and its leader former President Megawati Sukarnoputri, including over the appointment of ministers. However, as Marcus Mietzner notes in his Indonesia review chapter, unlike his predecessor, he did not shy away from conflict with Parliament and made bold decisions to fulfil his campaign promises on health, education and welfare issues.

Mietzner argues that the divisive 2014 elections would return Indonesia to its more "normal" state of politics in which the country's long standing tensions, between democracy and authoritarianism, Islam and Pancasila, would be played out more openly again after being bottled up under Susilo Bambang Yudhoyono's policies of inclusiveness and stability above all else.

In foreign policy, the initial indications were of a learning process at work, but clearly, as Mietzner notes, there is departure from Yudhoyono's consensus seeking approach to maintain calm to a more self-interested and nationalistic stance which was manifest on issues like foreign vessels fishing in Indonesian waters and Indonesian women employed as domestic workers in other countries. It was not clear if ASEAN would be accorded the same importance as before. Rizal Sukman, a foreign policy advisor of the President, said it would remain one of the key pillars of Indonesia's foreign policy, but not the only one, suggesting that Indonesia would be more likely to act outside the perceived constraints of ASEAN, if its national interests required it to do so.

Myanmar

In Myanmar, there was much domestic and international criticism of alleged backsliding in democratization and the reform process, including by democracy icon

Aung San Suu Kyi. However, as Morten Pederson demonstrates in his Myanmar review chapter, much of the criticism was ill-founded. For a country that had just emerged from half a century of authoritarian rule and internal conflicts, there were bound to be difficulties on the road to democratization. As the International Crisis Group said, "Bad news stories about Myanmar's transition are easy to find. But the good news stories reflect the broader trend." President Obama endorsed the progress, saying, "Myanmar's democratization process is real." Parliament performed well, the press remained vibrant, and there was growing civil space. While the military was unlikely to accept any constitutional amendment that diminishes its role, at least for the present, existing democratic institutions had continued to perform robustly, according to Pederson, "and the prospects for a freely elected government emerging in 2015 looked good."

However, the critically important peace talks with the two dozen or so ethnic minority groups that have fought the government on and off for nearly three quarters of a century, did not bear fruit by the end of the year despite the government's keenness to achieve a breakthrough. Pederson warns that unless an agreement can be reached early in 2015, the risk of more armed clashes and ethnic communities being denied participation in the coming elections would darken the future prospects for peace. In her chapter on the conflict in the Kachin State, Mandy Sadan provides illuminating insights into why it has been so difficult to reach an agreement with one particular ethnic group, the Kachins.

A particularly troubling feature of the Myanmar situation was the conflict between the country's Buddhist and Muslim communities, although there were no major outbreaks of communal violence in 2014. The situation in the Rakhine State remained tense and dangerous. Elsewhere in the country, "2014 will be remembered as the year when extremist Buddhist nationalism became a mainstream political force with potentially major negative implications for future community relations", Pederson contends. The authorities remained reluctant to take action against senior monks some of whom openly engaged in anti-Muslim "hate speech" which is forbidden by the country's new laws. The government (and Aung San Suu Kyi) regards the domestic political costs of ruffling Buddhist nationalist sensitivities as far greater than the costs of ignoring the rights of small Muslim minorities.

The Rest of Southeast Asia

The other countries of Southeast Asia saw no major political change in 2014 and were grappling with the familiar issues of economic growth and governance and in the case of Vietnam and the Philippines, also the South China Sea disputes.

After the shock election results of 2013 which saw the Cambodian People's Party (CPP) drop significantly in voter support after twenty years of virtually unchallenged rule, Prime Minister Hun Sen's government faced strong political pressures to be more accountable to the people. An important preoccupation of the government was to recover some of the lost popular support.

In the Philippines, the economy continued to look up with growth well above the Southeast Asian average for the year as reforms were being implemented and prospects for foreign direct investment looked healthy. In the arena of politics it was by and large more of the same. One troubling feature of the year was the slow progress in turning the Comprehensive Agreement on the Bangsamoro which was concluded with the Moro Islamic Liberation Front on 27 March into a draft law and having it passed and ratified. The delays allowed vested interests more scope to find fault with the agreement with the result that by the end of the year the initial high expectations gave way to concerns.

In Singapore, an important focus of the government was to address issues which had caused a decline in the votes for the ruling People's Action Party in the 2013 elections, including health care, housing and transport, and to better address the needs of the poor and the aged.

Timor Leste was relatively stable as it sought to build the institutions and the human resources to stand on its own feet after the withdrawal of UN peacekeepers and the Australian-led International Stabilisation Force in late 2012. Prime Minister Xanana Gusmão indicated that he would step down to pave the way for a new generation leader, but no leadership change took place in 2014.

In Vietnam, economic growth (estimated at 5.5 per cent) remained below its performance in the previous decade and the needed reforms were slow to materialize. Foreign direct investment continued to flow in but skills development was lacking and this could constrain future investments. In the political sphere, the Vietnam Communist Party was preparing for the next Party Congress due in early 2016. The most dramatic event of the year was the crisis in relations with China over the deployment of a giant Chinese oil rig in waters disputed with Vietnam.

Political Islam and the Trend Towards Islamic Conservatism

Islamic conservatism was gaining ground in Malaysia and Brunei, two of the three Muslim majority states in Southeast Asia. In Malaysia this has been noticeable since the 1980s, partly because of influences from the Middle East, including from Malaysian students returning from Islamic and other studies there, and partly because of the expansion of the Islamic bureaucracy at the state and federal levels from the Mahathir era to demonstrate that UMNO was no less than PAS in Islamic probity. The electoral setbacks of the BN in 2008 and 2013 made significant sections of the Malay community more insecure, resulting in more racialized politics, a turn to religion, and growing intolerance of other faiths.

Ahmad Fauzi Abdul Hamid in his chapter on "The *Hudud* Controversy in Malaysia: Religious Probity or Political Expediency?" sees the support by some UMNO officials to PAS implementing *hudud* laws in Kelantan as part of an UMNO design to win the crucially important next general election by capturing some of the rural Malay support from PAS and by splitting the opposition PR coalition, as discussed earlier. *Hudud* has become a political tool in the hands of UMNO and PAS, according to Fauzi, who does not think that in the final analysis UMNO will allow PAS to establish *hudud* in Kelantan.

Still, the controversies around *hudud* were disquieting to many. Islamic conservatism in Malaysia in recent years has been caused in significant measure by this competition between UMNO and PAS, each seeking to project itself as more pious than the other. In view of the hundreds, even thousands of *ulama* (religious teachers) trained in the Middle East in puritanical strands of Islam by the government, many in the Islamic bureaucracy of the BN government today may not be much different in their religious ideology from conservative elements in PAS who seek to impose *hudud* laws. This obviously has negative implications for Malaysia's multi-religious and multi-ethnic society and for the international image the government has been cultivating of Malaysia as a model of moderate Islam. It may also be providing more fertile ground for ISIS recruitment.

The conservatives in Malaysia no doubt also found encouragement from the new legislation on the Syariah Penal Code passed in Brunei in October 2013 which among other things prescribes punishments for criminal offences or *hudud* that include theft, sexual offences, apostasy and acting against Islamic beliefs. It came into force on 1 May 2014. Pushpa Thambipillai in her review chapter on Brunei says that implementation would be in stages. A greater part of 2014 was spent by the Sultan and religious experts explaining the new Syariah law. It was not yet clear to what extent the new elements would apply to non-Muslims, though it has been pointed out that non-Muslims can be punished under the system if they are party to an offence by a Muslim.

In Indonesia, as Ulla Fionna and Gwenael Njoto-Feillard show, the Islamic parties did slightly better in the 2014 legislative elections in terms of percentage of the popular vote they garnered than they did in in the previous elections, thereby arresting their downward trajectory, but "the appeal of 'Islamism' as an all-encompassing political solution to societal problems is declining. ... The relatively good results of these parties illustrates not so much the hold of an Islamic ideal in the electorate but rather the consolidation of their traditional patronage and clientelistic networks", say Ulla and Gwenael. In any case the ideologies and social bases of the Islamic parties are very different and they cannot be viewed as a monolithic whole.

President Widodo is heading a secular nationalist coalition, and according to Marcus Mietzner, a number of factors are likely to make the secular–Islamic divide in Indonesia's politics, papered over by former President Yudhoyono's accommodationist policies, sharper during Widodo's term of office. These include the appointment of secular nationalist and liberal figures to key positions in the Cabinet, and the fact that for the first time since 2001 the PKS (Partai Keadilan Sejahtera) is now outside the government and therefore free to push more strongly for Islamic interests.

Religious Extremism and Terrorism

Sidney Jones and Solahudin note a sharp decline in terrorist incidents in Indonesia in 2014. There had not been a successful bombing in five years and the three attempts at suicide bombings had killed only the would-be bombers. This was due to a number of factors, among them the decision by some extremist groups, including the Jemaah Islamiyah (JI), to refrain from violent attacks in Indonesia; weak capacity; and the diversion of interest to the Islamic State of Iraq and Syria (ISIS). But Jones and Solahudin caution that the lull could be temporary as extremist groups in the country cooperate, compete, divide, reunite, and change strategy and tactics. There were indications towards the end of the year that the JI, which Jones and Solahudin describe as having "the most resilient membership and the best capacity for thinking long term", was undertaking a systematic rebuilding in Indonesia, with emphasis on recruiting professionals from universities.

However, the more immediate concern of the authorities was the impact on Indonesian security of the Islamic State of Iraq and Syria (ISIS). By the end of 2014, at least 100 Indonesians were believed to have left for Syria, most to fight for ISIS, a smaller number for Al Nusra Front, the Al Qaeda affiliate fighting the Syrian government. For a variety of reasons ISIS held the greater fascination for extremist groups and some ordinary Indonesians, though JI was allied with the al-Nusra Front. The extremists groups that had sworn allegiance to ISIS were active in promoting the ISIS cause and engaging in recruitment for ISIS. They were also prepared to use violence against the Indonesian state. The worry was that Indonesians fighting with ISIS would eventually return to Indonesia battle-hardened and with weapons skills to give a boost to local extremists opposed to the Indonesian government. Further, Indonesians and Malaysians who had fought together in Syria could retain their bonds on return to their home countries and try to form a new transborder *jihadi* organization. On 4 August 2014, the government declared ISIS a banned organization. It is a problem that will not go away any time soon and may get worse.

Disaster Management

Southeast Asia is known to be prone to natural disasters like earthquakes, volcanic eruptions, typhoons or cyclones, and flooding. The massive 2004 Boxing Day earthquake and the resultant tsunami claimed hundreds of thousands of lives. The 2013 super-typhoon Haiyan, called Yolanda in the Philippines, which hit that island nation in November 2013 caused an estimated 6,300 deaths, over a thousand people missing, and about 7.5 million people displaced. In 2014, people in the affected areas, especially Tacloban city, which was the most severely hit, were still struggling to recover.

Lorraine Carlos Salazar, in her chapter on "Typhoon Yolanda: The Politics of Disaster Response and Management", describes the response to the typhoon as fraught with mismanagement and political tension. She highlights the issues and bottlenecks, both administrative and political, at national and local level, that blighted delivery of aid and start of reconstruction, especially in Tacloban City, whose mayor is from the same clan as Imelda Marcos and viewed as an archenemy by the Aquinos and the Roxases. Salazar underlines the importance of advance preparation and timely mitigation efforts in disaster management.

In an effort to be better prepared for natural disasters, the ASEAN Coordinating Centre for Humanitarian Assistance on disaster management (AHA Centre) deployed an Emergency Rapid Assessment Team (ERAT) to the Philippines ahead of Typhoon Hagupit in early December. Still, many worry whether the region has successfully digested the lessons from Typhoon Yolanda. Although some ASEAN states furnished crisis relief in response to Yolanda, they did so on their own national accord. The conspicuous lack of an ASEAN-led response revealed the dearth of collective capability or will, notwithstanding the availability of the AHA Centre and protocols like the ASEAN Agreement on Disaster Management and Emergency Response (AADMER), as well as the participation by the respective militaries of ASEAN members in joint humanitarian assistance and disaster relief (HADR) exercises.

Meanwhile, in April 2014, Singapore announced the setting up of a Regional Humanitarian and Disaster Relief (HADR) coordination centre to be based at the Changi Command and Control Centre. The offer by Singapore was first made during an ASEAN–U.S. Defence Ministers' informal meeting. The hope is that the new centre will allow for a coordinated regional military response to natural disasters.

Conclusion

During 2014 many Southeast Asian states faced serious domestic trials as well as more demanding major power attention. These domestic challenges combined with growing strategic tensions and an expanding ASEAN agenda stretched all states and ASEAN.

Acknowledgements

Several people made important contributions at some stage or other of the long preparation and production process of this volume.

Standing out among them was Research Associate Ms Veena Nair who helped the editor to manage the entire process from beginning to end, including compiling a list of potential contributors to this volume; handling correspondence with them; making valuable inputs to the editing process through two rounds of meticulous editing of the chapters; doing the proof-reading; and participating in the writing of the Introduction.

Thanks also go to our secretary Betty Tan and production editor Sheryl Sin for their efforts, and those research colleagues whose views the editor sought on some matter or other which they provided generously. They include Malcolm Cook, Mustafa Izzuddin, and Ulla Fionna. Finally a word of thanks too for ISEAS Director Ambassador Tan Chin Tiong, Deputy Director Ooi Kee Beng, and Head of ISEAS Publishing Mr Ng Kok Kiong for their support.

The Region

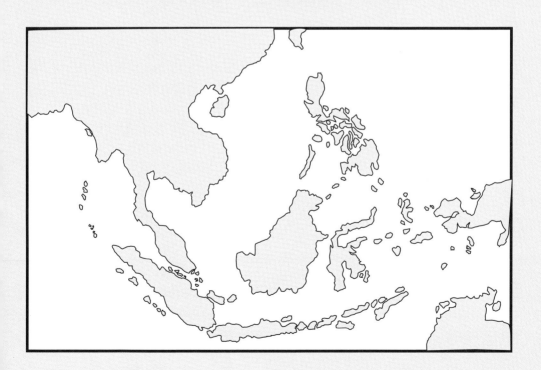

SEEKING STABILITY IN TURBULENT TIMES
Southeast Asia's New Normal?

See Seng Tan and Oleg Korovin

Political and security developments in Southeast Asia in 2014 reflect efforts on the part of Southeast Asian countries as well as ASEAN (the Association of Southeast Asian Nations) to adjust and adapt to the conditions and circumstances of a "new normal" in the wider Asia-Pacific region: a rapidly changing regional strategic environment where emerging powers display greater assertiveness and assurance of their newfound status, whilst established powers experience relative decline and seek to rebalance against the growing power and influence of their rivals. China's rising power and influence appears to have grown from strength to strength, notwithstanding putative efforts by the United States, Japan and others to balance against it partly through rallying Southeast Asian partners in support of their cause. Adding to the growing prospect of regional instability and turbulence was Russia's annexation of Crimea in March, which raised fears among some Southeast Asians over the prospective emulation of Russia's action by more powerful claimant states over the South China Sea region.

At the same time within Southeast Asia, a number of states and societies underwent political transition. Indonesia conducted a successful presidential election in July which saw a popular non-establishment figure, the then Jakarta Governor Joko Widodo (or "Jokowi"), win the presidency. It remains unclear at

SEE SENG TAN is Associate Professor and Deputy Director of the Institute of Defence and Strategic Studies at the S. Rajaratnam School of International Studies (RSIS), Nanyang Technological University, Singapore.

OLEG KOROVIN is an independent scholar whose research focuses on the international relations of the Asia Pacific and Russia's foreign policy.

this point what Jokowi's foreign policy will look like. However, there are early hints that Indonesia might not be as fixated with ASEAN as in the past. Going beyond the "Indo-Pacific" idea advanced by the Yudhoyono administration, the Jokowi administration's vision for Indonesia is as a global maritime fulcrum connecting the Indian and Pacific Oceans.[1] Known as "PACINDO", the area of engagement envisioned here is ostensibly geographically more extensive than the Indo-Pacific region the Yudhoyono administration had in mind. To that end, India and the Gulf states have been identified as countries with whom Jokowi would engage more deeply. As a foreign policy adviser to Jokowi has declared: "We used to say ASEAN is *the* cornerstone of our foreign policy. Now we change it to *a* cornerstone of our foreign policy."[2]

After considerable unrest in Thailand caused by the rift between the so-called "Red Shirts" and their "Yellow" rivals, senior officers of the Thai military launched a bloodless coup in May which brought temporary relief but left many questions unanswered. The coup appeared to sour relations between the new military regime and the Thai royalists that supported the coup, on one hand, and the United States on the other. With this downturn in Thai-U.S. relations and its potential ramifications for their security alliance — including the U.S. decision to scale back the Cobra Gold 2015 military exercise — there is growing concern over whether Thailand may seek to deepen further its already substantial ties with China — a step likely to worry Thailand's ASEAN neighbours given their apprehensions over China's actions in the South China Sea.[3] On the other hand, Washington would presumably repair its ties with Bangkok so as not to push the latter into Beijing's embrace.[4]

To be sure, post-colonial Southeast Asia is no stranger to turbulence, not least for a region born out of the Pacific War and forged in the furnace of great power collapse, war and political upheaval.[5] That said, the current regional situation is unprecedented in that at no time in the region's annals has there ever been the concomitant (albeit uneven) rise of three regional powers, China, Japan and India, and the complications that has posed to the post-World War Two hegemony long enjoyed by a United States. Of these, India remained the odd man out in 2014 in terms of involvement, although Indian Prime Minister Narendra Modi took advantage of the East Asia Summit (EAS) in November to signal his intent to recast India's decades-long "Look East" policy, defined mostly by missed opportunities, to an "Act East" policy under his premiership.[6] The growing strategic competition and alignments among the great powers have engendered uncertainty among Southeast Asian states, whose dedicated project of regional community formation has been confounded by the temptation to break ranks and undermine ASEAN cohesion through unilaterally siding with a particular great power so as to advance their own interests.

At least three noteworthy trends defined Southeast Asia's new normal in 2014. Firstly, China was the outstanding performer among the big powers in the regional diplomatic and economic stakes. A generation removed from the "keeping a low profile" approach that had dominated Chinese foreign policy since the time of Deng Xiaoping, the People's Republic appeared sufficiently self-assured to assert itself on the regional and global stages. Secondly, notwithstanding the presence of multiple players in the South China Sea, China remained the key without which there would be no progress in the maritime disputes among the claimant states. Finally, Southeast Asia and ASEAN continued to labour, frustratingly so in the light of a self-imposed 2015 deadline, for the formation of the ASEAN Community that is unlikely to be achieved in terms of depth of regional cooperation and integration that would satisfy the collective needs of the region.

The Great Game in 2014

The region has been marked by the growing rivalry between emerging and established powers, whose complex interactions threaten to muddy the distinction between what constitutes revisionist actions and what constitutes status quo. For a long time and as a consequence of its role as a strategic guarantor, the United States has occupied a privileged place in the security calculi of East Asian countries in general. The rise of China, the focus of considerable analysis among Asia watchers throughout the post-Cold War period, has often been discussed in terms of its "potential" to rival the United States — an as yet unrealized prospect further deferred by the relative alignment of interests between Beijing and Washington over the global war on terrorism. Two major dynamics are now changing that. The first involves the perceived relative decline of the United States, whose post-Afghanistan strategic "pivot" or "rebalance" to Asia — seen by many Chinese as a containment effort directed against China, even though U.S. officials have strenuously denied that — appeared to be a half-hearted proposition following the global financial crisis of 2007–08 and severe cuts to the U.S. defence budget. The second involves the considerably more recent development of Russia's annexation of Crimea and its ongoing support of the armed rebellion in eastern Ukraine. The chief beneficiary of both these trends, at least in 2014, has arguably been China.

America's Rebalance on Track?

It has been argued that East Asia's security order is undergoing transition from the Cold War-era great power bargains, namely the U.S.-Japan alliance, which made Japan dependent on America for its security and indirectly assured China its security through the restraining impact of the alliance on Japan's strategic ambitions and, the 1972 U.S.-China rapprochement, which paved the way to a tacit coalition against Soviet influence. However, the transition is as yet unformed or at best incomplete great power bargains.[7] The post-Cold War rise of China and the ongoing military "normalization" of Japan — the expectation for a more active and enhanced military role for Japan within the context of its alliance with the United States[8] — led to the dissolution of the older great power bargains. While it could conceivably be argued that the broad-based legitimacy enjoyed by the United States as the region's strategic guarantor constituted a bargain of sorts, its hegemony was at best incomplete given the potential challenge to its leadership posed by China. As the former head of Council for Security Cooperation in the Asia-Pacific (CSCAP) China, Ambassador Shi Chun-Lai, once declared at a CSCAP meeting, China does not accept America's preponderance in the region as much as it "tolerates" it for the time being.[9]

Against this backdrop, America's pivot or rebalance towards Asia, formally announced by President Barack Obama before the Australian Parliament in late 2011,[10] has elicited as many questions from, as it has furnished answers to, security allies and partners who wonder aloud whether their American friends have the stomach to see their commitment to Asia through in the face of serious fiscal constraints, political uncertainties and diplomatic distractions dogging the United States. In April, Obama undertook a four-nation visit to the region reassuring that the pivot "is real", while his then Defence Secretary — Chuck Hagel, who resigned in late November reportedly because the White House felt he was not the right man to handle shifting priorities like the rise of the Islamic State-led insurgency in Iraq and Syria and the Ebola pandemic in Africa[11] — argued that America "is a Pacific Power for many years. We've looked forward to a continuation of building those relationships and those partnerships [in the region] as we go forward".[12]

Obama's attendance at the Asia-Pacific Economic Cooperation (APEC) summit and the East Asia Summit (EAS) constituted a success in themselves, given his no-shows at both summits in 2013. On the sidelines of APEC 2014, a landmark climate change agreement with China that specifies a timetable for emission reduction was announced. However, Obama's international reputation appeared diminished among the Chinese; for example, a conservative Chinese periodical dismissed the U.S. president's leadership as "insipid" — a far cry from 2009 during Obama's first presidential visit to China where he reportedly dazzled a student audience at a town hall-style meeting in Shanghai.[13]

Russia Leans towards China

On the other hand, Ukraine, where a new pro-Western government came to power after a coup in February 2014, has become the locus of the trans-Atlantic stand-off. Sanctions and diplomatic pressure by the European Union (EU) and the United States have effectively forced Russia to gravitate towards China. Presumably, the Chinese are not particularly enthused by Russia's annexation of Crimea but, at the same time, they worry over the implications the February ouster of Ukrainian President Victor Yanukovich could have had on the region.[14] Moscow has concluded deals, unprecedented in scale, with Beijing to supply China with Russian oil and gas through projects totalling US$400 billion, and has opened the Russian market for Chinese strategic investments.[15] The original plan for Russia was to have two geopolitical support pillars on both ends of the Eurasian continent: China in the East, and Germany in the West. But with the scrapping of its EU-bound South Stream gas pipeline project, it appears Russia's ties with the EU — more specifically with Germany — are now in disrepair.[16] Although the Kremlin has undertaken steps to regroup *vis-à-vis* the EU, its heavy dependence on China is now undeniable, providing Beijing a putative strategic advantage against Washington.

Fairly or otherwise, some Southeast Asians view the Crimean annexation with concern in that it might embolden China to adopt a similarly aggressive approach towards its territorial claims in the South China Sea[17] — a view shared by some Americans.[18] However, on the whole, Southeast Asians are ambivalent over what the Ukraine question might mean for their region. Against those who worry over the prospect of enhanced Chinese assertiveness, there are others who believe U.S. inaction in fact indirectly mollifies China towards self-restraint over Ukraine. Whichever case, the perception cultivated has been that of a United States incapable and/or unwilling to do anything to prevent the belligerence of others despite being the world's sole global power. Arguably, America's troubled pivot and Russia's act of aggression and resulting isolation by the West has been to China's benefit.

China Gains

In many ways, 2014 marked China's emergence as an active and assertive global power. Nowhere has this been more apparent than in Chinese achievements garnered at international meetings, both those chaired by China and those in which it participated. At the APEC Summit in Beijing in November, China demonstrated economic leadership in calling for the creation of a Free Trade Area of the Asia-Pacific (FTAAP) and its "one belt, one road" plan — to which the Chinese have committed a Silk Road fund worth US$40 billion for infrastructure-related investments in addition to its Asian Infrastructure Investment Bank (AIIB) proposal that twenty-one countries have already joined.[19] Beijing's successful conclusion of free trade pacts with Australia and South Korea has only added to China's standing. China will reportedly invest US$1.25 trillion abroad over the next ten years, and import more than US$10 trillion in goods in the next five years.[20] "As its overall national strength grows", as China President Xi Jinping noted in his address to the APEC CEO Summit in November, "China will be both capable and willing to provide more public goods for the Asia-Pacific and the world, especially new initiatives and visions for enhancing regional cooperation." In language reminiscent of his so-called "Chinese dream",[21] Xi told his audience in Beijing, "We are duty-bound to create and fulfil an Asia-Pacific dream for our people."[22] That said, according to Alan Bollard, executive director of the APEC secretariat, "None of the economies want to start negotiating on the FTAAP. It is far too early to do that."[23]

Secondly, China demonstrated diplomatic finesse in improving its troubled ties with Japan. While much was made of the frostiness Chinese President Xi exhibited towards his Japanese counterpart Shinzo Abe at their bilateral exchange on the side of the APEC meeting, the exchange — the first in two years between the two leaders — was an affirmation of the agreement reached in early November between Chinese State Councillor Yang Jiechi and Japanese National Security chief Shotaro Yachi on a four-point consensus on improving Sino-Japanese ties.[24] Chinese nationalistic sentiment over the disputed islands and waters aside, greater stability in its relationship with Japan — particularly in the light of Abe's continued leadership following his successful re-election in mid-December — benefits China more than the prolongation of toxic ties. Thirdly, as noted, the landmark agreement with the United States on climate change is another feather in the Chinese cap.

Finally, China, arguably with less success, has persisted in its efforts to promote a vision for regional security that some see as exclusivist towards the United States. At the Conference on Interaction and Confidence-Building Measures in Asia (CICA) held in Shanghai in May 2014, Xi pledged that China would stick to peaceful methods to resolve its disputes over territory.[25] Echoing his predecessors, Xi has claimed that China would never seek "hegemony or expansion" in the Asia-Pacific, even as it strengthens its diplomatic and military footprint in the region.[26] The logic undergirding Xi's pledge, according to analysts, is a "new security paradigm" that China wishes to promote, where elements such as mutual respect and understanding and the search for common ground while shelving differences would provide the basis for Asian security to "be handled in the Asian way".[27] In much the same way during the Jiang and Hu presidencies, China consistently advanced its principles of peaceful coexistence and promoted a "new security concept" — first introduced in 1997 and subsequently reintroduced each time with slight modifications — that emphasizes equality, mutual trust, respect and cooperation, consensus through consultation and the peace settlement of disputes.[28]

Beyond 2014, whether the aforementioned developments point to a new Chinese charm offensive in the foreseeable future — or, at the least, a restrained version of the "tailored coercion" that Beijing's East and South China Seas policy has been called — remains to be seen, however.[29] At the CICA gathering referred to above, Xi issued a veiled threat against unnamed Southeast Asian countries over their alleged efforts at strengthening military alliances to counter China, reflecting Beijing's inherent suspicions. It raises the possibility that China feels that the United States — presumably having encouraged, if only indirectly, its allies Japan and the Philippines and even a former foe, Vietnam, to harden their stances on their respective islands disputes with China — has not shown it the respect it feels it rightfully deserves. At the Sunnylands summit between Xi and Obama in June 2013, the former outlined China's two key wishes: one, respect from the United States, and two, for "a new relationship among major powers" to be forged between the two countries. Although Obama acknowledged the need for a "new model of cooperation" at the time, others have nonetheless noted his studious avoidance of the Chinese phraseology of a "new model of major country relationships",[30] which perhaps hinted that Washington neither viewed Beijing as responsible nor major — at least not yet. Be that as it may, Southeast Asian countries have by and large taken care to eschew fostering the impression that they are bandwagoning with the Americans to contain China. The influential international relations scholar John Mearsheimer predicted in 2013 that:

> [I]f China continues to grow economically, it will attempt to dominate Asia the way the United States dominates the Western Hemisphere. The United States, however, will go to enormous lengths to prevent China from achieving regional hegemony. Most of Beijing's neighbours, including India, Japan, Singapore, South Korea, Russia, and Vietnam, will join with the United States to contain Chinese power.[31]

However, there has been no obvious taking of sides with the United States to contain China, although the actions of many Southeast Asian countries imply that they continue to subscribe to strategic hedging, institutional engagement through the ASEAN-based regional architecture, and maintaining a balance of the major powers in the region. In an interview with Yoichi Funabashi, the editor-in-chief of the Japanese news daily, *Asahi Shimbun*, Singapore's founding leader, Lee Kuan Yew, once complained about the unfortunate predilection of the conservative Chinese press to translate the phrase "to balance" (*pingheng*) as "to conscribe" (*zhiheng*), hence connoting containment.[32] Such mistakes arouse Chinese anger unnecessarily.

The South China Sea: Choppy as Ever?

As expected, the issue of territorial disputes in the South China Sea dominated the ASEAN Regional Forum (ARF) in Naypidaw in August. The divergence in perceptions and narratives on the South China Sea (hereafter SCS) was noticeably acute. On the one hand, the U.S. Secretary of State, John Kerry, noting the "provocative steps" taken by claimant states "aimed at changing the status quo" (to use Kerry's words), indirectly fingered China as the main culprit whose actions, according to Kerry, have purportedly caused regional trade to suffer and regional relations to deteriorate.[33] The provocations in question presumably included China's controversial placement of its Haiyang Shiyou-981 oil rig — owned by the China National Offshore Oil Corporation (CNOOC) — near the Vietnamese coastline in May, which elicited anti-Chinese violence in Vietnam and the forced evacuation of thousands of Chinese citizens. The Vietnamese Foreign Ministry claimed that Chinese ships "intentionally rammed" two Vietnamese Coast Guard vessels near the oil rig.[34] It has been argued that China's deployment of the oil rig was no strategic mistake but a considered decision to advance its economic interests.[35] That the placement of the oil rig took place a mere few months after the establishment of a wide-ranging agreement between China and Vietnam on trade, infrastructure, energy and maritime affairs in October 2013 suggests however that Beijing likely did not anticipate the extent of Vietnamese anger in reaction.

The Chinese subsequently removed the oil rig in July, one month ahead of the previously announced schedule.[36] This left room for speculation whether China sought to mollify its counterpart after a provocation, or if it achieved what it wanted anyway.

Going further, Kerry proposed a moratorium on provocative actions in the SCS, which his Chinese counterpart, Foreign Minister Wang Yi, roundly rejected as "premature".[37] Challenging Kerry's assessment, Wang insisted that the "situation in the SCS is generally stable, and the freedom of navigation there has never seen any problems", and "countries out of the region can have their legitimate concerns, but if they come here for finger-pointing, then we are opposed to that".[38] China similarly rejected calls by the Philippines and other ASEAN countries for disputes to be resolved through arbitration within the framework of the United Nations Convention on the Law of the Sea (UNCLOS).[39] Although China insisted that it would resolutely safeguard its sovereignty and maritime rights in the South China Sea, it nonetheless reiterated its commitment to a "dual track" policy — bilateral consultations and negotiations between claimant states, on the one hand, and between China and ASEAN in their joint pursuit of a binding code of conduct for the South China Sea on the other[40] — to resolve the situation in the South China Sea.

Hitherto, little progress has been achieved on the proposed code of conduct other than member countries of ASEAN reaching a consensus at the ASEAN Summit's leaders retreat in Naypidaw in November over "the need to expeditiously work towards early conclusion" of the code of conduct without specifying its possible contents much less a timeline for completion.[41] That ASEAN foreign ministers had affirmed as far back in August 2013 that the ASEAN states would from henceforth speak with "one voice" in their effort to press China for a speedier conclusion to the code is a stark reminder to the Southeast Asians that the progress in the negotiations is more or less determined by the Chinese.[42] Yet the process has not been without accomplishments like the establishment of "early harvest" measures, such as hotlines for maritime emergencies to enhance communication.[43]

ASEAN: Still More Neighbourhood than Community?

With the 2015 deadline for the official début of the ASEAN Community — with its economic, political-security and socio-cultural "pillars" — looming, ASEAN foreign ministers concurred at their leaders retreat in November on the need for their countries to speed up community building and ASEAN integration and to move forward to the realization of the "master plan" for the ASEAN connectivity. In practically every conceivable domain — economic, political, security — the regionalism project has encountered considerable challenges and constraints, many of which ASEAN and its member countries have yet to surmount.

Not Quite There Yet

Supporters and critics of the Association alike are agreed that the anticipated ASEAN Economic Community (AEC) is unlikely to be realized in terms of its envisaged targets, by the end of 2015. In response, ASEAN officials have insisted that the AEC will be pushed through as planned and that it has addressed 80 per cent of the required action lines — or as official reports have it, "ASEAN has implemented 82.1 per cent of the 229 AEC key deliverables targeted for completion by 2013"[44] — largely in areas such as tariff reduction and the facilitation of trade and investment liberalization.[45] Many are sceptical about the ability of the member states to complete the remaining and arguably more intractable issues — eliminating non-tariff barriers, creating the ASEAN Single Window, increasing cross-regional mobility of skilled labour and the like — in time for the launch of the AEC.[46]

Ironically, the delay comes at a time when the need for integration is greater than ever before as many Southeast Asian countries, once over-dependent on export-led growth, are now rebalancing their economies and shifting their development strategies toward growing domestic demand. ASEAN states will need to manage their capital flows better and foster deeper economic integration not only to reduce developmental gaps among member countries but also — particularly for Indonesia, Malaysia, the Philippines, Thailand and Vietnam — to overcome the "middle-income trap" as their pace of growth falters.[47] Sundram Pushpanathan, the former ASEAN Deputy Secretary General responsible for implementing the AEC, has urged the leaders of ASEAN countries to move beyond the "process-based regionalism" that had historically served their national needs but has become a bane in the way of regional progress. Calling for a new regionalism that emphasizes concrete results and outcomes based on a structured and rules-based regime, Pushpanathan argued that for the AEC to be ready by 2015, "it is imperative that ASEAN shifts aggressively towards 'result-based regionalism'. We must act now."[48] Likewise, Surin Pitsuwan, the Secretary General of ASEAN from 2008 to 2012, has declared that it is time for ASEAN to move beyond the provision of "the centrality of goodwill" to "the centrality of substance".[49]

Nagging Constraints

Nor, for that matter, would the ASEAN Political-Security Community (APSC), which has received considerably less attention from regional policymakers relative to the AEC, be ready by 2015. In the wake of challenges such as the Burmese junta's crackdown on the Buddhist clergy-led demonstrations in Yangon in 2007 (the so-called "Saffron Revolution"), ASEAN leaders amended their initial plan for the "ASEAN Security Community" — as originally stipulated in the 2003 Bali Concord II[50] — to the APSC in an apparent effort to scale back expectations. Recent developments have underscored the wisdom of that decision. They include border disputes among members like that between Cambodia and Thailand over the Preah Vihear promontory — which the International Court of Justice eventually ruled in Cambodia's favour in November 2013[51] — or intramural discord at the ASEAN Ministerial Meeting in Phnom Penh in July 2012 over the organization's position on the South China Sea disputes. The latter led to the ignominy of failing, for the first time in the Association's history, to produce an end-of-meeting communiqué. Subsequently, Indonesia exercised its *de facto* leadership in the Association to cobble together the so-called "six point agreement" as a compromise.[52]

While the ASEAN Coordinating Centre for Humanitarian Assistance on disaster management (AHA Centre) has deployed an Emergency Rapid Assessment Team (ERAT) to the Philippines ahead of Typhoon Hagupit in early December, many worry whether the region has successfully digested the lessons from last year's Typhoon Haiyan, which devastated wide swathes of the Philippines in November 2013. Although some ASEAN states furnished crisis relief in response to Haiyan, they did so on their own national accords rather than under the Association's aegis. Then, the conspicuous lack of an ASEAN-led response was equally revealing about the extent or dearth of collective capability and will,[53] notwithstanding the availability of the AHA Centre and protocols like the ASEAN Agreement on Disaster Management and Emergency Response (AADMER), as well as the participation by the respective militaries of ASEAN members in joint humanitarian assistance and disaster relief (HADR) exercises. The need for concerted and coordinated action among member states is equally true of all areas of intramural collaboration in general; the leader of a member nation has argued that ASEAN ought to respond in a decisive and coordinated fashion to geopolitical developments such as maritime disputes in the South China Sea and security issues like the rise of the Islamic State.[54]

Looking Outward, Not In

When Xi Jinping urged for Asia's security issues to be handled by Asians alone at the CICA meeting in Shanghai in May, few made the connection at the time that the Chinese leader's appeal implicitly recalled the Indonesian mantra of "regional solutions for regional problems".[55] The notion that Southeast Asians are best placed to manage their own security challenges has long captivated the regional imagination and, together with the Cold War concern against "interference" in Southeast Asia by outside powers, has served as a basis for ASEAN treaties and protocols like the 1971 Zone of Peace, Freedom and Neutrality (ZOPFAN) and the 1995 Southeast Asia Nuclear Weapons Free Zone (SEANWFZ). On the other hand, the emergence of ASEAN in the post-Cold War period as the region's leading facilitator of "open" and "inclusive" regionalism[56] — through its participation in the APEC and its formation of a suite of regional arrangements like the ARF, ASEAN+3, East Asia Summit (EAS) and the ASEAN Defence Ministers Meeting-Plus (ADMM-Plus) — has underscored a growing reliance on external powers, rather than their rejection, in the management of regional security.

In the case of the ADMM-Plus, for instance, ASEAN countries look to eight dialogue partners (America, Australia, China, India, Japan, Korea, New Zealand, and Russia) for assistance to develop their national and regional capacities in HADR, nuclear counter-proliferation, ensuring safety and security in the maritime domain, counter-terrorism, and the like. And as noted, despite the focus paid to the development of ASEAN's capabilities in HADR, the organization's relative inaction in response to Typhoon Haiyan — the efforts by individual ASEAN states were obviously nowhere near what America and Britain contributed — only served to underscore the extent and depth of their dependence. However, the aspiration for regional solutions still matters to the extent that the Association's members persist to ensure that the norm of ASEAN centrality in Asian regionalism continues to enjoy the support of all stakeholders, especially the non-ASEAN countries.

One Step Forward, Two Steps Back

The region's democratic transition, uneven at best, had mixed results in 2014. Promising to bring "true democracy" to Thailand, the coup leaders, led by General Prayuth Chan-ocha who had installed himself as prime minister, have formed a Cabinet made up of the junta and former officers — former army chief, Prawit Wongsuwan, is a deputy prime minister; Anupong Paochinda, another former army chief, is interior minister; and Tanasak Patimapragorn, the chief of Thai Defence Forces, is the new foreign minister — plus a few senior bureaucrats — including Pridiyathorn Devakula, a former central banker, as a deputy prime minister with special responsibility for overseeing economic strategy.[57] While most Bangkok residents are relieved that the bloodless military putsch engendered a return to normalcy, a host of problems remain, not least the poor performance of the Thai economy and uncertainty over how the junta will deal with the restive south and with former premier Yingluck Shinawatra and her supporters.[58]

In Indonesia, Joko Widodo defeated the controversial ex-general Prabowo Subianto in the July presidential election and became the first outsider to clinch the Indonesian presidency. Having campaigned on a reformist agenda, Widodo, popularly known as "Jokowi", raised expectations among many Indonesians regarding the prospect of much needed reforms to the nation's infrastructure, social welfare and level of corruption, among other things — a challenging task in the light of the odds stacked against him.[59] However, Jokowi's picks for his Cabinet marked the triumph of what one noted analyst has termed "realpolitik over reform", where requisite compromises to political parties and forces of patronage which backed his candidature had to be made.[60] The surprise, however, was in the extent to which he chose to go in making those compromises. A key example was the inclusion of Ryamizard Ryacudu, a former army chief often criticized by human rights groups, as defence minister; Ryacudu is an ally of former Indonesian President Megawati Sukarnoputri, on whose patronage Jokowi relied heavily. Be that as it may, the new President's decision to make good on his electoral promise to reduce state energy subsidies in an effort to free up funds for development plans is viewed by many economists as a good start.[61]

Myanmar's Chairmanship: Better Than Expected?

The year 2014 marked the first time that Myanmar became chair of ASEAN. The country joined the Association in 1997, but was denied its right to assume chairmanship in 2006 due to the international emphasis on Myanmar's poor track record in the area of human rights and the rule of law which resulted in pressure against the country's assumption of the chairmanship for the year. The decision against Myanmar in 2006 was unpleasant for ASEAN as a whole as it went against the members' general commitment to non-interference in each other's domestic affairs. But it also highlighted the Association's incremental shift towards that which it has termed "enhanced interaction" where particular instances of intramural interference if not interventionism are rationalized and justified.[62]

Notwithstanding the country's ongoing ethno-religious problems, the economic, social and political transformation that Myanmar has undergone under the leadership of President U Thein Sein has been nothing short of remarkable. There remain significant constraints against further change, to be sure. For example, for dissident turned parliamentarian Aung San Suu Kyi to become president — constitutionally she is barred because her late British husband was a foreigner, as are her children — her political party, the National League for Democracy (NLD), would have to win nearly three-quarters of all the seats contested in the upcoming election due (putatively) in late 2015.[63] But the positives achieved have not been insignificant. Freedom of information reforms, including the abolition of media censorship, facilitated in part the public outcry that led to Naypidaw's abrupt *volte face* in September 2011 over the construction of the Myitsone Dam, a Chinese-sponsored project which, when completed, would have supplied generated energy to China and likely caused adverse environmental damage to Burmese soil.[64] In 2013, Myanmar passed Cambodia on Transparency International's Corruption Perceptions Index, making Cambodia the lowest-ranking ASEAN member.[65] Myanmar was placed 157th in the Berlin-based group's 2013 study, an impressive climb of fifteen spots from its rank of 172nd of 176 countries in the 2012 study, while Cambodia tied for 160th place.[66] As ASEAN Secretary-General Le Luong Minh has noted, "Myanmar's chairmanship comes amidst the country's ongoing democratisation and reform process which has been enjoying strong support from ASEAN Member States and the international community at large."[67]

Myanmar came to the chairmanship mindful of the damage to ASEAN's reputation under Cambodia's chairmanship in 2012. "The lesson for Myanmar here is to respect ASEAN tradition, which is to take tiny little diplomatic steps without creating political friction among other ASEAN members, and to know its strategic limits", according to Peter Tan Keo, an independent analyst who focuses on ASEAN. "It would behove the country to understand its role in stewarding issues, not to stifle them for its own strategic gains or interests, as was clearly the case with Cambodia."[68] In that respect, Myanmar performed remarkably well for a first-timer. The most significant testament to Myanmar's diplomatic prowess in 2014 was the non-escalation of the dispute over South China Sea issues, which returned to the tentative status quo by the end of August. Considering how upset Vietnam, the Philippines, and the United States had been with China's behaviour, what the Burmese accomplished was no small feat. Furthermore, Myanmar managed to avoid antagonizing any of the parties involved. Beijing seemed sufficiently placated that ASEAN's joint statement on the matter did not contain any direct references to China.[69] On their part, Hanoi and Manila, the members most affected in the debacle in Phnom Penh in 2012, managed to get a dedicated ASEAN statement that addressed the South China Sea disputes.[70]

Finally, as ASEAN has increasingly done over the past few years, the organization has used its summits to stress the importance of upholding the principle of "ASEAN centrality" in East Asian regionalism and its supporting architecture. Under Myanmar's leadership, the 2014 ASEAN Summit was no different.[71] The centrality of ASEAN has come under challenge from within and without in the past few years. Crucially, the absence of new great power bargains in the immediate post-Cold War period, allowed ASEAN, from the early 1990s onward, to step into the breach as the region's convenor by providing a regional architecture and convention which brought together regional countries, including the big powers, and institutionalized regular dialogues on political and security issues among them. Put differently, ASEAN's centrality in East Asia's regional architecture has principally been dependent on the regional consensus concerning the Association's relevance to regional order and security. If anything, it is the regional grouping's professed neutrality and relative weakness that great powers, unable to form bargains among themselves, find most attractive because ASEAN threatens no one. However, as events in the Association's recent past suggest, the regional grouping's ability to persuade the external powers to maintain that consensus in a rapidly shifting regional strategic environment has been eroded.[72] Nevertheless Myanmar did what it could to ensure that ASEAN centrality meant something more than mere rhetoric.

Looking Ahead to 2015

It is the contention of this chapter, firstly, that 2014 has effectively been China's year in terms of its accomplishments amid an evolving regional strategic environment characterized by rising and rebalancing powers, and secondly, that ASEAN has lagged in delivering on its regional goals. With the United States likely to look increasingly inward as its polity gradually gears up to vote for a new president in 2016, China will presumably seize the opportunity furnished by a distracted America to cultivate and deepen its ties to Southeast Asia. With Malaysia assuming the chairmanship of ASEAN in 2015, the emphasis will be on mobilizing member countries to complete the task of delivering the AEC by the end of the year; concluding the negotiations for the Regional Comprehensive Economic Partnership (RCEP) comprising the ASEAN states and six of its dialogue partners (Australia, China, India, Japan, New Zealand and South Korea); and strengthening ASEAN and its suite of institutions by urging ASEAN members to agree to increase their contributions to the organization.[73] On the other hand, it remains to be seen what role Indonesia, which has long treated ASEAN as the cornerstone of its foreign policy, would want to play under its new president. Given that Indonesian intellectuals known for their advocacy of a "post-ASEAN foreign policy" for Indonesia are reportedly advising the new President on foreign policy raises the possibility that Indonesia's ties to ASEAN might not be as robust as before.[74]

Notes

1. Rendi A. Witular, "Jokowi Launches Maritime Doctrine to the World", *Jakarta Post*, 13 November 2014.

2. Rizal Sukma at a public conference in Washington in December 2014, emphasis added. Cited in Prashanth Parameswaran, "Is Indonesia Turning Away From ASEAN Under Jokowi?", *The Diplomat*, 18 December 2014, available at <http://thediplomat.com/2014/12/is-indonesia-turning-away-from-asean-under-jokowi/>.

3. Patrick Jory, "China is a Big Winner from Thailand's Coup", *The Diplomat*, 18 June 2014, available at <http://www.eastasiaforum.org/2014/06/18/china-is-a-big-winner-from-thailands-coup/>.

4. Achara Ashayagachat, "Irritation as Thailand Loses Its Charm", *Bangkok Post*, 1 February 2015, available at <http://www.bangkokpost.com/opinion/opinion/463130/irritation-as-thailand-loses-its-charm>.

5. Milton Osborne, *Region of Revolt: Focus on Southeast Asia* (London: Elsevier, 2013).

6. Ankit Panda, "Modi 'Acts East' at East Asia Summit", *The Diplomat*, 14 November 2014, available at <http://thediplomat.com/2014/11/modi-acts-east-at-east-asia-summit/>.

7. Evelyn Goh, *Japan, China, and the Great Power Bargain in East Asia*, EAI Fellows Program Working Paper Series No. 32 (Seoul: East Asia Institute, November 2011), pp. 3–5.

8. Christopher W. Hughes, *Japan's Re-emergence as a "Normal" Military Power*, Adelphi Series 368–9 (Abingdon, Oxon: Routledge, 2007).

9. See Seng Tan, *The Making of the Asia Pacific: Knowledge Brokers and the Politics of Representation* (Amsterdam: Amsterdam University Press, 2013), p. 131.

10. Lenore Taylor, "Changing Fortunes Dictate Another Presidential Pivot", *Sydney Morning Herald*, 17 November 2011, available at <http://www.smh.com.au/federal-politics/political-opinion/changing-fortunes-dictate-another-presidential-pivot-20111117-1nk3t.html>.

11. Perry Bacon, Jr., "A Shifting Battleground: Why Chuck Hagel Resigned", *NBC News*, 24 November 2014, available at <http://www.nbcnews.com/politics/first-read/shifting-battleground-why-chuck-hagel-resigned-n255056>.

12. U.S. Secretary of Defence Chuck Hagel in April 2014, cited in Zachary Keck, "US Swears Asia Pivot Isn't Dead", *The Diplomat*, 2 April 2014, available at <http://thediplomat.com/2014/04/us-swears-asia-pivot-isnt-dead/>.

13. Matt Shiavenza, "The 'Insipid' Mr. Obama Goes to China", *The Atlantic*, 6 November 2014, available at <http://www.theatlantic.com/international/archive/2014/11/obama-visits-china-global-times/382435/>. The Chinese commentary in question is from "Midterm Result Will Further Thwart Obama", *Global Times*, 5 November 2014, available at <http://www.globaltimes.cn/content/890056.shtml>.

14. Author's discussion with members of the China Institutes of Contemporary International Relations (CICIR) in Singapore on 19 December 2014.

15. Lucy Hornby, "Putin Snubs Europe with Siberian Gas Deal that Bolsters China Ties", *Financial Times*, 10 November 2014, available at <http://www.ft.com/cms/s/0/79eeabb0-6888-11e4-acc0-00144feabdc0.html#axzz3MQEmduSj>.

16. "Putin: Russia Cannot Continue South Stream Construction in Current Situation", *Sputnik*, 1 December 2014, available at <http://sputniknews.com/business/20141201/1015368062.html>.

17. Euan Graham, "Russia's Crimean Annexation: What It Means for East Asia", *RSIS Commentaries*, 25 March 2014; Zachery Keck, "Overseas Chinese and the Crimea Crisis", *The Diplomat*, 10 April 2014, available at <http://thediplomat.com/2014/04/overseas-chinese-and-the-crimea-crisis/>; Parameswaran Ponnudurai, "Will China Use Russian-Style Tactics to Settle Territorial Disputes in Asia?", *Radio Free Asia*, 20 April 2014, available at <http://www.rfa.org/english/commentaries/east-asia-beat/ukraine-04202014053612.html>.

18. David Brunnstrom, "U.S. Warns China not to Try Crimea-style Action in Asia", *Reuters*, 4 April 2014, available at <http://www.reuters.com/article/2014/04/04/us-usa-china-crimea-asia-idUSBREA322DA20140404>.

19. Dingding Chen, "China's 'Marshall Plan' is Much More", *The Diplomat*, 10 November 2014, available at <http://thediplomat.com/2014/11/chinas-marshall-plan-is-much-more/>.

20. Dexter Roberts, "Obama and Xi Spar Over Rival Free-Trade Pacts at APEC Forum", *Bloomberg Businessweek*, 10 November 2014, available at <http://www.businessweek.com/articles/2014-11-10/obama-and-xi-spar-over-rival-free-trade-pacts-at-apec-forum>.

21. "Chasing the Chinese Dream", *The Economist*, 4 May 2013, available at <http://www.economist.com/news/briefing/21577063-chinas-new-leader-has-been-quick-consolidate-his-power-what-does-he-now-want-his>.

22. "Chinese President Proposes Asia-Pacific Dream", *China Daily*, 9 November 2014, available at <http://www.chinadaily.com.cn/china/2014-11/09/content_18889698.htm>.

23. Shannon Tiezzi, "China's Push for an Asia-Pacific Free Trade Agreement", *The Diplomat*, 30 October 2014, available at <http://thediplomat.com/2014/10/chinas-push-for-an-asia-pacific-free-trade-agreement/>.

24. The two countries agreed to the following: (1) continue to develop a mutually beneficial relationship based on common strategic interests; (2) agree to overcome political difficulties by "facing history squarely and looking forward to the future"; (3) mutually address the Senkaku/Diaoyu Islands; and (4) agree to gradually resume political, diplomatic and security dialogues through various multilateral and bilateral channels. Shannon Tiezzi, "A China-Japan Breakthrough: A Primer on Their 4 Point Consensus", *The Diplomat*, 7 November 2014, available at <http://thediplomat.com/2014/11/a-china-japan-breakthrough-a-primer-on-their-4-point-consensus/>.

25. John Ruwitch, "China's Xi Issues Veiled Warning to Asia over Military Alliances", *Reuters*, 21 May 2014, available at <http://news.yahoo.com/chinas-xi-says-committed-peacefully-resolving-territorial-disputes-024633860.html>.

26. Jeremy Blum, "Former Foreign Minister Says 'China will Never Seek to become a Hegemonic Power'", *South China Morning Post*, 18 September 2013, available at <http://www.scmp.com/news/china-insider/article/1312346/former-foreign-minister-says-china-will-never-seek-become>; Patrick Donahue and Brian Parkin, "Xi Says China's Military Expansion Not Aimed at Asian Hegemony", *Bloomberg News*, 29 March 2014, available at <http://www.bloomberg.com/news/2014-03-28/xi-says-china-s-military-expansion-not-aimed-at-asian-hegemony.html>.

27. Kor Kian Beng, "China Puts Low-key Summit in Spotlight", *Straits Times*, 10 May 2014, p. A18.

28. David Capie and Paul Evans, *The Asia-Pacific Security Lexicon*, 2nd ed. (Singapore: Institute of Southeast Asian Studies, 2007), pp. 169–72.

29. Patrick M. Cronin, Ely Ratner, Elbridge Coby, Zachary M. Hosford, and Alexander Sullivan, *Tailored Coercion: Competition and Risk in Maritime Asia* (Washington, D.C.: Center for New American Security, 2014); Robert Haddick, "Salami Slicing in the South China Sea", *Foreign Policy*, 3 August 2012, available at <http://www.foreignpolicy.com/category/section/small_wars>.

30. Elizabeth Economy, "The Xi-Obama Summit: As Good as Expected — and Maybe Even Better", *The Atlantic*, 11 June 2013, available at <http://www.theatlantic.com/china/archive/2013/06/the-xi-obama-summit-as-good-as-expected-and-maybe-even-better/276733/>.

31. John J. Mearsheimer, "Can China Rise Peacefully?", *The National Interest*, 25 October 2014, available at <http://nationalinterest.org/commentary/can-china-rise-peacefully-10204>.

32. "On Power and Stabilising Forces", *Straits Times*, 17 May 2010, available at <http://xinkaishi.typepad.com/a_new_start/asia/page/14/>.

33. John Kerry, "Opening Remarks at ASEAN Regional Forum", *United States Mission to ASEAN*, 10 August 2014, available at <http://asean.usmission.gov/remarks08102014-02.html>.

34. Nguyen Phuong Linh and Michael Martina, "South China Sea Tensions Rise as Vietnam says China Rammed Ships", *Reuters*, 7 May 2014, available at <http://www.reuters.com/article/2014/05/07/us-china-seas-fishermen-idUSBREA4603C20140507>.

35. Dingding Chen, "China's Deployment of Oil Rig is Not a Strategic Mistake", *The Diplomat*, 20 May 2014, available at <http://thediplomat.com/2014/05/chinas-deployment-of-oil-rig-is-not-a-strategic-mistake/>.

36. "Spotlight: China Rebuffs U.S. 'Freeze' Proposal on South China Sea, Raising 'Dual-track' Approach", *Shanghai Daily*, 10 August 2014, available at <http://www.shanghaidaily.com/article/article_xinhua.aspx?id=234543>.

37. "Beijing Hits Out at US South China Sea Proposal", *Straits Times*, 12 August 2014, available at <http://www.straitstimes.com/news/asia/east-asia/story/beijing-hits-out-us-south-china-sea-proposal-20140812>.

38. Thuc D. Pham, "Implications of the US-China Split at the ARF", *The Diplomat*, 5 September 2014, available at <http://thediplomat.com/2014/09/implications-of-the-us-china-split-at-the-arf/>.

39. David Tweed and Sangwon Yoon, "China Rejects Push at Asean to Curb South China Sea Activity", *Bloomberg*, 10 August 2014, available at <http://www.bloomberg.com/news/2014-08-09/south-china-sea-tension-seen-dominating-asean-ministers-meeting.html>.

40. "China Supports 'Dual-track' Approach to Resolve Dispute", *Xinhua*, 10 August 2014, available at <http://usa.chinadaily.com.cn/china/2014-08/10/content_18280191.htm>.

41. "Press Release by the Chairman of the ASEAN Foreign Ministers' Retreat (AMM Retreat)", <http://asean-summit-2014.tumblr.com/post/73949814893/press-release-by-the-chairman-of-the-asean-foreign>.

42. "ASEAN Vows Unity on South China Sea", *Yahoo! News*, 14 August 2013, available at <https://sg.news.yahoo.com/asean-vows-unity-south-china-sea-142838507.html>.

43. Dylan Loh, "ASEAN Must Respond in Decisive, Coordinated Way to Regional Issues: PM Lee", *Channel NewsAsia*, 12 November 2014, available at <http://www.channelnewsasia.com/news/singapore/asean-must-respond-in/1468054.html>.

44. "The 46th ASEAN Economic Ministers' (AEM) Meeting Joint Media Statement", 25 August 2014, p. 2, available at <http://www.asean.org/images/Statement/2014/aug/JMS%20AEM%2046%20_Final.pdf>.

45. "Myanmar Hosts ASEAN Summit for the First Time", *ASEAN Secretariat News*, 9 May 2014, available at <http://www.asean.org/news/asean-secretariat-news/item/myanmar-hosts-asean-summit-for-the-first-time>.

46. Dario Agnote, "Talks to Build ASEAN Economic Community Slows, ADB Says", *Kyodo News*, 25 September 2014, available at <http://english.kyodonews.jp/news/2014/09/313608.html>; Jayant Menon, "An ASEAN Economic Community by 2015?", *Vox*, 27 September 2014, available at <http://www.voxeu.org/article/asean-economic-community-2015>.

47. *Economic Outlook for Southeast Asia, China and India 2014: Beyond the Middle-Income Trap* (Paris: OECD Development Centre, 2013), available at <http://dx.doi.org/10.1787/saeo-2014-en>.

48. Sundram Pushpanathan, "Opinion: No Place for Passive Regionalism in ASEAN", *Jakarta Post*, 7 April 2010, available at <http://www.thejakartapost.com/news/2010/04/07/no-place-passive-regionalism-asean.html>.

49. Cited in Malminderjit Singh, "Asean Must Do More to Boost Competitiveness: Surin", *Business Times*, 2 June 2011, available at <lkyspp.nus.edu.sg/aci/.../20110602_ACR_Launch-Business_Times.pdf>.

50. "Declaration of ASEAN Concord II (Bali Concord II)", 7 October 2003, available at <http://www.asean.org/news/item/declaration-of-asean-concord-ii-bali-concord-ii>.

51. "UN Court Awards Disputed Preah Vihear Temple Area to Cambodia, Orders Thai Security Forces to Leave", *Australian Broadcasting Corporation (ABC) News*, 12 November 2013, available at <http://www.abc.net.au/news/2013-11-11/un-court-awards-flashpoint-border-temple-area-to-cambodia/5084504>.

52. Donald K. Emmerson, "Beyond the Six Points: How Far Will Indonesia Go?", *East Asia Forum*, 29 July 2012, available at <http://www.eastasiaforum.org/2012/07/29/beyond-the-six-points-how-far-will-indonesia-go/>.

53. Euan Graham, "Super-typhoon Haiyan: ASEAN's Katrina Moment?", *PacNet*, no. 82, 20 November 2013.

54. Dylan Loh, "ASEAN Must Respond in Decisive, Coordinated Way to Regional Issues: PM Lee", *Today*, 12 November 2014.

55. Michael Leifer, "Regional Solutions to Regional Problems?", in *Towards Recovery in Pacific Asia*, edited by Gerald Segal and David S.G. Goodman (London: Routledge, 2000), pp. 108–18.

56. Amitav Acharya, "Ideas, Identity and Institution-Building: From the 'ASEAN Way' to the 'Asia-Pacific Way'?", *The Pacific Review* 10, no. 3 (1997): 319–46.

57. James Hookway, "Veterans of Thai Military Government Take Key Posts in New Cabinet", *The Wall Street Journal*, 1 September 2014, available at <http://www.wsj.com/articles/thai-leaders-name-cabinet-1409488985>.

58. "Uniform Reaction: The Generals Introduce 'True Democracy', Thai-style", *The Economist*, 13 September 2014, available at <http://www.economist.com/news/asia/21616970-generals-introduce-true-democracy-thai-style-uniform-reaction>.

59. "Jokowi Should Act Swiftly on Reform Agenda", *FT View* (*Financial Times*), 2 November 2014, available at <http://www.ft.com/intl/cms/s/0/a1251a90-611f-11e4-b935-00144feabdc0.html#axzz3LfMAgE5t>.

60. Edward Aspinall, "Jokowi Fails His First Test", *New Mandala*, 27 October 2014, available at <http://asiapacific.anu.edu.au/newmandala/2014/10/27/jokowi-fails-first-test/>.

61. Rieka Rahadiana, Agus Suhana, and Herdaru Purnomo, "Bank Indonesia Raises Key Rate After Fuel-Price Increase", *Bloomberg*, 18 November 2014, available at <http://www.bloomberg.com/news/2014-11-17/indonesia-s-widodo-increases-subsidized-gasoline-diesel-prices.html>.

62. Jurgen Haacke, "'Enhanced Interaction' with Myanmar and the Project of a Security Community: Is ASEAN Refining or Breaking with Its Diplomatic and Security Culture?", *Contemporary Southeast Asia* 27, no. 2 (August 2005): 188–216; See Seng Tan, "Herding Cats: The Role of Persuasion in Political Change and Continuity in the Association of Southeast Asian Nations (ASEAN)", *International Relations of the Asia-Pacific*, vol. 13, no. 2 (2013), pp. 233–65.

63. "A Choice of Sorts: Myanmar Gets Ready for Elections", *The Economist*, 20 November 2014, available at <http://www.economist.com/news/21631852-myanmar-gets-ready-elections-choice-sorts?zid=309&ah=80dcf288b8561b012f603b9fd9577f0e>.

64. Peter Chalk, *On the Path of Change: Political, Economic and Social Challenges for Myanmar, ASPI Special Report* (Barton, ACT: Australian Strategic Policy Institute, December 2013), pp. 6–7.

65. Justine Drennan, "Myanmar's ASEAN Chairmanship: Lessons from Cambodia", *The Diplomat*, 13 January 2014, available at <http://thediplomat.com/2014/01/myanmars-asean-chairmanship-lessons-from-cambodia/>.

66. Simon Lewis, "Reforming Burma Moves Up Global Corruption Rankings", *The Irrawaddy*, 3 December 2013, available at <http://www.irrawaddy.org/burma/reforming-burma-moves-global-corruption-rankings.html>.

67. Cited in "Myanmar Hosts ASEAN Summit for the First Time".

68. Justine Drennan, "Myanmar's ASEAN Chairmanship: Lessons from Cambodia".

69. "Joint Communiqué 47th ASEAN Foreign Ministers' Meeting", 8 August 2014, p. 48, available at <http://www.asean.org/images/documents/47thAMMandRelatedMeetings/Joint%20Communique%20of%2047th%20AMM%20as%20of%209-8-14%2010%20pm.pdf>.

70. "ASEAN Foreign Ministers' Statement on the Current Developments in the South China Sea", 10 May 2014, available at <http://www.asean.org/news/asean-statement-communiques/item/asean-foreign-ministers-statement-on-the-current-developments-in-the-south-china-sea?category_id=26>.

71. "Press Release by the Chairman of the ASEAN Foreign Ministers' Retreat (AMM Retreat)", 17 January 2014, available at <http://asean-summit-2014.tumblr.com/>.

72. Evelyn Goh, "ASEAN-led Multilateralism and Regional Order: The Great Power Bargain Deficit", *The Asan Forum* (Special Forum), 23 May 2014, available at <http://www.theasanforum.org/asean-led-multilateralism-and-regional-order-the-great-power-bargain-deficit/>.

73. Prashanth Parameswaran, "Malaysia as ASEAN Chair in 2015: What To Expect", *The Diplomat*, 22 November 2014, available at <http://thediplomat.com/2014/11/malaysia-as-asean-chair-in-2015-what-to-expect/>.

74. Rizal Sukma, "Indonesia Needs a Post-ASEAN Foreign Policy", *Jakarta Post*, 30 June 2009; Rizal Sukma, "A Post-ASEAN Foreign Policy for a Post-G8 World", *Jakarta Post*, 5 October 2009.

CHINA'S TWO SILK ROADS INITIATIVE
What It Means for Southeast Asia

David Arase

Introduction

In 2013, Chinese President Xi Jinping announced a pair of initiatives that aims to restructure the economy and geopolitics of Eurasia. The Silk Road Economic Belt announced by Xi Jinping in September 2013 during a tour of Central Asian neighbours is a programme to build land transportation corridors that connect China to Europe and all other major Eurasian subregions, including Indochina, South Asia, and Southwest Asia.[1] Then in October 2013, Xi visited Indonesia and announced the 21st Century Maritime Silk Road, which is a port development initiative to broaden Chinese trade channels targetting the maritime regions of Southeast Asia, South Asia, the Middle East, East Africa, and the Mediterranean. Xi Jinping's two Silk Road programmes are a package called the "One Belt — One Road" [*yidai-yilu*] initiative.[2]

Both Xi Jinping and Premier Li Keqiang spent great effort in the year 2014 launching concrete measures to advance the silk roads agenda of Eurasian connectivity and regional cooperation. They hope to build a comprehensive trans-Eurasian network of economic corridors that could sustain China's economic growth and strengthen China's political leverage for decades to come. The consequence would be to draw the countries of Eurasia into China's economic orbit to form what Xi Jinping calls a "community of shared destiny". Members' fortunes would rise as China's own rise continued. A culturally and politically

David Arase is a Visiting Senior Fellow at the Institute of Southeast Asian Studies (ISEAS), Singapore. He is also Resident Professor of International Politics at The Hopkins-Nanjing Centre at Nanjing University, The John Hopkins University — School of Advanced International Studies.

diverse but economically integrated division of labour harmoniously organized by China's trade and financial interests is what China promises. If this vision is fully realized, China's silk roads vision will help realize "the great rejuvenation of the Chinese nation" and the "China Dream" of a wealthy society grounded on Chinese values.

It should be noted that this *yidai* — *yilu* agenda is a work in progress rather than a fully drawn up master plan. That is, as previous Chinese leaders have done, Xi Jinping is providing a grand strategic vision or agenda for China. The Chinese Communist Party and government must work to realize this agenda to the best of their ability. So, for the rest of Xi Jinping's years in power — expected to last until 2022 — we will hear about the two Silk Roads at every meeting that Xi Jinping or Li Keqiang attends in Europe, Africa, the Middle East and Asia.

The Year of the Silk Roads

Even the briefest summary of high-profile Chinese initiatives that advanced the Silk Roads agenda in 2014 amounts to a long list. Premier Li Keqiang made five overseas tours that highlighted this agenda. In May, Li made a four-nation African tour. In Kenya, he signed a US$3.8 billion agreement to use Chinese high-speed railway technology to connect Nairobi to Mombasa, the largest port in East Africa.

In June, he visited Greece to discuss purchase of both the Greek port Thessaloniki and the Greek state-owned railway. He also negotiated to purchase full ownership of the massive new Piraeus Container Terminal, which is already half-owned and managed by Chinese state-owned shipping giant COSCO.[3] In all, Li signed new deals with Greece valued at US$5 billion.

In October, Li visited Germany, Russia, and Italy, and attended the Asia-Europe Summit (ASEM). China and Germany's signed agreements on bilateral trade, mutual investment and technological cooperation are valued at US$18.1 billion; in Russia, Li Keqiang witnessed the signing of thirty-nine bilateral cooperation agreements and contracts, including a high-speed rail project connecting Moscow and Kazan via the Volga River (to be extended through Kazakhstan to Beijing by 2018 providing another trans-Eurasian rail link from China to Western Europe via Moscow), worth US$10 billion; in Italy, he witnessed Chinese and Italian corporations signing more than ten agreements totaling more than US$10 billion.[4]

In November, Li went to Myanmar to attend the annual ASEAN Summit meetings. During his visit, China signed US$8 billion in agreements with Myanmar and pledged US$10 billion for China-ASEAN infrastructure investment.

In December, Li visited Kazakhstan, Serbia, and Thailand. In Kazakhstan Li attended the Shanghai Cooperation Organization Summit and witnessed the signing of US$18 billion worth of economic cooperation and infrastructure construction agreements with Kazakhstan. Li then attended the third China–Central and Eastern European Leaders' Meeting in Serbia and announced a US$10 billion Chinese credit line for infrastructure development as well as a US$3 billion Chinese equity investment fund. He also signed an agreement to finance 85 per cent of a new Chinese-built railway linking Budapest to the Greek port of Piraeus on the Mediterranean Sea with intervening stops in Belgrade and Skopje. This deal is worth almost US$3 billion and will open Western, Central, and Eastern Europe to cheap container traffic with China.[5] Li Keqiang then departed for Thailand where he signed a US$10.6 billion financing deal to build a railway segment between Bangkok and the Chinese border that is part of a planned larger north-south railway network that runs from Kunming down the western, middle, and eastern axes of Indochina. Li also pledged US$3 billion at the Greater Mekong Subregion Economic Cooperation Summit to finance infrastructure connectivity, Chinese machinery exports, and Indochina poverty reduction efforts.

In the course of his five overseas tours, Li Keqiang signed bilateral and multilateral cooperation agreements worth some US$140 billion to advance China's interest in exporting railway and port infrastructure construction and management services that boost Chinese industrial exports and create transportation access to export markets, natural resources, and investment opportunities across and around Eurasia.[6]

The year 2014 also saw landmark initiatives by Xi Jinping that begin to provide an institutional and normative foundation for China's vision of a Eurasian community.

On 21 May 2014, Xi Jinping proposed the New Asian Security Concept to the twenty-six member states of the Conference on Interaction and Confidence Building Measures in Asia (CICA). This organization was originally founded by Kazakhstan and its membership mainly consists of continental rather than maritime Eurasian countries.[7] He stated, "To beef up and entrench a military alliance targeted at a third party is not conducive to maintaining common security."

Rather than traditional security, he asked members to focus on cooperative Asian development as the core security concern for Eurasia. He also asserted that, "it is for the people of Asia to run the affairs of Asia, solve the problems of Asia, and uphold the security of Asia."[8]

In September, Xi Jinping visited India and pledged to invest US$20 billion in upgrading India's infrastructure, especially its railways. China subsequently offered — at no cost to India — to do a feasibility study for a 1,750 km high-speed railway between Delhi and Chennai, a port city on the Bay of Bengal.[9] Xi also pledged to support India's full membership in the Shanghai Cooperation Organization.

In October, Xi Jinping and twenty other national representatives signed a Memorandum of Understanding (MOU) to establish the Asian Infrastructure Investment Bank (AIIB) with an initial capitalization of US$50 billion and authorized capitalization of US$100 billion. Xi had announced plans to establish such a bank a year earlier in a visit to Indonesia. The AIIB is expected to emphasize ASEAN infrastructure development.

At the November APEC Summit Meeting, Xi Jinping announced the Silk Road Development Fund to finance infrastructure and trade creation, for which he pledged US$40 billion in funding, of which 65 per cent will come from China's foreign currency reserves, and the rest from China's sovereign wealth fund, the Export-Import Bank of China, and the China Development Bank.[10] The Silk Road Development Fund seems destined to help finance the overland Silk Road Economic Belt.

China's Search for Great Power Status Leads to the Silk Roads

To understand China's Eurasian Silk Roads initiative, one needs to put it into a larger geo-strategic and historical context. China's rise to great power status causes a transition from a unipolar situation of U.S. "hyper-power" to structural bipolarity in the international system. The defining characteristic of a great power is the ability to determine the nature of international order. That is, it has an ability to determine the kinds of principles, norms, and institutions that smaller states will follow, and it begins to exercise this power first of all in its home region. As China figures out how and why it will use its power to restructure the world around it, it must first of all consider the adjustment of relations with the existing great power that has created the present international order, that is, the United States.

The 2008–09 financial crisis seemed to signal the end of U.S. global predominance and greatly accelerated the speed at which China would overtake the U.S. in GDP terms.[11] The Chinese foreign policy stance that emerged in 2009 continued the basic line of peaceful development, but it became much more independent and assertive in demanding certain changes in global and regional governance.[12] By the time leadership passed from Hu Jintao to Xi Jinping in 2012, the emphasis was on the need to establish a "new type of great power relationship" with the U.S. The critical element was gaining U.S. recognition of China's core interests in East Asia while avoiding armed conflict, especially with the U.S. and its allies.

To expand its control of strategic space in East Asian waters, China pursued what the Pentagon called an "Anti-Access/Area Denial" (A2/AD)[13] offshore maritime control strategy. At the same time, it loudly argued a historical case for its exclusive right to maritime territorial jurisdictions that neighbouring states claimed on the basis of rights uniformly accorded to all coastal states by the U.N. Convention on the Law of the Sea (UNCLOS). Simultaneously, China paraded new types of naval, air force, and space capabilities. Maritime skirmishes and incidents began in 2009, and in 2012 China launched paramilitary campaigns to establish civilian maritime occupation and patrol around Scarborough Shoal (Huangyandao) in the South China Sea and the Senkaku (Diaoyu) islets in the East China Sea. The months-long and controlled use of civilian coercive force successfully overcame resistance and established Chinese control (partial in the Senkaku/Diaoyu case but total in the Scarborough/Huangyandao case), while remaining below the threshold that could lead to a military confrontation with the United States.

China continues to use this formula in the East China Sea and the South China Sea to expand its sphere of maritime control against the opposing jurisdictional claims of neighbouring coastal states. In November 2013, China added a new dimension to this formula by declaring a militarily enforceable air defence identification zone (ADIZ) over the Senkaku/Diaoyudao islets in the East China Sea. It appears to be preparing to establish an ADIZ over the South China Sea, if the construction of artificial islands with landing strips is any indication.

Having established a formula for incremental strategic expansion that avoided direct conflict with the U.S., China turned to the reshaping of the Asian regional order to ensure its continuing economic rise and eventual political leadership.

The Economic and Political Agenda in Asia: Community of Shared Destiny

Xi Jinping's announcement of the *yidai-yilu* initiative in September–October 2013 marked a turn of attention toward the restructuring relations with Asia to secure China's future as a great power. Speaking in Indonesia in October, Xi Jinping chose the term 命运共同体 (*mingyun gongtongti*), which translates as "community of common destiny" or "community of shared fate", to express his vision of a China-centred regional community.[14] He then presided over the 23–24 October 2013 Chinese Communist Party Central Leadership Work Forum on Diplomacy Toward the Periphery, which was attended by the entire Standing Committee of the Politburo. Xi Jinping used the occasion to explain the kind of regional order that China aspired to create, and the role that the *yidai — yilu* initiative would play in it.

Xi explained the core idea is that neighbours must link their economic future to the "China Dream", that is, China's continuing rise, especially in economic terms. He then laid out the following framework:

- The use of China's advantages in economy, trade, technology, and finance to build "win-win" cooperation with neighbours;
- Construction of the two Silk Roads;
- The use of trade and investment to create a new kind of regional economic integration;
- An Asian Infrastructure Investment Bank, internationalization of the Chinese currency, renminbi (RMB), and regional financial stability;
- The development of Chinese border areas as gateways to neighbouring countries;
- A new concept of security, based on mutual trust, reciprocity, equality, and coordination through enhanced cooperation mechanisms.
- Public diplomacy and people-to-people exchanges including tourism, technology, education, and provincial level cooperation.[15]

The Silk Roads Agenda

The infrastructure that constitutes the two Silk Roads is both hard and soft. Hard infrastructure is the steel, concrete, computers, and equipment that go into building railways, highways, ports, energy pipelines, industrial parks, border customs facilities, and special trade zones. Soft infrastructure refers to the social and institutional foundations of trade and investment promotion such as diplomacy, development finance institutions, economic cooperation agreements, multilateral cooperation forums, academic research, cultural exchange, tourism, etc.

The Eurasian countries along the Silk Road routes number over sixty, and over fifty have already signed Silk Road cooperation endorsements with China — with notable exceptions such as India. China expects these countries to link their development strategies to China's growing trade and investment. This will lead them to ongoing policy dialogue and coordination, and membership in the China-centred community of shared destiny.

China has a number of reasons to invest in the two Silk Roads. It has become a net importer of energy, industrial commodities, and food, so it needs to secure access to new sources. Moreover, China can now export higher value-added goods and services, including electronic parts, consumer durables, heavy equipment, and construction and engineering services, but it needs to break into export markets. Ports and railway lines not only promote Chinese exports of advanced machinery and engineering services, but also open the way for Chinese trade and investment in as yet unfamiliar markets.

The *yidai — yilu* agenda also addresses the problem of geographically imbalanced development inside China. Inland border provinces have lagged behind the coastal provinces. The Silk Roads given them a chance at prosperity and a better quality of life as outward-looking Eurasian trade hubs. Beijing has designated the following provinces as Eurasian gateways: Jilin facing Mongolia, the Russian Far East, and the Japan Sea sub-region of Northeast Asia (via Russian and North Korean ports); [16] Guangxi working with Hainan and Guangdong facing maritime Southeast Asia; Yunnan facing the Mekong River sub region as well as the Bay of Bengal rim of the Indian Ocean (via Myanmar); and Xinjiang facing Central Asia with onward linkages to the Caspian Sea region, the Arabian Sea region, the Black Sea region, the Mediterranean Sea region, and Eastern and Northern Europe. Each of these Chinese gateway provinces has begun hosting an annual international Expo and a wide range of other regular events to develop trade and investment with foreign partners.

Financing the Silk Roads Agenda

The current tidal wave of Chinese state-guided overseas capital investment began at the end of the 1990s when China articulated a "going out" policy. The idea was to channel surplus savings abroad to secure energy and raw materials.[17] As will be noted below, the size of China's savings surplus and the reasons to invest overseas have only multiplied since then. The result today is a new era of Chinese "South-South cooperation", which means that China as a developing country gives economic aid to meet China's own development needs while also serving the development needs of recipients. This "win-win" economic cooperation formula fits the two Silk Roads agenda because countries along the routes tend to be lower and middle-income developing countries that lack adequate infrastructure. The Asian Development Bank has estimated that developing Asia will need US$8 trillion in infrastructure development from 2010–20 just to keep up with anticipated demand. Economic infrastructure is not a high priority among Western aid donors, and so China has found a special role to play in shaping the economic integration of Eurasia.

China's foreign exchange reserves have grown to US$3.9 trillion, and there is a desire to invest it in more than just U.S. Treasury bills. Growing doubts about the future of the U.S. dollar motivated China to diversify the investment of its in foreign exchange reserves and to plan for the internationalization of the RMB. The accumulation of domestic debt has grown so quickly since 2008 that the marginal productivity of domestic investment in the macro-economy is such that it takes RMB5.0 of investment to produce RMB1.0 of GDP growth. This makes attractive the investment of foreign exchange reserves in overseas projects and export finance that not only yields decent financial returns, but also stimulates domestic production and promotes higher value-added industrial export-substitution. Multi-billion dollar Silk Road infrastructure projects also allow the promotion of RMB trade invoicing, trade settlement, and project financing across Eurasia. Sustainability of this investment agenda seems feasible if domestic growth can be maintained. The national savings rate is around 40 per cent of GDP, and China runs a chronic current account surplus at around 2 per cent of GDP. China's banking system and international financial flows remain mostly under state control, so the Central Bank can provide liquidity or bailouts in the case of a crisis. China's Development and Reform Council is considering investing as much as US$800 billion over the next ten years in the two Silk Roads. This seems doable. In 2014, Premier Li Keqiang alone committed at least US$94 billion in new government financing to specific Silk Road projects and programmes at leadership meetings in Silk Road countries.[18]

Governance of the Community of Shared Destiny

The difference in economic scale between China and its neighbours means that deepening economic interdependence gives China more bilateral leverage, and military superiority gives China additional leverage. As a newly risen great power, Beijing is laying out a vision of regional order that fits its unique set of cultural norms, political values, and core interests. How is it likely to govern a China-centred international community?

The West's favoured approach to regional integration (for example, NAFTA and the EU) is economic liberalization. This uses multilateral treaties to remove legal and institutional barriers to trade and investment, and it creates legally binding rules, standards, and dispute resolution mechanisms that states must follow to create a free open space for private sector activity. It does not focus on the provision of physical infrastructure or the channelling of trade in any particular direction; this is left to the free market.

In contrast, China's approach to regional integration centres on policy-led trade facilitation. This features the improvement of trade connectivity by building more efficient transportation linkages, providing more trade and investment finance, streamlining trade and investment approvals, and multiplying human exchange opportunities. It requires policy dialogue between states to shape the direction of development rather than the negotiation of a multilateral trade liberalization agreement that sets uniform and legally binding rules for states to follow and enforce.

China's Silk Roads agenda is to create railways and ports that connect China to points across the Eurasian land mass (the Silk Road Economic Belt) and along the maritime rim of Eurasia (the 21st Century Maritime Silk Road). The result will be to channel Eurasian economic transactions toward China to deepen interdependence between individual countries of Eurasia on the one hand, and the massive Chinese economy on the other. This economic interdependence will give China superior leverage over any other Eurasian country in a one-on-one negotiation, and will give China a leadership position in any Eurasian multilateral economic policy setting.

Advancement of this agenda does not require multilateral treaty negotiations or supranational bureaucratic authority. It merely requires China to supply leadership in the form of initiating discussion, advancing cooperation proposals, lowering information and transaction costs for cooperation partners, and providing them with material incentives such as new infrastructure, credit, investment, and trade opportunities. The allocation of resources is done on an individual, case-by-case basis by Chinese authorities. Other things being equal, this should induce potential partners to voluntarily cooperate with China's Eurasian integration project.

What are some of the key principles that will guide China's governance of the new Eurasian order? Besides the afore-mentioned South-South mode of economic cooperation, we can point to at least three other principles.

First, there is the practice of bilateralism with reciprocity in Chinese diplomacy. In any matter that affects important Chinese interests, China strongly prefers reliance on bilateral negotiation. In China's view, if others respect China's interests, this respect will be paid back; but if others do not respect China, it will find ways to punish them. Countries that reject Chinese interpretations of history and territorial sovereignty, criticize Chinese human rights practices, or welcome visits of the Dalai Lama may suffer various forms of Chinese punishment such as reduced market access, Chinese obstructionism in international organizations, and diplomatic snubs.

Second, "the principled bottom line" (原则底线 *yuanze dixian*) corollary in China's commitment to peaceful development means that China will fight before it sacrifices its "core interests".[19] These core interests include the preservation of absolute power in the hands of the Chinese Communist Party and the state apparatus; the sovereignty and territorial integrity of the Chinese state; and the continuing stability and development of China's economy.[20] This means that China will not tolerate criticism for lacking liberal democracy and human rights principles; making illegitimate territorial sovereignty claims; or threatening disruption of China's continuing economic development. It reserves the right to use any means at its disposal if anyone challenges these core interests.

Finally, the international rule of law is meant to act as a brake on the arbitrary exercise of state power, and to establish an international community of states with agreed norms and procedures for managing relations. However, in explaining China's concept of the international rule of law, Foreign Minister Wang Yi stated: "Such principles as respect for sovereignty and territorial integrity, peaceful settlement of international disputes and non-interference in the internal affairs of others, as enshrined in the UN Charter, are the foundation stones upon which modern international law and conduct of international relations are built." [21] This definition omits core legal norms in the UN Charter such as state accountability to law, respect for human rights, and the resort to independent adjudication of disputes.[22]

With respect to international judicial institutions, Wang Yi warned: "[they] should avoid overstepping their authority... Still less should they encroach on the rights and interests of other countries under the pretext of 'the rule of law' in total disregard of objectivity and fairness." This begs the question, who will apply international law with objectivity and fairness when China's interests conflict with those of its neighbours?

The answer is found in China's diplomatic practice. China does not turn to international tribunals to resolve sovereignty disputes. Instead, it insists on direct bilateral negotiations with individual disputants, holding in reserve "the principled bottom line". This maximizes China's leverage and minimizes the procedural and substantive normative constraints on international dispute resolution.

The implication of reciprocity in Chinese bilateral diplomacy, the principled bottom line, and China's insistence on the sovereign interpretation of legal rights beyond the reach of international adjudication is that smaller countries will lack the protection of the full range of international legal norms and institutions when disputing with China. They will need to accommodate themselves to the values and interests of China in order to avoid the loss of rights and privileges in the community of common destiny.

This approach to regional community is different from ASEAN-style community in important respects. China promises prosperity in association with its continuing growth and development. But the core-periphery structure of connectivity, governance, and member status in China's community of shared destiny differs from the kind of non-coercive, equal, and impartial multilateralism that ASEAN has developed.

The Silk Roads Agenda in Southeast Asia

At the 2013 China-ASEAN Summit, Premier Li Keqiang introduced China's 2+7 Initiative. China's two fundamental principles of engagement with ASEAN are mutual security and economic cooperation. Based on these principles, China proposes seven ideas: a new China-ASEAN treaty of good neighbourliness and cooperation; an annual China-ASEAN defence ministers' meeting; a goal of US$1 trillion in trade by 2020; the Asian Infrastructure Investment Bank; more reliance on the RMB in Central Bank reserves, trade invoicing, and bank finance; maritime cooperation in the South China Sea; and cultural exchange. This framework strengthens Chinese influence over Southeast Asia.

On his trip to Malaysia and Indonesia in October 2013, Xi Jinping announced the 21st Century Maritime Silk Road initiative. Though the nearest target is maritime Southeast Asia, the agenda of expanding port access to support maritime trade extends across the Indian Ocean to the Persian Gulf, East Africa, and through the Red Sea into the Mediterranean.

Guangxi as a Maritime Silk Road Hub

In geo-economic terms, Guangxi has a 637km land border with Vietnam and three deep seaports on the South China Sea that can be a main terminus for the Maritime Silk Road. Together with Hainan and Guangdong provinces, Guangxi supports the Pan-Beibu Gulf Economic Cooperation Forum and it hosts the annual China-ASEAN Exposition in Nanning. Guangxi's main cooperation partners are Vietnam, Malaysia, Singapore, the Philippines, Indonesia and Brunei. Talk of a high-speed railway from Guangxi along the Vietnam coastline leading all the way to Singapore is eye-catching, but the Maritime Silk Road focus is investment by Chinese firms such as China Merchant Holdings, COSCO, CITIC, and China Communication Construction Company in port development and operation to develop maritime trade in Southeast Asia, South Asia, East Africa, the Middle East, and the Mediterranean. Table 1 summarizes recent Maritime Silk Road port projects in these subregions, using media reports available in January 2015.

TABLE 1
Maritime Silk Road Port Investments

Port	Country	Investment Value (US$ billion)
Kuantan	Malaysia	2.0
Batam	Indonesia	2.0
Kyaukpyu	Myanmar	2.4
Chittagong	Bangladesh	8.7
Colombo	Sri Lanka	1.3
Hanbantota	Sri Lanka	1.0
Gwadar	Pakistan	1.6
Djibouti	Ethiopia	0.185
Port Bashir	Sudan	0.215
Lamu	Kenya	0.480
Bagamoyo	Tanzania	10.0
Suez Canal corridor	Egypt	1.8
Piraeus	Greece	0.880

Yunnan as a Silk Road Hub

Landlocked Yunnan has always been a remote and backward border province of China. But the Silk Road Economic Belt agenda now makes Yunnan China's "strategic bridgehead" into Indochina. It borders on Vietnam, Laos, and Myanmar, and the province is a member of the Greater Mekong Sub-region (GMS) Economic Cooperation Programme. The GMS programme brings Yunnan into cooperation with Myanmar, Thailand, Vietnam, Laos, and Cambodia to manage a variety of Mekong River watershed issues. Kunming, the capital of Yunnan, is the hub of land transport corridors. An all-weather highway leads to Bangkok, and another leads to Hanoi. Planned electrified railways will link Kunming to Vientiane, Bangkok, Hanoi, Ho Chi Minh City, Kuala Lumpur, and Singapore.

Yunnan also serves as China's bridgehead to the Bay of Bengal and the wider Indian Ocean region. Myanmar is an indispensable partner in this plan. A high-speed rail link between Yunnan and Yangon is planned. More land corridors will link Kunming to Kyaukpyu on Myanmar's coastline. This is a deep-sea port developed by Chinese firms. Oil and gas pipelines from Kyaukpyu to Kunming are roughly 1,000 km long and can carry more than 22 million tons (20 million tonnes) of oil and more than 420 billion cubic feet (11.89 million cubic metres) of natural gas per year. The pipelines bring China energy from the Middle East and Africa that bypasses the long route through the Malacca Strait and South China Sea. In addition, an 868 km railway is to be built between Kunming and Kyaukpyu, as well as a highway.

Yunnan is looking beyond Myanmar to link up with Bangladesh and India. Planning to implement the Bangladesh-China-India-Myanmar Economic Corridor began in December 2013. The core element is a 2,800 km highway linking Kunming to Kolkata in India. Special customs, trade, and industrial zones along the route are intended to develop industry and build supply chains across China, Myanmar, Bangladesh, and India. The ASEAN Free Trade Area, the ASEAN-China Free Trade Area, and the ASEAN-India Free Trade Area agreements, as well as India's own Bay of Bengal initiatives, have created a low tariff environment for the BCIM corridor. This paves the way for, and will leverage the benefits of, Chinese investment through better connectivity.

Xinjiang-Greater Eurasia

Xinjiang Province borders Mongolia, Russia, Kazakhstan, Kyrgyzstan, Tajikistan, Afghanistan, Pakistan, and India. China's trade with Central Asian countries reportedly climbed 13 per cent to reach US$40 billion in 2013.[23] The province hosted the third annual China-Eurasia Exposition and the China-Eurasia Economic Development and Cooperation Forum in Urumqi on 2–7 September 2013 with ministers and officials from the Ministry of Agriculture, Central Bank, Ministry of Tourism, Ministry of Science and Technology, Department of Public Information, Department of Customs putting organizing a variety of forums and seminar, and representatives from over twenty countries attending them.[24]

China's Central Asia diplomacy goes back to the mid-1990s when it settled border disputes with newly independent neighbours. In 1996 China hosted the first Shanghai Five Summit involving China, Russia, Kazakhstan, Uzbekistan, and Kyrgyzstan to develop strategic trust and cooperation. In 2001, this group added Uzbekistan and became the Shanghai Cooperation Organization. Subsequently, a number of countries have joined as observers (Afghanistan, India, Iran, Mongolia, and Pakistan), and China has used the SCO to combat the "3 evils" (terrorism, religious extremism, and separatism) and to advance its economic interests in Eurasia.

Xi Jinping used his historic tour of Central Asia in September 2013 to launch the Silk Road Economic Belt from China through Central Asia to reach Europe.[25] The Ministry of Commerce is working out ways to promote cargo transportation, personnel exchange, e-commerce, RMB trade settlement and new cross-border economic cooperation zones. Other ministries are working out ways to promote trade and development in agriculture, tourism, and culture. In November 2013, some twenty-four cities from eight countries signed an agreement to cooperate in building this trans-Eurasian economic belt. During his tour, Xi also proposed the creation of a SCO development bank and signed new investment deals worth US$56 billion, on top of some US$30 billion in existing Chinese FDI in Central Asia.

Central Asian Energy Pipelines

The Turkmenistan-China gas pipeline and the Kazakhstan-China oil pipeline are the two major examples of trans-continental scale infrastructure projects spanning Central Asia. The West-East Gas Pipeline Project (WEPP) connects the eastern markets of China with sources in the Tarim Basin, Uzbekistan, Kazakhstan, and Turkmenistan. With the completion of Phase II, it measures 8,704 kilometres and travels through fifteen provinces. Two additional phases are planned or under construction. The 298km-long Kazakhstan-China oil pipeline transports crude oil from oil fields located in western Kazakhstan to the Dushanzi refinery in Xinjiang. It met its design capacity in 2011.[26]

Trans-Eurasian Railways

With respect to land transportation, which will be the backbone of the New Silk Road Economic Corridor, in December 2012 the Second Eurasian Land Bridge running from Lianyungang on the East China Sea through Urumqi to Rotterdam on the Atlantic, Riga on the Baltic, and the Mediterranean region via Istanbul was completed. A German firm using it today needs only sixteen days to ship a container from a Chongqing factory to Germany. Trans-Eurasian high-speed rail development is also contemplated now that Urumqi is linked to China's domestic network.

Xinjiang-Gwadar (Arabian Sea) Economic Corridor

The Xinjiang-Gwadar Port road and rail construction project now underway runs from Kashgar to the Arabian Sea near the Persian Gulf.[27] It parallels the already widened and improved Karakorum Highway linking China to Pakistan. This is to be the backbone of a China-Pakistan (Arabian Sea) economic corridor, in view of the unsettled conditions in Afghanistan that prevent secure investment in pipelines and railways through that country.

Security Implications

When Xi Jinping explained China's New Asian Security Concept at the May 2014 Conference on Interaction and Confidence Building in Asia (CICA) Summit in Shanghai, he did not offer military alliances or security guarantees to other CICA members. In fact, he urged members to turn away from military alliances altogether. Instead, he offered to develop CICA into a multilateral security forum for Eurasian countries to discuss mainly their economic developmental needs. The notion is that economic interdependence, cooperation, and development brings peace and stability, and that China's continuing growth will enhance the security of any countries linked to it. There is a hint that if any of China's neighbours are troubled by China's military rise and assertiveness, they would do better to put aside their fears in order to benefit from closer economic association with China. However, given the well-known weaknesses of informal multilateral cooperation forums, CICA would not be the first place anyone facing a threat of armed aggression would go to seek help. However, for China the point would be to lead an informal Eurasian security community devoted to common, cooperative, and comprehensive non-traditional security and economic development — without incurring any military obligations or international security commitments.

It would be naïve to believe that China's great power identity, which requires a massive and well-publicized build-up of advanced warfare capabilities, fails to consider traditional security and geopolitical interests. With the construction of Chinese connectivity to the whole of Eurasia's inland regions and maritime rim lands, the consequence of organizing Eurasian security solely as soft cooperation in non-traditional security, is to leave an unconstrained and massively armed China facing no other Eurasian state or alliance of states able to resist its will — unless it possessed a nuclear deterrent capability. Before conceiving of Eurasian security cooperation purely in terms of non-military commitments, it would be advisable that China and every other member limits the legitimate exercise of military power and commits to peaceful dispute resolution by impartially administered justice based on the international rule of law.

The connection of China's *yidai — yilu* programme to geopolitical theories of world domination is also worth noting. The geopolitical theories of Halford Mackinder and Nicolas Spykman focus on the pivotal role of Eurasia.[28] The basic idea is that Eurasia is divided into two macro-strategic zones: the heartland or pivot area of continental power roughly corresponding to the former Soviet Union, and the inner crescent or rimland that is divided into sections and oriented toward the surrounding seas. If any single state were to establish hegemony over the whole of the Eurasian land mass, the scale of resources and the geo-strategic advantages available to that state would allow it to dominate the entire world. The implication of this way of thinking is that, Great Britain before World War I, and the U.S. after World War II played the role of an offshore balancer to Tsarist Russia or the Soviet Union to prevent the consolidation of Eurasian hegemony under a single state. Today there are only two Eurasian states that might have the capacity and will to seek Eurasian hegemony: Russia and China. As explained above, the *yidai — yilu* agenda extends China's economic presence across the Eurasian heartland and around the Eurasian rimlands. This penetration of Chinese economic interests may motivate China to build a Eurasian political association and military presence. [29] Perhaps in a sign of things to come, the Chinese Navy is already patrolling off the coast of East Africa to control pirates, and China has deployed a battalion of armed soldiers to join U.N. forces in South Sudan where China's oil interests have been affected by instability.[30]

Complicating Factors

China's effort to become the Eurasian great power fits the Chinese style of realism, but it confronts certain challenges. First, soft power — the ability to cause others to admire, respect, and emulate — is critically important when trying to build a new kind of international order. Without it, a would-be hegemon has only carrots, sticks, and deception with which to manage the behaviour of others. Does the way Beijing governs its own citizens and national minorities indicate how Beijing would treat other peoples? What one sees is China deploying its growing military and civilian power in intimidating ways to get neighbours to cede their maritime territorial rights granted under the U.N. Convention of the Law of the Sea (UNCLOS) — which China has signed. It is possible that China may decide to embrace the international rule of law and rely on UNCLOS dispute resolution provisions at some point in future, but if it does not, neighbours both large and small will face difficult choices. It is already apparent that few, if any, of China's neighbours are willing to see China govern the region single-handedly.

Second, China may assume that the U.S. will recognize the primacy of China's interests in Asia and cede to it a "sphere of influence". However, the U.S. sees a vital interest at stake in maintaining a strategic defensive perimeter in the Western Pacific and naval supremacy in the world's oceans. Other powers, such as Russia, India, and Japan, may also prudently wish to prevent the kind of Eurasian predominance that China may eventually seek, especially if China continues to demonstrate the "great power autism" of bullying smaller neighbours for marginal territorial gains.[31]

Third, given China's endemic environmental crisis, systemic financial risks, institutional corruption, labour unrest, aging population, and civil society pressures for democratization, it is far from certain that there will be no "black swan" event in China's future that will derail its rapid upward trajectory.

Conclusion

China's Eurasian geo-strategic vision is plausible if one assumes that China's fast-paced economic growth and development can be maintained, and if China's continuing rise does not call forth counter-balancing coalitions of states. Based on a successful programme of Silk Road development, China may command the markets and resources of Eurasia and neighbouring Africa. China's community of shared destiny is simple and easy to manage — for China. It relies on the ability to finance the construction of economic corridors and to incentivize economic cooperation with China, and it puts China at the centre of a Eurasian hub-and-spoke structure of power relations with few legal and strategic constraints on its exercise of sovereign power. A look at what China has done so far shows that it is quickly advancing this agenda both across the heartland and around the margins of the Eurasian land mass.[32] Though China faces many daunting obstacles and uncertainties, the impact of its Eurasian strategy could be lasting, and is today certainly changing the existing Eurasian order.

Notes

1. Map of Yuxinou Railway connecting China with Europe, available at <http://www.therakyatpost.com/wp-content/uploads/2014/03/rail_M.jpg>.

2. Map comparing the Silk Road Economic Belt and the 21st Century Maritime Silk Road, available at <http://www.chinadaily.com.cn/china/images/attachement/jpg/site1/20140411/00221917e13e14b179190f.jpg>.

3. "Chinese Carrier Cosco is Transforming Piraeus — and Has Eyes on Thessaloniki", *The Guardian*, 19 June 2014, available at <http://www.theguardian.com/world/2014/jun/19/china-piraeus-greece-cosco-thessaloniki-railways>; "China's 21st Century 'Maritime Silk Road' Ambitions", *Seatradeglobal.com*, 19 December 2014, available at <http://www.seatrade-global.com/news/asia/chinas-21st-century-maritime-silk-road-ambitions.html>.

4. "China on Track in Russia", *Chinadaily.com*, 14 October 2014, available at <http://www.chinadaily.com.cn/world/2014livisitgrl/2014-10/14/content_18735207.htm>.

5. "China is Planning to Build a Bullet-train that Connects Eastern and Western Europe", *Business Insider*, 16 December 2014, available at <http://www.businessinsider.com/afp-china-steps-up-plan-for-new-export-corridor-into-europe-2014-12>; Press Release: "Five Containers Already Arrived from the Port of Piraeus, Rail Cargo Hungaria", 16 June 2014, available at <http://www.railcargo.hu/en/press-room/press-releases/1962-press-release-five-containers-already-arrived-to-hungary-from-the-port-of-piraeus.html>.

6. "中国'超级推销员'签约1,400亿美元" [China's Super Salesman Closes Deals Worth US$140 Billion], 广州日报 [*Guangzhou Daily*], 29 December 2014, available at <news.xinhuanet.com/world/2014-12/29/c_1113804346.htm>.

7. CICA website, available at <http://www.s-cica.org/index.html>.

8. Statement by H.E. Mr Xi Jinping, "Conference on Interaction and Confidence Building Measures in Asia", 21 May 2014, available at <http://www.s-cica.org/page.php?page_id=711&lang=1>.

9. "China to Offer India Aid for High Speed Rail Study", *Reuters*, 25 November 2014, available at <http://in.reuters.com/article/2014/11/25/china-india-railway-idINKCN0J90EF20141125>.

10. "With New Funds, China Hits a Silk Road Stride", *Caixin*, 3 December 2014, available at <http://english.caixin.com/2014-12-03/100758419.html>.

11. Wu Xinbo, "Understanding the Geopolitical Implications of the Global Financial Crisis", *The Washington Quarterly* 33, no. 4 (October 2010): 155–63.

12. Elizabeth C. Economy, "The Game Changer: Coping with China's Foreign Policy Revolution", *Foreign Affairs* 89, no. 6 (November/December 2010), available at <http://www.foreignaffairs.com/articles/66865/elizabeth-c-economy/the-game-changer>.

13. Andrew F. Krepinevich, et al., *Meeting the Anti-Access and Area Denial Challenge*, Center for Strategic and Budgetary Assessments, 2003, available at <http://csbaonline.org/publications/2003/05/a2ad-anti-access-area-denial/>.

14. "China Vows to Build Community of Common Destiny with ASEAN", *Xinhua*, 3 October 2013, available at <http://news.xinhuanet.com/english/china/2013-10/03/c_132770494.htm> (accessed 21 March 2014).

15. "Xi Jinping: Let the Sense of Community of Common Destiny Take Deep Root in Neighbouring Countries", Ministry of Foreign Affairs of the People's Republic of China, 25 October 2013, available at <http://www.fmprc.gov.cn/mfa_chn/zyxw_602251/t1093113.shtml>. This agenda was reaffirmed in a broader and more confident vision of Chinese great power leadership at a Central Work Meeting on Foreign Affairs in November 2014. See "习近平出席中央外事工作会议并发表重要讲话" [Xi Jinping attends the Central Work Meeting on Foreign Affairs to make an important speech], *Xinhua Online*, 29 November 2014, available at <http://news.xinhuanet.com/politics/2014-11/29/c_1113457723.htm>.

16. Zarubino port on the Japan Sea will be jointly developed by China and Russia into a 60 million ton/year port linked by road and rail to Jilin Province at the border city of Hunchun. "Russia Port Has Big Regional Goals, Especially for Northeast Asia", *Global Times*, 18 September 2014, available at <http://en.people.cn/business/n/2014/0918/c90778-8784185.html>. Jilin already has road and rail links to the North Korean port of Rajin where it has a long-term lease on pier facilities.

17. Charles Wolf, Jr., Xiao Wang, and Eric Warner, *China's Foreign Aid and Government-sponsored Investment Activities: Scale, Content, Destinations, and Implications* (Santa Monica, CA: RAND National Defense Research Institute, 2013), available at <http://www.rand.org/content/dam/rand/pubs/research_reports/RR100/RR118/RAND_RR118.pdf>.

18. "The Chinese Premier's US$140 Billion Trips Abroad", *China Development Gateway*, 26 December 2014, available at <http://en.chinagate.cn/2014-12/26/content_34416924.htm>.

19. "习近平阐明中国和平发展原则底线" [Xi Jinping Explains the Principled Bottom Line in China's Peaceful Development], *Xinhua Online*, 30 January 2013, available at <http://www.chinanews.com/gn/2013/01-31/4535125.shtml>. Timothy Heath, "Diplomacy Work Forum: Xi Steps Up Efforts to Shape a China-Centered Regional Order", *China Brief*, vol. 13, issue 22 (7 November 2013), available at <http://www.jamestown.org/single/?tx_ttnews[tt_news]=41594&no_cache=1#.VJGRfqbdVRA>.

20. In 2009, speaking at the U.S.-China Strategic and Economic Dialogue, State Councilor Dai Bingguo defined China's core interests in the following way: "中国的核心利益第一是维护基本制度和国家安全，其次是国家主权和领土完整，第三是经济社会的持续稳定发展" [First Round of the U.S.-China Economic Dialogue: Other Important Issues Discussed Besides the Moon], 首轮中美经济对话:除上月球外主要问题均已谈及, 中国新闻网 [*China News Online*], 29 July 2009, 9:29 a.m., available at <http://www.chinanews.com.cn/gn/news/2009/07-29/1794984.shtml>.

21. "Full Text of Chinese FM's Signed Article on Int'l Rule of Law", *Xinhua*, 24 October 2014, available at <http://en.people.cn/n/2014/1024/c90883-8799769-2.html>.

22. The U.N.'s definition of the international rule of law starts off this way: "a principle of governance in which all persons, institutions and entities, public and private, *including the State itself*, are accountable to laws that are publicly promulgated, equally enforced and *independently adjudicated*, and which are consistent with *international human rights norms and standards*…." (italics added). "What is the Rule of Law?", United Nations Rule of Law website, available at <http://www.unrol.org/article.aspx?article_id=3>.

23. "China-Central Asia Trade Seeing Fast Growth", *Xinhua*, 13 February 2014, available at <http://news.xinhuanet.com/english/china/2014-02/13/c_133112941.htm> (accessed 21 March 2014).

24. "China-Eurasia Expo, Urumqi, Xinjiang, China-Britain Business Council", China-Britain Business Council, available at <http://www.cbbc.org/cbbc_calendar/event/view?id=610> (accessed 21 March 2014).

25. "China Proposes New Silk Road Free Trade Zone", *China Briefing*, 17 September 2013, available at <http://www.china-briefing.com/news/2013/09/17/china-proposes-new-silk-road-free-trade-zone.html> (accessed 21 March 2014); Aleksandra Jarosiewicz, "A Chinese *Tour de force* in Central Asia", *OSW*, 18 September 2013, available at <http://www.osw.waw.pl/en/publikacje/analyses/2013-09-18/a-chinese-tour-de-force-central-asia> (accessed 21 March 2014).

26. "The World's Longest Oil and Gas Pipelines", *hydrocarbons-technology.com*, 18 October 2012, available at <http://www.hydrocarbons-technology.com/features/featureworlds-longest-oil-gas-pipelines-imports/> (accessed 21 March 2014).

27. Martin W. Lewis, "Balochistan and the New 'Great Game' in Central Asia?", *Geo-Currents*, 20 May 2012, available at <http://www.geocurrents.info/geopolitics/balochistan-and-a-new-great-game-in-central-asia> (accessed 21 March 2014); Shabaz Rana, "Building on Ties: New Premier Indicates Plan to Link Gwadar with China", *The Express-Tribune*, 6 June 2013, available at <http://tribune.com.pk/story/559370/building-on-ties-new-premier-indicates-plan-to-link-gwadar-with-china/> (accessed 21 March 2014).

28. Halford J. Mackinder, "The Round World and the Winning of the Peace", *Foreign Affairs* 21 (1943): 595–605. Nicolas J. Spykman, *America's Strategy in World Politics: The United States and the Balance of Power* (New York: Harcourt, Brace and Company, 1942). See also, Zbigniew Brzezinski, *The Grand Chessboard: American Primacy and Its Geostrategic Imperatives* (New York: Basic Books, 1998).

29. Shannon Tiezzi, "The Maritime Silk Road vs. the String of Pearls", *The Diplomat*, 13 February 2014, available at <http://thediplomat.com/2014/02/the-maritime-silk-road-vs-the-string-of-pearls/>.

30. "Chinese Troops Ready to Join South Sudan UN Force", *BBC News*, 22 December 2014, available at <http://www.bbc.com/news/world-africa-30577294>; "China Oil Fears Over South Sudan Fighting", *BBC News*, 8 January 2014, available at <http://www.bbc.com/news/world-africa-25654155>.

31. Edward N. Luttwak, *The Rise of China vs. the Logic of Strategy* (U.S.: Harvard University Press, 2012).

32. Map of China's proposed Silk Road Routes, available at <http://www.wsj.com/articles/chinas-new-trade-routes-center-it-on-geopolitical-map-1415559290>.

SOUTHEAST ASIAN ECONOMIES
Striving for Growth

Arief Ramayandi and Megananda Suryana

Growth prospects for Southeast Asia in 2014 turned out to be less than what many expected earlier in the year. The International Monetary Fund (IMF) and the Asian Development Bank (ADB) lowered the growth forecast for regional economies in their fourth quarter 2014 flagship publications by 0.2 and 0.4 percentage points respectively relative to what they had perceived earlier in the year (see Table 1). These changes imply more pessimistic perceptions about how the region's economies will fare in terms of their growth as more data became available. As a consequence, according to ADB estimates, aggregate GDP growth for all Southeast Asian economies in 2014 moderated to 4.6 per cent relative to 5.0 per cent in 2013, marking the second consecutive slowdown in economic activities of the region. Inflation, however, is projected to be relatively stable at slightly above 4 per cent.

Despite the trend of general slowdown, there are differences in the performance of each individual country (Table 1). Downward corrections for the projection of 2014 growth rate were obvious in the case of Indonesia, Philippines, Singapore and Thailand. Malaysia, on the contrary, is marked with an upward correction, an improvement in economic growth performance relative to the previous year. This paper provides a discussion on what is behind the general slowdown in growth of the region and a glimpse at the prospects going forward.

ARIEF RAMAYANDI is a Senior Economist at the Asian Development Bank, the Philippines.

MEGANANDA SURYANA is a Researcher at the Center for Economics and Development Studies, Department of Economics, Padjadjaran University, Indonesia.

TABLE 1
Southeast Asia's GDP Growth Rates: 2013–14

	2013 (ADB)	2014 (ADB)		2014 (IMF)	
	ACTUAL	ADO 2014	UPDATE 2014	WEO 2014	UPDATE 2014
ASEAN	5.0	5.0	4.6	4.9	4.7
Brunei Darussalam	−1.8	1.1	1.1	5.4	5.3
Cambodia	7.2	7.0	7.0	7.3	7.2
Indonesia	5.8	5.7	5.3	5.4	5.2
Lao P.D.R.	7.9	7.3	7.3	7.5	7.4
Malaysia	4.7	5.1	5.7	5.2	5.9
Myanmar	7.5	7.8	7.8	7.8	8.5
Philippines	7.2	6.4	6.2	6.4	6.2
Singapore	3.9	3.9	3.5	3.7	3.0
Thailand	2.9	2.9	1.6	2.5	1.0
Vietnam	5.4	5.6	5.5	5.6	5.5

Notes: Data for 2013 taken from Asian Development Bank; ADO = Asian Development Outlook; WEO = World Economic Outlook.
Source: ADB's Asian Development Outlook Update 2014 and IMF's Asia and Pacific Economic Outlook: October 2014 Update.

Large Economies Dominated the Slowdown

Aggregate GDP growth rate in the ten Southeast Asian economies decelerated for a second year in a row, to 4.6 per cent in 2014 from 5.0 per cent in 2013 and 5.7 per cent in 2012. The softer growth rate was primarily driven by slower growth in the region's four biggest economies, which occupy about 76 per cent of the Southeast Asia's total output (see Figure 1). Indonesia and Thailand, the two largest economies in Southeast Asia, have dragged down the region's growth over the past two years. In particular, the regional growth performance in 2014 was affected by political instability in Thailand that saw a contraction of the economy

FIGURE 1
Average GDP Share 2009–12

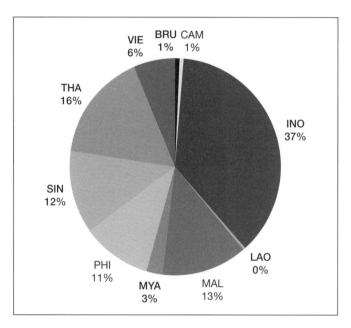

BRU = Brunei Darussalam, CAM = Cambodia, INO = Indonesia, LAO = Lao P.D.R., MAL = Malaysia, MYR = Myanmar, PHI = Philippines, SIN = Singapore, THA = Thailand, VIE = Viet Nam.

Source: Processed from CEIC database.

in the first half of the year and an unexpectedly sharp slowdown in Indonesia that brought growth to its weakest in five years. By contrast, Malaysia, the third largest economy in the region, was performing much better than expected and was forecast to expand at its strongest pace in four years.

Figure 2 displays the trends in economic growth rate and its private domestic demand components by focusing on Southeast Asia's five largest economies: Indonesia, Malaysia, the Philippines, Singapore and Thailand — the Southeast Asia-5. The declines in growth momentum of these economies were generally accompanied by declines in the total growth of domestic private consumption and investment. Worse still, growth in domestic demand components for the Southeast Asia-5 was generally showing an even more persistent declining trend than GDP growth since 2012. Fixed investment decelerated in Indonesia,

FIGURE 2
Growth of GDP and Private Domestic Demand in
Southeast Asia-5: 2012–14

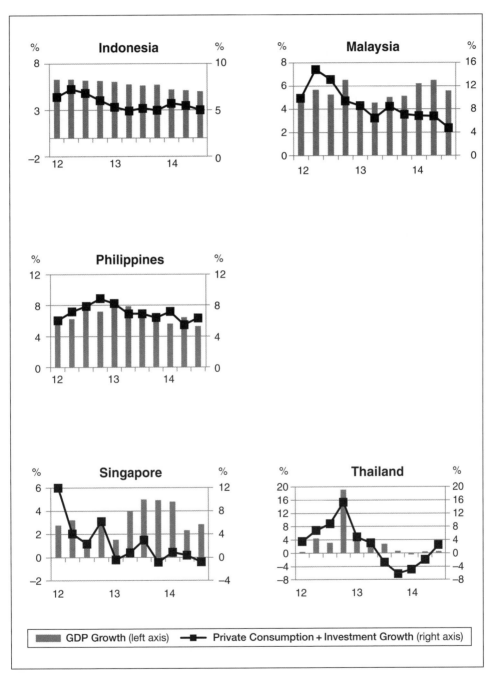

Malaysia, and the Philippines in the first half of 2014 and actually fell in Singapore and Thailand. Growth in private consumption in these economies also tended to moderate throughout 2014. Dimmer growth momentum in private consumption and investment, which played a major role in supporting the region's growth during the global financial crisis, means less support for the aggregate economic activity recently.

Thailand seems to differ from other cases as growth in domestic demand components picked up in 2014. The pick-up, however, took place after an interruption in the growth of domestic demand following political disruptions and government paralysis that eroded confidence and undermined domestic consumption and investment through the second half of 2013 and into the first half of 2014. Therefore, the pick-up is more appropriately seen as a correction as domestic demand started to recover gradually, sending its growth back to positive territory in the third quarter of 2014. Private consumption contracted by 1.4 per cent in the first half of 2014 and private investment slid by 7.2 per cent in the same period as companies postponed decisions due to political uncertainty. That said, the trivial pick-up in the growth of private domestic demand in the third quarter was mainly due to a low base, and did not reflect genuine strengths of rebound in private consumption and investment.

The problems emanating from weaker domestic demand in Southeast Asia were amplified by weak external demand as economic recovery in major industrialized economies remained sluggish. Figure 3 displays year-on-year growth rates of export and import activities of the Southeast Asia-5. Feeble external demand generally weakened export performance in 2014, but imports deteriorated even more, helping countries to improve their trade balance position. Again, variations were observed in trade performance as exports rebounded in Malaysia, the Philippines and Singapore in the first half of 2014, but fell in Indonesia and Thailand (see Figure 3). Declining imports, however, are often a sign of weak investment in most countries as the bulk of imports in these economies consist of capital goods and raw materials, and hence making the prospect for future pick-up perhaps even grimmer.

In sum, the recent deceleration of growth prospects in Southeast Asia is a result of less vibrant domestic factors and sluggish progress in the global economic recovery. The combination of these lethargic external and internal factors complicates the policy challenges faced by authorities in the region for sustaining a high growth momentum going forward.

FIGURE 3
Growth of Total Export and Import in Southeast Asia-5: 2012–14
(Percentage)

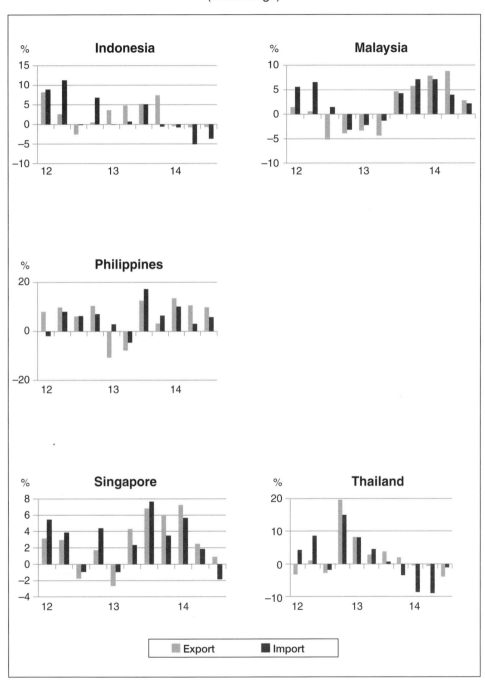

Source: Processed from CEIC database.

The External Environment

For the Southeast Asian economies, support for growth from the external environment is currently not very encouraging. This section discusses external challenges faced by the region, starting from the feeble economic recovery in the major industrial economies that prevented a faster rebound in the global economy; slower growth performance of China; and Southeast Asian countries' own deceleration in the momentum of economic growth.

In its 2013 report, the ADB showed a change in the structure of trade between the Southeast Asian economies and their trading partners (see Figure 4). Although the traditional trading partners — the major industrial economies of the U.S., Euro zone and Japan — still absorbed a large chunk of the region's exports, the two Asian giants, particularly China, have become increasingly important markets

FIGURE 4
Trade Shares of ASEAN Countries' Major Trading Partners

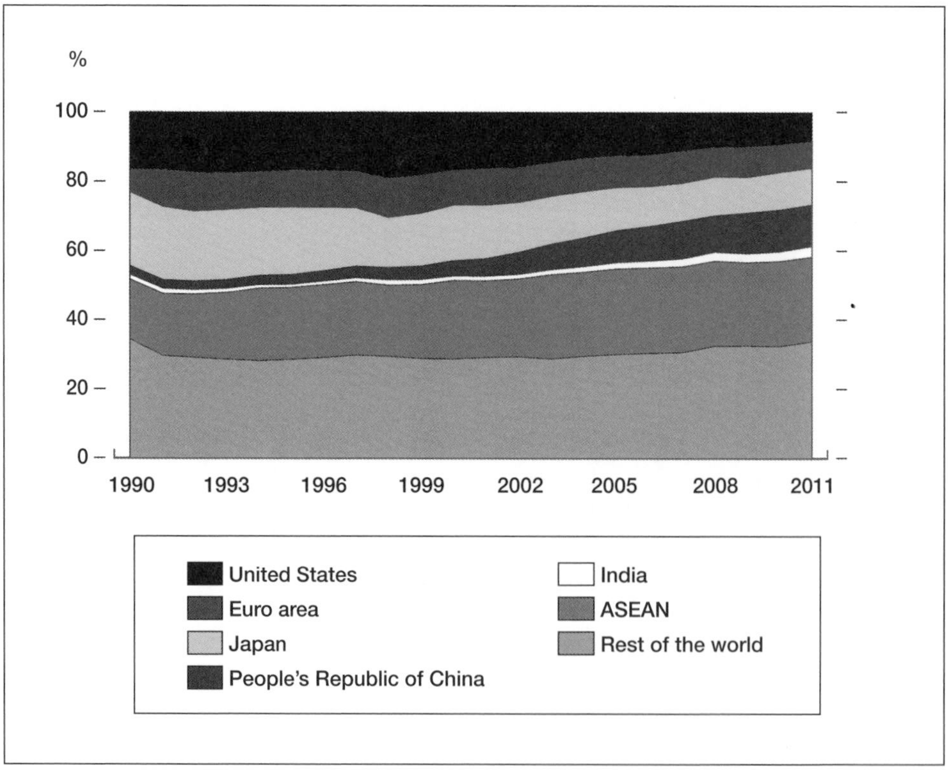

Source: Asian Development Outlook 2013, p. 12.

for the Southeast Asian economies. The share of exports from Southeast Asia to both China and India has grown rapidly in the 2000s, and China has now become the most important single trading partner for the region. In addition, trade within the region has also become increasingly important for each of the Southeast Asian countries as a result of their intensified involvement in global value chains.

During the global financial crisis in 2008–09, this change in trade structure helped to secure trade for the region. Greater trade within developing Asia helped to cushion the impact of soft export demand from traditional markets during the crisis. But with the recent trend of slower growth in China and in the Southeast Asia region in general, the challenge of upholding growth through export demand from within Asia also has become more challenging. Weak demand from the traditional markets for final goods exports — Europe and the United States — has seemed to finally negate the support for export demand from higher trade within Asia following weaker demand for intermediate goods exports as the markets for final durable goods remained sluggish.

Major Industrial Economies

Economic recovery continued in the major industrial economies, albeit slowly. The recovery pace was somewhat disrupted in the first half of 2014 as growth weakened due to a the slower U.S. first quarter because of a severe winter, a stalled second quarter growth rate in Europe, and a second quarter contraction in Japan that turned into a technical recession which continued into the third quarter. All these suggest that global trade would remain muted as the growth in major industrial economies may not be strong enough to compensate slowing demand from emerging economies.

Prospects for the strength of economic recovery going forward diverge among the major industrial economies. Recovery in the U.S. is back on track after a disappointing first quarter with strong rebound of 4.6 per cent at a seasonally adjusted annualized rate (saar) in the second quarter, driven by private consumption and investment. This trend was expected to continue throughout the year as the economy was estimated to grow at 3.9 per cent (saar) in the third quarter. Imports quickened, outpacing exports as domestic demand propelled the overall economic growth. Unemployment declined continuously from 6.6–6.7 per cent at the beginning of 2014 to 5.6 per cent by the end of the year. Inflation, however, remained low, averaging 1.8 per cent for the year.

The momentum for recovery in the Euro zone slowed as GDP growth stalled in the second quarter of 2014. GDP growth declined in the major European economies — Germany, France, and Italy — except for Spain, which recorded a positive growth. Investment was a drag on the second quarter growth, and was expected to remain weak. Consumption, despite its positive contribution to growth in the second quarter, also appeared to be weak as the consumer confidence index remained negative throughout 2014. Unemployment remained stubbornly high at 11.5 per cent. Deflation remained a threat for the area as the inflation rate remained close to zero, well below the ECB's inflation target of 1.0 per cent.

In Japan, a robust growth in the first quarter of 2014 was followed by GDP contractions in both the second and third quarter. As households and firms brought spending forward before the value-added tax (VAT) rate hike in April, private consumption and investment fell sharply in the second quarter. The weakness continued in the third quarter as investment fell further and consumption rebounded only mildly. Consumer price index inflation was around 1.0 per cent excluding the VAT effect, but inflationary effects from the yen depreciation of 2013 would gradually fade. The decline in international oil prices may also complicate Japan's effort to move away from its deflation trap.

The uneven progress in economic recovery among the major industrial economies pointed to moderate, if not weak, demand for final export products from other economies. Even the U.S. economy, which showed the strongest signs of recovery, was still growing at a moderate pace that did not guarantee a huge jump in demand for exports from other economies, including those from Southeast Asia.

China

China has played a key role in the region's development over the past three decades. The region's dependence on China has increased sharply over the past five years as China emerged as a key source of end demand at a time when the U.S., Europe and Japan slowed significantly after the global financial crisis. China has become an important export destination for the Southeast Asian economies, particularly in relation to the region's production network where China as the final goods producer absorbed the intermediate goods produced by most of the region's economies.

After three decades of rapid expansion at around 10 per cent annually, growth started to decelerate. Despite its still enviable rate of GDP growth of

7.4 per cent in 2014, China's economic expansion has continued to moderate along with its recent policies to promote more sustainable growth that relies more on domestic potentials. This prospect of controlled deceleration in growth matters to Southeast Asian economies given the importance of China as their major export destination. The ADB, in two consecutive publications,[1] discussed the possible spillover implications from the lower growth in China to other economies in Asia. A one percentage point growth slowdown in China is estimated to drag down growth in the Southeast Asian economies by about 0.17 percentage point.[2] The spillover effect is even higher when one considers only the five largest economies in the region (Indonesia, Malaysia, Philippines, Singapore and Thailand), where growth is at risk of falling by about 0.25 percentage point for each point of growth slowdown in China.[3]

The moderation of GDP growth in China is likely to continue in 2015 as the government lowers its growth target to concentrate on structural reforms. These reforms are aiming at a more sustainable long-term growth rate for the economy by changing the country's growth model into one that is less capital and energy-intensive, and less dependent on credit and real estate booms. Despite being lower on average, the growth rates need to continue to be high enough to generate employment for the economy. Nevertheless, at least in the short run, the transition would still bring an adverse impact to the growth prospects of China's important trading partners, including those in Southeast Asia.

Trade would be the primary channel through which the slowdown in China is transmitted to the region, but it is not the only one. In line with its growing economic power, China has emerged as an important source of foreign direct investment (FDI) to the region. FDI from China into Singapore, for example, reached US$3 billion in 2011. Growth deceleration in China may also be translated into a decline in FDI from China to the region, causing an adverse effect on Southeast Asian economies in general. Thus there would be a significant impact of a slowing China on the region. The effect on individual countries, certainly, will not be uniform. Countries tied up more intensively with China in terms of production networks will likely be hit harder than others.

Within Southeast Asian

Although the region's recent general slowdown of growth is not entirely attributable to external environment, the sluggish economic recovery in the major

TABLE 2
Top 5 Export Destinations for Southeast Asian Economies: 2009–13

Top 5 Export Destination	1	2	3	4	5
Brunei Darussalam	Japan	S. Korea	Australia	Indonesia	India
Cambodia	US	Hong Kong	UK	Canada	Germany
Indonesia	Japan	China	Singapore	US	S. Korea
Lao P.D.R.	Thailand	China	Viet Nam	UK	Japan
Malaysia	Singapore	China	Japan	US	Thailand
Myanmar	Thailand	China	India	Japan	S. Korea
Philippines	Japan	US	China	Singapore	Hong Kong
Singapore	Malaysia	Hong Kong	China	Indonesia	US
Thailand	China	Japan	US	Hong Kong	Malaysia
Viet Nam	US	China	Japan	S. Korea	Germany

Source: Processed from CEIC database.

industrial economies and a slower China have certainly played some role by at least slowing the growth of exports of the regional economies.

Table 2 shows the top five export markets for each of the Southeast Asian countries. It clearly shows that, during the past five years, the top five export market destinations were either the major industrial economies, China or some other Southeast Asian countries. Adverse events in any of these economies would bring about negative implications for exports of the region. In particular, aside from the weak performance in its traditional markets and China, the region's recent exports have also been penalized by the region's own weaker growth performance.

Effects Beyond Trade

Beyond trade, the external developments discussed above would also have other implications for growth stability in the region. First and foremost, the recovery momentum taking place in the United States would eventually prompt its monetary authority to tighten the monetary policy stance to normalcy after the ultra-loose policies since the outbreak of the global financial crisis. The action may induce distortions to the region's financial markets and disturb the pace of growth in Southeast Asian economies.

Financial market volatility in emerging economies, including those in Southeast Asia, intensified following the remark from the U.S. Federal Reserve chairman in late May 2013 about the possible tapering of the third wave of their quantitative easing policy. The comment shocked markets and provoked a large and sudden stream of capital outflow from emerging economies, including Southeast Asia, heightening volatility and disrupting the growth momentum of these economies. The news was however not followed by an actual tapering — let alone tightening — until the end of 2013.[4]

With the rebound of economic activity, interest rates in the U.S. may eventually start to rise sometime in 2015. This would be an actual tightening of monetary policy that follows a sequence of asset purchase tapering that still leaves the economy with ample liquidity. While the May 2013 talk of tapering was not anticipated by the market, the potential start of liquidity contraction in the U.S. is now widely anticipated. Due to this reason, it is argued that the region's economies are better prepared to face such a liquidity contraction, making the risk of heightened volatility to be less severe when the event unfolds. To avoid excessive capital outflows, the economies in the region may need to appropriately adjust their interest rates upward. Consequently, domestic cost of capital would rise and narrow the scope for faster growth in the regional economies going forward.

However, not all the major industrial economies would start to tighten their liquidity condition in 2015. Due to the slow progress of the economic recovery, particularly relative to that of the United States, economies in the Euro zone and Japan will continue with their liquidity expansion to stimulate their economy further. This may, to some extent, limit the effects of the possible reduction of liquidity in the U.S., and its volatility implications for the financial markets in emerging economies.

Further, the decline in oil and other commodity prices will help to keep aggregate prices in check and therefore reduce the necessity to raise interest rates too quickly to combat inflation. The risk of deflation in some advanced economies could prompt them to continue maintaining their accommodative monetary policy, which eventually would help sustain the easy liquidity condition of the global economy. Such a situation, if managed properly, could benefit emerging markets — Southeast Asia included — as capital inflows that follow could then be channelled into productive uses to encourage faster economic growth in the receiving economy.

The weak commodity prices can also be seen as presenting valuable opportunities for implementing necessary reforms to benefit the economic development of countries in the region. Declining oil prices make it easier for countries to reform their unproductive domestic fuel subsidy programmes to provide additional fiscal space for more productive government spending. Indonesia, for example, has taken a series of domestic fuel subsidy reforms that could benefit the country's future economic development. Large commodity exporters can also seize the opportunity to enhance the development of their manufacturing sectors to provide wider means for future economic expansion and compensate for low commodity prices that lessen commodity exports value, which has traditionally acted as the main pillar for their economic growth.

For most of the Southeast Asian economies, the lower global commodity prices tend to bring more benefit than harm. Table 3 shows that, except for Brunei Darussalam, the shares of commodity net trade in GDP are small if not negative. While lower commodity prices would certainly benefit countries with negative net trade — like the Philippines, Singapore and Thailand — the relatively small costs to countries like Indonesia, Malaysia and Vietnam would likely be more than compensated by the benefit of lower domestic aggregate price inflation. In other words, lower international commodity prices would tend to be growth enhancing for most of the Southeast Asian economies as the low prices reduce trade deficits for some countries and lower the inflation rate, which increases domestic purchasing power in most of the countries in the region.

TABLE 3
Primary Merchandise Trade, 2013 As % to GDP

Economy	Primary Products Net Trade	Fuel, Net Trade
Brunei Darussalam	51.5	54.4
Indonesia	3.2	1.0
Malaysia	4.2	3.2
Philippines	−2.1	−2.2
Singapore	−13.5	−12.3
Thailand	−4.0	−7.7
Viet Nam	1.3	−0.2

Source: UNCOMTRADE SITC Revision 3 and IMF-WEO database.

Although lower international commodity prices generally benefit economic growth, this trend does not come without downsides. For large commodity exporters like Brunei Darussalam, lower commodity prices would certainly tax the country's capacity to grow faster. In addition, a prolonged trend of weakening commodity prices would also suggest lingering weakness in global demand. Despite the fact that the current trend of declining international oil prices is mostly viewed as being due to the supply factors, an extended period of falling oil prices would also reflect failure of the global demand to pick up. Sluggish demand in the global economy would be a great concern for Southeast Asian countries as it will stall demand for exports, which is an important factor for growth of the region.

The Internal Environment

Aside from its direct implications for the Southeast Asian economies, the unfavourable external environment has also indirectly brought up issues that may threaten domestic economic stability of these countries. The ultra-loose monetary policy in the advanced economies has led to a massive expansion in global liquidity that spills into emerging economies, including those in Southeast Asia, resulting in rapid domestic credit expansion. On the one hand, the credit expansion supported the economy by pushing up aggregate demand, which was needed to compensate for the weaker demand for exports from the traditional markets during the global financial crisis. On the other hand, excessive credit expansions could harm economic stability by pushing prices up, particularly those of assets, beyond what is supported by the economic fundamentals. Worse still, excessive increases in asset prices could worsen the situation by creating a vicious circle of continuing credit expansion, as it provides borrowers with increasing value of collaterals to back up more debt. If not appropriately managed, such events could easily send an economy into crisis.

Asset prices in the large Southeast Asian economies were rapidly inflated following massive liquidity expansion policies in the advanced economies. This is what partly explains the large fall in the region's financial markets during the taper tantrum discussed earlier. Such large fluctuations intensified the financial markets' volatility in the region, which in turn increased the perception of risk for investing in these markets. In consequence, countries were forced to compensate for the higher risk premium by raising their interest rates in order to maintain their attractiveness as investment destinations. The region has witnessed interest rates rises quite sharply since the taper talk, most notably in Indonesia. As also discussed earlier in the text, this tendency of higher interest rates in the

Southeast Asian economies is eventually going to be translated into higher domestic cost of capital that may put tighter limits on growth potential.

The other type of asset that experienced rapid growth in prices following the massive stream of capital inflows to the region is property. In association with rapid increases in domestic credit, home prices have risen markedly since 2009 in most of the large Southeast Asian economies (see Figure 5). Different countries have reacted differently to such conditions. Singapore is among the countries that reacted aggressively to contain house prices from going out of control. It went beyond the standard policies to contain the growth of credit for housing by applying various measures to contain demand. Even with such responses, the current level of house prices in the region remains high, making them less affordable which may need correction at some point in the future. To avoid massive corrections that may be followed by an economic crisis, efforts to contain excessive increases in property prices would have to be conducted prudently.

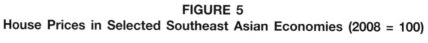

FIGURE 5
House Prices in Selected Southeast Asian Economies (2008 = 100)

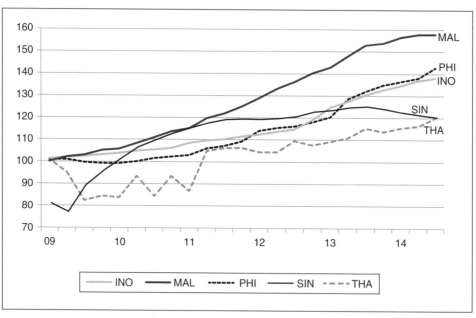

INO = Indonesia; MAL = Malaysia; PHI = Philippines; SIN = Singapore; THA = Thailand

Data Source:
Indonesia = Bank Indonesia; Malaysia = Valuation and Property Services Department; Philippines = Colliers International; Singapore = Urban Redevelopment Authority; Thailand = Bank of Thailand

FIGURE 6
Inward Foreign Direct Investment
(US Dollars at current prices and current exchange rates in millions)

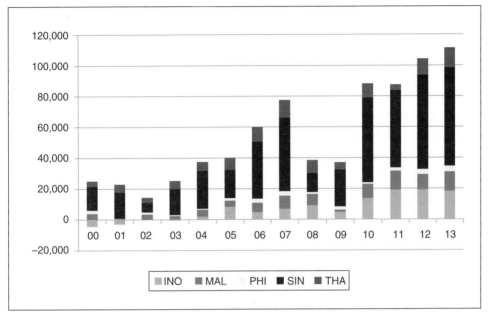

INO = Indonesia; MAL = Malaysia; PHI = Philippines; SIN = Singapore; THA = Thailand

Source: United Nations Conference on Trade and Development (UNCTAD).

Thus far, Southeast Asian economies have also been quite successful in maintaining their attractiveness as foreign investment destinations. Figure 5 suggests that inward FDI to the five largest regional economies has generally increased steadily after the peak of the global financial crisis impact in 2009. This is a good trend as FDI is considered the type of foreign capital inflow that jells very well with enhancing the economic growth of a country. Maintaining this trend in the future would be a challenge, particularly given the prospects of monetary policy tightening in the U.S. that may prompt a reversal in global investors' sentiment towards the region.

To maintain the momentum of investment in the region, countries need to continue preserving their level of economic competitiveness. Although specific policies may differ from country to country, maintaining a competitive level of the cost of doing business should be a common target for the region. In particular, countries need to enhance the productivity of their input factors, while maintaining the costs of these inputs at the same time. Countries with poor infrastructure should proceed to expedite their infrastructure development programme in order to avoid the competitiveness of their production sector being undermined by the inadequacy of their supporting infrastructure.

Maintaining labour productivity and its competitiveness is another issue for the region. Recently, some have argued that Southeast Asian economies are regaining their labour competitiveness following the rapid increase of real wages in China. While real wages are also rising in Southeast Asia, the recent average increase is less than that of China. In the last five years, China's annual rate of growth of real wages was averaging at about 7.9 per cent, which is much higher than Indonesia's that saw the steepest annual average increase in growth post the global financial crisis (Table 4). From this standpoint, it thus seems reasonable to expect that some of the FDI flows to China may slowly be diverted to Southeast Asia. In the near term, however, this is not very likely.

Despite its higher growth in real wages during the past five years, labour productivity in China also grew relatively at par — by about 7.6 per cent — in the same period. The story for Southeast Asia is, unfortunately, somewhat different. Table 4 highlights that in three out of the five largest Southeast Asian economies, the average annual growth of real wages way outpaced the average annual growth in labour productivity — measured as the average of the total output per worker — in the past five years. The higher increase in China's real wages actually does less harm to its labour competitiveness relative to those in the three Southeast Asian countries. The accommodation of workers' demand for higher nominal wages in Indonesia, Malaysia and Thailand, has not come with comparable increase in productivity. Consequently, the degree of labour competitiveness in these countries fell substantially as the real cost of employing workers per unit of output increased substantially. Thus, finding ways to increase labour productivity to boost competitiveness is also necessary for the Southeast Asian economies.

TABLE 4
Average Growth in Output per Worker and
Real Wages: 2009 to 2013
(per cent)

	Output per Worker	Wages
Indonesia	3.1	6.1
Malaysia	0.6	3.7
Philippines	3.5	0.7
Singapore	2.6	0.6
Thailand	2.9	4.5

Source: Processed from Haver database.

Moving Forward: Striving for Growth

Looking forward, the picture for growth momentum does not look rosy for the Southeast Asian economies. Sluggish economic recovery in the advanced economies and continuation of the orchestrated slowdown in China are incompatible with possible boost for export demand from Southeast Asia. The trend of less vibrant domestic demand factors recently observed may also continue into 2015. As a result, additional efforts by the regional economies to boost the growth momentum are certainly needed.

On the other hand, the picture for the Southeast Asian economies is not all that gloomy, though this does not apply to all countries. The recent decline in oil prices brings some good news. Low oil prices free up some space for a much needed fiscal consolidation in countries like Indonesia, whose fiscal position has long been burdened by unproductive energy subsidies. The resulting savings can then be allocated to more productive spending that lends more support to the country's capacity to grow, such as spending on infrastructure to remove some of the clogs that have prevented the economy from working more efficiently. However, for countries whose budgets depend more on oil revenue, progress in fiscal consolidation may be adversely affected. Malaysia, for example, would find some difficulties in achieving its target of reducing its fiscal deficit as prices of oil continue to decline. To proceed with its fiscal consolidation objectives, the country would have to restructure its budget and compensate for the loss in revenue by resorting to alternative sources of revenue and/or more efficient spending behaviour.

Aside from providing scope for fiscal reforms, the lower international oil prices also add a downward pressure on domestic inflation. Reduced inflationary pressures would allow monetary authorities to take a more accommodative stance to stimulate the economy, and hence to some extent balance the region's need for interest rates increase to manage capital flows volatility. In other words, as there are opposing forces at work in guiding the direction for monetary policy, regional economies may end up being able to avoid the need for aggressive monetary tightening that could put additional limits on economic growth. Eventually, striking a delicate balance between maintaining the attractiveness for foreign capital and keeping domestic cost of capital low enough to stimulate the economy is what the region requires.

In the real sector, preserving and improving the level of economic competitiveness is unavoidable. Continued investment in human capital is necessary. Keeping adequate employment during the process is also important for ensuring the stability of the purchasing power of domestic consumers. For the longer term, the authorities should adopt policies that will induce innovations to create a wider spectrum of growth prospects. All these, should also be put in the context of more integrated Southeast Asian economies, as the region embraces the ASEAN Economic Community (AEC) which should be established by the end of 2015. The AEC is a rather ambitious economic agenda that envisages the Southeast Asian economies as a highly competitive single market and production base that is fully integrated into the global economy and pursues equitable economic development. The agenda will promote the free flow of goods and services, investments, and skilled labour among its member countries.

Along with all the opportunities opening up with the establishment of AEC, the agenda also posits some difficult issues. Implementing the AEC accords will not be all that smooth as they require changes to domestic laws that may lead to possible non-compliance from member states, in view of the loosely binding characteristics of the accords. However, the AEC also has the potential to help the region to capitalize more on its intensive production network to quicken its regional integration. Getting to that stage, though, would require a lot of adjustments from the regional countries that may involve asymmetrical gains among different countries during the transitional process. This is not going to be easy, but it is also not impossible to achieve.

In sum, it is not impossible for the Southeast Asian economies to resume their growth momentum going forward. This would, however, require some re-orientation from their traditional export-led growth model that entails more efforts to maintain both short- and long-term economic competitiveness.

Notes

The content of this paper is entirely the views of the authors and does not necessarily reflect the views of any of the organization to which the authors are affiliated with.

1. *The Asian Development Outlook 2013* and *The Asian Development Outlook 2013 Update*.
2. *The Asian Development Outlook 2013 Update: Government and Public Service Delivery*, ADB, October 2013, p. 13.
3. *The Asian Development Outlook 2013: Asia's Energy Challenge*, ADB, April 2013, p. 13.
4. *The Asian Development Outlook 2013*, ADB, October 2013.

Brunei Darussalam

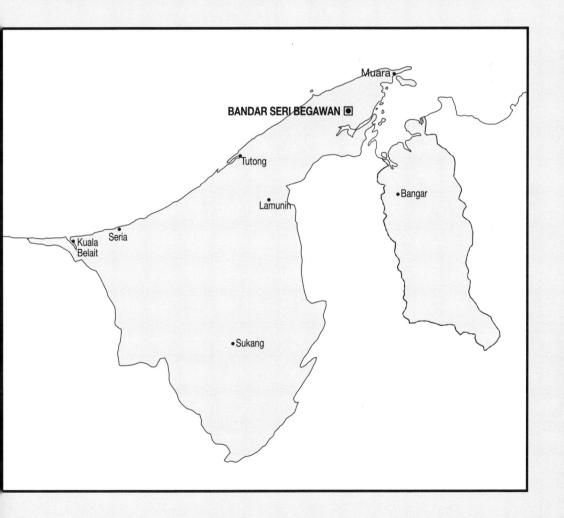

BRUNEI DARUSSALAM
A Time for Stock Taking

Pushpa Thambipillai

After a year of busy schedules as ASEAN Chair in 2013, Brunei Darussalam settled into its more routine national activities and concerns in 2014. It was also a year of reflection as it observed its thirtieth year of full sovereignty. As the year progressed it was evident that two main areas of national interest would preoccupy policymakers: the economy, and the recently gazetted *Syariah* law. In other areas of domestic and international affairs, the sultanate fared reasonably well in accordance with its projected policies.

Hauling the Economy Forward
Economy's Pillars

The long-term forward looking *Wawasan 2035* (Vision 2035) continued to provide the national goals for economic and social development while the 10th Five Year Development Plan (2012–17) provided the more immediate targets in development. By 2035, Brunei aims to achieve a sustainable and dynamic economy, with a well-educated and skilled people enjoying a high quality of life. The integrated approach calls for strategic development in such areas as domestic business, education, environment, infrastructure, institutions and social security. Progressive and sustainable growth has been identified as vital in achieving the goals of Vision 2035. Some strategies seem to be working while others are still lagging. For instance, educational, infrastructural and institutional development have been given more emphasis, while economic development, as

PUSHPA THAMBIPILLAI is an Associate Fellow at the Institute of Southeast Asian Studies (ISEAS), Singapore and a Visiting Adjunct Fellow at the East West Center in Hawaii. She was formerly with the Faculty of Business, Economics and Policy Studies, University of Brunei Darussalam.

a result of structural inadequacies and external dependencies has not contributed to a comfortable growth rate. In a *titah* (speech), Sultan Haji Hassanal Bolkiah, Head of State and Government, announced the establishment of the Council for Vision 2035 (Majlis Wawasan 2035) to assess and ensure the targets of the Vision were realized.[1]

The national economy grew at a slow pace, reaching an average of about 1 per cent. According to the Department of Economic Planning and Development, Brunei's second quarter recorded a growth of 0.8 per cent. It noted that the prevailing conditions in the third and fourth quarters were not favourable to Brunei's GDP growth.[2] A report from the OECD stated that ASEAN can expect an average of 5.6 per cent while Brunei is expected to average 1.6 per cent from 2015–19; that would be higher than the 0.9 per cent growth between 2011 and 2013.[3]

Income from hydrocarbon sources — crude oil and natural gas — has continued to fuel the economy. In the last few years over 90 per cent of export earnings have been derived from the export of these two basic commodities. However reduced earnings have been recorded as a result of a reduction in oil production and exports and falling oil prices, especially in the third quarter. According to the Department of Economic Planning and Development, there was a decline from the previous 135,000 barrels per day to 121,000 in July 2014. For the third quarter Brunei had nevertheless increased its exports due to demand and to the surplus of crude oil in its reserves. Globally, from a high of US$106 in the beginning of the year, the price for Bent crude had dropped to below US$70 by November (for January's future trade).[4]

The oil and gas industry was also in the national limelight as a source of employment to the local job seekers. A few years earlier the Minister of Energy in the Prime Minister's Office (PMO) had chided the oil industry (especially the major player, Brunei Shell Petroleum Company) for not employing more Bruneians. Over the last two years there has been a marked increase in local interest in the industry through various schemes. The number of local and joint-venture companies engaged in the hydrocarbon sector has increased, thus providing more opportunities at various levels of employment. The First Energy White Paper was launched by the Sultan in March 2014 during the opening of Energy Week. This paper attempts to take stock of the country's energy sources, needs and prospects.[5] The Energy Department had revealed that the planned recruitment of 3,000 locals in the energy sector in 2014 would most likely exceed expectations; 2,473 jobs had already been secured and another 2,000 jobs were available at the industry's job fair in November 2014. The sector was confident of locals filling another 3,000 expected jobs in 2015 as well.[6] The private sector in general has not been successful in recruiting or retaining the local workforce due to a number of factors, ranging from preference of Bruneians for the public sector, and lower remuneration and job dissatisfaction. The Energy Department was thus proactive in undertaking its own internal auditing to ascertain the employment situation in the industry and assess how many of those it employed since 2012 had remained on the job.

While some of the existing infrastructure and institutions in the hydrocarbon sector has been around for more than fifty years and thus need reassessment, new actors — local and foreign — are entering the industry, both in the allied services sector and in deep-sea exploration. Two examples from 2014: The Energy Department together with the Ministry of Oil and Energy of Oman organized a seminar in Brunei that brought together about thirty industry-related firms. One of the results was a joint-venture agreement between Brunei and Oman companies in "well service activities" in the Brunei market, while another three joint ventures are also expected.[7] Another large international company was poised to begin deep-well operations in Brunei's Exclusive Economic Zone (EEZ) in 2016 based on seismic data it had acquired recently that indicated the economic viability of the venture.[8] The resident hydrocarbon player, the Brunei Shell Petroleum Company, entered into a venture with two Japanese firms (Nippon Steel and Sumitomo Corporation) to set up an oil-pipe threading plant by mid 2016 in one of the designated industrial sites in the Brunei-Muara district. The major task of threading for imported steel pipes is aimed at creating further economic spin-offs for local SMEs besides the transfer of technology.[9]

Local players in the hydrocarbon sector have had valuable experience through collaboration with international firms, and through the employment of professional talent from abroad in addition to locals. Local companies are also venturing abroad; an example is the government-owned company PetroleumBrunei (the Brunei National Petroleum Company Sdn Bhd) that acquired 87.25 per cent share in the operation in central Myanmar. It had signed an oil production sharing contract with two of Myanmar's private companies in Naypidaw in September 2014 after winning the bid in November 2013.[10]

Employment-wise it was a new area of opportunity for Bruneians as the Oil and Gas Job Fair in the past two years has shown. It also called for reforms and restructuring of technical training in the country. Technical institutions have been integrated for better management and quality control of the products. However, other than the oil and gas industry which the Energy Department has closely monitored and apparently has an estimate of labour demand, the other sectors have not been specific. Thus there might be an overproduction of technical diplomas without a corresponding demand; for instance, under the new integrated scheme, there were about 2,000 youths who completed their technical and trades-related education in 2014 alone.

Diversification

The target of diversification (moving beyond the oil and gas industry) and the development of domestic business enterprises saw some modest progress in 2014. The frequent reminders by leaders on the topic and encouragement for its people to take on productive activities have slowly shown some effect. Progress can be seen at three clusters: (i) small/micro industries in services or products; (ii) Information and Communications Technology (ICT)-related enterprises, especially those dealing in e-business, and (iii) large industries through foreign investment and joint ventures. Brunei-based small industries have largely been related to the oil and gas sector, mainly as service providers and suppliers of industry-related equipment. Over the past five years or so, a number of successful small enterprises that produce consumer products for the home and foreign markets have emerged. They are found in the food, handicraft and other light industries. A few women entrepreneurs have successfully carved out a niche, for example, in the production and export of a variety of chilli sauces and products from soy beans. With government support for the ICT industry (mainly from the Brunei Economic Development Board, BEDB and the Authority for Info-Communications Technology Industry, AITI), a number of enterprising young individuals have embarked on e-business, media and computer-related services for the home market while gathering experience before venturing abroad. The bigger industries are in the transport sector (construction of road, bridge, port and other infrastructure) and in the oil and gas sector (exploration and other upstream activities, downstream activities like the production of methanol, urea, and a planned refinery for petroleum and diesel products). Tourism that had been promoted since the 1990s as an alternate source to diversify the economy performed dismally; the number of *bona-fide* tourist arrivals has not shown any major improvement in the past few years.

Brunei still has a long way to go in order to promote itself as a business venue as it does not compare well with other ASEAN countries in the global "competitiveness index" by the World Economic Forum. Its bureaucracy is still not geared up to eliminating unnecessary procedures that inhibit the business start-ups. Official procedures for businesses to begin operation may take anywhere from a month to three months, unlike in leading economies like New Zealand or Singapore where it might be as short as three days. Efforts are still underway to streamline the requirements; it must be pointed out that several modifications have been introduced with modest success although the international indices do not seem to indicate any positive outcome.

The fall in global prices for crude Brent in the later half of 2014 would have an impact on the national income; if the government was concerned, it did not show it. As for the consumers, they had always enjoyed fixed, subsidized prices at the pump and thus the fall in crude oil prices did not directly matter. However, energy was very much in the limelight as the earlier section showed. As the number of players in the oil and gas sector increased, so did the number of available jobs. The government ensured that it would be the locals who would receive the benefits in the job market.

Trade and Investment

There were no major changes to the usual trade pattern of the country: commodity export dominated by hydrocarbon, constituting about 90 per cent of export earnings. There was a slight variation in the direction of trade. According to the latest available data for international merchandise trade (2013), total exports had decreased by 11.8 per cent while imports had increased by 1.5 per cent as compared to the previous year.[11] A number of regional trade agreements will be coming into force in the next few years, beginning with the ASEAN Economic Community (AEC) in December 2015 that may see some changes to its trade and investment patterns. Currently, outside of ASEAN, Brunei has a bilateral free trade agreement with Japan; other potential links are still under negotiation, for example with the United States and with Pakistan.[12] A number of agreements were signed with foreign investors to commence manufacturing in the next year or two. For instance, a Chinese company intends to commence steel-pipe manufacturing while a South Korean firm will be building an aluminium manufacturing plant and a Canadian company is geared to produce *halal* pharmaceuticals. China's Zhejiang Hengyi is by far the largest investor with about US$4 billion project for an integrated refinery-cum-industrial centre at Pulau Muara Besar.[13]

Annual Budget

The Legislative Council met in March, as per routine, to consider various policy pronouncements and expenditures for each of the ministries. The 2014 session, the tenth since the council was reinstated in 2004, was presented with the annual budget (2014–15) of B$5.98 billion, an increase of 10 per cent from the previous year (the budget year is from April 2014 to March 2015). As the premier institution, the Ministry of Finance had the largest share with B$1.167 billion (US$856.23 million), followed by the Ministry of Education with B$770.777 million, Ministry of Defence with B$719.15 million, the Prime Minister's Office with B$647.82 million and followed by other ministries. The main function of Brunei's Legislative Council is to approve the budget after a few days of open discussion.[14]

According to the Second Minister of Finance, the year's budget was expected to focus on a number of vital issues that would: enhance education and training; stimulate investment; promote private sector growth; increase economic productivity, and ensure the welfare of the people is provided for through the various governmental schemes. These are not new areas of concern, but highlight the emphasis on national action.

A sum of B$1.15 billion was allotted for the Tenth National Development Plan for the 2014–15 period. The largest allocation of B$336.8 million (29 per cent) was earmarked for social services such as education, health, national housing and human resource development. The next highest at B$266 million (23 per cent) was for development expenditure in public facilities like projects on sewage, clean water supply, drainage improvement, flood protection and electricity supply. The other major allocation of B$226.6 million was for the transportation and communication sector (which includes roads, telecommunications and civil aviation). The trade and industry sector would receive B$118.4 million while the security sector was assigned B$31.5 million. About 1 per cent of the development fund for the year was for research in science and technology and development innovation.

The legislative session offers one of the rare opportunities for members of the council (three quarters of whom are appointed, while the rest are elected at village and district levels) to query policies and issues of implementation by the various ministries. It allowed ministers to respond directly to queries by members of the council under the watchful eyes of the media and the public.[15]

Domestic Environment

Social Policies

The year began with anticipation to celebrate Brunei's thirty years of independence with a wide variety of activities, topped off with the special National Day celebrations on 23 February. However, 2014 started with one of the worst floods in Brunei's history when most of Tutong and Belait districts were badly inundated for a few days. Causing large financial losses in property and infrastructure, it did not, fortunately, cause any loss of lives.

Issues related to economic development were also linked to other concerns in domestic development, especially social development. The government continued to focus on ensuring that its population was well housed, served (with subsidized rice, sugar, and energy) and educated. Education at the primary and secondary school level continued to be hotly debated as the SPN21 (the National Education System for the twenty-first century), which made certain structural revisions to the existing educational system, did not meet the expectations of all sectors of society. The Minister responsible assured concerned parents and teachers that it was still being modified. An encouraging step towards relevant youth training came with the centralized coordination of the seven technical schools under Brunei Technical Education. Its aim was to upgrade technical education as an alternate mode of education to produce marketable workers. The government has been generous in allocating free education for its citizens up to tertiary level and beyond for those who qualify for university education. Beginning in 2014, the government also approved an education loan scheme for students (who did not meet the scholarship criteria) to pursue their higher education in local or foreign universities.[16]

While English remained the medium of instruction in secondary and tertiary education, citizens were also reminded of the use of the Malay language. A recent phenomenon has been the popularity of Arabic language schools from preschool to secondary level (as distinct from the already existing mandatory religious and Arabic language education up to a certain grade in public schools).[17] Brunei also observed its 100 Years of Formal Education anniversary from 1914–2014. The sultanate ranks high in the UN Millennium Development Goal at about 98 per cent literacy level.

With a youthful population — those below the age of forty accounting for about 60 per cent — issues related to education, employment, housing and health continued to be highlighted in public policies. The National Service Programme (*Program Khidmat Bakti Negara*, PKBN) for school leavers of both sexes in its second year of implementation was still on a voluntary basis; there was no indication that it would be made compulsory for all youths despite the fact that its aim was to instil moral values and other leadership qualities. Begun in 2011 on a pilot scheme, the past two years have seen about 300 youths undergoing the training that imparts social values, religious reinforcement and physical fitness (non-military). The programme is coordinated by the Ministry of Culture, Youth and Sports. An encouraging sign amongst the youth is a discernable growth in volunteerism and civic organizations dedicated to humanitarian and environmental concerns, partly due to the greater awareness of social issues and partly because of the emphasis given to the role of youth by national leaders.

National housing schemes were notoriously slow in meeting the demands from registered applicants. More developers were assigned for the housing industry while high-rise accommodation of at least six storeys was initiated to meet the housing needs of those on the waiting list. For the past three decades, government subsidized dwellings have been distributed under the National Housing Scheme and the Landless Indigenous Citizen Housing Scheme. In 2014, for example, 1,542 new home owners were personally handed the keys by Sultan Hassanal Bolkiah.[18]

Limiting Foreign Labour

The uneasy realization that more than 65 per cent of those in the private sector were foreigners prompted the government to introduce new measures in 2014 to provide more opportunities to locals in search of employment and to reduce the dependence on external sources beyond what was necessary. The Ministry of Home Affairs (in charge of labour matters) announced at the end of May that it was revoking all unused foreign labour quotas (which actually numbered about 71,000 approved positions). A foreign worker levy was also imposed for several sectors as of the end of June. Other policies included the freezing of foreign labour quotas in specific areas like wholesale and retail trade, sales and other service sectors, reducing foreign labour quota upon renewal and not issuing licences for businesses in residential areas unless the business is run by locals. Employers were to seriously pursue localization through training programmes to ensure their businesses would not be adversely affected; meanwhile they complained of problems in hiring locals for certain jobs, or to fill up the quota of 70 per cent locals in their enterprise.[19]

Law, Justice and Punishment

As a Malay Muslim Monarchy (*Melayu Islam Beraja — MIB*), Islam according to the teachings of *Ahli Sunnah Wal Jamaah* under the *Shafiee* school of thought, has been the core belief of the sultanate. The British, who imposed the Residential System with their system of administration during their rule, allowed some elements of the Islamic legal system (*Syariah*) to be continued alongside the imported judicial system — Islamic jurisprudence was confined to issues related to civil matters like marriage, divorce and property rights.[20] The 1959 Constitution established the supremacy of the Islamic religion and since independence in 1984, various aspects of the practice of Islam and related Islamic jurisprudence have been cumulatively added. Brunei aims to be *Negara Zikir* — a nation that adheres closely to the teachings of Islam in everyday life. Thus it came as no surprise when the Sultan a few years ago proposed the intention to revise and expand the existing *Syariah* law to cover a larger component of the judicial system.

The Sultan had signed the new legislation, the Syariah Penal Code in October 2013, that among others, laid out the punishments for criminal offences or *hudud* that include theft, illicit sexual relations, apostasy and acting against Islamic beliefs, that appeared to catch the attention of observers inside and outside the country. The new legislation also tightened existing *Syariah* laws for offences, for example, on observing the tenets of the fasting month, *khalwat* (close proximity of persons of the opposite sex) or the consumption of alcohol. It was to have come into effect six months later but due to some delay it came into force on 1 May 2014. However the implementation of the punishment would be in stages. In the first year it would only apply to the offences that would require heavier penalties of fines or imprisonment, while the more serious criminal justice system would be implemented later. It was not yet clear to what extent the new components of the *Syariah* law would be applicable to non-Muslims; however it has been pointed out that non-Muslims can be punished under the system if they are party to an offence by a Muslim. There were reminders to non-Muslims with regards to certain words and actions that they are forbidden from using.

A greater part of the year was spent by leaders, including the Sultan and other religious experts, explaining the basics of the intended *Syariah* law as most observers only paid attention to the severity of punishments, for example, the amputation of the hand for theft or stoning for adultery, without understanding the actual process in arriving at the final punishment for offenders. Brunei's dual system — *Syariah* and civil criminal justice system — is expected to be in effect in the next three to four years, after the Syariah Courts Criminal Procedure Code is gazetted. In the meantime, there was only one reported case of an offender during the month of Ramadan prosecuted under the new Syariah Penal Code.[21] Following the introduction of the Penal Code in 2013, external reactions from some quarters had been negative and became more vocal after it came into force in May 2014. Reactions were reported from such diverse groups as human rights organizations, Hollywood personalities who would boycott hotels owned by the government/Sultan of Brunei and United States congressmen who called on their President to review relations with Brunei that was implementing such harsh punishments under the *Syariah* system of justice. After a month or two of intense publicity the international attention gradually dissipated.

Strengthening External Linkages
Multilateral Relations

It was a good year for Brunei's international relations as it marked several significant anniversaries on the occasion of its third decade of independence. Partner countries recalled the close ties spanning the thirty years; these included the ASEAN Five, Australia, Japan, and the United States. Brunei had also joined a number of international organizations in 1984 that included ASEAN and the United Nations. As the state's leading diplomat, Sultan Hassanal Bolkiah was in New York in September to address the 69th U.N. General Assembly, recalling the day when he first attended the assembly in September 1984.[22] Prior to that, he had delivered the sultanate's policies to the U.N. Climate Summit. He mentioned that Brunei had reduced energy consumption by 13.9 per cent the previous year and that the target would be 63 per cent by 2035. Brunei was committed to conservation, including that of forests as evidenced by the allocation of 58 per cent of its land area to the "Heart of Borneo" forest conservation initiative with Indonesia and Malaysia and the participation of the World Wide Fund for Nature. He also touched on climate change and its adverse effects, phenomena that Brunei and its neighbours had experienced of late and which called for better shared facilities and cooperation. The Bali Democracy Forum, the seventh in the series and the last hosted by President Susilo Bambang Yudohono, also heard the Sultan's views on political, economic and social development that can promote greater interaction between the government and the people resulting in a partnership that is peaceful, inclusive, and consultative. The Sultan has attended all the previous democracy forums held since 2008, reflecting his personal friendship with the former Indonesian President.

ASEAN and its related activities took up most of the country's external engagement, involving various levels of participation — from summits, to ministerial meetings, to officials' meeting and youth, women, academic and private sector dialogues. As the 2015 target for the ASEAN Economic Community draws near, there were attempts to ensure that the relevant national stakeholders would be ready to take advantage of the opportunities. The subregional grouping of the Brunei Darussalam-Indonesia-Malaysia-Philippines East ASEAN Growth Area (BIMP-EAGA) gave Brunei a more direct role in promoting access for the private sector to explore the ties with its immediate neighbours like Sabah and Sarawak in Malaysia. ASEAN has also enabled more economic and diplomatic linkages with China, Japan, South Korea and increasingly in the past year, with the United States. Collective negotiations in Regional Comprehensive Economic Partnership (RCEP), East Asia Summit (EAS), Trans-Pacific Partnership (TPP) and Asia-Pacific Economic Cooperation (APEC) provided the small state with a wider network to explore its national interests. Brunei has pursued an active role and is not put off by other bigger players as it is accorded its full recognition as an equal partner.

Bilateral Ties

The year saw Brunei strengthening its bilateral relations with a number of partners. Malaysia under Prime Minister Datuk Seri Najib Tun Razak has continued to foster good ties in the diplomatic and economic spheres. In 2013, Premier Najib was in Bandar Seri Begawan in early December for the 17th Annual Leaders' Consultation where two major agreements dealing with the joint development of oil assets in the South China Sea were signed. At this meeting, the Friendship Bridge was also launched, a joint development project linking Temburong in Brunei with Sarawak, across the Pandaruan River. The bridge provides convenient access to the Pan Borneo Highway; previously drivers had to wait for ferries to cross the narrow river. In August 2014 representatives from the two countries signed an agreement on the maintenance and management of the Friendship Bridge, which included sharing the construction cost of the 189-metre long and 14-metre wide bridge. For 2014, the 18th Annual Leaders' Consultation led by the two leaders was held in Malaysia in November. The leaders took note of the progress in implementation of the earlier initiated Exchange of Letters concluded in 2009 and other areas of mutual cooperation in oil, maritime, territorial boundary, and joint business ventures. As a symbol of the close educational collaboration, the Sultan was conferred an Honorary Doctorate in Law by Universiti Sains Malaysia during its fiftieth convocation ceremony. The Malaysia-Brunei relationship has long been cemented at the royalty, governmental and societal levels. This is especially so with the neighbouring states of Sabah and Sarawak who share historical and cultural traditions with Brunei.

The close relationship between Brunei and Singapore was evidenced by the regular exchange of visits at the highest levels. Singapore President Tony Tan made his first official state visit to the sultanate in April where he suggested several areas for further cooperation, including exchange programmes. The Singapore-Brunei Youth Leadership Exchange Programme was the direct result of it. Fifteen Brunei and fifteen Singapore youths participated in the inaugural programme in Singapore in November, to be reciprocated in Brunei in 2015. Ongoing links between the two states are in defence, trade, education, civil service matters and the long-standing financial and monetary linkages. The Currency Interchangeable Agreement (since June 1967) has brought the two economies closer. As part of their ongoing exchanges, the Monetary Authority of Singapore and Autoriti Monetari Brunei Darussalam signed a Memorandum of Understanding on cooperation in capital market development and capacity building.[23] The 34th Singapore Lecture was delivered by the Sultan of Brunei where he recalled his personal ties with Singapore leaders as well as Brunei's relations with its neighbours and suggested ways to make ASEAN a more responsive organization.

Relations with China have increased substantially over the past few years in both the diplomatic and economic fields. On the occasion of his visit to

Beijing for the APEC Summit, the Sultan, in an interview with *Xinhuanet*, noted that "Our bilateral partnership has been progressing well especially now that we have raised it to the level of a Strategic Cooperative Relationship following my visit last year (2013)."[24] He pointed out that the frequent exchanges between both sides had resulted in the signing of a number of MOUs in several sectors including energy, infrastructure, agriculture, fisheries, defence and education.[25] Although Chinese nationals make up one of the smaller groups of foreigners in Brunei, China has intensified its bilateral cultural and educational linkages and is one of the largest foreign investors in recent years. The development of Pulau Muara Besar is undertaken by a Chinese conglomerate that is readying the infrastructure before building refineries and other hydrocarbon related industries. The Brunei-Guangxi Economic Corridor is also exploring the joint participation of Chinese and Brunei entrepreneurs in agriculture, fisheries and port development.[26] It was reported that Brunei will be participating in the Chinese-sponsored Asian Infrastructure Investment Bank, a development bank with assets of US$100 billion, to finance regional infrastructure projects.

The Sultan also undertook a state visit to South Korea, prior to attending the (25th) ASEAN-Korea Commemorative Summit in December 2014. Korea is an important bilateral partner for trade and investments as well as for educational and cultural exchanges. The Foreign Minister, Prince Mohamed Bolkiah had earlier in October undertaken an official visit, noting that the celebrations of Brunei-Korea 30th anniversary would result in a number of agreements in education, double taxation and joint-venture agreement on agriculture.[27] As for the other long-term ally, Japan, that was also observing thirty years of diplomatic relations, the scene had already been set in December 2013 when the Sultan visited Japan. Together with Prime Minister Shinzo Abe, he unveiled the logo for special activities in 2014.[28]

The United States on the other hand has not aggressively pursued political and economic relations as it is quite comfortable with the existing good ties in diplomatic, defence and security cooperation while already being the largest gross investor in the energy sector. Lately, the U.S. Embassy has been actively promoting educational and training opportunities in the United States as it lags behind the more successful United Kingdom and Australian initiatives. Among fellow Islamic countries, relationships with Oman and Turkey saw new areas of cooperation. The former is an old ally of the sultanate with similar political and religious traditions and shared interests in the energy sector, while the latter had only recently established a resident diplomatic mission and is eager to explore bilateral ties.

Security and Defence Landscape

Security Concerns

While Brunei has its share of local security issues mostly linked to petty criminals, illegal immigrants, human traffickers, smugglers of illicit items and poachers of its natural resources like timber and marine resources, 2014 saw an alarming realization that it could be a "hub" for external-based terrorists and religious extremists.

There were at least two known cases of Malaysians intending to use the Brunei airport as their "transit" on their way to Turkey to join the Islamic State (IS) in Syria. Both had been apprehended in Malaysia's international airport, KLIA, before their departure to Brunei. One was a young woman on her way to marry a militant in Syria while the other was intending to leave for Syria, both of whom were suspected to have been recruited through social media influences.[29] At the ASEAN Summit in Myanmar in November, the Sultan had called upon ASEAN to be vigilant against the influence of terror and extremist groups on people in the region.

Earlier in the year it was reported in the local media that a "man with terror links" had been detained. The foreign national, engaged in herbal business as a "front", apparently had links to Jemaah Islamiyah and other militant groups and had intended to use Brunei as a "safe haven" for other individuals.[30] The disclosure caused concern among the public. Even the regular Friday sermon's theme was on the "terror threat", warning about teachings that might advocate terror and the need to be vigilant against such activities. For a nation that has often been generous in its donations to deserving causes, the *imams* urged caution in making donations especially to external recipients in case they were used for militant activities.[31] At a joint Prime Minister's Office-U.S. Government sponsored counter-terrorism course for Brunei's enforcement officers, a senior member of the Royal Brunei Police Force pointed out that Brunei remained "vulnerable" to regional security threats and terrorism especially with training camps located nearby in southern Philippines and Indonesia.[32]

Community "policing" was also expanded under the "neighbourhood watch" by the Police Force to provide a participatory role for the people in their security environment.

The Armed Forces

Meanwhile the Royal Brunei Armed Forces, on its 53rd year since its formation, emphasized skills training and bilateral exercises to enhance its efficient operability. New hardware was added to its maritime defence forces with the commissioning of the Royal Brunei Navy's new Darussalam Class patrol vessel, *KDB Daruttaqwa*. The ship, built in Germany, is the fourth in the Darussalam fleet of vessels. Meanwhile the Air Force put into operation the S-70i Sikorsky Blackhawk helicopter. The currently serving Bell 212s, in service for forty years, will be gradually replaced with twelve Blackhawk helicopters. There had also been plans to order a number of C-130J Hercules military transport aircraft. It is expected that the large aircraft, already in operation by its ASEAN neighbours, will be used for Brunei's regional humanitarian mission. Apparently U.S. government approval had already been given for the sale of the aircraft to Brunei.

There are also plans to establish a Blackhawk S-70i Simulator Centre, a first of its kind that would attract potential global clients. The Brunei Government in cooperation with Canadian Aviation Electronics (CAE) has established the CAE Brunei Multi-Purpose Training Centre and the proposed Simulator Centre and other training facilities, like the Emergency Management and Crisis Management Centre of Excellence to provide Brunei and ASEAN partners with disaster preparedness, emergency response and disaster management capabilities.

There were various joint military exercises with partner countries throughout the year. The Brunei and Singapore air forces conducted the 20th Exercise Air Guard at Bukit Agok Range in Tutong. The Brunei Navy probably had the busiest schedule. As a sign of increasing bilateral military relations with China, Brunei for the first time participated in the Multilateral Maritime Exercise in Qingdao where naval drills involving China's nine partner countries took place. The *KDB Daruehsan* also participated in the International Fleet Review to mark the 65th anniversary of the founding of China's Peoples Liberation Army (PLA) Navy. Brunei was also represented in the Western Pacific Naval Symposium that was held in conjunction with the Exercise and Review, expanding the local personnel's international exposure. At home, navies of Brunei and the U.S. conducted their 20th Cooperation Afloat Readiness and Training (CARAT) at the Muara Naval Base while other forces from the

Brunei Land Forces and Brunei Air Force also trained with U.S. Marines and U.S. helicopters (from a U.S. navy ship) respectively. With Malaysia, the annual Exercise Hornbill got underway in Brunei, it being the sultanate's turn to host the exercise. It is expected to strengthen the relationship between the two navies and facilitate mutual cooperation.

Perhaps the biggest moment for small Brunei was when 140 officers on two patrol vessels (*KDB Darussalam* and *KDB Darulaman*) joined the 24th U.S. Pacific Fleet's Rim of the Pacific (RIMPAC) maritime exercise in the Hawaiian Islands between June and August. Enroute the Brunei Navy participated in Exercise Pelican with the Singapore Navy. The five-week training in Hawaii involved multilateral naval exercises including anti-surface, anti-air and anti-submarine warfare in one of the world's largest maritime exercises. Brunei was one of thirty-one states and 25,000 personnel involved in enhancing their skills in naval warfare. The value of participation in such exercises for skills training and defence diplomacy has been undermined in the sultanate's Defence White Paper. Regular workshops, exchange of visits and the offering of places to foreign military participants in the Defence Ministry's executive training programmes, English language courses and friendly competitions have promoted Brunei's defence diplomacy within and outside the region. Brunei has continued participating with the International Monitoring Team in Mindanao and with the United Nations Interim Force in Lebanon (UNIFIL) where Brunei's soldiers are embedded with the Malaysian contingent.

Conclusion

Promoting greater economic diversity and surmounting the volatility of the hydrocarbon market remained the major concerns as Brunei concluded 2014, despite the fact that its foreign reserves were substantial and inflation was minimal. Its generally stable macroeconomic and social environment will be sustained for the near future. The various reviews and assessments of national policies have provided better guidelines to leaders to address concerns in economic development, youth employment, the nurturing of new actors in business, like young entrepreneurs and women in industry, and the national adherence to the Islamic faith in finance, law and everyday life. In external relations, its practice of being friendly with important external states and its undivided support for ASEAN, regarded as the cornerstone of its foreign policy, have provided a stable field for interactions.

Notes

1. The Sultan's *titah* delivered on the occasion of his sixty-eighth birthday, Istana Nurul Iman, 14 August 2014 (the celebrations were observed later than the actual date of 15 July as the fasting month of Ramadan fell in July). For details of the speech, see <www.pmo.gov.bn>.

2. See <www.jpke.gov.bn> for further information on the economy for 2014.

3. For the annual OECD report on Economic Outlook for Southeast Asia, China and India, see <www.oecd.org/site/seao/BruneiDarussalam>.

4. There were already increased supplies from the United States and other major producers, while the OPEC countries continued to keep up their normal output level despite the fall in prices as a result of the glut in supplies. OPEC member states account for one-third of the world's oil. In a related issue, the South Korean Ambassador to Brunei, in a farewell interview with a local daily, pointed out that his country would probably buy less liquefied natural gas (LNG) from Brunei after the current contract ends in 2018 as it was much cheaper to source it from the United States. See details of the interview in *Brunei Times*, 26 October 2014.

5. The Energy White Paper, 2014, is available at <www.energy.gov.bn>.

6. Rachel Thien, "We'll Exceed Job Targets for Locals", *Brunei Times*, 27 November 2014, quoting the Minister of Energy. The first job fair organized by the Energy Department was held in 2012 where the recruitment target was 1,000 and 1,600 for the following year. The job fairs resulted in a successful recruitment of 1,302 and 2,610 for 2012 and 2013 respectively.

7. See Danial Norjidi, "Joint Venture Forged at Brunei-Oman Seminar", *Borneo Bulletin*, 29 November 2014.

8. See Rachel Thien, "SDB Expects to Drill Wells in Blocks A, Q", *Brunei Times*, 29 November 2014. SDB or Shell Deepwater Borneo Ltd. is a Shell-owned company set up in 2011.

9. See Koo Jin Shen, "Oil Pipes Threading Plant to be Set Up in Brunei by Mid 2016", *Brunei Times*, 27 November 2014.

10. This is provided by Rachel Thien, "PetroleumBRUNEI Acquires Stake in Myanmar Oil Block", *Brunei Times*, 17 September 2014.

11. Detailed information is available at <www.jpke.gov.bn>.

12. See ADB Asia Regional Integration Centre, Free Trade Agreements, available at <www.aric.adb.org>.

13. For further information on foreign investments, see the Brunei Economic Development Board at <www.bedb.gov.bn>.

14. The session began on 6 March 2014, with the *titah* by the Sultan; it ended on 22 March with the passing of the annual budget. More information is available

at <www.majlis-mesyuarat.gov.bn>. The local dailies, *Borneo Bulletin* and *Brunei Times*, also carried daily accounts of the sitting.

15. The Legislative Council has 33 members, including the Sultan as Head of State and Government, the Crown Prince, the *Perdana Wazir*-cum-Foreign Minister, 11 cabinet ministers, and 19 appointed members who represent the nobles/titled or *ceterias*, various professionals, social and religious figures and representatives from all four districts — the only members who are elected by their respective residents. As of the last three sessions, the Council has included two prominent women members.

16. This was announced by the Sultan in his *titah* on the occasion of his birthday. See <www.pmo.gov.bn> and the local dailies of 15 August 2014 for his full speech.

17. The government had introduced the Compulsory Religious Education Order 2012 to ensure that all children of Muslim citizens and permanent residents would be given religious education for a stipulated number of years. Muslim parents have to register their children in a religious school for a period of seven years, or they would be subject to a fine or imprisonment. The child's compulsory religious education, under the Ministry of Religious Affairs is in addition to the normal school enrolment, which is the responsibility of the Ministry of Education. For further information, see <www.mora.gov.bn>.

18. See for example the report on the meeting of the recipients with the Sultan in *Brunei Times*, 3 June 2014.

19. For further insight, see the following articles: Rafidah Hamit, "Expats Make Up 64.9% of Workforce"; Rafidah Hamit, "MoHA Cancels Unused Expat Labour Quotas"; Rachel Thien and Debbie Too, "Employers Worry about Job Localisation Policy". Available at <www.bt.com.bn>, 26 and 30 May 2014.

20. See the series of articles by B. A. Hussainmiya, for instance, "Administration of Law and Justice in Brunei before the Coming of the British" in *Borneo Bulletin*, 9 November 2014.

21. A foreign Muslim worker was charged under the new law; he was fined for smoking during the fasting month of Ramadan. As reported in *Brunei Times*, 22 July 2014.

22. See "News — 25.09.14 General Debate on the 69th UN General Assembly", available at <www.pmo.gov.bn>.

23. *Business Times*, 22 April 2014, available at <www.businesstimes.com.sg>.

24. *Borneo Bulletin Weekend*, 8 November 2014.

25. Ibid.

26. This is according to the out-going Chinese Ambassador, Zheng Xianglin, in a discussion with the local media. See *Brunei Times*, 27 December 2014.

27. Rabiatul Kamit, "South Korea Set to Sign Several New Agreements with Brunei", *Brunei Times*, 2 October 2014. For details on the official activities of the

Foreign Minister promoting Brunei's foreign policy throughout the year, see <www. mofat.gov.bn>.

28. For an overview of the Brunei–Japan bilateral relations and the list of planned activities in the two countries, see <www.bn-emb-japan.go.jp>.

29. As reported in <www.thestar.com.my>, 19 December 2014.

30. *Brunei Times*, 27 February 2014.

31. *Brunei Times*, 1 March 2014.

32. *Brunei Times*, 12 August 2014.

Cambodia

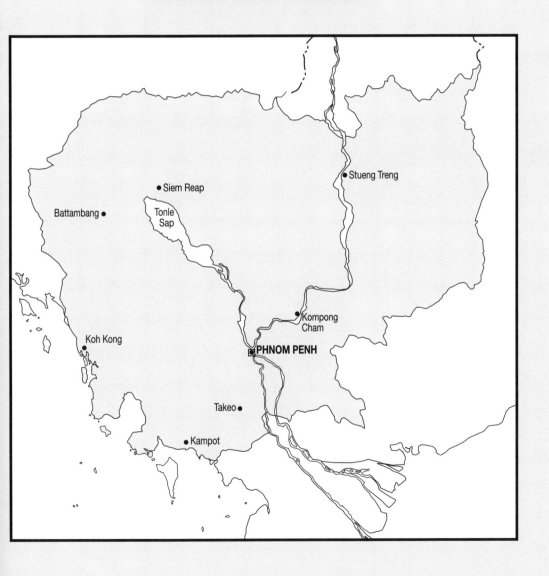

Southeast Asian Affairs 2015

CAMBODIA IN 2014
The Beginning of Concrete Reforms

Vannarith Chheang

The July 2013 General Elections was a critical turning point in the modern history of Cambodian political development and democratization. The predominant role of the Cambodian People's Party (CPP) with the long-serving Prime Minister Hun Sen was challenged for the first time in twenty years. The results of the 2013 election illustrated the narrowing political power base of the ruling CPP and the increasing popularity of the opposition Cambodia National Rescue Party (CNRP).

It is the first time the opposition party gained such a strong power base. The popular votes for both parties were roughly equal (CPP received 3,235,969 votes — 48.83 per cent and CNRP received 2,946,176 votes — 44.46 per cent). In terms of seats at the National Assembly, the CPP got sixty-eight seats while the CNRP got fifty-five seats, signifying the narrowing of political gap and the emergence of political power transformation in Cambodia.

2014 was a year full of controversies and complexities but was also a year of hope. There are strong political pressures and impetus to reform state institutions to be accountable to the people. Fruitful reform results are expected if both parties can effectively work together to serve their people and national interests.

Economic growth rate remains high and the current 20 per cent poverty rate is expected to be reduced by 1 per cent per annum. However, bureaucratic capacity, political leadership, good governance and human capital are the main constraints in maintaining high economic growth and promoting socio-economic equity and inclusiveness.

VANNARITH CHHEANG is a Senior Fellow at the Cambodian Institute for Cooperation.

Social dynamics (socio-economic inequality, social injustice, and social trust issues) are posing a serious threat to national stability and well-being. Without efficiently and effectively addressing such social issues, Cambodia may fall into political, social and economic crisis in the coming years. Clean and accountable government needs to be strengthened at both the national and local levels in order to improve the trust between society and state.

In terms of diplomacy, Cambodia has strengthened bilateral ties with Thailand, Vietnam and China. Bilateral relations with Thailand face new challenges after the coup in Thailand in May although both sides are trying to carefully manage ties. Relations with Vietnam have strengthened remarkably especially in economic cooperation although they face certain challenges coming from the opposition party in Cambodia. Relations with China continue to develop fast.

Propelling Forces of Reform

Since the 1998 election, the Cambodian People's Party had consolidated its power. No significant political changes or transformations were expected for Cambodia. In the 2008 election, the CPP further strengthened its power base especially in the rural areas through a multi-layered patronage system. The power of the Prime Minister had become more concentrated while the opposition forces were sidelined. Different scholars share similar views on power consolidation by the CPP and PM Hun Sen over the years.

> The Cambodian People's Party (CPP) consolidated legislative control with a decisive election victory in 2008. Four contributing factors are identified: CPP control of local authorities who can deliver the vote, its marginalization of the opposition, the mass patronage enabled by an economic boom and exploitation of a border dispute with Thailand.[1]
>
> The economy expanded but was said to need diversification. Inequality intensified conflicts, but development generated legitimacy, while the political opposition and civil society were attacked.[2]
>
> Hun Sen and the ruling Cambodian People's Party further consolidated power via the exercise of rule by law and patronage politics.[3]
>
> Hun Sen's Cambodian People's Party further consolidated its power, sidelining opposition parties and coopting disgruntled workers and farmers.[4]

With great confidence that it would never lose its grip on power, CPP neglected the fast-changing social dynamics and people's aspirations. It underestimated the opposition parties, in particular the two main parties Sam Rainsy Party (SRP) and the Human Rights Party (HRP), which merged in 2012 and posed a greater threat to the CPP.

The 2013 election was a wake-up call for the ruling CPP to urgently carry out comprehensive reforms, or end up losing power in the next election. At the first Cabinet meeting on 25 September 2013, Prime Minister Hun Sen warned the new ministers to practise self-criticism and to be more responsible. He said, "Look at yourself in the mirror, take a bath, and rub off dirt from your body, if there is any." He also told his Cabinet members to change their leadership style and attitude by listening to the voice of the people and not running their ministries as if they were their own family business. "We must change or we will fail", he said. "We must change our attitude, way of thinking and action in delivering on our election promises."[5]

In another remark at the official launching of Cambodia's trade integration strategy 2014–18 on 18 February 2014, he reasserted that: "We continue to strengthen good governance, move up the value chains and participate in regional production networks, and create a favourable environment for the private sector and investment to enhance its competiveness."[6] Such political statement and commitment aims at restoring public trust and investor confidence. Moreover, the government has since also focused more on educational reform by emphasizing vocational training and skills development.

The government's national development plan for 2014–18 has four goals, namely, average annual growth of 7 per cent, more jobs for the people especially the youth, annual poverty reduction rate at more than 1 per cent, and strengthening institutional reform and good governance. To achieve these goals, Cambodia will invest more in human resources development and physical infrastructure. It aims to strengthen governance and capacity of the public institutions in order to improve the efficiency of public service and the investment climate.

Cambodia also launched the Industrial Development Strategy 2014–19 to promote manufacturing and agro-processing through attracting foreign direct investment and enhancing the capacity of small and medium enterprises, further develop industrial zones, and harness opportunities to integrate Cambodia's manufacturing into regional and global production network.

From Political Standoff to Political Reconciliation

Cambodia went through a period of political instability for almost one year. The opposition CNRP rejected the election results, claimed it should have won sixty-three seats, boycotted the National Assembly, demanded independent investigation of the election results, called for a snap election and the resignation of Prime Minister Hun Sen, and demanded a deep reform of the National Election Committee, which was accused of being the tool of the ruling CPP.

CNRP organized a series of mass street protests, some of which resulted in deadly violence. The government suppressed the protests and imposed a ban on public demonstrations, and this included the closure of the Freedom Park in January. After several unfruitful rounds of negotiations between the two parties, Cambodia was stuck in a political stand-off that was almost a year long. In the first half of 2014, political distrust between the two parties deepened, social fragmentation driven by political polarization was on the rise, and economic development prospects were uncertain.

2014 is regarded as a critical year in the political reform and power transformation process. Under mounting domestic and international pressures to find a political solution, on 22 July, both parties finally reached a comprehensive political settlement agreement, breaking a year-long political deadlock. The agreement reflected political compromises from both sides. A new power-sharing arrangement and political reconciliation paved the way for promised political reforms and the implementation of the national development programmes.

The agreement involved reform of the National Election Committee (NEC) and the National Assembly (NA). Each party was to elect four members to the NEC and one independent member was to be selected based on the consensus of both parties. A prominent human rights activist, Pung Chhiv Kek, the president of a local non-governmental organization, was selected as the ninth independent member of the NEC. In early October, the Constitution was amended in order to pave the way for the reform of the NEC. The new mandate and budget policy made the NEC a more independent and neutral institution, but its performance in the next election will determine its credibility.

NEC reform was one of the top priorities in resolving the post-election political crisis. Should the NEC lack accountability and reliability, Cambodia will once again face post-election political impasse. The preliminary report of a survey conducted by the Asia Foundation in May 2014 shows that two-thirds of the respondents were dissatisfied with the NEC.

> The poll results suggest that the NEC is a good place to start establishing working relations between the parties, but at the same time, voters expect much more. The parties' first step should be to clearly outline the guiding principles for electoral reform and open up the process to public input through national dialogue. If they fail to do so, the parties again risk raising party interests above the interests of the electorate, only to find themselves staring at another stalemate.[7]

With regard to the power-sharing arrangement at the National Assembly, the position of vice-president and chairperson of five commissions out of ten in the National Assembly went to CNRP. These five commissions are: (a) Commission on Human Rights, Complaints and Investigation; (b) Commission on Planning, Investment, Agriculture, Rural Development, Environment and Water Resources; (c) Commission on Education, Youth, Sport, Religious Affairs, Culture and Tourism; (d) Commission on Health Care, Social & Veterans' Affairs, Youth Rehabilitation, Labour, Vocational Training & Women's Affairs; (e) Commission on Investigation and Anti-Corruption. Such institutional arrangement provides the CNRP with a roughly equal playing field in the National Assembly, although the CPP still holds the majority of seats with sixty-eight Assemblymen.

On 8 August, opposition MPs ended the boycott and attended the extraordinary session of the 5th National Assembly. Prime Minister Hun Sen called on the public to note down the CPP-CNRP leaders' commitment, and requested the CNRP to stop slandering and both parties to reduce criticism of each other. In the meantime, opposition leader Sam Rainsy appealed to CPP and CNRP to adopt a culture of dialogue, cooperation and negotiations for national interests.[8]

Expectations are high on the future performance of both parties with regard to structural reforms and people-oriented development. Fruitful results are expected to come from the working partnership between the two parties. A number of Cabinet ministers were called upon and questioned by the National Assembly, mainly led by the MPs from the opposition party. This was part of building a strong democratic institution through the strengthening of checks and balances.

The on-street protesters, especially the victims of the land grabbing, and factory workers, submitted their petitions through the commissions chaired by the opposition. Such measures help build state-society trust and resolve some of the emerging social and economic issues confronting the local community. However, some doubts remain especially among the supporters of the opposition party. They are afraid that CNRP might fall into the political trap of the ruling CPP, as happened to its former coalition party FUNCINPEC. Some independent observers also raise cautious optimism and urge both parties to implement their commitment and promises.

Economic Reforms

The renewed economic reform momentum and the end of political stand-off created an impetus for economic growth in the country. Both the Asian Development Bank and the World Bank estimated the GDP growth rate for Cambodia in 2014 to be slightly above 7 per cent. Some other forecasts predicted the real GDP growth to average 7.4 per cent a year from 2014 to 2018, mostly driven by faster private consumption growth. Agriculture, garment industry, tourism, construction and infrastructure development are the main economic sectors while the development of small and medium-sized firms would help to sustain and diversify economic growth.

Inflation was estimated to be around 3.5 per cent in 2014, amidst the high inflation in the region and increase in food and oil prices on the international market. The banking system remains robust with high liquidity. The international reserves reached US$4.5 billion in 2014. The flow of foreign direct investment still concentrates on the garment industry, rice milling, construction and tourism industries. Such a narrow base of economic development cannot sustain medium- to long-term economic growth projection and therefore the country needs to diversify its growth base.

If Cambodia can maintain an annual growth rate of over 7 per cent, the poverty reduction is expected to be reduced by 1 per cent per annum. There are about 3 million people living below the poverty line of US$1.25 per day and over 8.1 million are in the category of the near-poor, making them vulnerable to falling back into poverty. Without having an effective universal social protection, it is impossible to realize inclusive and sustainable development, which in turn leads to social and political instability.

The labour market instability caused by labour strikes and demonstrations by the garment workers demanding higher wage adversely impacts investor confidence and disrupts some production of garment and footwear. The garment industry employs about 620,000 workers and exports more than US$5 billion worth of goods. For instance, in early January, mass labour protests turned deadly after the security forces opened fire into the crowd of striking workers and killed at least four people. The international community, including the big retailers of garment and footwear products made in Cambodia, condemned the violence and called for a peaceful and comprehensive settlement of labour disputes.

With regard to the economic freedom (including monetary freedom, business freedom, labour freedom, and freedom from corruption) measured by the Heritage Foundation in 2014, Cambodia's economic freedom score is 57.4, ranking twenty-third out of forty-two countries in the Asia-Pacific. Its overall score is lower than the regional average which is 58.5.[9]

The investment climate in Cambodia is not yet attractive to foreign investors due to high level of corruption and the weak rule of law. According to the 2014 report of the Transparency International, Cambodia is one of the most corrupt countries in Southeast Asia. The Judiciary and the law enforcement agencies are the two weakest institutions.[10] Good governance is a core issue, and needs to be urgently addressed in order to improve the investment climate in the country. Corruption is a chronic and structural issue. Kheang Un puts it this way:

> Corruption is hierarchically institutionalized in a way that Cambodians characterize as "*thum si tarn thum touch si tarn touch*" (the big eat big, the small eat small). Although both kinds of acts are detrimental to the overall social, political and economic development of the country, high-level corruption is an underlying cause of the lack of democratic consolidation in Cambodia.[11]

Moreover, the electricity cost remains one of the key problems in attracting investment. In 2014, the price of electricity for businesses and industries was US$18.18 per kilowatt. It is relatively high compared with neighboring countries. For example, in Vietnam, it costs US$9.21 per kilowatt. The main issues facing the energy sector in Cambodia are low electrification rate, high energy import, narrow energy resource base, and the mismanagement of the energy sector due to corruption.

Social Dynamics

Demographic Changes

The demands of the Cambodian youth engenders a new political landscape and social change. In the 2013 election, about 3.5 million of Cambodia's 9.6 million registered voters were between the ages of 18 and 30; and of those, around 1.5 million were first-time voters. The majority of these young voters look beyond the country's tragic past and are demanding concrete political and economic reforms, more freedom of expression, social justice, inclusiveness, and a clean and accountable government. Their aspirations are higher than their parents' generation and they want to see "change".

The rapid development of communications technology, especially through social media and smartphones, allows young voters to receive updated information and actively exchange their views online. Such a widespread proliferation of social media has broken down the effectiveness of state media control and propaganda in shaping public opinion on national issues. Although CPP has been reasonably successful in maintaining peace and stability, economic growth and infrastructure development, there are still serious shortcomings that are now more widely acknowledged. Those shortcomings include weak state institutions, nepotism, corruption, social injustice and impunity, rapid deforestation, and rampant land grabbing.

Social Trust

The year 2014 marked a critical political development — a gradual decrease in social trust or social capital. This social trust deficit is generally driven by the rapid development of materialist culture, capitalism and individualism, widening development gap (income inequality, spatial development) and social injustice.

Moreover, increasingly more people do not trust or have lost confidence in the state institutions and local authority. Corruption is viewed as the main issue within the state power apparatus. The social fabric is confronted with emerging challenges deriving from political polarization and the breakdown of the village structure due to internal and international migration, landlessness, environmental degradation, deforestation and the depletion of natural resources. Such social dynamics adversely impacts on social cohesion and political stability.

Migration

Domestic and cross-border migration increased in 2014 due to the lack of job opportunities, rural poverty, indebtedness and landlessness. 80 per cent of Cambodia's population live in rural areas, and many of them have decided to immigrate to the urban areas and other neighbouring countries to find job opportunities and incomes to sustain their livelihood. Some of them even take risks by illegally crossing the border to Thailand. Usually they face labour exploitation, serious human rights abuses, and become the victims of human trafficking. Women and children are the most vulnerable group.

In early June, around 250,000 Cambodian migrant workers were deported or fled from Thailand amid panic and fear of arrests and violence. It was a human disaster given that there was not enough support particularly in terms of food, water, medicine, transport and shelter provided to such a sudden influx of migrants.

To facilitate the legalization process of migration, Cambodian and Thai governments have created a one-stop-service along the border, and set up other institutional arrangements to prevent human trafficking. The one-stop-service at the border was created to facilitate paper credentials for migrant workers. By September, there were 190,000 Cambodian migrants returning back to Thailand, mostly through the legal channels.[12]

Emerging Public Voices

Politically active civil society groups and people movement are challenging the existing state apparatus and power hierarchy. Civil society groups and the grass-roots have become more politically savvy and more actively involved in shaping the country's political life. Kheang Un argues, "In Cambodia, the countervailing force to the elite networks is the civil society, constituted predominantly of non-governmental organizations (NGOs)."[13]

After the 2013 elections, a wave of movements taking shape in different forms started to demand justice and accountability from the state institutions and private corporations. Such movements suggests new dynamics of democratization and power struggle between state and society.

The victims of land grabbing and factory workers are the most active groups. They frequently mobilized and organized street protests and demonstrations to seek government intervention in resolving chronic land disputes, finding social justice, ending impunity, or demanding an increase in minimum wage (from the current rate of US$100 to US$177).

Public opinion, still in the early stage of formulation, will play a significant role in promoting democratic participation and is a "game changer" in Cambodia's politics.[14] For instance, in October this year a new network called "Khmer for Khmer" was established to promote public debates in its demand for democratic consolidation particularly the strengthening of internal democratic practices within the two main political parties (CPP and CNRP).

Geopolitics and Foreign Policy

Located in the most dynamic region in the world, Cambodia can harness external opportunities and quickly develop the economy through regional integration and opening up. It can leapfrog its economic development path through right leadership and strong institutions.

Deepening economic integration, peaceful settlement of disputes, non-interference, strengthening strategic trust and confidence through dialogues and negotiation, promoting rules-based international relations, and diversification of strategic partners are the norms and principles of Cambodia's foreign policy.

Strengthening good relations with neighbouring countries is the top priority of Cambodia's foreign policy. Maintaining and strengthening stable and good relations with Thailand and Vietnam are fundamental to national security and development. Border tension, which led to bloody armed conflict, between Cambodia and Thailand from 2008-2011 prompted Cambodia to take all measures necessary to strengthen mutual trust and confidence with Thailand through dialogues at different levels and sectors.

After the military coup in Thailand in May 2014, Cambodia-Thailand relations faced a new turn. PM Hun Sen, who has strong personal relationship with the former Thai PM Thaksin Shinawatra and close cooperation with the previous Yingluck administration, found it challenging to maintain stable and peaceful cooperation with the new regime in Thailand.

After gaining its power, the Thai junta regime started to proactively reach out to and engage with regional countries especially China, Myanmar, and Cambodia. During his visit to Cambodia in early July, the Thai Acting Foreign Minister Sihasak Phuangketkeow reached out to Cambodian leaders and tried to convince them that NCPO intended to maintain good relations with Cambodia and that they do not have any policy to crack down on migrant workers, but instead have properly regulated those foreign migrant workers in order to protect their benefits and rights under Thai law. To further improve relations between the two neighbours, Cambodian Defence Minister Tea Banh visited Thailand in the same month to exchange views on the border issues, migrant workers, transnational crimes, and ASEAN community-building 2015.

In his state visit to Cambodia in late October, Thai Prime Minister Prayut Chan-o-cha promised to strengthen bilateral ties between the two countries especially in the field of economic cooperation along the border and migration management. Three MOUs were signed on Bilateral Cooperation in Eliminating Trafficking of Children and Women and Assisting Victims of Trafficking; on Rail Route Connection, and on Bilateral Cooperation in Tourism. However, both countries failed to address sensitive and complicated issues such as the enforcement of the International Court of Justice's decision on the surrounding areas of the Preah Vihear Temple, and the overlapping maritime claims in the Gulf of Thailand.

Bilateral relations with Vietnam are strong despite certain challenges created by the opposition group and the Khmer Krom community in Cambodia. After the controversial 2013 election, Prime Minister Hun Sen made his first state visit to Vietnam in December 2013, and in January 2014, Vietnamese Prime Minister Nguyen Tan Dung visited Cambodia to deepen bilateral ties between the two countries and peoples. Vietnam is now one of the top investors and the largest trader with Cambodia.

In 2013, bilateral trade volume hit US$3.43 billion and Vietnam's foreign direct investment in Cambodia totalled over US$3 billion. Vietnam is Cambodia's third largest trading partner and its fifth biggest foreign investor. By 2015, bilateral trade is expected to reach US$5 billion, and Vietnam's total investment is projected to hit US$4 billion. However, the two issues both countries need to resolve are border demarcation and Vietnamese illegal immigrants in Cambodia.

Cambodia regards China as the most important development and strategic partner. In 2014, Prime Minister Hun Sen visited China twice in May and in September. China is now Cambodia's top donor and investor, and key trading partner. China has provided about US$3 billion to Cambodia to mainly develop infrastructure without many conditions attached. In 2013, the bilateral trade amounted to more than US$3 billion. It is projected that by 2017, bilateral trade will reach US$5 billion. The cumulative Chinese investment in Cambodia amounted to US$9.6 billion from 1994 to 2013. The investment projects focus on labour-intensive industry, particularly the garment sector and natural resource extraction.

In May, Prime Minister Hun Sen met President Xi Jinping in Shanghai, ahead of the fourth summit of the Conference on Interaction and Confidence Building Measures in Asia (CICA). China provided a grant of US$114 million and an interest-free loan of US$33 million to construct an Olympic-size stadium, a government building and a pandemic prevention centre in Cambodia. Hun Sen acknowledged China's long-term support and reaffirmed Cambodian commitment to strengthen bilateral friendship.

China is slated to be the main market for the Cambodian rice exports. The target volume to be exported is set at one million tons by 2015. At the bilateral meeting between Sun Chanthol, Cambodian Minister of Commerce, and his Chinese counterpart in Beijing in August, Cambodia requested the Chinese government to provide duty and quota free concessions to Cambodia. Cambodia hopes to see an increase of duty-free rice export to China from 100,000 to 500,000 tons. At the meeting between Cambodian Prime Minister Hun Sen and Chinese Vice-Premier Zhang Gaoli at the 11th China-ASEAN Expo in September 2014, China agreed to promote the import of agricultural products from Cambodia.

Notes

1. Caroline Hughes, "Cambodia in 2008: Consolidation in the Midst of Crisis", *Asian Survey* 49, no. 1 (2009): 206.
2. Stephen Heder, "Cambodia in 2010: Hun Sen's Further Consolidation", *Asian Survey* 51, no. 1 (2010): 208.
3. Kheong Un, "Cambodia in 2011: A Thin Veneer of Change", *Asian Survey* 52, no. 1 (2011): 202.
4. Kheang Un, "Cambodia in 2012: Beyond the Crossroads?", *Asia Survey* 53, no. 1 (2012): 142.
5. Hun Sen, "Remarks at the Cabinet Meeting", Phnom Penh, 25 September 2013.
6. Hun Sen, "Speech on the Occasion of Official Launching of Cambodia's Trade Integration Strategy 2014–2018", Phnom Penh, 18 February 2014.
7. Silas Everett, "Electoral Reform Breathes New Life in Cambodia", *The Asia Foundation*, 23 July 2014, available at <http://asiafoundation.org/in-asia/2014/07/23/electoral-reform-breathes-new-life-in-cambodia/>.
8. Agence Kampuchea Press (AKP), "NA Holds an Extraordinary Session", 8 August 2014, available at <http://www.akp.gov.kh/?p=49601>.
9. Heritage, "2014 Index of Economic Freedom, Cambodia", available at <http://www.heritage.org/index/country/cambodia>.
10. Transparency International Cambodia, "Corruption and Cambodia's Governance System, the Need for Reform", available at <http://www.ticambodia.org/files/2014EN-NISA-WEB.pdf>.

11. Kheang Un, "State, Society and Democratic Consolidation: A Case Study of Cambodia", *Pacific Affairs* 79, no. 2 (2006): 225–45.

12. Mekong Migration Network, "Migrants Skipping Gov't Plan for Thai Alternative", August 2014, available at <http://www.mekongmigration.org/?cat=20>.

13. Kheang Un, "State, Society and Democratic Consolidation: A Case Study of Cambodia", *Pacific Affairs* 79, no. 2 (2006): 234.

14. Phoak Kung, "The Rise of Public Opinion in Cambodia's Politics", *The Diplomat*, 31 October 2014, available at <http://thediplomat.com/2014/10/the-rise-of-public-opinion-in-cambodias-politics/>.

THE CAMBODIAN PEOPLE HAVE SPOKEN
Has the Cambodian People's Party Heard?

Kheang Un

Introduction

The 2013 national elections could be seen as a transformative event for Cambodian politics. Given its massive grassroots organizations, strong symbiotic relations with domestic tycoons and its control of state resources and institutions — particularly the security apparatus, the judiciary, and the National Election Committee (NEC) — the ruling Cambodian People's Party (CPP) was expected to win a landslide victory over the opposition Cambodian National Rescue Party (CNRP). This expectation was up-ended as large numbers of Cambodian people voted against the CPP, forcing the party to do some soul searching. This article addresses four points.

The first examines factors that led many people to expect CPP victory. The second focuses on reasons underlying the protest votes against the CPP and the CNRP's popularity. The third documents the popular protests organized by the CNRP and the CPP's responses that culminated in a political compromise; and the fourth addresses CPP's reform efforts since the election. It then concludes by outlining expected trends for the coming years.

The Expectations

The CPP went into the 2013 election cycle with strong prospects. First, the economy was strong, growing at a rate of over 7 per cent propelled by the agriculture,

KHEANG UN is an Assistant Professor of Political Science and an Associate of the Center for Southeast Asian Studies at Northern Illinois University.

textile and tourism sectors. The CPP controlled all government institutions from the national to local levels including the National Election Committee. It also had a monopoly over the media; major television and radio stations are either affiliated with or owned by the CPP. As the Cambodian state has been synonymous with the CPP, the party was able to manipulate public goods transforming them into partisan resources. The CPP has strong organizational capacity with networks that link the state and business tycoons to local communities, creating a massive patronage-based vote-driving machine. The core of this structure is the party working groups comprising central party officials, senior government officials, and sub-national government officials with funding from these government officials and businesses. These working groups contributed resources for the construction of schools, roads, bridges, and offered a variety of small gifts including cash, monosodium glutamate (MSG), clothing and reading glasses. Nationwide opinion polls conducted by the National Republican Institute found 79 per cent of Cambodians believed that their country was headed in the right direction. Top reasons for people's confidence included the country's infrastructural improvement.[2] Cambodia watchers generally believed that the CPP would win a comfortable majority even in the absence of electoral manipulation.

The Outcome: Cambodians Have Spoken

The 2013 election was a surprise for Cambodia watchers and a shock to the CPP. The official results showed that the CPP won 68 seats with 3,235,969 votes and the CNRP 55 seats with 2,946,176 votes. This was a significant loss for the ruling CPP whose share of parliamentary seats dropped from 90 — a two-thirds majority, the threshold for amending the Constitution. The CPP's shockingly disappointing result can be attributed to a number of reasons. First, social stability and economic growth has been based largely on crony capitalism. The economic boom over the past decade has created a rich class — business tycoons, government elites and security forces — while dispossessing the rural and urban poor. Yet instead of addressing rising discontent over inequality, injustice, and corruption, the CPP campaigned on the memory of its battles against the Khmer Rouge, emphasizing the party's role in liberating Cambodians from their genocidal grip and using the brutal regime as a yardstick for its own achievements. This message had worked in the past with the generation of Khmer Rouge era survivors.

Second, demographic shifts occurred within Cambodia which worked against the CPP. Cambodia has experienced a youth bulge since the end of the 1980s; by 2013 over 50 per cent of eligible voters were under the age of 25. While during the previous elections Cambodian youth were politically apathetic, in the 2013 elections many of them became politically exuberant. Unlike older voters, these youth were looking for new options. Although they acknowledge that Cambodia has made progress, they believe that Cambodia's real potential is undermined by entrenched corruption, nepotism, and cronyism whose associated ills are social inequality, land grabbing, depletion of natural resources, and the presence of illegal Vietnamese immigrants. For many youths, their concerns were amplified through social media, most particularly Facebook. Their online political activities were found to be correlated with their electoral participation. The majority of these youths gave their support to the CNRP. A survey of youth who hold Facebook accounts indicated that 55.24 per cent supported CNRP while only 6.67 per cent supported the CPP and 36.19 per cent expressed non-partisanship.[3] This author's field observations during the election campaign period support this finding. The majority of the tens of thousands who participated in campaign rallies organized by the CNRP were youth. Many of the supporters, who had made small donations and volunteered to canvas for the party, were answering the CNRP's populist and nationalist appeals to mobilize against CPP's entrenched interests.[4]

Third, a number of changes have also occurred in the countryside, the CPP's traditional base. Previously, people in rural Cambodia credited the CPP for bringing about peace. Their apparent support for the CPP also stemmed in part from the control by CPP of local authorities who were able, in large measure, to control access to information in their communities. Since the early 2000s, better road conditions, improved communications and political decentralization have enabled local opposition activists to engage with the rural people.[5] Furthermore, NGOs have worked to build community-based organizations which attempted—in the face of intimidation and harassment by the authorities—to promote and protect local interests. These developments have not only reduced villagers' fear of local authorities, but also contributed to increased political awareness among rural populations.

Fourth, Cambodia's recent integration into the regional and global economies transformed the country's economy and social structure. Rural households have increasingly relied on the migrant labour of their children. Anecdotal information seems to suggest that international and internal labour movements have helped to change the political culture in rural Cambodia as more progressive views have been transmitted to rural areas via migrant workers.[6] Although Cambodian farmers remain cautious, many have become more tactically astute, and while they might still express outward support for the CPP, many wanted change. When the party offered them gifts in exchange for promises to vote for the CPP, they took the gifts and promised. But come election day, many cast their ballots against the ruling party.[7] The election results and the ensuing protests (discussed below) are testimony that the Cambodian people are no longer satisfied by the CPP's justification for its continuing rule in the name of peace and aggregate economic growth.

A fifth factor is the unity of the opposition to the CPP. The CPP's strength in past elections lay in part in the division among opposition parties. The merger of the Human Rights Party (HRP) and the Sam Rainsy Party (SRP) into the CNRP was pivotal to strong opposition electoral gains. This merger provided the opposition a unified front of urban and rural bases. Kem Sokha — the leader of HRP — had a rather strong rural base because of his work as a human rights activist from 2002 to 2007. As head of the International Republican Institute-funded Cambodian Center for Human Rights, Kem Sokha criss-crossed Cambodia, and his brief imprisonment in 2005 for his anti-government views earned him a national reputation.[8] Sam Rainsy — head of the SRP — had strong support from urban areas, particularly from garment workers and small shop owners. His popularity derived from his fearlessness in pushing for expansion of public debate and determination to use urban protests to expose government failings and corruption.[9] The union of Sam Rainsy and Kem Sokha served as a source of hope for many Cambodians inside and outside of Cambodia that it might be possible to topple the CPP. This allowed the CNRP to mobilize financial and moral support, especially abroad.

Sixth, the opposition also ran a better campaign than the ruling party. Its campaign platform was simple and focused on people's immediate concerns, that is, better healthcare, higher salaries for state employees and factory workers, lower prices for commodities such as fertilizer and gasoline, and illegal Vietnamese immigrants. Under the current CPP-controlled government, although overall progress was made toward providng healthcare services, the health sector continues to face structural challenges which include low salaries for health staff, "drug shortages and under-funded, under-maintained health facilities".[10] Although incomes increased over the past two years, civil servants' salaries remain below livable wages. Workers in the garment industry — a critical export sector — have also demanded higher wages from the minimum monthly wage of US$100 to US$160.

The opposition party contended that the inability of the government and factory owners to increase public sector wages was the result of widespread corruption that amounted to US$800 million per annum.[11] The opposition party's claim resonated with popular discontent over Cambodia's rampant corruption. An IRI survey in January 2013 showed that for those who said Cambodia was headed in the wrong direction, corruption was listed as one of their top reasons.[12] The opposition party also capitalized on Cambodians' animosity toward Vietnam and Vietnamese immigrants in Cambodia.[13] Cambodians dissatisfied with the country's direction, listed illegal immigration as their second top concern. This animosity has long historical roots dating back to the annexation of the Mekong Delta by the Vietnamese in the eighteenth century, the brutality of Vietnamese forces against Cambodians during the anti-French resistance, and the recent Vietnamese occupation of Cambodia between 1979 and 1989. This animosity was intensified by the general belief in a continuing Vietnamese encroachment on Cambodian territory and the large number of Vietnamese illegal immigrants living in Cambodia. Although no formal census had ever been undertaken, according to the U.S. Central Intelligence Agency's estimation, the number of Vietnamese living and working in Cambodia accounted for 5 per cent of Cambodia's total population or 770,000.[14] The CNRP promised immigration reform to curb what it called the uncontrolled influx of illegal Vietnamese immigrants to Cambodia.

Importantly, the opposition for the first time was successfully able to link the issue of Vietnamese immigration to the hot button issue of land grabbing. The last decade saw dramatic increases in land consolidation following Cambodia's economic transformation and deeper integration into regional and global economies. Key individuals within the business sector have shifted their investments as Cambodia moved away from dependence on illicit trade in timber, gems, and narcotics, towards more respectable industries.

Foreign investors too have partaken in the land rush.[15] By the end of 2012, approximately 2.6 million hectares of land were granted to foreign and local firms — 1.2 million of which were used for rubber plantations.[16] Moreover, the Cambodian Government has provided concessions since the year 1993 to 121 companies, 82 of which were foreign.[17] Among these 82 foreign firms, 34 were Vietnamese, the group that obtained the most land concessions (253,623 hectares); followed by 25 Chinese, with 203,960 hectares granted. The land rush on the part of large investors — both Cambodian and foreign — has prompted a mass expropriation of land from Cambodian farmers and from the urban poor, often violently with the assistance of the military and police.[18]

Land concessions have negatively affected about 400,000 people.[19] Land conflicts have led to "displacements, deaths, and imprisonments of human rights and community activists".[20] Previously, Cambodians had narrow social consciousness whereby incidents of land grabbing generated protests only in the affected communities. However, by the 2013 election, the CNRP successfully linked popular fears over "Vietnamese swallowing Cambodian land", to the rapid granting of land concession to Vietnamese companies. That argument allowed the CNRP to cast discrete reports about farmers and villagers being expropriated into a much broader case about the wholesale exploitation ofCambodia's natural resources by an ill-intentioned neighbour.

Electoral Impasse and Settlement

What was broadly anticipated to be a sweeping electoral victory for the CPP developed instead into a year-long political deadlock as the CNRP refused to recognize the electoral result due to what it labelled as "massive fraud". The CNRP led a series of mass protests with three demands: an independent investigation into the alleged electoral fraud with participation from the United Nations and civil society groups; new elections; and — if these two conditions are not met — the resignation of long-time Prime Minister Hun Sen.

In order to put pressure on the CPP, the CNRP organized a series of demonstrations attended by tens of thousands of people. The CPP initially tolerated these mass protests, assuming they would soon run out of steam. As the intensity and spontaneity of the protests rose, with the potential of evolving from discontent over the electoral result toward outbursts of broader discontent over wages and land grabbing, the CPP became fearful of the contagious effects of these protests. They had the potential to culminate in nationwide demonstrations against the CPP's long-term grip on power, which would inevitably force the CPP-controlled government to resort to a large-scale violent crackdown. In early January 2014, the suppression of protests by garment factory workers demanding higher wages and better working conditions resulted in up to five deaths and dozens of injuries.[21]

This lethal crackdown was immediately followed by a nationwide ban on demonstrations including the closure of Freedom Park — a government designated space for democratic expression. The CNRP continued to challenge the ban by organizing smaller-scale meetings with grass-roots supporters. While attempting to seek international support for its demand for an electoral investigation, the

CNRP repeatedly challenged the government ban on public protest with attempts to reoccupy Freedom Park which was ringed by barbed wire-fence. On 18 July, clashes between security forces and CNRP supporters erupted at the park. Following the incident, the government arrested seven CNRP lawmakers-elect who were charged with leading an "insurrection".[22] Soon after the incident, the two parties resumed negotiations and reached an agreement centred on overhauling the NEC and sharing power in the National Assembly to end the political impasse due to the CNRP's boycott of the National Assembly. According to the agreement, the CNRP would exercise control over half of the parliamentarian commissions, including the anti-corruption commission. Second, the NEC, widely believed to be CPP-controlled, will have nine members, four of whom will be chosen by the CPP and four by the CNRP, with the remaining seat to be selected by consensus; surprisingly, the two parties had seemingly already agreed in principle upon the ninth member, removing what was expected to be a sticking point to the deal. The CNRP accepted when the CPP agreed to appoint Pung Chhiv Kek — a long-time human rights advocate — as the ninth member. But then in November the CPP insisted that members of the NEC should only hold Cambodian citizenship, eliminating Pung Chhiv Kek from contention. At the time of writing this chapter, the new draft law on the NEC remains under negotiation.

To many analysts, the CPP used the arrest of the seven CNRP lawmakers-elect to pressure the CNRP to resume negotiations, which had previously been stalled. Arguably, the reasons underlying the resumption of negotiations were more complicated. In the months following the elections, differences emerged within the CNRP over the party's continuing boycott of the National Assembly. While Kem Sokha, CNRP's vice-president, intended to prolong the boycott, Sam Rainsy wanted to join the National Assembly. The latter believed that with popular support behind it, the party could more effectively engage with the CPP by working from within the system than by protesting from without. Sam Rainsy argued that "no other option was better" for the CNRP than reaching a compromise with the CPP.[23] The CNRP's initial strategy of using its boycott of the National Assembly to delegitimize the CPP had been ineffective. The European Union publicly registered its dissatisfaction with the CPP government whilst taking no concrete actions. In January 2014, President Barak Obama signed a spending bill which froze only a small segment of the US$80 million in foreign aid channelled directly to the Cambodian Government. Other major donors like Japan and China, continued their engagement with the CPP-led government; in fact China increased its financial aid to Cambodia to off-set any Western financial punishment.

Second, the CNRP had little room for manoeuvre given the CPP's tight control over the security forces and the judiciary, which allowed it to intimidate the opposition. Furthermore, CNRP's efforts to organize nationwide protests akin to the Arab Spring events did not materialize. Although there was widespread popular resentment against the CPP, Cambodia did not have the dire conditions that motivate people to risk their lives when confronting a potential government-armed crackdown. CNRP's hope for a split within the CPP in the midst of popular protests was unrealistic. Despite speculation of internal divisions, CPP leaders' political and economic interests were better served by party unity. Moreover, the strong bonds among CPP members are cemented by the memory of hardships during the time of struggle against the Khmer Rouge regime and the civil war of the 1980s and 1990s, reinforced by marriages among their children.

The CPP had its own reasons to compromise. First, although it has been able to conduct government affairs as usual, the Hun Sen government has continued to face pressure from the United States, the European Union and the World Bank to reach a political settlement with the CNRP. Second, based on the 2013 national elections, the CPP realized that its popularity had substantially declined, and its bullying tactics against the opposition party would further alienate voters (especially young voters who seemed fearless during street protests). Third, any deal that allowed the CPP to remain in the driver's seat was preferable to continued gridlock and protests. Given its strong organizational structure, internal cohesion, and resources, the CPP believes — as past experience in its dealing with political rivals has shown — that despite its compromise with the CNRP, it will remain a dominant force.

Furthermore, although Cambodia's economy has not been affected by the political impasse, anecdotal evidence suggested that the business community had adopted a wait-and-see strategy as far as new investment was concerned.[24] Any economic decline could further strengthen the opposition. The government's rapid response to the over 200,000 returned illegal migrant workers from Thailand in June 2014 following the Thai military government's crackdown on illegal migrant workers was a clear example of the Cambodian Government's concern over potential unrest associated with rising unemployment. Following the return of illegal immigrants, Prime Minister Hun Sen ordered the Ministry of Interior to expedite passport issuance to workers and drastically reduce fees from US$124 to US$4 as a way to facilitate these returnees' re-application for legal work permits in Thailand.[25]

CPP's Reform Efforts

There is a growing realization within the CPP leadership that for the party to stay in power without relying on the use of force, it needs to ensure that its government is responsive to people's changing expectations, which include the government's willingness to address social inequality, injustice and poor public services.

The sign of reform began with a reshuffle of the Cabinet. Some old guards who had for years ruled government ministries as their fiefdoms — were replaced by younger, more dynamic, reform-leaning leaders. Most noticeable are Hang Chuon Narong and Say Samal — the new Ministers of Education and Environment respectively. Dr Hang's first action was to curb widespread and well-known bribery and cheating that had infested Cambodia's baccalaureate exam over the past thirty years. For the first time the Anti-Corruption Unit was employed along with security forces to monitor the exam. The effect of Dr Hang's action was a high fail rate of over 75 per cent among the examinees.[26] Procurements at the ministry have become more transparent, resulting in more efficient reallocation of resources.[27] The Ministry of Environment, under Say Samal, has taken some concrete steps to address environmental issues associated with economic land concessions. There are indications of attempts to instil new practices at these two ministries such as the utilization of evidence-based policy formulation and promotion of technocrats.[28]

The Ministry of Economic and Finance — known to be the most lucrative ministry for rent seeking — also showed signs of reform. Long-serving Director General of the Department of Taxation — Pen Siman, was replaced by Kun Nhim. There have been significant reforms in public financial management. A senior official of a multilateral financial institution said: "Since the 2013 elections, the reforms in public finance amounted to the combined reforms of the previous five years."[29] In the first quarter of 2013, tax revenue rose by 9.5 per cent.[30] The government planned to increase tax revenue by 14.5 per cent in 2014.[31] But by November 2014 taxes received reached US$959 million — an increase of 20 per cent compared to last year's revenue.[32]

As indicated above, illegal Vietnamese immigrants were a major concern among many Cambodians and a rallying cause for the opposition. In response to this issue, in 2014 the CPP-controlled government also took initiatives to address this issue for the first time. The government undertook a limited census of foreigners and conducted raids of businesses suspected of employing illegal immigrants. By 6 November 2014, 700 foreigners had been arrested, among whom were over 500 Vietnamese.[33] Since June, Cambodia has deported approximately 344 illegal Vietnamese immigrants back to Vietnam.[34]

Changes have also taken place in the National Assembly. A survey showed that Cambodians wanted to see the National Assembly play a more active oversight role.[35] Before the 2013 elections, despite the opposition parties' persistent demands for government ministers to answer questions from members of the National Assembly, as required by the Constitution, very few government ministers appeared at the National Assembly. Following the 2013 elections, news reports show more government ministers appearing to answer questions including on sensitive issues such as national budgets and alleged non-transparent management of the sale of tickets to the Angkor Wat temple complex. More interestingly, some CPP members of the National Assembly took action to assist victims of land grabbing — an unusual move. For example, Lor Peang villagers have been in a prolonged conflict with KDC — a company owned by Chea Kheng, the wife of the Senior Minister of the Ministry of Industry. Villagers had suffered for years from abuse by security forces, and trumped up legal charges as they attempted to fight against unjust deals imposed upon them by the politically well-connected companies. In August 2013, three protesting villagers were arrested.[36] In a rare show of responsiveness, CPP lawmaker Ker Chanmony used her position as a bond to bail out the three arrested villagers. She promised to help mitigate their feuds if villagers agreed to stop their public protests.[37]

To safeguard against abusive concession policies, regulations on land concessions include a clause stipulating the government's right to confiscate undeveloped concessions. However, up until 2013 there was no known case of enforcement of this clause. In September 2014, Land Management Minister, Im Chhun Lim, intervened on behalf of embattled villagers who had fought for years against Horizon Agriculture Development by taking 1,562 hectares of land from the company and distributing it to villagers.[38]

Another action taken by the government in response to voters' concern was wage increases. Before the 2013 elections, although some concessions were made in responding to garment workers' demands for wage increases, the government was seen to side with investors. While opposition parties and unions claimed that low wages were associated with widespread corruption within the government, the latter claimed that higher wages and constant strikes would undermine Cambodia's global competitiveness. Cambodian garment factory workers had fought for wage increases for years and had endured frequent and at times violent government crackdown. Undeterred, the workers continued to organize protests that have produced contagious effects on other private and public sectors workers. As argued above, these developments have generated concerns among CPP leaders over potential cross-sectoral mass protests. Such protests could possibly lead the party to resort to excessive use of force if it does not want to see its entrenched power challenged which in turn would de-legitimize the CPP's legitimacy nationally and internationally. As a result, since the last election, the government has actively engaged in mediating negotiations between unions and investors. In November this year, the government recommended a wage increase from the base salary of US$100 per month to US$128.[39] Teachers also saw their salaries increase from US$105 to US$128.[40]

Conclusion

By 2005, with National United Front for an Independent, Peaceful, Neutral and Cooperative Cambodia's (FUNCINPEC) inevitable demise and Chea Sim's[41] declining health and weakened patronage networks and therefore increasing irrelevance in Cambodian politics, Prime Minister Hun Sen had consolidated his power. Such power consolidation could have ushered in the beginning of political reform in Cambodia. However, no significant reform emerged for three reasons. The first is the presence of entrenched patronage that has become, in the words of Steve Heder, "enormously institutionalized".[42] Many government ministers treat their ministries as personal domains choked with nepotism and cronyism. The second is the CPP's confidence in its patronage-based development as an agent of rural economic growth and hence political legitimacy. Third, the CPP has portrayed itself as the stabilizer of Cambodia; arguing therefore that its defeat could mean renewed civil war. The CPP hoped that this could continue to discourage Cambodian voters from voting against it.

The CPP went into 2013 elections with confidence, but the result caught them by surprise. The entrenched patronage has created a new mechanism wherein the state depends on the party, the party depends on individuals and individuals rely on rent seeking. This mechanism has consequently produced injustice and inequality — conditions that undermined CPP's achievements in maintaining social order and aggregate economic growth. The result showed that Cambodians could no longer be "manipulated in the name of stability".[43] Many Cambodians used their voting rights to challenge the status quo. Since the 2013 elections, societal pressure has ignited a sense of urgency in the CPP to initiate reform. The CPP devised new strategies. Patronage handouts seemed to have halted. Instead the party has shifted its focus to searching for reasons underlying popular discontent, ordering its officials to listen to villagers' concerns and provide suggestions for reforms. As this essay demonstrates, the CPP also carried out reform at the national level, most noticeably the Cabinet reshuffle (the replacement of some aging ministers with more dynamic and better educated ones); the appearance of an oversight role for the National Assembly and the restructuring of NEC; and the improvement of revenue collection.

However, the extent to which these reforms will usher further democratization remains to be seen. From the start of the introduction of democracy by the United Nations in early 1993, the CPP has been sceptical of Western-style democracy. Rather it insisted that Cambodia should follow other Asian models like Singapore and Malaysia wherein economic development takes precedence over full-fledged democracy.[44] Up until 2013, despite the CPP's rhetoric of leading Cambodia toward a developmental state — a state with strong capacity and inclusive economic institutions — the Cambodian state can be characterized as a crony capitalist state. Such states possess extractive economic institutions wherein access to state resources and government position is awarded on the basis of patronage. There is a growing realization within the CPP leadership that for the party to stay in power without relying on the use of force, it needs to ensure that the government is responsive to people's changing expectations, which now include its willingness to address social inequality, injustice and poor public services. As the above discussion shows, there are emerging signs of reform. Given the government's highly institutionalized patronage system, widespread corruption and sluggish bureaucracy, meaningful reform continues to be a daunting task for the CPP. Effective reform requires restructuring of the government bureaucracy by replacing incompetent bureaucrats with competent ones. However, this has not been systematically adopted due partly to a long history of the CPP never discarding its loyalists. Although this culture has helped unify the CPP, it remains an impediment to reform efforts.

In the final analysis, it might be premature to dismiss Prime Minister Hun Sen's reform efforts as disingenuous. After all he is a pragmatist who has in the past readily adapted to changing circumstances to stay on top of the political game. Meanwhile, the CNRP hopes to capitalize on its rival's structural problems and increase political activism to gather more popular support. The presence of all these conditions, coupled with a better balance of representation within the National Assembly and a more inclusive electoral institution, could help move Cambodia toward, if not a genuine democracy, a more inclusive society.

Notes

1. Part of the data for this article was collected while the author served as a research fellow at the Center for Khmer Studies, Cambodia in the summer of 2013. He is grateful for their support.
2. International Republican Institute, "Survey of Cambodian Public Opinion", Phnom Penh, 13 January–2 February 2013.
3. Virak Thun, "Youth Political Participation in Cambodia: Role of Information and Communication Technologies (ICTs)", Master's Degree thesis, Northern Illinois University, 2014.
4. Author's interview with youth working for CNRP's election campaign, Phnom Penh, June 2013.
5. Interview with Sun Chhay, former SRP parliamentarian (currently CNRP parliamentarian). See also Eng, Netra. "The Politics of Decentralization in Cambodia: The District Level", PhD dissertation, School of Politics and Social Inquiry, Monash University, 2013.
6. This information is based on the author's conversation with a number of political activists and villagers.
7. Author's conversation with members of CPP working groups.
8. Author's interview with human rights activist, Phnom Penh, June 2014.
9. For detailed discussion of Sam Rainsy see Kheang Un, "Sam Rainsy and the Sam Rainsy Party: Configuring Opposition Politics in Cambodia", in *Dissident Democrats: The Challenge of Democratic Leadership in Asia*, edited by John Kane, Hague Patapan and Benjamin Wong (New York: Palgrave Macmillan, 2008), pp. 105–28.
10. Harry Jones, "Building Political Ownership and Technical Leadership: Decision Making, Political Economy and Knowledge Use in the Health Sector in Cambodia" (London: Overseas Development Institute, 2013), p. 20.
11. Kem Sokha's campaign speech, Kampong Chhnang, July 2013.
12. International Republican Institute, "Survey of Cambodian Public Opinion", Phnom Penh, 13 January–2 February 2013.
13. Ibid.
14. Central Intelligence Agency, "East and Southeast Asia: Cambodia", available at <https://www.cia.gov/library/publications/the-world-factbook/geos/cb.html>.

15. Caroline Hughes and Kheang Un, *Cambodia's Economic Transformation* (Copenhagen: Nordic Institution of Asian Studies, 2011).

16. "Rubber Barons: How Vietnamese Companies and International Financiers Are Driving a Land Grabbing Crisis in Cambodia and Laos", Global Witness, available at <http://www.globalwitness.org/sites/default/files/library/Rubber_Barons_lores_0.pdf>.

17. May Titthara, "Kings of Concessions", *Phnom Penh Post*, 25 February 2014, available at <http://www.phnompenhpost.com/national/kings-concessions>.

18. Kheang Un and Sobunthoeun So, "Land Rights in Cambodia: How Neopatrimonial Politics Restricts Land Policy Reform", *Pacific Affairs* 84, no. 2 (June 2011): 289–308.

19. Global Witness, "Rubber Barons".

20. Kheang Un, "Cambodia in 2012: Towards Developmental Authoritarianism?", *Southeast Asian Affairs* (2013): 79.

21. Thomas Fuller, "Cambodia Cracks Down on Protest with Eviction and Ban on Assembly", *New York Times*, 4 January 2014, available at <http://www.nytimes.com/2014/01/05/world/asia/cambodia.html?_r=0>.

22. Alex Willemyns and Dara Mech, "Parties to Meet for 'Final Talks' on Basis of February 28 Election", *Cambodia Daily*, 21 July 2014, pp. 1 and 2.

23. "Sam Rainy Party: Explanation of Sam Rainsy after Explanation", available at <https://www.youtube.com/watch?v=HcgSe3dQ580>.

24. Author's conversation with Cambodian economists and researchers, June 2014.

25. Bopha Phorn, "Gov't Effort to Send Workers Back to Thailand", *Cambodia Daily*, 23 June 2013, pp. 1 and 17.

26. Radio Free Asia, "More Than 70 percent Cambodia's High School Students Fail Key Exam", available at <http://www.rfa.org/english/news/cambodia/exam-08292014201054.html> .

27. Interview with official at the Ministry of Economic and Finance, July 2014.

28. This author had on a few occasions in 2014 participated in such discussions with government technocrats and members of civil society groups.

29. Conversation with author, Phnom Penh, October 2014.

30. Reaksmey Hul, "Tax Revenue Up 9.5 percent in First Quarter", *Cambodia Daily*, 12 May 2014, p. 17.

31. Reaksmey Hul, "Government Expects 14.5 Percent Rise in State Revenue", *Cambodia Daily*, available at <http://www.cambodiadaily.com/archives/government-expects-14-5-percent-rise-in-state-revenue-46807/>.

32. *Xinhua*, "Cambodia's tax revenue reaches nearly 1blm USD in 11 month", 12 December 2014, available at <http://news.xinhuanet.com/english/2014-12/12/c_133851068.htm>.

33. Sokhean Ben, "Workshop Raid Nets Illegal Vietnamese Immigrants", *Cambodian Daily*, 6 November 2014, p. 13.

34. *Xinhua*, "Cambodian, Vietnamese PMs vow to deepen ties, cooperation", available at <http://news.xinhuanet.com/english/world/2014-11/25/c_133813536.htm>.

35. International Republican Institute, "Survey of Cambodian Public", Phnom Penh, 22 October–25 November 2008.

36. Naren Kuch, "Fresh Arrests for Embattled KDC Villagers", *Cambodian Daily*, 13 August 2014, pp. 1 and 2.

37. Naren Kuch, "LorPeang Villagers Bailed after CPP's Lawmaker's Intersection", *Cambodian Daily*, 30 August 2014, p. 5.

38. Aun Pheap and George Wright, "After Prolong Protest, Villagers Win Back Land", *Cambodia Daily*, 1 September 2014, pp. 1 and 2.

39. Reaksmey Hul and Peter Zsombor, "Government Sets Minimum Wage for Garment Workers at \$128", *Cambodia Daily*, 13 November 2014, pp. 1 and 7.

40. Eng Mengly, "Ministering Simplified Teacher Salary Payment", *Cambodia Daily*, 11 September 2014, p. 17.

41. Chea Sim is the President of CPP. Chea Sim commanded a faction within the CPP which includes Deputy Prime Minister Sar Kheng.

42. Personal communication, November 2014. See also Steve Heder, "Hun Sen's Consolidation: Death or Beginning of Reform?", *Southeast Asian Affairs* 2005, no. 1 (2005): 111–30.

43. Kheang Un, "The Cambodian People Have Spoken", *New York Times*, 9 August 2013.

44. On this discussion, see Judy Ledgerwood and Kheang Un, "Global Concepts and Local Meaning: Human Rights and Buddhism in Cambodia", *Journal of Human Rights* 2, no. 4 (December 2003): 531–50.

Indonesia

INDONESIA IN 2014
Jokowi and the Repolarization of Post-Soeharto Politics

Marcus Mietzner

After a decade in power, Susilo Bambang Yudhoyono retired from the Indonesian presidency in October 2014. Arguably, his rule was the most stable period of governance in Indonesian democratic politics — counting both the sixteen years following Soeharto's fall and the seven-year parliamentary democracy in the 1950s. Accommodating a wide array of ideological, religious and social interests, Yudhoyono has been a master political integrationist. The slogan of his party ("nationalist-religious") symbolized Yudhoyono's determination, and ability, to bridge the key divide in Indonesian society, that is, that between nationalists, who believe that religion needs to take a backseat to larger societal issues, and devout Muslims, who favour a stronger role for Islam in political life. While balancing these two groups, Yudhoyono also neutralized a host of other conflict spots. Handing out patronage posts to all major parties that sought them, and refraining from conflict with forces critical of him or democracy overall, Yudhoyono ensured that almost everyone accepted, or at least tolerated, his rule. The result of this decade-long political equilibrium looked impressive: Indonesia recorded economic growth rates last seen under Soeharto, communal violence was kept at very low levels, and one major separatist conflict — Aceh — was resolved.

Yet Yudhoyono's quiet rule was followed by the most divisive elections since the end of Soeharto's New Order regime in 1998. The struggle for Yudhoyono's succession saw renewed tensions between the nationalist and Islamic camps, and supporters of a return to some form of autocratic governance faced off with

MARCUS MIETZNER is Associate Professor at the Department of Political and Social Change, Coral Bell School of Asia Pacific Affairs, Australian National University. At the time of writing, he was also Fellow, Southeast Asian Studies (funded by BMBF), Albrechts-Ludwigs-Universität Freiburg, Germany.

defenders of the democratic status quo. Both candidates in the 2014 presidential elections, Joko Widodo (Jokowi) and Prabowo Subianto, styled themselves as populists who promised — in very different ways — to address public dissatisfaction with Yudhoyono's steady but uninspiring government. Clearly, then, Yudhoyono's presidency had not ended the country's long-standing tensions and conflicts — it had simply bottled them up.[1] The 2014 elections returned Indonesia to a more "normal" state of politics — one in which the heterogeneity of views and interests played out in the open instead of being absorbed into Yudhoyono's quest for societal harmony. This article describes the repolarization of Indonesian politics by evaluating the "battle of the populists" in the 2014 elections, the state of the economy as a main driver of the populist surge, and the new, more aggressive foreign policy rhetoric under the Jokowi administration.

Politics: The End of Yudhoyono's Moderating Presidency

The dramatic events of 2014, during which Indonesia briefly flirted with a return to authoritarianism, had their roots in Yudhoyono's interpretation of the presidency throughout his decade in power. For Yudhoyono, the key role of an Indonesian president was to "establish balance" between the myriad competing forces in the country.[2] This meant that all groups, regardless of their agenda, needed to be accommodated and given access to patronage resources — as long as they did not violently challenge the legitimacy of the state. In Yudhoyono's view, his tasks as president included guaranteeing that the main constituencies felt satisfied with the resources and influence given to them, and thus refrained from creating instability. "I love order, I love stability", Yudhoyono stated in a December 2014 interview, explaining his approach to presidential leadership.[3] When balancing the various interests proved impossible, Yudhoyono felt that he, as president, had to follow the majority view — in the name of democracy and to prevent unrest in society. Thus, Yudhoyono defined himself as a moderator, rather than a leader, of the political process, overseeing that everyone had a say and that no one lost face or felt disrespected. Through this arbitrating role, Yudhoyono in essence relinquished the executive and decision-making dimension of the presidency, instead celebrating politico-ideological equilibrium as the *raison d'être* of politics.

Yudhoyono's belief in the arbitrating function of the presidency led him to build an oversized government coalition — at the end of his rule, six out of nine parliamentary parties were in Cabinet. Traumatized by his experience as a minister under Abdurrahman Wahid (1999–2001), when he watched the president being impeached by the Legislature, Yudhoyono was obsessed with avoiding a similar fate. A smaller alliance of government parties, he contended, would have risked legislative threats to his rule.[4] For him, the downsides of "promiscuous power-sharing" (namely, protracted policymaking processes and low levels of democratic accountability)[5] were preferable to instability. Similarly, Yudhoyono sought to manage inter-constituency relations by appeasing both sides in a conflict with concessions, rather than by ruling on the basis of constitutionality. In the controversy over the Islamic sect Ahmadiyah, which began in the mid-2000s and stretched to the very end of his presidency, Yudhoyono felt trapped between conservative Muslims on one side and liberal human rights defenders on the other. In Yudhoyono's eyes, this was not a case that could be decided based on the Constitution alone (which guarantees freedom of religion). Instead, presidential action needed to give both groups enough so that they would not disturb the peace[6] — irrespective of which party had the stronger legal position.

At the surface, Yudhoyono's moderating presidency appeared successful. He escaped impeachment proceedings, maintained stability in his government, and reduced communal violence. For a country with a long history of political conflict, Indonesia's decade of stability should not be taken for granted — and Yudhoyono deserves credit for presiding over it. Yet after two presidential terms, Yudhoyono did not end his rule amidst collective praise. Instead, in the words of an Australian commentator in October 2014, Yudhoyono was "booed off stage".[7] In May 2013, only 30 per cent of Indonesians were still satisfied with Yudhoyono's performance, down from 75 per cent in November 2009.[8] Apparently, what Yudhoyono himself proudly perceived as prudent, consensus-oriented executive management was now widely condemned as unwillingness to make tough decisions and, indeed, refusal to carry out presidential responsibilities. More seriously for Indonesia, it turned out that Yudhoyono's ostensible pacification of the country's deep-seated tensions had been temporary at best; at worst, Yudhoyono aggravated these conflicts by creating an environment in which a populist, belligerent challenge to the political stasis was almost inevitable. Paradoxically, then, Yudhoyono's major legacy was to provoke public calls for the dismantling of the artificial calm he had imposed on Indonesian politics.

The first to profit from this Yudhoyono legacy was Prabowo Subianto, Soeharto's former son-in-law and a leading general in his military. Dismissed from the Armed Forces in 1998 for the kidnapping of pro-democracy activists, Prabowo channelled his bitterness over his dismissal into a ferocious populist campaign for the presidency. He had been unsuccessful in 2004, when he failed to secure Golkar's nomination, and in 2009, when he was only vice-presidential candidate to Megawati Sukarnoputri. However, 2014 seemed to be his year: between 2010 and early 2013, Prabowo topped most of the opinion polls on Yudhoyono's presidential succession. His radical rhetoric, which condemned Indonesia's democracy as corrupt, exploited by foreigners and beyond repair, resonated with many voters who had grown wary of Yudhoyono's leadership. In the legislative elections of April 2014, Prabowo's party Gerindra (Gerakan Indonesia Raya, Great Indonesia Movement) more than doubled its 2009 result to 11.8 per cent, making it Indonesia's third-largest party (see Table 1). In order to be nominated for the presidential elections in July, however, Prabowo needed a coalition of parties that had achieved either 20 per cent of the seats or 25 per cent of the votes in the preceding parliamentary polls. He had no problems in getting this coalition together. He ultimately controlled an alliance that held 63 per cent of the seats in Parliament.

While Prabowo had developed a classic populist campaign of the kind Hugo Chavez had run in Venezuela and Thaksin Shinawatra in Thailand, his main rival, Jokowi, offered a more moderate version of populism. This "populism-lite" was critical towards the inability of the Yudhoyono government to significantly improve public services for the citizenry, but it did not aim at the destruction or replacement of the democratic regime *per se*.[9] Instead, Jokowi — the then sitting governor of Jakarta and former mayor of Solo — promised to be a more hands-on president than Yudhoyono had been, and he indicated that he would discontinue the tradition of oversized coalitions and "promiscuous power-sharing". Jokowi had overtaken Prabowo in most presidential opinion surveys since January 2013, and by December of that year, he had opened a 39 per cent lead over him (62 to 23 per cent).[10] But Jokowi still needed a nominating party. While he was a member of Megawati's PDIP (Partai Demokrasi Indonesia Perjuangan, Indonesian Democratic Party of Struggle), Megawati was widely believed to still hold presidential ambitions herself, and her daughter, Puan Maharani, also intended to run in the elections, most likely as a vice-presidential candidate to the nominee of another party. Eventually, however, Megawati announced on 14 March 2014 that Jokowi was PDIP's presidential candidate. In the subsequent legislative elections, PDIP finished first with 18.95 per cent, but like Prabowo's Gerindra, it needed allies to officially nominate its candidate. Jokowi, and PDIP,

TABLE 1
Parliamentary Elections, 9 April 2014, Results

Party	Percentage	Seats	Post-Election Nomination
Indonesian Democratic Party — Struggle (Partai Demokrasi Indonesia Perjuangan, PDI–P)	18.95	109	Joko Widodo
Party of the Functional Groups (Partai Golongan Karya, Golkar)	14.75	91	Prabowo Subianto
Great Indonesia Movement Party (Partai Gerakan Indonesia Raya, Gerindra)	11.81	73	Prabowo Subianto
Democratic Party (Partai Demokrat, PD)	10.19	61	None*
National Mandate Party (Partai Amanat Nasional, PAN)	7.59	49	Prabowo Subianto
National Awakening Party (Partai Kebangkitan Bangsa, PKB)	9.04	47	Joko Widodo
Prosperous Justice Party (Partai Keadilan Sejahtera, PKS)	6.79	40	Prabowo Subianto
United Development Party (Partai Persatuan Pembangunan, PPP)	6.53	39	Prabowo Subianto
Nasdem Party (Partai Nasdem, Nasdem)	6.72	35	Joko Widodo
People's Conscience Party (Partai Hati Nurani Rakyat, Hanura)	5.26	16	Joko Widodo

Note: *But supported Prabowo Subianto.
Source: Indonesian Election Commission.

quickly assembled a coalition that represented 37 per cent of the seats in the Legislature.[11]

The building of the Prabowo and Jokowi coalitions occurred along politico-ideological fault-lines that the Yudhoyono presidency had tried to overcome.[12] The first fault-line was defined by the two camps' divergent positions on the role of Islam in politics and society. Prabowo's coalition contained Indonesia's only openly Islamist parties, that is, parties that demanded a stronger formal role for Islam in state organization: PKS (Partai Keadilan Sejahtera, Prosperous Justice Party), PPP (Partai Persatuan Pembangunan) and PBB (Partai Bulan Bintang or Crescent Moon Party). It also consisted of PAN (Partai Amanat Nasional, National Mandate Party), a Muslim-based party whose patron, Amien Rais, had a history of politicizing Islam when it suited him. The same was true of Prabowo himself. Prabowo came from a multi-religious family and had little theological interest in Islam. However, in the dying days of the Soeharto regime, Prabowo had aligned with radical and conservative Islamic groups to counter more nationalist elements in the Armed Forces, including its then commander, Wiranto.[13] For his 2014 presidential campaign, Prabowo revived these connections. As a result, he could not only count on Islamist parties, but also on radical Muslim militias such as the FPI (Front Pembela Islam, Front of the Defenders of Islam).

In Jokowi's coalition, the more nationalist-secular forces of Indonesian politics assembled. In addition to PDIP, the standard bearer of pluralism, there was the traditionalist Muslim party PKB (Partai Kebangkitan Bangsa), whose constituency was a long-time ally of nationalist parties since the 1950s; the pluralist Nasdem (Nasional Demokrat, National Democrats) founded by media mogul Surya Paloh; and Hanura (Hati Nurani Rakyat or People's Conscience), led by Wiranto. And indeed, the alliance's main task in the presidential campaign was to fend off accusations from the Prabowo camp that Jokowi's election would lead to the marginalization of Islam from the political arena. Among others, Prabowo's campaign spread rumours that Jokowi was the son of a Singaporean Chinese; that he would appoint a member of the Shi'a minority as Minister of Religion; and that he planned to legalize same-sex marriage. In Jokowi's view, this smear campaign was Prabowo's most effective political weapon, and it was mainly responsible for Jokowi's dramatic decline in the polls. From the 39 per cent margin in December 2013, Jokowi's advantage had shrunk to less than 1 per cent three weeks before the elections.[14] Fittingly, however, it was the non-Muslim constituency's massive support for Jokowi that helped him over the line. An exit poll showed that 70 per cent of non-Muslim voters had opted for Jokowi, and only 12 per cent for Prabowo (the rest refused to reveal their choice).[15]

The second fault-line visible in the campaign was that between supporters of the democratic status quo and forces that wanted to either roll back reforms or demolish democracy entirely. In the 1999 elections, this fault-line was of some relevance, but had since then faded away. In the 2014 elections, however, it was stronger than ever before. Jokowi led the alliance that defended the democratic status quo, with an emphasis on improving its effectiveness; Prabowo, by contrast, proposed returning to the 1945 Constitution that had served as the foundation of Indonesia's pre-1998 autocratic regimes, annulling all constitutional amendments since 1999.[16] In this restorative agenda, Prabowo enjoyed the support of Abdurizal Bakrie, the chairman of Soeharto's electoral machine Golkar. Other parties in Prabowo's alliance were not as enthusiastic about this platform, but went along. Similarly, not all parties and figures in Jokowi's coalition were reformers, but were opposed — for a variety of reasons — to a Prabowo presidency. In contrast to the religious fault-line, however, voters did not recognize the democracy-authoritarian divide as being one: nominal support for democracy was as high among Prabowo voters as it was among Jokowi's, indicating that many believed Prabowo would not follow through with his plans.[17] This was also the view of Yudhoyono, who threw his support behind Prabowo as well.[18]

After the elections, though, the schism between democratic status quo forces and proponents of a roll-back turned out to be more resilient than the religious cleavage. Jokowi won the elections with 53.15 per cent against Prabowo's 46.85 per cent, deeply frustrating the latter. Believing that Jokowi had betrayed him (Prabowo had supported Jokowi in the 2012 gubernatorial elections in Jakarta), the former general was determined to offer fierce opposition to Jokowi's government. Unlike in the elections, the theme of Prabowo's post-election campaign was not Jokowi's lack of Islamic credentials — instead, he focused his efforts on restoring some elements of pre-democratic rule. Two months after his defeat, Prabowo used his coalition in Parliament to torpedo the regime of direct elections for local heads of government — a major post-Soeharto reform introduced in 2005. Arguing that direct elections were violence-prone and too expensive, Prabowo wanted to return the power to select regional leaders to their respective parliaments. Yudhoyono, who at the time of the vote still controlled the largest caucus in the Legislature, did not support Prabowo's move, but did not want to vote with Jokowi's camp either — which wanted to maintain the existing mechanism. In the vote on 25 September 2014, Yudhoyono's caucus abstained, handing Prabowo's camp victory. It was only after Yudhoyono suffered unprecedented abuse on social media that the outgoing president issued an emergency regulation to re-establish direct local elections.

Thus, the 2014 elections re-ideologized and repolarized Indonesian politics in significant ways. The illusion of harmonious ideological balancing and amalgamation, upheld by Yudhoyono for a decade, has given way to the return of major debates about Indonesia's fundamental direction. For the first time in many years, discourses about re-introducing authoritarian rule went mainstream, with key party leaders openly propagating the advantages of Soeharto's "Pancasila Democracy".[19] And while the Islamist-secular cleavage appeared less sharp after the polls (largely because Prabowo had lost interest in it, for the time being), it is set to be more pronounced under Jokowi's government than under Yudhoyono's. For one, PKS is outside of government for the first time since 2001, creating a major incentive for the party to put a stronger emphasis on Islamic interests than under Yudhoyono's presidency, when government participation moderated PKS' rhetoric and actions. Second, the appointment of secular, nationalist and liberal figures to key positions in Cabinet — for instance, Interior Minister Tjahjo Kumolo, who met with Ahmadis, Shi'as and other minorities in his first week in office[20] — is certain to provoke Islamist and other religiously conservative circles, who have held these posts under Yudhoyono.

To be sure, the new polarization has had its limits. Jokowi, in trying to build a coalition to confront Prabowo's challenge, had to make numerous compromises with established elites. This began with lobbying Megawati to grant him the presidential nomination, continued with his acceptance of oligarchic support during the campaign (among others, from his vice-presidential candidate, Jusuf Kalla and his long-time business partner, retired general Luhut Panjaitan), and culminated in a Cabinet that contained many ministers his sponsors had imposed on Jokowi. These sponsors are mostly parties and elite figures who are politically conservative but correctly believe that the majority of the population want to maintain the democratic system, and are convinced — also correctly — that Prabowo would seek to re-establish a personal autocracy if handed the presidency. Nevertheless, they view Jokowi's middle-class background and his "populism-lite" with suspicion, and have thus tried to constrain his presidential freedoms. Megawati, for instance, reportedly threatened to withdraw her support from Jokowi if he did not heed her wishes during the formation of the Cabinet. As a result, conservative political interests are represented in government, making the divide between democrats and supporters of neo-authoritarianism less manifest than would otherwise be the case.

Despite these compromises, however, Jokowi used his first months in office to display clear differences between his and Yudhoyono's presidency. Unlike Yudhoyono, Jokowi has not shied away from conflicts with Parliament (in which he does not have a majority). Jokowi made two landmark decisions early in his presidency, fulfilling key campaign promises. First, he issued new health, education and welfare cards that expanded the social security net for millions of Indonesians. Parliament protested against this move, saying that it required legislative approval. Jokowi ignored those calls, and prevailed. "Let parliament oppose my policies, I don't care", Jokowi stated in September, "I'll tell the people who it was that rejected more benefits for them."[21] Second, Jokowi reduced fuel subsidies in November, less than a month after his inauguration. In his decade, Yudhoyono had tried in vain to permanently lower the level of subsidies, often failing to convince Parliament that this was necessary to fund additional social and infrastructure projects. Jokowi, by contrast, decided to not even ask Parliament — once again earning him strong but ultimately inconsequential legislative protests. Overall, Jokowi's presidency may not be the revolutionary breakthrough that many of his voters hoped for; but it has shaken up Indonesian politics, promising less consensus and more politico-ideological battles in the years ahead.

The Economy: Declining Commodities, Rising Nationalism

As Yudhoyono left office in October 2014, the Indonesian economy showed clear signs of weakening — both in the short and medium term. GDP growth, while the second-highest among the G20 states, fell to 5.0 per cent in the third quarter of 2014 — only slightly better than in the crisis year of 2009 and, ironically, the same growth rate as in 2004, when Yudhoyono had taken power.[22] The currency, the rupiah, lost 25 per cent of its value between mid-2013 and mid-2014, and slipped further towards the end of the year. Similarly, Indonesia's current account registered a deficit in October 2014 for the twelfth continuous quarter, pointing to declining exports (overall 2014 exports were 2.2 per cent lower than at the end of 2013).[23] Two major developments were responsible for these downward trends. First, the end of the commodity boom hit Indonesia hard. Yudhoyono's presidency had coincided with the resource boom from the early 2000s to the early 2010s, producing relatively high growth rates for most of the time. The global collapse in the price of palm oil and coal, Indonesia's two main commodity exports, had a major impact on the economy, turning current account surpluses into deficits from late 2011 onwards. The second factor was the so-called Bernanke shock, that is, the announcement of the U.S. Federal Reserve chair in May 2013 that the end to quantitative easing in the United States was near.[24] This led to significant capital outflow from developing economies, including Indonesia.

To some extent, the end of the commodity boom revealed Indonesia's failure to make itself less dependent on natural resource exports. Under Yudhoyono, this dependency did not decline significantly. Indeed, the manufacturing sector even deteriorated, from a share of 28 per cent to GDP in 2004 to 24 per cent at the end of Yudhoyono's rule.[25] Thus, growth rates of around 6 per cent concealed the fact that this growth was largely driven by the capital-intensive commodity sector, and not by manufacturing and services. In a similar vein, positive unemployment and poverty figures masked deep-seated structural problems. In 2014, official unemployment continued to decline — from 6.2 per cent in August 2013 to 5.9 per cent in August 2014 (and down from 9.9 per cent in 2004, when Yudhoyono became president).[26] But these statistics distracted from a less impressive figure: in 2014, 59.4 per cent of Indonesians remained trapped in lowly paid informal sector jobs[27] — a percentage higher than Nigeria's. The same applied to poverty numbers: these declined in 2014, from 11.46 per cent in September 2013 to 11.25 per cent in March 2014. Using this measure, poverty decreased substantially under Yudhoyono — it was 16.7 per cent in 2004. However, the government's definition of poverty has been traditionally low. Under the World Bank's standard of US$2 a day, 43 per cent of Indonesians were still poor or near-poor at the end of Yudhoyono's government.[28]

The gulf between Yudhoyono's rhetoric of high economic growth and the social reality was also reflected in increasing inequality levels. The Gini coefficient, which measures a society's level of inequality in income distribution, rose to new record levels in the 2013-14 period — it stood at 0.41, up from 0.32 in 2004.[29] Yudhoyono's Indonesia also had the fastest growth rate of millionaires in Asia, with its numbers tripling to 100,000 between 2010 and 2015.[30] By the same token, the household consumption share of the upper 20 per cent of income earners rose from 42.1 per cent in 2004 to 49 per cent in 2013–14, while the share of the lowest 40 per cent of income earners fell from 20.8 per cent to 16.8 per cent.[31] Even *The Economist*, not known for its sentiments against income inequality, concluded in May 2014 that Indonesia's "rich are getting richer much more rapidly than the poor are".[32] The inability of the Indonesian economy under Yudhoyono to translate the commodity boom into real sector jobs and to distribute the rising prosperity equally goes a long way to explain the outgoing president's declining popularity and, at the same time, the appeal of both Prabowo's radical populism and Jokowi's "populism-lite". In December 2013, as Indonesia prepared for the 2014 elections, only 36 per cent of citizens thought that the economy was improving; 55 per cent believed it was not moving at all or getting worse.[33]

Indonesia's response to the decline in commodity prices, capital outflow and rising inequality did not come in the form of urgently needed economic reforms; instead, the Yudhoyono government, and the political elite as a whole, pursued exceedingly nationalist and protectionist policies. Between 2009 and 2014, seven key laws were passed that imposed restrictions on foreign investors, established new tariffs and allowed ministries to set import quotas.[34] These seven laws were Law 4/2009 on Mineral and Coal Mining, Law 13/2010 on Horticulture, Law 18/2012 on Food, Law 19/2013 on the Protection and Empowerment of Farmers, Law 3/2014 on Industry, Law 7/2014 on Trade, and Law 39/2014 on Plantations. As a result of Law 4/2009, Indonesia began an export ban on unprocessed minerals in January 2014, trying to force large mining companies to build in-country processing facilities. Some mining firms suspended operations as a result, and a compromise was only reached at the end of Yudhoyono's term. This compromise is likely to lead to "lower government revenue (as compared with a tough mining-tax regime), some country reputational damage, and the impending establishment of what will in all likelihood be high-cost processing facilities".[35] Moreover, the passing of three new protectionist laws in 2014 — Laws 3, 7 and 39/2014 — indicates that Indonesia's Government and Parliament have no intention to change course anytime soon.

In the 2014 elections, economic nationalism was a key theme, with both candidates trying to outbid each other as the more patriotic manager of the economy. Prabowo's claim that foreigners exploited Indonesia's natural resources, and that only iron-fisted leadership could end this outrage, was well received by many Indonesians. His camp distributed maps in which foreign flags were attached to Indonesia's natural resource extraction sites, implying that the country was under external control. Jokowi's team was only slightly less nationalistic. Jokowi, a former furniture entrepreneur with many foreign business partners, was generally sympathetic to open market policies; however, such policies do not win elections in Indonesia, especially not if pitched against Prabowo's populism. Accordingly, Jokowi styled himself as an economic nationalist as well, promising that Indonesia would achieve self-sufficiency in food under his presidency. His party was an enthusiastic supporter of this approach too; a PDIP advertisement during the legislative elections, presented by Puan, featured a variety of food items, each decorated with a flag of the country from which Indonesia had imported it. The protectionism rhetoric did not dissipate after the elections either: as president, Jokowi reiterated that food autonomy would be reached within three years,[36] suggesting that the issue will be one of his priorities.

The rise of economic nationalism in Indonesia is dubious not because it hurts the interests of foreign investors and violates the spirit of free trade. As Yudhoyono stated, many foreign investors in Indonesia are excessively self-interested, and the government needs to ensure that the country gets its fair share in every deal.[37] The problem with Indonesia's new wave of protectionism, however, is that it is unlikely to benefit consumers, farmers, low-income citizens or the unemployed. Rather, the main beneficiaries are mostly oligarchs with interests in natural resource extraction, agriculture and horticulture. Not coincidentally, among these oligarchs are many elite politicians whose companies profit from the state's restrictions on competition in the market. Thus, Prabowo's call for expanded economic protectionism was not only a clever electoral strategy to impress the masses with his unwavering nationalism; in what Edward Aspinall (2015) has called "oligarchic populism", Prabowo in fact advanced the policies that best suited his own business empire, that of his tycoon brother, Hashim Djojohadikusumo, and the struggling conglomerate owned by Golkar's Bakrie.[38] In Jokowi's case, economic nationalism does not benefit him personally, but will help many of his sponsors who control natural resource concessions.

The focus on protectionism also threatens to undermine Jokowi's otherwise prudent socio-economic agenda. This agenda has four core pillars: first, to increase infrastructure spending; second, to improve the health system; third, to enhance the quality of education; and fourth, in order to pay for these goals, to reduce fuel subsidies and budget waste. In the area of infrastructure spending, Indonesia has fallen behind under Yudhoyono. Between 2004 and 2014, Indonesia spent only around 4 per cent of GDP on infrastructure — half of what China and India allocated in those periods, and half of what the New Order regime used to expend.[39] Jokowi wants to overcome this deficit by building more ports and other key facilities. Similarly, spending on public health was dismally low under Yudhoyono: 3 per cent of GDP in 2012, compared to China's 5.4 per cent and Turkey's 6.3 per cent.[40] For Jokowi, investments in a good health system are investments into the productivity of Indonesia's workforce, and he therefore has prioritized this sector since his time as mayor of Solo. Equally, Indonesia's expenditure on education was small under Yudhoyono: 3.6 per cent of GDP in 2012, compared to Brazil's 5.8 per cent.[41] Jokowi has made it clear that he wants to dramatically increase this figure, once again in order to produce more skilled workers.

In order to finance these policies, Jokowi has — as indicated above —reduced fuel subsidies in his first month in office, and abolished subsidies for premium petrol altogether in early January 2015. In Yudhoyono's final budget, fuel and electricity subsidies had consumed a whopping US$29 billion, or 19 per cent of total expenditure.[42] For Jokowi, fuel subsidies were "nonsense — they benefit the middle class, the people with cars. We need to free up the money tied to these subsidies to fund programs that benefit the poor".[43] Thus, Jokowi pledged during the campaign to cut the subsidies and shift the newly available funds into infrastructure, health and education spending. He delivered — the November cuts to fuel subsidies alone, which came at a time of falling international oil prices, saved the state US$10 billion for the 2015 fiscal year.[44] The success of Jokowi's economic agenda, however, will depend to no small measure on his ability to circumvent the dominant protectionist discourse, shift Indonesia's economic base from commodities to manufacturing and services, and stir Indonesia through the manifold problems of the global economy in the years ahead.

Foreign Policy: Ending the "Million Friends, Zero Enemies" Paradigm?

The end of Yudhoyono's presidency not only discontinued harmonious consensus-seeking as the premise of domestic politics — it also phased out a similarly inspired foreign policy. Yudhoyono's principle had been "A Million Friends, Zero Enemies", opening up Indonesia for contacts and trade with a wide variety of nations — from the United States to China, from Australia to North Korea. Yudhoyono was well aware that his paradigm was vulnerable to accusations of geopolitical arbitrariness. "I have been criticized for this concept", Yudhoyono stated shortly after his retirement in December 2014. "People said: why are nations who steal our [fish] considered our friends [...] This is a stupid interpretation [of my concept]. Of course, if it comes to territorial integrity, there can be no compromise."[45] Nevertheless, Yudhoyono was a strong believer in quiet diplomacy to resolve issues in personal discussions between leaders. "If only small issues were involved, should I really say 'you're not my friend, you're my enemy?' [...] I can call [Malaysian Prime Minister] Najib [Razak], Abdullah

Badawi [...] that is the ASEAN way, that is our framework of agreement." Thus, like in the domestic context, Yudhoyono tried to accommodate all interests and avoid confrontation, and like in domestic affairs, this earned him some praise for maintaining stability, but also much criticism for presiding over a stagnant status quo.

For Yudhoyono, however, his foreign policy was one of his biggest achievements. Calling himself a "foreign policy President" who was more active in that field than any of his predecessors (with the exception of Sukarno), Yudhoyono believed that he had developed Indonesia's traditional foreign policy doctrine "free and active" [*bebas dan aktif*] into a new "free and active plus" [*bebas dan aktif plus*] concept. This new notion, in Yudhoyono's view, maintained Indonesia's non-block position but extended it by intensifying outreach and engagement. Under his leadership, Yudhoyono contended, Indonesia had grown into a "regional power and global player", and as such, "we can't remain passive, we need to think about the fate of this world."[46] For Yudhoyono, his foreign policy contributed to this goal in five major ways: first, by turning Indonesia into a US$1-trillion economy and a member of the G20, Yudhoyono ensured that the country was part of global discussions on economic reform; second, Indonesia became an active player in debates on climate change — or so Yudhoyono claimed; third, Yudhoyono felt that he had positioned Indonesia as a mediator between the West and the Islamic world; fourth, Yudhoyono saw Indonesia as a key actor in discussions on development issues; and fifth, Yudhoyono thought he had strengthened Indonesia's role as a safeguard of peace and stability in Asia.

There is no doubt that Indonesia's international profile has increased substantially under Yudhoyono, and that the President contributed to this rise. But a critical review of Yudhoyono's claims reveals a continued gap between Indonesia's self-perception and geopolitical realities. To begin with, Indonesia's persistently high poverty rates continue to obstruct its ability to play a major role in high-level economic debates at the global level. While 43 per cent of Indonesians live on less than US$2 a day, this rate is 19 per cent in China, 7 per cent in Brazil, and 3 per cent in Turkey.[47] Similarly, Indonesia's continuously rising carbon emissions — despite a promise by Yudhoyono in 2009 at the G20 meeting in Pittsburgh to decrease them by 26 per cent by 2020 — has eroded its credibility to mediate on this issue, and it therefore had almost no role in international climate change summits.[48] Indonesia's significance as a bridge between the West and the Islamic world also remained limited, with Yudhoyono's assertion of being prominent in the crisis diplomacy on Syria sounding hollow.[49] Indonesia, and Yudhoyono personally, did get active on development themes, but once again, with few concrete results. And while Indonesia has been a factor of stability in Asian security, this was largely because it lacks the military capacity to be a force of its own. Indonesia's defence expenditure continues to be less than 1 per cent of GDP, about half of what other large nations spend.[50]

Jokowi's rise as Indonesia's central political figure also had a tremendous impact on its foreign policy outlook. Initially, it appeared as if Jokowi had little interest in foreign policy, and he said as much to his campaign and post-election advisers. Rather than a "foreign policy President", he pledged to be fully focused on people's daily-life problems, such as healthcare, schooling, transportation and jobs. For his only televised foreign policy debate with Prabowo, Jokowi was heavily coached by his adviser Rizal Sukma, the Executive Director of the Centre of International and Strategic Studies (CSIS) and Indonesia's leading foreign policy scholar. While Jokowi did well in this debate, surprising Prabowo and everyone else, his lines sounded rehearsed, and he clearly had little passion for the subject. After the elections, he continued to rely on Sukma for foreign policy advice, and he still seemed reluctant to take on a prominent role in this area. He dreaded the prospect of having to attend three major international events shortly after his inauguration: the summits of the Asia-Pacific Economic Cooperation (APEC) in Beijing, from 10–11 November, the Association of Southeast Asian Nations (ASEAN) in Naypyidaw, Myanmar, from 12–13 November, and the G20 in Brisbane, from 15–16 November. He publicly pondered whether it was necessary for him to attend all three meetings,[51] but was eventually convinced to do so.

Once Jokowi got a taste of international summits, however, he became determined to change Indonesia's overall foreign policy strategy. Believing that Indonesia had been shortchanged by many of its foreign partners in the past, he vowed to put a stronger emphasis on defending the country's own interests. He immediately did so in his summit meetings with U.S. President Barak Obama and the Chinese leader Xi Jinping, astonishing them (and his advisers) with his frank, non-diplomatic language.[52] Sidelining his Foreign Minister, Retno Marsudi — who Megawati had imposed on him — Jokowi took the lead in conceptualizing a new foreign policy that prioritized Indonesia's economic and political agenda above the "Million Friends, Zero Enemies" approach. In this post-Yudhoyono foreign policy, the people's interests — that is, that of Indonesian migrant workers, job-seekers and the poor — take precedence over lofty state goals, and Jokowi's vision of a maritime nation is a primary pillar. Presented with these cornerstones of foreign policy, Retno could do little else than summarize them. Returning from the summits, Retno stated that "What differentiates us now is that we will become more definitive in our demands. In the past, our [...] counterparts usually asked what Indonesia actually wanted [but] Indonesia could not make up its mind. But now, [...] we have already provided them with our stance — the maritime doctrine."[53]

Thus, as its domestic politics, Indonesia's foreign policy has become more polarized as a result of the 2014 elections. In essence, Yudhoyono's consensus-seeking policy made way for a more nationalist and self-interested approach to foreign affairs. Jokowi emphasized this new paradigm by sinking a number of foreign fishing vessels, mostly from Vietnam and Thailand, in November and December 2014. Yudhoyono recognized this as a momentous departure from his own practice: "[in my time], many Indonesian fishermen got caught in Australia, in Malaysia, [and their boats] were not immediately destroyed, only seized; I called Najib [and said] 'please set them free', and they were set free — and when we caught theirs, we set them free."[54] However, while Jokowi is likely to drive a more Indonesia-centred foreign policy, this does not mean that he is going to launch into a new Indonesian chauvinism. Jokowi is set to continue Indonesia's reliable and predictable foreign policy, and he shares his predecessor's reluctance to use bombastic and hostile rhetoric. Indeed, his election saved Southeast Asia, and the wider region, from a major destabilization of geopolitical affairs. Had Prabowo been elected, Indonesian foreign policy would have become a tool in the hands of an erratic president with a penchant for anti-foreign rhetoric and political adventurism. Jokowi, that much is clear, is a safer pair of hands.

Indonesia in 2014: The Survival and Polarization of Democracy

The year 2014 was arguably Indonesia's most important watershed since the fall of authoritarianism in 1998. At no other point since the regime change had Indonesian voters faced such a stark difference between the two main contenders for the presidency. On the one side stood Jokowi as the representative of the democratic status quo, supported by an alliance of moderate Muslims and non-Muslim forces; on the other side was Prabowo, the proponent of returning Indonesia to its pre-democratic Constitution, backed by the country's Islamist parties, Soeharto's former party and Yudhoyono. Had Prabowo prevailed, Indonesia would have embarked on a path of neo-authoritarian experimentation and political instability. Jokowi's victory guarantees the continuation of the democratic system, with all its deficiencies and pitfalls. Already, Jokowi's compromises with conservative elements in his own alliance have highlighted these continued weaknesses. Such continuities notwithstanding, Jokowi's Indonesia will most definitely look different from Yudhoyono's. The elections have repolarized Indonesia after a decade of static Yudhoyono rule, producing a more dynamic, but also more conflict-prone polity. Crucially, this polarization has also extended to foreign policy, with Jokowi's Indonesia determined to prioritize national interest over consensus-seeking multilateralism.

Notes

1. See John Sidel, "Men on Horseback and Their Droppings: Yudhoyono's Presidency and Legacies in Comparative Regional Perspective", Paper delivered at the Indonesia Update Conference 2014, Canberra, 19 September 2014.
2. Interview with Susilo Bambang Yudhoyono, Cibubur, 2 December 2014.
3. Ibid.
4. Ibid.
5. Dan Slater and Erica Simmons, "Coping by Colluding: Political Uncertainty and Promiscuous Powersharing in Indonesia and Bolivia", *Comparative Political Studies* 46, no. 12 (2013): 1366–93.
6. Interview with Susilo Bambang Yudhoyono, Cibubur, 2 December 2014.
7. Michael Bachelard, "Susilo Bambang Yudhoyono's Legacy: The Great Democratic Leader who Became a Follower", *Sydney Morning Herald*, 18 October 2014.
8. "Majority of Public Dissatisfied with SBY", *Jakarta Post*, 27 May 2013; "LSI: Popularitas SBY Semakin Anjlok", *Viva News*, 26 June 2011; "SBY's Popularity Dips Further", *Jakarta Post*, 3 September 2010.
9. Marcus Mietzner, "Jokowi: Rise of a Polite Populist", *Inside Indonesia* 116, April–June 2014; Marcus Mietzner, "Reinventing Asian Populism: Jokowi's Rise, Democracy and Political Contestation in Indonesia", *Policy Studies* (Honolulu: East West Center, 2015).
10. Saiful Mujani Research and Consulting (SMRC), "Koalisi untuk Calon Presiden: Elite vs. Massa Pemilih Partai, Temuan Survei: 20–24 April 2014" (Jakarta: SMRC, 2014).
11. For a more detailed account of Indonesia's 2014 legislative and presidential elections, see Marcus Mietzner, "Indonesia's 2014 Elections: How Jokowi Won and Democracy Survived", *Journal of* Democracy 25, no. 4 (2014): 111–25; and Edward

Aspinall and Marcus Mietzner, "Indonesian Politics in 2014: Democracy's Close Call", *Bulletin of Indonesian Economic Studies* 50, no. 3 (2014): 347–69.

12. Thomas Power, "Ideology Resurgent in Indonesia's Presidential Coalitions", *East Asia Forum*, 9 June 2014.

13. Marcus Mietzner, *Military Politics, Islam and the State in Indonesia: From Turbulent Transition to Democratic Consolidation* (Singapore: Institute of Southeast Asian Studies, 2009).

14. Interview with Joko Widodo, Jakarta, 15 September 2014; Saiful Mujani Research and Consulting (SMRC), "Survei Nasional Pemilihan Presiden — Wakil Presiden, 30 Juni–3 Juli 2014" (Jakarta: SMRC, 2014).

15. Indikator Politik, "Hasil Exit Poll Pemilu Presiden RI 2014, Rabu, 9 Juli 2014" (Jakarta: Indikator Politik, 2014).

16. Simon Butt, "Returning to the 1945 Constitution: What Does it Mean?", *New Mandala*, 18 June 2014.

17. Saiful Mujani Research and Consulting (SMRC), "Kinerja Demokrasi dan Pilpres 2014: Evaluasi Pemilih Nasional, Temuan Survei: 21–26 Juli 2014" (Jakarta: SMRC, 2014).

18. Interview with Susilo Bambang Yudhoyono, Cibubur, 2 December 2014.

19. "Bakrie: Pilkada Lewat DPRD Kikis Demokrasi Liberal", *MetroTV News*, 11 September 2014.

20. "Tjahjo to Protect Minorities", *Jakarta Post*, 6 November 2014.

21. Interview with Joko Widodo, Jakarta, 15 September 2014.

22. Badan Pusat Statistik, "Laporan Bulanan Data Sosial Ekonomi Desember 2014", Jakarta, BPS (2014); Stephen Howes and Robin Davies, "Survey of Recent Developments", *Bulletin of Indonesian Economic Studies* 50, no. 2 (2014): 160.

23. Badan Pusat Statistik (BPS), "Laporan Bulanan Data Sosial Ekonomi Desember 2014" (Jakarta: BPS, 2014).

24. Haryo Aswicahyono and Hal Hill, "Survey of Recent Developments", *Bulletin of Indonesian Economic Studies* 50, no. 3 (2014): 322.

25. World Bank, "Manufacturing, Value Added (% of GDP)", available at <http://data.worldbank.org/indicator/NV.IND.MANF.ZS>.

26. Badan Pusat Statistik (BPS), "Laporan Bulanan Data Sosial Ekonomi Desember 2014" (Jakarta: BPS, 2014); Stephen Howes and Robin Davies, "Survey of Recent Developments", *Bulletin of Indonesian Economic Studies* 50, no. 2 (2014): 160.

27. Badan Pusat Statistik (BPS), "Laporan Bulanan Data Sosial Ekonomi. Edisi 55" (Jakarta: BPS, 2014), p. 44.

28. World Bank, "Poverty Headcount Ratio at $2 a Day (PPP) (% of population)", available at <http://data.worldbank.org/indicator/SI.POV.2DAY>.

29. Stephen Howes and Robin Davies, "Survey of Recent Developments", *Bulletin of Indonesian Economic Studies* 50, no. 2 (2014): 160.

30. "World's Biggest Millionaire Boom? It's in Indonesia", *MNN Post*, 28 September 2012.

31. Stephen Howes and Robin Davies, "Survey of Recent Developments", *Bulletin of Indonesian Economic Studies* 50, no. 2 (2014): 160.

32. "Poverty in Indonesia: Muted Music", *The Economist*, 3 May 2014.

33. Saiful Mujani Research and Consulting (SMRC), "Kinerja Demokrasi dan Pilpres 2014: Evaluasi Pemilih Nasional, Temuan Survei: 21–26 Juli 2014" (Jakarta: SMRC, 2014).

34. Stephen Howes and Robin Davies, "Survey of Recent Developments", *Bulletin of Indonesian Economic Studies* 50, no. 2 (2014): 160; "New Plantation Law Limits Foreign Ownership", *Jakarta Post*, 30 September 2014.

35. Haryo Aswicahyono and Hal Hill, "Survey of Recent Developments", *Bulletin of Indonesian Economic Studies* 50, no. 3 (2014): 338.

36. "Jokowi: Tidak ada Impor Beras Lagi Tiga Tahun Mendatang", *Tempo*, 26 December 2014.

37. Interview with Susilo Bambang Yudhoyono, Cibubur, 2 December 2014.

38. Edward Aspinall, "Oligarchic Populism and Economic Nationalism: Prabowo Subianto's Challenge to Indonesian Democracy", *Indonesia* (forthcoming).

39. Raoul Oberman et al., *The Archipelago Economy: Unleashing Indonesia's Potential* (Seoul and Washington, D.C.: McKinsey Global Institute, 2014); Henry H. McVey, *Indonesia: Transitioning Potential Into Reality* (New York: KKR Global Perspectives, 2013).

40. World Bank, "Health Expenditure, Total (% of GDP)", available at <http://data.worldbank.org/indicator/SH.XPD.TOTL.ZS>.

41. World Bank, "Public Spending on Education, Total (% of GDP)", available at <http://data.worldbank.org/indicator/SE.XPD.TOTL.GD.ZS>.

42. Edward Aspinall and Marcus Mietzner, "Indonesian Politics in 2014: Democracy's Close Call", *Bulletin of Indonesian Economic Studies* 50, no. 3 (2014): 349.

43. Interview with Joko Widodo, Jakarta, 15 September 2014.

44. "Harga BBM Naik, Negara Hemat Subsidi Rp 120 Triliun", *Tempo*, 18 November 2014.

45. Interview with Susilo Bambang Yudhoyono, Cibubur, 2 December 2014.

46. Ibid.

47. World Bank, "Poverty Headcount Ratio at $2 a Day (PPP) (% of population)", available at <http://data.worldbank.org/indicator/SI.POV.2DAY>.

48. *The Guardian*, "World Carbon Dioxide Emissions by Country", available at <http://www.theguardian.com/news/datablog/interactive/2013/jul/16/carbon-emissions-carbon-tax>.

49. Interview with Susilo Bambang Yudhoyono, Cibubur, 2 December 2014.

50. World Bank, "Military expenditure (% of GDP)", available at <http://data.worldbank.org/indicator/MS.MIL.XPND.GD.ZS>.

51. "Jokowi Akan Hadiri Acara APEC dan ASEAN Summit, untuk G20 Belum Pasti", *Detik.com*, 8 October 2014.

52. "Jokowi Bikin Obama Kaget", *Tribun News*, 11 November 2014.

53. "Discourse: RI Now has Firm Foreign Policy Standpoint, says Retno", *Jakarta Post*, 17 November 2014.

54. Interview with Susilo Bambang Yudhoyono, Cibubur, 2 December 2014.

Southeast Asian Affairs 2015

JUNCTURES OF THE OLD AND NEW
The 2014 Indonesian Elections

Ulla Fionna and Gwenael Njoto-Feillard

Introduction

The fourth democratic election in post-Soeharto Indonesia was a display of inter-connections between the old and the new. The 9 April legislative and 9 July presidential elections were the first that saw the maximum impact of the implementation of decentralization and direct elections, and the abolishment of the party-ranking list system.[1] These new schemes have created more open and competitive polls for Parliament. The rise of Joko Widodo (Jokowi), first as Solo mayor, then Jakarta governor, and subsequently as Indonesia's president, is the strongest evidence of the possibilities that have been opened by direct local elections and disbursement of authority to the regions. These have now allowed local leaders to project their career to the highest administrative level. The effect of personalism and leaders' charisma has strengthened alongside this trend, particularly as parties still lack clear ideological platforms and programmes.

Meanwhile, old campaign tactics and means have interacted with the new realities and challenges of these elections. The prevalence and evolution of money politics — particularly during the legislative round — was evidence of old tactics evolving to sophistication. At the same time, new trends and realities, such as the dominance of legislative candidates, the role of volunteers, and the extent of the utilisation of social media as a means to campaign in the presidential rounds — are new trends, some of which may well become permanent fixtures in the coming elections.

ULLA FIONNA is a Fellow at the Institute of Southeast Asian Studies (ISEAS), Singapore.

GWENAEL NJOTO-FEILLARD is a Visiting Fellow at the Institute of Southeast Asian Studies (ISEAS), Singapore.

Contrasts between the two presidential candidates were the epitome of the "old versus new". While Jokowi represented the new breed of leader offering a fresh start, the other candidate Prabowo Subianto, characterized the growth of the sense of longing to return to the old system. The intense campaigning and the results that ensued also demonstrated how divisive the polarizing differences have been.

Legislative Elections: Candidate-centred, Money Rules

The legislative election in April provided strong indications of the emergence of new trends in campaigning at the grass-roots level. Spurred by the abolishment of the party-ranking system introduced just before the 2009 elections, the authority and control of the campaign mechanism have shifted firmly to the candidates. In previous elections, parties controlled candidacy by determining where each candidate would be placed in the ranking list that appeared in ballot papers — the higher the ranking, the better chance to be elected. The Constitutional Court annulled Article 214 of Law No. 10 of 2008 which regulated this system, introducing an open system where each candidate has equal chance to be elected regardless of his placement in the ballot list. As such, the role of parties was overshadowed by the role of the candidates and their individual initiatives and efforts, demonstrating the segregation between parties and candidates. Individual legislative candidates (*caleg, calon legislative*) ran much of the course of the campaign.

Parties had a very minimal authority in setting up — but did not enforce — the criteria for selection of candidate (such as levels of education and organizational experience); and lending their name, symbol, and attributes.

While criteria such as level of education, commitment to the party, past achievement, experience and funding were common features of what parties wanted in candidates, in reality these were not enforced by the parties. Basically parties were keen on having a popular candidate who had the financial means, while ensuring they met the 30 per cent female candidate requirement. Once candidacy was confirmed, parties provided some minimal briefing on technicalities of rules and limitations on the use of party symbols and attributes in the campaign. Theoretically, parties could cancel a candidacy for violations, but such action would be risky and possibly costly. Indeed, the cancellation of a candidacy would mean that they have to find a candidate of equal or better merit — while risking the wrath of voters who liked the cancelled candidate and the possibility of their being swayed to another party's candidate. Another important feature of the legislative campaign was the abandonment of mass rallies, and the increasing adoption of voter-focused campaign activities. Mass rallies (*pawai* and *konvoi*), traditionally a prominent feature of an election campaign,[2] have been dropped by the parties for various reasons. The rallies are expensive exercises, and perceived as no longer effective in drawing crowds and votes. So, parties only scheduled them when they had the best chance to draw crowds, particularly when national campaigners (*jurkamnas, juru kampanye nasional*) were in town. Even then, parties had to bribe supporters to come — at the minimum to refund supporters' transport costs, or provide some sort of enticement in door prizes — and yet, it was still a struggle to fill the venues.[3] Thus, while rallies were seen as an important way to show the power of parties in the past, it was increasingly difficult to use them in the same way during the 2014 elections.

Candidates had their own constituents to focus on. This enabled them to tailor their campaign methods to the various interests groups that they could draw votes from. As such, a direct approach was highly preferred. In particular, the *blusukan* (literally going through difficult passages to directly meet and talk to the locals) has become an increasingly popular feature of the legislative campaign. It must be noted here that the direct method could vary from genuine dialogue to find out what the community needed, to outright vote-buying tailored to the needs of specific groups. Consequently, there were often two teams on the ground — the candidates' and the parties'. The two only met during rallies. Even on these rare occasions, when parties tried to exert their influence by making it compulsory for candidates to attend, many did not; and there was no sanction for non-attendance.

Despite the fact that most parties were forced to take the back seat in the campaign, one party was able to defy the trend. The Prosperous Justice Party (Partai Keadilan Sejahtera or PKS) was able to manage candidacy more authoritatively. It selected only internal cadres as candidates. In the campaign, the party also assigned and scheduled campaign activities across different candidate constituencies. PKS utilised a range of candidate occupations, and rotated the candidates to campaign in different constituencies. For instance, a candidate who is a doctor would give health information sessions while a lawyer would offer free legal advice. In this way, candidates had to campaign for the party as, more often than not, they had to deal with other candidates' constituencies. PKS supporters were encouraged to vote for a cadre, it mattered not which one — as long as he or she was from the party. This was starkly different from other parties where competition, especially among candidates from the same party was stiff – and parties did nothing to resolve the tensions.

One developing negative effect of the candidate-centred election is that the open competition has encouraged candidates to take short-cuts to votes — most notably by buying them. The trend has grown so strong in this election that it has been dubbed the most "massive, vulgar, and brutal".[4] Observers on the ground have testified to the high degree of organization and sophistication of these vote-buying tactics. A new profession has flourished in these elections: intermediaries were paid by candidates to identify different kinds of voters and employ a range of strategies to get or buy votes from communities for an agreed price. These intermediaries have developed a set of skills that candidates take advantage of, and which have skewed the voting decisions significantly.[5] Deciding which candidate(s) to vote for was often reduced to which candidate was the highest bidder and gave the biggest tangible and immediate benefits. This situation has been enabled by the socio-economic background of many voters and the lack of ideological and programmatic platforms among parties.

The Results: Fragmented Parliament, Resilient Islamic Parties

On 9 April, twelve national parties contested the Assembly's 560 seats. A month later, the official results came in with some predictable outcomes, but also a few surprises. The first lesson learned from this election was the confirmation that political power in the DPR is experiencing a continuous process of fragmentation.[6] The foremost winner of the 2009 election (20.85 per cent of the vote, 148 seats), the Democratic Party (PD, Partai Demokrat), suffered a major defeat (down to 10.19 per cent, 61 seats). This was due to the party's inability to find a suitable personality to succeed Susilo Bambang Yudhoyono (SBY) and the fact that some high-profile PD politicians had been involved in major corruption scandals.

After ten years in the opposition, the PDIP was destined to take over PD's place on the top spot, thanks in great part to the so-called "Jokowi effect". However, internal party rivalry between the old guard supporting Puan Maharani (the daughter of Megawati Soekarnoputri) and the Jokowi camp rendered PDIP's campaign ineffective. This rift appeared clearly when TV ads for the party showed Megawati and Puan, while Jokowi — the party's most popular figure — was nowhere to be seen, except in the final days of the campaign. The party's results were respectable, but lower than some had expected: 18.95 per cent of the popular vote (a 5-point increase from 2009) and 109 parliamentary seats (a 15-seat increase).

TABLE 1
Comparison of Votes and Seats for Parties in 2009 and 2014 Elections

Political Parties	2009		2014	
	Votes (%)	Seats	Votes (%)	Seats
Partai Demokrasi Perjuangan (PDIP)	14.03	94	18.95	109
Golkar	14.45	106	14.75	91
Gerindra (Partai Gerakan Indonesia Raya)	4.46	26	11.81	73
Partai Demokrat (PD)	20.9	148	10.19	61
Partai Kebangkitan Bangsa (PKB)	4.94	28	9.04	47
Partai Amanat Nasional (PAN)	6.01	46	7.59	49
Partai Keadilan Sejahtera (PKS)	7.9	57	6.79	40
Partai Persatuan Pembangunan (PPP)	5.32	38	6.53	39
Nasdem (Partai Nasional Demokrat)	—	—	6.72	35
Hanura (Partai Hati Nurani Rakyat)	3.77	17	5.26	16
Total	81.78	560	97.63	560

Source: Komisi Pemilihan Umum (KPU).

The PDIP thus ended up sharing the top tier with two other parties, Golkar Party (Functional Groups Party) and Gerindra Party. Golkar Party, stagnated at 14.75 per cent of the popular vote, but lost 15 seats in the DPR. Responsibility for this failure was attributed to its chairman, Aburizal Bakrie, who led a dismal PR campaign for the party. Indeed Lapindo, a company majority owned by the Bakrie Group, was involved in a 2006 mud flow disaster that had displaced thousands of villagers in East Java. Bakrie's image deteriorated further when he appeared in a viral video in the company of young female artists en route to a Maldives vacation in his private jet.

For the Gerindra Party, however, the legislative election was a clear success. The young party (created in 2009) succeeded in garnering 11.81 per cent of the popular vote (a 7.35 point increase) with 73 seats in the DPR. Unlike PDIP in relation to Jokowi, Gerindra managed to make full use of Prabowo's popularity. Moreover, the party had the great advantage of benefiting from the funds of Prabowo's brother, wealthy businessman Hasyim Djojohadikusumo.[7] Gerindra, along with Nasdem (National Democrat Party, founded by media mogul Surya

Paloh) and Hanura (People's Conscience Party, originally an alliance between ex-general Wiranto and Indonesian-Chinese tycoon Hary Tanoesoedibjo[8]), epitomised the growing investment of wealthy businessmen in national-level politics as a means of advancing their own economic interests.[9]

The second lesson learned from the results was that Islamic parties have resisted an earlier downward trend, but that the appeal of "Islamism", as an all-encompassing political solution to societal problems, is declining. In the 2009 election, Islamic parties (PAN/Partai Amanat Nasional/National Mandate Party, PBB/Partai Bulan Bintang/Crescent Star Party, PKB/Partai Kebangkitan Bangsa/National Awakening Party, PKS/Partai Keadilan Sejahtera/Prosperous Justice Party and PPP/Partai Persatuan Pembangunan/United Development Party) totalled 25.85 per cent of the popular vote (35.12 per cent in 2004). Observers and polling institutes had suggested that they would fare even more poorly in 2014, but with a total of around 32 per cent of the popular vote, their score was closer to that of the 1999 and 2004 elections. However, the ideologies and social bases of these parties are so distinct that grouping them into a single analytical unit is debatable.[10] The relatively good results of these parties illustrate, not so much the hold of an Islamic ideal in the electorate, but rather the consolidation of their traditional patronage and clientilistic networks. PKB managed to garner 9 per cent of the popular vote (a 4 per cent point increase, adding 19 seats) by ending its long-standing rift with the leadership of Nahdlatul Ulama, the mass organization that forms its social base. Similarly, PAN, linked to Muslim mass organization Muhammadiyah, and PPP respectively managed to slightly increase and maintain their score by consolidating their traditional electoral base.

PKS, for its part, avoided the backlash that could have resulted from the party leadership's involvement in a beef-import graft scandal in 2013. Appealing to its core constituents, PKS presented the scandal as a conspiracy to destroy the party. It also relied on its dedicated cadres on the ground and its long-term strategy of humanitarian aid among local communities. Thus, the party managed to maintain its vote share of 6.79 per cent, losing just around one percentage point from 2009. While in the process, PKS lost 17 seats, it gained 273,249 voters compared to 2009. The relative success of this damage control strategy has been largely attributed to its new chairman, Anis Matta, who chose to pursue PKS' "normalization"[11] process engaged in 2004, that is, the toning down of the party's Islamist identity in favour of more inclusiveness.

In the weeks following these surprisingly decent results, some Muslim personalities called for the creation of a united front that would allow Islamic parties to nominate their own presidential candidate.[12] However, this initiative failed. As noted previously, acute ideological differences played a role in this lack of unity, but this reflected more generally the great social diversity (in terms of culture and class) that is typical of the Islamic landscape in Indonesia.[13] In the competitive electoral process, Islam is now more than ever a selling point for political marketing used both by nationalist and Islamic parties, but much less a programmatic platform. As such, it would have an important role in the run-up to the presidential election, particularly in the context of parliamentary fragmentation.

Presidential Candidates: The Old Elite Versus the New Breed of Leader

The results of the legislative elections have forced parties to realistically assess the prospects of their candidates. For instance, while many in PDIP leadership may have wanted to grant presidential candidacy to chairperson Megawati Sukarnoputri, their weaker-than-expected performance in the legislative round forced them to form a coalition with other parties. At the same time, the leadership also had to consider that many elements within the party favoured the candidacy of the much more popular Jokowi. Meanwhile, although Golkar Party came second and despite strong party machinery, its candidate Aburizal Bakrie had been struggling to boost his popularity. Prabowo Subianto on the other hand, was gaining ground as a prominent candidate, and his Gerindra Party came third. Thus, although there was speculation on other candidates, eventually only two prevailed as presidential candidates: Jokowi and Prabowo. After much discussions behind closed doors, Jusuf Kalla and Hatta Rajasa were selected as vice-presidential candidates respectively.

The campaign that ensued demonstrated the wide contrast between the two candidates. While Jokowi relied on his humble common man persona, Prabowo symbolized a strong leader who promised decisiveness. Jokowi was a furniture businessman from a small town of Solo, while Prabowo had an illustrious military career, came from an aristocrat family and had been married to Soeharto's daughter, Titiek. Jokowi wore cheap clothing and kept an unrefined persona typical of a village dweller (*ndeso*), while Prabowo rode a pure-bred stallion, with an expensive *keris* (traditional dagger) to his thigh, in the campaign. Beyond their appearance, the two political contenders also represented opposing groups of leaders in a country that had only started its democratic transition process in 1998. Prabowo had the pedigree of a typical New Order (1966–98) leader. His involvement in the kidnapping of student activists in 1998 which led to his discharge from the military, proved both a burden but also a "selling point" for his campaign. For some voters, it was evidence of Prabowo's firmness in contrast to outgoing President Susilo Bambang Yudhoyono's perceived indecisiveness.

Prabowo's campaign featured an announced return to the original version of the 1945 Constitution. The amendments to the original version have seen the introduction — among others — of direct presidential and local elections, a human rights charter. Prabowo's proposals further strengthened his anti-reform credentials. While both candidates ran on populist themes, Prabowo emphasized the urgency of returning to a stronger nationalism to protect Indonesia's political and economic interests. Frequently referring to foreigners as "thieves", he vowed to restore the country's control over its own natural resources.

Jokowi on the other hand, was a directly-elected local leader from Solo before taking over Jakarta's governorship and rose to be the presidential candidate from PDIP. While Prabowo's electoral promises seemed more like a collection of concepts, Jokowi listed the various initiatives that he had implemented in Solo and Jakarta as the backbone of his campaign promises. His health and education cards have benefited the poor and he built on these for his campaign track-record. In contrast to Prabowo's denouncement of direct elections, Jokowi's campaign promised to pursue the path of democratization and work for public service improvement within the existing system.

As such, the old elite was represented by the candidacy of Prabowo, while Jokowi embodied the opportunities for a "nobody" to emerge as the country's leader — a new possibility in a reformed Indonesia. After the legislative election results, Jokowi announced that his alliance of parties would be strictly based on the support for his agenda of reforms, and not the usual promise of ministerial positions. Joining him and the PDIP were the PKB, Nasdem and Hanura (old politics, however, proved hard to replace as Jokowi's Cabinet would later include many members from his coalition parties). Prabowo and the Gerindra united behind them a larger coalition of parties that had no qualms about openly using patronage politics: Golkar, PAN, PPP and the PKS. The Partai Demokrat played an ambiguous role, while leaning towards Prabowo. Both camps engaged in conventional and new campaign strategies.

The Polarizing Effect of New Campaign Strategies

In terms of campaign strategies, the Prabowo camp had a clear head start, one that Jokowi would find hard to catch up with. There was an obvious reason for this: Gerindra had been preparing for this moment for years, when the PDIP was still marred by internal rivalries. While the Jokowi camp relied on a network of volunteers,[14] who were often mobilized through social media, Gerindra had the necessary funds to deploy thousands of salaried campaigners on the ground. The Prabowo camp also benefited from Golkar's political machine, known to be the country's most organized and efficient, as well as the quasi-propaganda of Aburizal Bakrie's TV One and Harry Tanoe's MNC group (RCTI, MNC TV and Global TV). In terms of coverage, these pro-Prabowo channels far outweighed Surya Paloh's Metro TV, a pro-Jokowi channel that caters mostly to the urban upper middle-class elite. In the history of Indonesia's presidential campaigns, this was the first time that the media would have such a critical role in polarizing the electorate or the country.

Gerindra's understanding of the importance of political marketing was clearly illustrated by the fact that it recruited an American consultant, Rob Allyn, who played a key role in creating an aggressive campaign for candidate Vincente Fox during Mexico's presidential elections in 2000.[15] This strategy would be used against Jokowi as well. Through *Obor Rakyat* (The People's Torch), a tabloid specially printed for the election, Prabowo supporters argued that Jokowi was a mere puppet of Megawati Soekarnoputri, that he was supported by big Chinese conglomerates and that the PDIP was the "Party of the Cross" (that is, working for the interests of Christians). While the paper was meant to be distributed mostly in East Java, particularly in Islamic schools (*pesantren*), the wide media coverage of the controversial issue made the message heard on a national scale. On the Internet, the black campaign was no less intense: Facebook and Twitter messages accused Jokowi of being a closet Christian or of being of Chinese descent. On this battleground for popularity, PKS-linked activists seem to have played a key role, as they are known to be well-versed in new technologies.

The Jokowi camp first chose to ignore the attacks, but, with the declining popularity of its candidate, a counter-strategy was rapidly put in place. Jokowi reaffirmed in the various media that he was an experienced and firm leader, contrary to what the Prabowo camp suggested. During TV debates, figures in the Jokowi campaign directly attacked Prabowo on his past of alleged human rights abuses or on more personal issues, such as the fact that he was unmarried. Because the attacks often took a religious turn, putting in doubt Jokowi's "Islamness", his campaign team worked to reinforce his religious credentials. For this, it relied mostly on the traditionalist camp, as the PKB had earlier pledged allegiance to Jokowi. The party distributed its own bulletin (*Obor Rahmatan Lil' Alamin*, or the "Torch of the Blessing for All Mankind") in the *pesantren* (Islamic boarding school) milieu to challenge the *Obor Rakyat* tabloid.

Both candidates thus rivalled in displaying a pious public image, visiting well-known *ulemas* (Muslim scholars), *pesantren* and pilgrimage sites. Islamic organizations, such as the NU, the Muhammadiyah and the Indonesian Council of Ulemas (MUI, Majelis Ulama Indonesia), were lobbied for support. It is noteworthy that in this race for religious legitimacy, Jokowi managed to hold firm to his ideal of defending a tolerant form of Islam. The Prabowo camp, for its part, was more pragmatic and did not hesitate to garner the support of ultra-conservatives and sometimes radical elements of Islam, such as the Islamic Defenders Front (Front Pembela Islam).

In the last days of the campaign, when polls were showing that Jokowi's lead had all but vanished, three determining factors came into play that possibly swayed the crucial weight of undecided voters. First, the Jokowi campaign organized a massive concert in Jakarta for its campaigners and the general public, featuring a popular band (Slank). The event was widely covered by the national media and may have played a role in drawing more votes from the young middle-class urbanites. Second, the final television debate (from a series of five) resulted in a relatively poor performance from Prabowo and Hatta, in contrast to the performance of Jokowi and Kalla, who both gave the image of being indeed firm, experienced and knowledgeable on the main issues facing the country. Finally, on the last week of the campaign, a cooling down period when political activity is supposed to be idle, Jokowi strategically chose to go a "minor pilgrimage" to Mecca (*Umroh*), again showing the ever-growing importance of Islam as a political marketing instrument.

The Results: Battling for Legitimacy

On 9 July, the election took place peacefully, with a voter turnout of 69.58 per cent. This was less than the 71.91 per cent of 2009, but still impressive by international standards. The process was deemed by experts as "the best in Indonesia's history".[16] There were a number irregularities and technical issues in the 470,000 voting booths spread all over the country, but none of these were considered to have been able to change the outcome.

On the evening of the voting day, quick-count results from eight trusted polling institutes showed that Jokowi had won the election by a modest but comfortable margin. The public had to wait till 22 July, however, for the Electoral Commission to announce the official results. In the meantime, the Prabowo camp did everything in its power to delegitimize the results from the quick count to show that its champion had in fact won the election. For this, it relied on quick-count results of four shady institutes that were suspected of having been financed by Prabowo supporters. While the eight polling institutes that declared Jokowi the winner announced that they were ready to be officially audited, three institutes in favour of a Prabowo victory refused to give access to their data.

During this tense period, researchers and "netizens" played a novel and interconnected role. Recognizing the danger posed to Indonesian democracy by the tactics of the Prabowo camp, two scholars from Australia's National University (ANU), Edward Aspinall and Marcus Mietzner, published a piece on the New Mandala blog covering the elections, accusing Prabowo of wanting to "steal the election" by influencing the complex counting process and possibly corrupting KPU officials at the local level. At the height of the election period, the site had a readership of around 100,000. It was not surprising therefore that Prabowo intervened to defend himself in an interview published on the very same blog, to which the two ANU scholars quickly responded by reaffirming their accusations.

These pieces were translated in Indonesian and had a manifest influence on some within the new generation of local netizens. After reading the commentaries, five young computer engineers decided to create the KawalPemilu.org website (Guard the Election) which allowed the ballots to be counted by a crowd-sourcing system made up of hundreds of volunteers. Through this system, the results were available to the public and the media about a week before the official KPU announcement and undermined Prabowo's efforts in delegitimizing earlier quick counts.

On 22 July, the KPU made the official announcement: Jokowi had won by a margin of 53.1 per cent to 46.9 per cent. Of 33 provinces, 23 saw a majority for Jokowi. Soon after, Prabowo declared that he was withdrawing from the process altogether, as the results had supposedly been marred by widespread fraud from the Jokowi camp and the KPU. The next day however, he retracted this declaration and announced that he was challenging the results in the Constitutional Court, a common initiative in the Indonesian elections' recent history.[17] After a long and tedious process, the court concluded that the evidence given by the Prabowo team was unsubstantial, thereby officially validating the election of Joko Widodo as the country's next president.

Acknowledging that the initiative to challenge the results at the Constitutional Court might fail, the parties behind Prabowo united in a "Red-and-White Coalition" with the intention of taking the fight to the Parliament, where they occupied, at that time, a majority of seats (314 of 560).

Conclusion: The Rise of a New Government and the Resistance of Old Elites

The legislative round has seen the evolution of a system that is open and competitive, but that also produces rampant and organized money politics. It has highlighted the weaknesses of political parties who had to relinquish their authority to candidates and could do little to support or control the campaigns — with the exception of PKS.

Similarly, there are benefits and disadvantages that the presidential elections elucidated. Jokowi's election has shown how far Indonesia has come in its democratic transition process — that a local leader could rise to national leadership is no small feat. However, the closely fought election has left some divides among Indonesians. Alongside this pressure, President Jokowi has been forced to balance various interests in his Cabinet appointments, and his choices have strongly indicated that he cannot escape some vested party interests and influences especially from Megawati herself and National Democratic Party chairperson, Surya Paloh.

Meanwhile, the continuing divide in the Parliament between the government and coalition opposition may continue to threaten the work efficiency and various reform programmes that the new President has promised. Certainly, the opposition's success in temporarily[18] overturning direct local elections demonstrated the potential of the old elites in the Parliament to preserve their own interests at the expense of democratic progress.[19] While Jokowi's Great Indonesia coalition and the Red-and-White coalition have managed to negotiate a compromise on power sharing,[20] it remains to be seen whether this will suffice to lower the tension between the two camps and promote further cooperation.

Overall, there are some positives that are noteworthy. The elections have tested the strength and independence of state institutions such as the General Election Commission (KPU, Komisi Pemilihan Umum) and the Constitutional Court (MK, Mahkamah Konstitutional). More importantly, never before has there been such involvement from Indonesians in assessing their government, Parliament, and ministers. As such, the next election will see an intense scrutiny of the parties, elected candidates, and the President himself. While there may be further challenges, greater participation and involvement should only strengthen this young democracy further. This will be needed in the face of the old elites' ongoing attempts to hold on to power.

Notes

1. Under this system, parties decided the ranking placement of candidate — the higher-ranked candidates had better chance to be elected as they would receive the first votes. Once the top-ranked candidate had enough votes for a seat, then votes would go to the subsequent candidate(s) on the list.

2. See Jennifer Lindsay, "The Performance Factor in Indonesian Elections", in *Elections as Popular Culture in Asia*, edited by Chua Beng Huat (London: Routledge, 2007), pp. 55–71.

3. Mass rallies of PAN and PKB in Malang attended by party chairmen were relatively empty, with only small number of paid crowds attending. Only when then-President Susilo Bambang Yudoyono came, was there a much bigger crowd for Partai Demokrat's rally.

4. "Pemantau Pemilu: Politik Uang Kali Ini Sangat Masif, Vulgar dan Brutal", *Kompas.com*, 21 April 2014, available at <http://nasional.kompas.com/read/2014/04/21/2000277/Pemantau.Pemilu.Politik.Uang.Kali.Ini.Sangat.Masif.Vulgar.dan.Brutal>.

5. See for example, Edward Aspinall, "Money Politics: The Distribution of Money, Goods, and Other Benefits is an Integral Part of Electioneering in Indonesia", *Inside Indonesia*, Edition 116 (April–June 2014), available at <http://www.insideindonesia.org/weekly-articles/money-politics-2>; and Ulla Fionna, "Vote-buying in Indonesia's 2014 Elections: The Other Side of the Coin", *ISEAS Perspective*, 4 June 2014, available at <http://www.iseas.edu.sg/documents/publication/ISEAS_Perspective_2014_35-Vote-buying_in_Indonesia's_2014_Elections.pdf>.

6. Stephen Sherlock, "House of Cards", *New Mandala*, 17 July 2014, available at <http://asiapacific.anu.edu.au/newmandala/2014/07/17/house-of-cards/>.

7. Marcus Mietzner, "How Jokowi Won and Democracy Survived", *Journal of Democracy* 25, no. 4 (2014): 117.

8. The pair separated after Hanura's poor results in the legislative election. Wiranto joined the Jokowi coalition, and Hary Tanoesoedibjoe left the party to join the Prabowo camp.

9. Eve Warburton, "The Business of Politics in Indonesia", *Inside Indonesia* 117, July–September 2014, available at <http://www.insideindonesia.org/feature-editions/the-business-of-politics-in-indonesia>.

10. For example, PKS appeals mostly to the new urban middle-class and, while it has normalized its discourse, its ideology is still influenced by a Muslim Brotherhood-type internationalist orientation. The PKB's constituents are mostly rural segments of Indonesian society. It is the vehicle of traditionalist Islam (quite different from PKS' puritanical Islam) and has a strong nationalist element to its ideology.

11. Julie Chernov-Hwang, "Patterns of Normalization: Islamist Parties in Indonesia", in *Islamist Parties and Political Normalization in the Muslim World*, edited by Quinn Mecham and Julie Chernov-Hwang (Pennsylvania: University of Pennsylvania Press, 2014): 58–83.

12. A presidential ticket must be supported by a party or a coalition of parties winning at least 20 per cent of the seats or 25 per cent of the popular votes in the legislative election.

13. Vedi R. Hadiz, "The Organizational Vehicles of Islamic Political Dissent: Social Bases, Genealogies and Strategies", in *Between Dissent and Power: The Transformation of Islamic Politics in the Middle East and Asia*, edited by Khoo Boo Teik, Vedi R. Hadiz, and Yoshihiro Nakanishi (London: Palgrave Macmillan, 2014), p. 49.

14. Mietzner, "How Jokowi Won and Democracy Survived".

15. "The selling of Prabowo", *Tempo*.co, 5 July 2014, available at <http://en.tempo.co/read/news/2014/07/05/080590630/The-Selling-of-Prabowo>.

16. Available at <http://www.ifes.org/Content/Publications/News-in-Brief/2014/July/Final-Results-of-the-2014-Presidential-Election-in-Indonesia-Announced.aspx> and <http://www.idea.int/vt/countryview.cfm?CountryCode=ID>.

17. Rizal Sukma, "Indonesia's 2009 Elections: Defective System, Resilient Democracy", in *Problems of Democratisation in Indonesia: Elections, Institutions, and Society*, edited by Edward Aspinall and Marcus Mietzner (Singapore: Institute of Southeast Asian Studies, 2010), p. 59.

18. In early 2015, Parliament decided to revert to direct elections.

19. On 26 September 2014, the outgoing parliament passed a law overturning direct local elections (to an indirect system, through local parliaments). The outgoing President Susilo Bambang Yudhoyono (SBY) issued a government regulation in lieu of the law (Perppu) to annul it. This will only take effect when passed by the new Parliament — which is scheduled to hold its session in January 2015. In the new Parliament, there are currently more parties who support the return to the indirect system. However, some of these parties (notably the United Development

Party or PPP and Partai Golkar) are experiencing leadership struggles that may see them cross over to the government coalition and support the Perppu in favour of the direct system.

20. Ending a two-month stand-off, in which ministers and other officials from the government coalition refused to attend hearings held by the House, a plenary session of the House of Representatives on 5 December 2014 passed an amendment to the Legislative Institutions (MD3). Under the amendment that essentially is about power-sharing, Jokowi's Great Indonesia Coalition will now have 21 out of 64 leadership posts in the House, while previously they were denied any.

ISIS IN INDONESIA

Sidney Jones and Solahudin

A steep decline in terrorist acts in Indonesia in 2014 should have been good news, especially because it underscored that police vigilance was high and extremist capacity was weak. But a third factor was also involved that was not such good news: more extremists were focused on getting to Syria and joining what they believed was a more important jihad than any they could wage at home. By late 2014, about 100 Indonesians, possibly more, were believed to have left to fight in Syria, some with their wives and children, and most to join the Islamic State.

Violent Extremists in Indonesia in 2014

By early 2014, Indonesia's jihadist community was divided between those who supported violence inside Indonesia, with the police as the primary target, and those who believed that at least for the moment, violence at home was counter-productive. The former generally supported the Islamic State and its predecessor, the Islamic State in Greater Syria and Iraq (ISIS). The latter were more likely to support IS's main rival in Syria, the al-Nusra Front, and its allies.

Prominent in the first group was Mujahidin Indonesia Timur (MIT), a group of some thirty armed men led by Santoso alias Abu Wardah in the hills outside Poso, Central Sulawesi. Santoso had run a series of military-style training camps in Poso beginning in 2011, and graduates and supporters are now scattered across Java, Sumatra, Sulawesi and Nusa Tenggara Barat (NTB). Despite being effectively under police siege during the year in his jungle camp, Santoso managed to smuggle out videos periodically to YouTube and radical websites. While neither he nor any other group managed any bombings in 2014, the few attacks on police during the year were all linked to MIT.[1] Santoso was the

---

SIDNEY JONES is Director and Solahudin is Co-Director at the Institute for Policy Analysis of Conflict (IPAC), Jakarta, Indonesia.

first Indonesian to publicly pledge loyalty to the Islamic State after its leader, Abubakar al-Baghdadi, announced the establishment of the new caliphate on 29 June 2014 (1 Ramadan).

The pro-violence group also included remnants of Mujahidin Indonesia Barat (MIB), many members of which had previous ties to an old Darul Islam network led by the now-imprisoned Abdullah Umar. It included some but not all members of Abu Bakar Ba'asyir's organization, Jamaah Anshorul Tauhid (JAT), and many followers of the imprisoned cleric Aman Abdurrahman who had no specific organizational affiliation.

The group that argued most strenuously that the costs of jihad in Indonesia outweighed the benefits was Jemaah Islamiyah (JI), best known for its involvement in the 2002 Bali bombing. Since 2007, it had forbidden its members to engage in attacks on the grounds that there was no community support, and there was no justification for collateral Muslim deaths since Indonesia was under neither occupation nor attack. It was vilified as a result by other jihadists for having abandoned jihad but its early and strong support for anti-Assad Islamists in Syria reburnished its jihadi credentials and strengthened its recruitment potential. Through 2014 JI remained strongly anti-ISIS but it also remained the only jihadi group with the capacity for long-term strategic thinking and the question was what its ultimate goals were.

The Attraction of Syria

From the beginning, the conflict in Syria had exerted a strong pull for Indonesians, stronger than other conflicts such as in Afghanistan, Somalia, Yemen and elsewhere that were seen as part of the global jihad. The reasons were several. First, according to several prophetic traditions (*hadith*), the final battle at the end of time, called *Malhamah al-Kubra*, would take place in Sham (Greater Syria), when the Imam Mahdi would lead the forces of Islam to victory.[2] The appeal of taking part in that victory was high, especially as radical Indonesians were avid readers of books on Islamic eschatology, with one Jemaah Islamiyah-affiliated publisher in Solo, Central Java, issuing a whole series on events that would mark the end of the world. Many of the discussions on the Syrian conflict that took place around Indonesia from 2012 onwards were explicitly linked to these apocalyptic predictions.

Second, many Indonesians were moved by the humanitarian suffering of Sunni Muslims in Syria and wanted to help. These included many in the radical community. Two groups close to JI became active in 2012. One was Syam

Organizer <www.syamorganizer.com>, which sponsored lectures and fund-raising events across Indonesia. Another was the Red Crescent Society of Indonesia (Hilal Ahmar Society Indonesia, HASI). In late 2012, HASI began sending delegations to Syria to provide medical assistance, initially to Ahrar al-Sham, a group that was initially independent but some factions of which eventually allied with al-Nusra.

Some, particularly in the Salafi community, were attracted to the idea of fighting Shi'ism and saw Assad, a member of the Alawite sect, as a murderous Shi'a massacring Sunnis.

Finally, some of Indonesia's most militant extremists saw in the struggle of ISIS in particular a chance for the re-establishment of a caliphate that would unite all Muslims in a single political entity. Many Muslims who see a caliphate as the most perfect form of governance reject violence as a means of achieving it. But in Indonesia, some have long believed that it would be achieved only through jihad and the creation of individual Islamic states. They closely followed the creation of the "Islamic State of Iraq" in 2006 — an entity that existed in name only — and admired its leader, the late Abu Musab al-Zarqawi. (Santoso of MIT, for example, calls himself the Zarqawi of Indonesia.) Thus when ISIS, the successor to ISI, began to control territory and apply a draconian form of Islamic law, the hopes of these militants rose. When al-Baghdadi declared a caliphate, they immediately pledged support.

The Syrian conflict thus stirred interest among many different Islamist groups in Indonesia, but the common concern masked different motivations and deep differences about which faction in Syria to support.

How Support for ISIS Spread in Indonesia

Early support for ISIS in Indonesia spread through two related channels: the website www.al-mustaqbal.net, run by a man named M. Fachry, and the teachings of detained cleric Aman Abdurrahman. Fachry had been initially inspired in 2005 by the teachings of a then U.K.-based cleric named Omar Bakri Muhammad, founder of an organization called al-Muhajiroun. Bakri taught that a caliphate could be built through the establishment, by force if necessary, of territorial zones called *imarah Islam*, in which Islamic law would be applied.[3] Fachry and a few friends were determined to set up such a zone in Indonesia, and they became increasingly hostile toward other Islamists whose views differed from theirs. They also became increasingly interested in developments in the Middle East.

When Arab Spring activism led to the fall of authoritarian leaders in Tunisia, Egypt and Libya, Fachry and several friends were convinced that the caliphate was at hand, because they saw these developments as fulfilment of a prophecy about the political cycle of Islam. In the prophecy, the Prophet's own rule would be followed by a government of his successors (caliphate), then by inherited kingdoms, then by dictators and finally, at the end of time, by a return to the caliphate (*khilafah minhajul nubuwah*). Fachry's friends included a few followers of Aman Abdurrahman.

Aman Abdurrahman himself, a superb Arabic linguist, became the main translator of ISIS propaganda, and though serving a nine-year sentence in a maximum-security prison, those translations appeared regularly on radical websites, including Fachry's. His support for ISIS was ironic. He had long been a critic of al-Zarqawi, faulting him for lacking a long-term strategy and only concerned with striking at the enemy. He called this approach *qital nikayah* which he contrasted with what he clearly believed to be the superior strategy, *qital tamkin*, which used jihad as a way of removing barriers to the establishment of an Islamic state. But as Zarqawi's successors began to hold territory and apply Islamic law, he strongly supported them and suggested that any Muslim who did not was tantamount to being an unbeliever (*kafir*). He also used his authority in prison to bring other prisoners around to his point of view. Outside prison, his many followers distributed his analyses as leaflets and kept his blog, millahibrahim.wordpress.com, updated.

Fachry and friends had initially taken a wait-and-see attitude after the rift between the al-Nusra Front and ISIS exploded into the open in April 2013, unsure of which to support. But Fachry's mentor, Omar Bakri Muhammad, came out in support of ISIS in October 2013 and from that point on, he and other ISIS supporters began organizing discussions designed to build local support for the pro-ISIS position. One of the activists who appeared frequently as a discussant or moderator in these events was a young preacher named Bahrum Syah, one of Aman Abdurrahman's disciples. On 16 March, Fachry and Bahrum Syah together organized a big pro-ISIS demonstration around central Jakarta's main traffic circle; two months later, Bahrum Syah left for Syria. Two months after that, he appeared in an ISIS recruiting video, posted on YouTube, urging other Indonesians to join.

By the time Bahrum Syah left, a critical mass of Indonesians was already there. Some had left from study abroad. One group of four had left from the International Islamic University in Islamabad; they were all from the school founded by former JI head Abu Bakar Ba'asyir in Ngruki, Solo. Another left from a university Yemen, two others from technical institute in Turkey. Another contingent had left from West Java. Several had left with families, attracted by the prospect not just of taking part in an exciting political and religious enterprise but by the stipends offered for housing and schooling. The Facebook and Twitter posts sent back to friends in Indonesia almost certainly attracted others, but most of those who left from Java already had ties to radical groups.

After victories in Mosul and other Iraqi cities and al-Baghdadi's declaration of the caliphate just as the fasting month was starting, Fachry and al-Mustaqbal started organizing induction ceremonies across Indonesia, where anywhere from a dozen to several hundred participants would take an oath of allegiance to the new leader. These ceremonies took place from Jakarta to Poso, from Malang to Bima. To the shock of many Indonesians, one such ceremony took place in mid-July in one of Indonesia's supposedly most tightly controlled prison complexes, where both Aman Abdurrahman and Abu Bakar Ba'asyir were detained. A photo of the inductees, together with an ISIS flag, was posted on the Internet.

It remains unclear whether anyone who attended the pledging ceremonies left for Syria on the strength of the oath alone, but the number of people believed to have taken part in the ceremonies across Indonesia in July and August alone was estimated to be about 2,000.[4]

In Syria

Information on how to get to Syria was available from several different sources. One was from social media sources. One of the teenagers who left his studies in Turkey to join the fighting was particularly active, sending photos and information back to his friends in Indonesia. Another husband-wife team, known on Facebook as Abu Qaqa and Siti Khadijah, wrote detailed accounts of how they left, where they crossed, how much money they spent, how they made contact and what their lives were like when they finally reached Aleppo.

Another source was prison networks. It became clear in early 2014 that some of the extremist prisoners were a key node in the sending networks. One such individual was Iwan Dharmawan alias Rois, the field coordinator for the 2004 Australian embassy bombing. Rois remains an important leader of the old West Java Darul Islam network known as Ring Banten that split off from the main DI body in 1999. He was sentenced to death for his role in the bombing and remains on death row in the same prison as Aman Abdurrahman, where he has become a strong pro-ISIS ally. Sometime in January, a former prisoner from Ring Banten, who had been by all accounts fully rehabilitated and not interested in conducting attacks in Indonesia, visited Rois as an old friend. He spoke to Rois about wanting to go to Myanmar to help defend Muslims under attack from Buddhists. Rois convinced him to go to Syria instead and gave him a contact number in Bogor. He followed up the lead, left for Turkey via Doha and by February was in Syria, on his way to battle in Iraq. He died in Ramadi in May 2014.

In Porong prison, Surabaya, another prisoner named Sibghotullah played a similar role, advising would-be mujahidin in the East Java area who came to visit whom to contact. After he was released in mid-2014, he wasted little time in leaving himself, except that he was caught en route and returned to Indonesia. Another prisoner was reportedly playing a similar role in Malang prison.

The prison network was only one of several operating in Indonesia for assisting those who wanted to leave to join ISIS. Unlike the generation that left for the Pakistan-Afghan border twenty-five years earlier, the fighters going to Syria have to pay their own way. Neither the Saudi funding, nor an equivalent of the "services bureau" set up in Peshawar to guide foreign fighters to the training camps, exists for the thousands making their way to the ISIS armed forces. A rudimentary system of vetting takes place, however, so that Indonesians leaving have to have a recommendation from someone already there before they are given the contact number on the Turkish-Syrian border and helped to cross over.

ISIS has made appeals for women to join, as teachers, nurses, cooks and wives for the fighters. All of Indonesian women known to be with ISIS in late 2014, however, were wives of men who went to fight.

These men seemed to have mostly joined a unit for Indonesian and Malaysian fighters initially called Kabila Nusantara and as of 26 September 2014, called Majmu'ah Persiapan Al Arkhabily, or the "Archipelago Group-in-Preparation". The goal of the new unit was to facilitate the incorporation of Malay- and Indonesian-speaking fighters into the ISIS forces because language had proved to be a serious problem, with few Indonesians fluent in either Arabic or English. It would also help widows and women left behind when their husbands went to fight; offer religious instruction; and provide the basis for a future Indonesian-Malaysia army of the Islamic state.

An announcement posted on Indonesian websites noted that "the new group is recruiting members so that it can meet the qualifications that IS requires for all its elite units: each *majmu'ah* must include fighters with combat experience and skills in sniper shooting, heavy weaponry, field engineering, military strategy and war tactics, and military management."[6]

The exact size of the unit was not known but one estimate was that it had or was aiming to have the strength of a military company, about 100 men.

Impact on Terrorism at Home

The fact that those most committed to violence in Indonesia have been those most excited about going to join ISIS in Syria has advantages and disadvantages for the Indonesian Government. On the one hand, it has meant that the groups most focused on committing terrorist attacks in Indonesia now have another goal that may be at least temporarily diverting them from planning operations at home, especially as very few of those operations have worked. As of late 2014, there had not been a successful bombing in five years, and the three attempts at suicide bombing had killed only the would-be bombers.

If the Indonesian Government turned a blind eye to departures of men who wanted to fight, some of them might well be killed. At least eight Indonesians and probably more had died either in battle or as suicide bombers between November 2013 and October 2014, three of them killed by Kurdish forces in the battle for Ras al-Ayn near the Turkish border in October. If they did not return, one view held, that meant fewer terrorists to worry about.

But the bigger worry was what would happen if even a small percentage returned with the leadership credentials, ideological commitment, combat experience and weapons skills to turn the largely incompetent Indonesian extremists into a more serious risk. The danger was high enough to warrant trying to prevent anyone from leaving; the problem was that Indonesia had no tools to do so. It is not against the law in Indonesia to go overseas to fight or even to join an organization that has been put on a terrorist list by the United Nations. There is no precedent for cancelling passports, as some other countries have done.

Even though the government's concern was high enough to declare ISIS a banned organization on 4 August 2014, the declaration had no force of law. It was more a policy directive and was followed by instructions to step up security at prisons, be more selective in the issuance of passports and improve monitoring of those known to be in Syria and those who had returned. One challenge for the new government of President Jokowi installed in October 2014 was whether additional legal tools could be developed.

The Corrections Directorate of the Indonesian Ministry of Law and Human Rights, responsible for overseeing prisons, was well aware of the problems it faced, with terrorists detained or serving sentences in twenty-seven different institutions, and most having access to handphones. By mid-2014 it had begun a concerted effort to improve security and training for prison officials, with some indication by the end of the year that it was paying off, as support for ISIS seemed to be declining.

Jemaah Islamiyah

Another challenge for the Indonesian Government is how to respond to the many extremist groups in Indonesia who rejected the caliphate announced by al-Baghdadi but supported the al-Nusra Front, the official al-Qaeda affiliate in Syria. These groups included JI, Majelis Mujahidin Indonesia (MMI) and a significant part of JAT. Indeed, when Abu Bakar Ba'asyir as the founder of JAT declared his support for ISIS, many in the organization, led by its chair, Mochammad Achwan, broke away to found a new group, Jamaah Anshorul Syariah (JAS).

If the groups who support al-Nusra in Syria do not support violence in Indonesia, what is the problem if they go there to fight? The problem is that al-Nusra, while focused more on bringing down Assad than on establishing a global caliphate, also employs brutality and a harsh system of Islamic law, and has also engaged in terrorism. Anyone fighting with al-Nusra is also likely to return to Indonesia with increased skills and ideological commitment and could well move away from the positions now espoused by the JI leadership. Moreover, there have been many reports of defections from al-Nusra to IS since the caliphate was announced; at least one Indonesian from IS has defected the other way. The point is that al-Nusra is not a moderate organization, and Southeast Asian governments, including Indonesia, should also be monitoring their nationals allied with it.

The alliance of JI with al-Nusra raises a particularly difficult set of issues. JI since 2007 has focused on *dakwah* (religious outreach) and education. Its imprisoned leaders have been models of cooperation with prison authorities and have preached that if jihadists do a cost-benefit analysis of attacks, they will see that at the moment, without community support, the costs far outweigh the benefits. The problem is that no one is quite sure when the calculus will shift. Of all extremist organizations in Indonesia, JI has the longest history, the most resilient membership and the best capacity for thinking long term. Its leadership remains committed to the establishment of an Islamic state in Indonesia. What impact will Syria have on that goal?

A partial answer was provided in March 2014 when police discovered a military camp in Klaten, Central Java where new JI recruits were training. In September they arrested a man who had been taking part in monthly JI fitness trainings in the hills outside Bandung and Semarang in Java. The man in question had been inducted into JI at the height of its strength in 2000 but became inactive after 2007. In early 2011, he was approached by a JI leader and asked to resume his activities in the organization, suggesting that a systematic rebuilding was underway. In late 2013, police discovered an end-of-year report that showed the extent that JI was concentrating on attracting professional recruits from universities — engineers, doctors, linguists, chemical technicians and IT specialists.

If the recruitment has been successful, JI's link to Syria and its early involvement in providing humanitarian aid through HASI may have contributed to its appeal. As of late 2014, police and prison authorities saw the senior JI leadership as partners in combating IS and generally had no problem with their going back and forth. Senior JI figures were indeed very critical of IS. They argued that IS was an organization, not a state, and that al-Baghdadi had not been selected as caliph by a religious council (*majelis syuro*), as Islamic law mandates. They also strongly objected to IS's practice of declaring anyone who did not swear a loyalty oath as an enemy and a legitimate target for killing.

But JI's rejection of IS does not make them moderate. Especially given its past, it is important that the organization not be seen as having abandoned violence or jihad. They decided in 2007 it was counter-productive, not illegitimate, and conditions could change.

Looking Forward

The Syrian conflict will reverberate in Indonesia for years to come. There are several ways it could have an impact. As noted, fighters could return with skills. Indonesians and Malaysians who fought together could retain those bonds at home and attempt to found a cross-border alliance for jihad — something that has not existed since JI had a presence in five countries just before the 2002 Bali bombing (Indonesia, Malaysia, Singapore, Philippines and Australia). IS could try to set up a structure in Southeast Asia through returning fighters or sympathizers. In the near term, would-be fighters who have not had the chance to leave for

Syria could decide to undertake an action in Indonesia to attract the attention of IS leaders and demonstrate their own commitment.

All of this suggests that the current lull in terrorist activities could be temporary. Just as there were no major attacks in Indonesia between 2005 and 2009, the lull could be shattered as it was then by the attack on two luxury hotels in Jakarta.

The government of Jokowi may have been given some breathing room to decide on a strategy but this is a problem that is not going to go away.

Notes

1. These included three killings of police in Bima; the fatal shooting of an informer allegedly linked to the military; and an armed clash with the police in Poso that led to the death of a paramilitary police officer.
2. Institute for Policy Analysis of Conflict, "Indonesians and the Syrian Conflict", IPAC Report No. 6, 30 January 2014.
3. Institute for Policy Analysis of Conflict, "The Evolution of ISIS in Indonesia", IPAC Report No. 13, 24 September 2014.
4. Some of the pledging ceremonies, announced on radical websites and through text messaging, were as follows: Poso, 1 July 2014; Kembang Kuning prison, Nusakambangan (Aman Abdurrahman), 2 July 2014; Ciputat, Jakarta, 6 July 2014; Solo, Central Java, 15 July 2014; Ambon, 16 July 2014; Pasir Putih prison, Nusakambangan (Abu Bakar Ba'asyir), 18 July 2014; Bima, Sumbawa, 20 July 2014; Malang, East Java, 20 July 2014; Bekasi Selatan, outside Jakarta, 3 August 2014. Ceremonies also reportedly took place in Lampung and East Kalimantan.
5. "Update on Indonesia-Malaysia Military Unit in Syria", IPAC Update, 6 October 2014. The update is based on an Indonesian website source, available at <http://panjimas.com/citizens/2014/09/29/allahu-akbar-majmuah-al-arkhabiliy-cabang-daulah-islamiyyah-terbentuk/>.
6. Ibid.
7. These were the attempted bombings of the police mosque in Cirebon in April 2011, a church in Solo in September 2011, and the police command in Poso in June 2013.

Laos

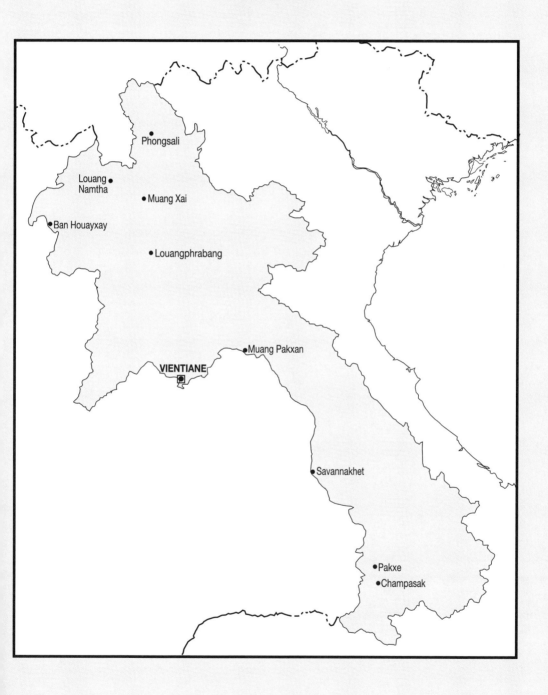

LAOS
The Dangers of Developmentalism?

Brendan M. Howe and Seo Hyun Rachelle Park

Developmentalism in Laos

The sub-regions of Northeast Asia and Southeast Asia have seen many development success stories. Often, however, East Asian countries have prioritized economic development over social or political development. While this "econophoria" —whereby the solution of all society's ills is sought through economic development — has contributed to remarkable patterns of economic growth, it has also seen the rise in importance of challenges to human security in both absolute and relative terms.[1] Kenneth Christie and Denny Roy also highlight the prioritization of macroeconomic development, noting that it "has assumed cult-like status" in East Asia.[2] Thus it is not surprising that Laos has followed the well-trodden path of developmentalism.

For the Lao People's Democratic Republic (PDR), the graduation from least developed country status has been an overarching goal. To this end, the government has emulated the strategies of its Communist allies such as China, by implementing National Socio-economic Development Plans (the first in 1976, the seventh for the years 2011–15) which sought to strike a balance between economic and social development. Laos has also derived inspiration from non-Communist regional economic powerhouses such as Japan,

BRENDAN M. HOWE is former Department Chair at the Graduate School of International Studies, Ewha Womans University in Seoul, and has served there as a Professor of International Relations since 2001.

SEO HYUN RACHELLE PARK is a graduate student and research assistant majoring in development cooperation at Ewha Womans University, Graduate School of International Studies.

South Korea, and Taiwan, looking to develop its way out of post-conflict poverty. Finally, Laos has looked to neo-liberal growth models, and sought to integrate ever more closely into the regional and global economic regimes. A notable example has been Laos' membership into the World Trade Organization (WTO) on 2 February 2013, achieved after fifteen years of long, arduous negotiation. These divergent sources of inspiration, as they have been actualized in Lao PDR, have in common the primacy of state driven, macroeconomic infrastructure projects.

Natural resources such as forestry, agricultural land, and hydropower comprise more than half of Laos' total wealth and generate approximately one third of economic growth.[3] Despite such natural resource wealth, and its steady exploitation by the government, Laos remains on the list of least developed countries (LDCs) prepared by the United Nations Conference on Trade and Development (UNCTAD). To graduate from LDC status by 2020, the government in 2011 proposed the seventh five-year economic plan, which aims to achieve a growth rate of at least 8 per cent each year. This target was indeed met in the first two years, but since then the government has struggled to reach its goals, due to expenditure constraints, which have delayed implementing macroeconomic infrastructure projects and put the country at the risk of financial instability. For the year 2014–15, the government has estimated that targeting economic growth at 7.5 per cent would be enough to stimulate the economy while avoiding the risk of financial crisis.[4]

Indeed, domestic and international institutional analyses of the economic outlook in Lao PDR have generally predicted positive outcomes. The National Economic Research Institute (NERI) of Laos expects economic growth to be higher for the fiscal year 2014–15, based on performance of the domestic production base and the electricity sector. It expects growth to reach as much as 8.2 per cent, compared to the 7.8 per cent in the previous fiscal year of 2013–14. Inflation has been forecast at 4.5 per cent in 2014–15, falling from 6.6 per cent in 2013–14.[5] The Asian Development Bank (ADB) has put economic growth at 7.3 per cent in 2014, from a revised 7.9 per cent in 2013. The forecast for growth in 2015 is reduced to 7.4 per cent, to reflect persistent fiscal difficulties. Resource development supporting such growth has included robust mining and hydropower investments, and investment increases in special economic zones. Copper production rose by 6.7 per cent and silver by 29.3 per cent in the first half of the year. Gold production, on the other hand, fell by a quarter when the Sepon mine ceased gold production in December 2013. These resource developments are constrained by fiscal deficits which initially forced the government to delay wage and utility payments. Such delays eased somewhat in 2014, but substantial barriers remain on public infrastructure developments, which will constrain spending on future projects. Given this economic context, the reported inflation rate is 5 per cent, and the current account balance −27.4 per cent. The full economic outlook is summarized in the table below.[6]

The World Bank (WB) has projected growth at 7.2 per cent in 2014, down from the 8.1 per cent recorded in 2013. The primary source of growth continues to be development of natural resources — in particular, FDI-financed investment in hydropower and accommodative macroeconomic policies. The resource sector, however, is expected to contribute less to growth as expansionary macroeconomic policies hinder management of resources. Worthy of attention are project delays and lower gold production, which offset the gains expected from higher copper production.[7] The International Monetary Fund (IMF) also predicted growth at roughly 7.8 per cent, and reports that the annual inflation rate has reached 4.2 per cent, as of August 2014. This inflation rate is expected to rise to 7.5 per cent by the end of the year. Nonetheless, medium-term economic prospects have remained generally positive due to robust natural resource exports and post-WTO accession expansion in non-resource sectors.

Foreign direct investment for natural resource development amounts to US$750 million with twenty-one ongoing projects. The exchange rate has also remained stable, with Kip/US dollar exchange rate only slightly depreciating by 2.1 per cent. Credit growth has been 20.69 per cent as of June 2014. In addition

TABLE 1

Selected Economic Indicators (%) — Lao People's Democratic Republic	2014		2015	
	ADO 2014	Update	ADO 2014	Update
GDP Growth	7.3	**7.3**	7.5	**7.4**
Inflation	5.5	**5.0**	6.0	**5.5**
Current Account Balance (share of GDP)	−7.4	**−27.4**	−26.0	**−26.0**

Source: ADB. 2014. *Asian Development Outlook 2014.*

to resource wealth, the context for such growth can be attributed to fiscal and monetary policies. On the fiscal front, the government has amended value-added tax and accounting laws, improved its public finance strategy for 2020 and vision to 2030, and upgraded its financial information systems to address the previous year's fiscal challenges. On the monetary front, the government sought to maintain price stability by controlling the exchange rate. Initiatives included setting annual targets for the exchange rate as well as reference rates for commercial banks and paying close attention to the credit market by suspending foreign currency loans to firms not generating incomes in foreign currency.[8] Despite these developments, however, challenges have remained in overcoming the serious fiscal constraints, which also pose risks to people's livelihoods.

The widening fiscal deficit, debt distress, credit growth and the unstable exchange rate all contribute to macroeconomic instability which together form barriers to transforming natural resource wealth into public investments. The World Bank notes that the significance of overcoming these macroeconomic challenges will rise to the fore as growth stabilizes to 7.5 per cent at the end of 2014, from lower contribution of resource sectors. Following sharp expansion during 2012–13 financial year, the fiscal deficit is expected to narrow in 2013–14, in part due to newly adopted fiscal consolidation measures. Continued, these fiscal measures are predicted to ease the fiscal deficit to around 4.2 per cent, for the 2014–15 financial year.[9] On the other hand, it remains to be seen whether the risk of debt distress will stay moderate, as predicted in the Joint International Monetary Fund-World Bank Debt Sustainability Analysis (DSA) in 2013.[10] Formidable obstacles remain, especially with the government failing to meet revenue collection targets over the 2013–14 fiscal year amid budget constraints. Total revenue collection during this time amounting to 23.544 trillion kip (US$123.5 million) and representing only 96.72 per cent of the amended budget plan, has slowed payment on public wages and prolonged chronic debt.[11]

Changes in credit growth and foreign exchange rate have both been moderate. Credit growth has hovered around 20.69 per cent, raising concerns on the health of the banking system. The foreign exchange rate which fell sharply in the third quarter of 2013, has largely retained nominal exchange rate stability. To maintain this rate, the government must ensure that foreign exchange reserves and net foreign assets stay competitive.[12] Here we need to turn to the key role played by Lao foreign relations in the development of the country.

International Relations and Development

Laos' foreign policy has also been dominated by "econophoria" and the development imperative. Lao PDR has looked to partner with international organizations and neighbouring countries to achieve its three geo-economic aims of integration into the regional and global economic regimes, national economic growth and poverty reduction, and becoming "land-linked". Hence Deputy Prime Minister and Minister of Foreign Affairs Thongloun Sisoulith has highlighted the need to safeguard political stability for national development, and noted that the Government of the Lao PDR has deployed its utmost efforts in pursuing a consistent foreign policy and promoting international cooperation at all levels.[13] Laos has played an active part in ASEAN community-building and in the Asia-Europe Meetings (ASEM). It lies literally at the heart of the Greater Mekong Subregion (GMS), being the only country bordering all other members.

The first of Laos' international geo-economic and strategic aims has substantially been achieved with WTO accession. WTO membership has promoted economic growth by reducing investment risks coming from weak and unpredictable law enforcement. Internationally, as the last ASEAN member to join the WTO, Lao's accession has aided the country's integration into the regional economy and added momentum to the formation of an ASEAN Economic Community.[14] Laos has also formed partnerships with key international organizations in an attempt to graduate from United Nations' list of Least Developed Countries.

Partnering with the ADB, Laos has received assistance to cater to its differing development needs, "from an early emphasis on agriculture in the 1980s, to roads and transportation in the 1900s, and education, energy, and regional integration in the 2000s". The two approved projects for 2014 included, "Nam Ngiep 1 Hydropower Project" and "Greater Mekong Sub-region Tourism Infrastructure for Inclusive Growth".[15] The ADB agreed on 15 August 2014 to finance US$50 million in direct loans for the Nam Ngiep 1 Hydropower Project, set to begin construction in 2019. Once online, the Nam Ngiep 1 will provide the bulk of its cost-efficient electricity to Thailand while generating revenues for Laos' economic and social development.[16] The ADB also agreed on 8 September 2014 to provide US$40 million in direct loans for the Greater Mekong Sub-region Tourism Infrastructure for Inclusive Growth Project. The project is expected to generate as much as US$330 million in revenue and create 27,000 new jobs, boosting the tourism sector's contribution to the economy.[17]

The United Nations Development Programme (UNDP) has been an active proponent of advancing human development in the region. It reports that as of 2014, Laos remains in the medium human development category and ranks 139 out of 187 countries in terms of human development. Laos' human development index as of 2013 was 0.569, which is below the 0.614 average countries in the medium human development category usually score. The UNDP currently has sixteen active projects in Laos, in the areas of poverty reduction, democratic governance, environment and energy, crisis prevention and recovery. All of these projects are conducted in consultation with national stakeholders and contribute directly to the Millennium Development Goals (MDGs) as well as the government's own National Socio-Economic Development Plans.[18]

Geographically, the Lao PDR is the only country in Southeast Asia faced with Collier's "poverty trap" of lacking direct access to the sea.[19] Being landlocked has presented a challenge for Lao residents' ability to participate in transnational trade since the sixteenth century.[20] Laos' status as a landlocked state has become the focus of ongoing development proposals for the country to become "land-linked" or a crossroads for trade.[21] In attempting to become land-linked, the Government of Laos has forged partnerships with neighbouring countries. These include two major railway projects linking the country with Thailand, Vietnam and China. Giant Consolidated, a Malaysian company in charge of constructing the 220-kilometre railway linking Laos' western border with Thailand to Vietnam, finally began construction operations after minor hitches which had postponed the ground-breaking ceremony. Laos has also been in negotiations to borrow US$7.2 billion from China to fund the 430-kilometre railway stretching from the capital Vientiane to Vietnam and ultimately to southwestern China. China initially pulled out of the partnership after assessing that the project would be unprofitable, but in October 2014, agreed once more to finance the project. Guan Huabing, China's Ambassador to Laos, has noted that the project may boost bilateral ties between the two countries, characterizing it as "strategic" and "historic".[22] Furthermore, implementation of large-scale public infrastructure projects at the macro level often in partnership with neighbouring countries has been the focus of the Lao Government's National Development Plan. Projects have typically been in the form of either (1) hydropower projects to generate electric power and revenue or (2) commercial exploitation of land to boost growth.

Energy-hungry Thailand has invested heavily in the Lao hydro-electric industry, and also forms the major market for the export of surplus energy produced as a result of damn construction. As first out of eleven dams proposed to be built on the Lower Mekong, the Xayaburi Dam is situated between Laos and Thailand, in the Xayaboury Province of northern Laos. Standing 810 metres tall, it is expected to generate 1,260 megawatts of electricity, most of which will be exported to Thailand. The total cost of building the dam is estimated to be US$3.5 billion.[23] As of March 2014, the Xayaburi has been reported to be 30 per cent complete, with the final dam to be constructed in February 2015.[24] The second and most recent dam proposed to be built on the Mekong River Basin, the Don Sahong Dam, is to be situated on the Siphandone area of southern Laos, approximately two kilometres north of the Laos-Cambodia border. The dam would stand between 30 to 32 metres high and generate 260 megawatts of energy for export to Thailand and Cambodia.[25]

The Government of Laos has also encouraged the development of rubber plantations in partnership with Vietnamese and Chinese interests. Further Chinese investment has come through the development of casinos and tourist infrastructure, and Vietnamese companies have partnered with the Government of Laos in logging ventures. Martin Stuart-Fox has explored the importance of these international partnerships for Laos, terming them the "Vietnamese Connection" and the "Chinese Connection".[26] Official sources report that roughly 1.1 million hectares or 5 per cent of the country's arable land, has been subjected to 2,600 land deals since 2010.[27] These land leases take the form of foreign investment projects brokered between the government and private enterprises.

Taken together with the econophoria of national developmentalism, however, these macroeconomic projects pursued in conjunction with other members of the international community can have serious negative consequences upon human security and human development of the most vulnerable sections of Lao society, as well as detrimental effects upon the environment. Either human needs are neglected as a result of the prioritization of macroeconomic policies, or they are sacrificed for the "collective good". The next section explores the detrimental impact of domestic and international developmentalism upon the people of Laos.

The Dangers of Developmentalism

The Xayaburi Dam has been criticized for being a threat to aquatic biodiversity and fisheries productivity as well as people's livelihoods.[28] The dam will block the migration paths for 23 to 100 species of fish. By destroying the river's ecosystem, the dam will put at least forty-one species of fish at the risk of extinction. More than 2,100 people will have to be resettled as a result of floods created by the dam and 202,000 people who meet their basic needs through fishing or cultivating rice on the riverbank's farmlands would be facing challenges to their livelihoods. The government promised financial assistance to those who have had to resettle since 2013, with aid packages totalling 5 million kip (US$670) per family per year. Families were granted up to 20 kilograms of rice per adult and up to 15 kilograms per child. The assistance and resettlement process was poorly managed, however, and could not replace access to river's resources which provided a natural source of sustainable income and food.[29] The combination, therefore, of low quality resettlement programmes, environmental degradation and a lack of viable livelihood options have directly contributed to further impoverishment of the most vulnerable.

There are also concerns that the Don Sahong Dam poses significant risks to food security and reduces the region's popularity as a tourist destination, thereby dramatically impacting the local economy. The threat to food security comes from the dam's impact on local fisheries. Blockage caused by the dam would threaten the migration, feeding and breeding patterns of the 201 species of fish living between Laos and the neighbouring countries. For people living in the Lower Mekong Basin, their livelihoods would be greatly affected because fish is a major source of food as well as revenue.[30] The Don Sahong Dam also reduces the allure of Siphandone's two main tourist attractions — the Khone Phapheng waterfalls and the Irrawaddy dolphins. The dam would reduce the aesthetic value of the Khone Phapheng fall, when most of the water is diverted to the dam for electricity generation.[31] As for the Irrawaddy dolphins who inhabit the Laos-Cambodia border, the noise from constant bombing for rock excavation would damage the dolphins' sensitive hearing and their environment will be greatly altered as a result of increased boat traffic, changes in water quality and habitat destruction.[32]

Put together, the environmental impacts of the Xayaburi and the Don Sahong dams threaten people's livelihoods, by either endangering food security or resettling indigenous people. These socio-economic and environmental effects, however, also have transboundary effects when the government chooses to bypass regional consultations and notify neighbouring countries of its decision to construct the dams. This has been the case for the Xayaburi and the Don Sahong. Responding to demands for consultation, Laos has embarked on an official consultations process for both dams since June 2014. The government, however, went ahead with dam-building as planned, violating the regional body's Mekong River Agreement and going against neighbouring countries' wishes for a more thorough assessment of the dams' impact. Therefore, although the 2014 decision for consultation was a significant step towards regional cooperation, more action is needed to ensure that dam-building over the shared Mekong River is "based on scientific knowledge, transboundary impact assessment and respect for the rights of all riparian nations".[33]

There are also problems associated with land leases, or "land grabs". These are twofold: for ethnic minorities or indigenous people, their displacement puts them at risk of increased poverty and higher mortality; and for land deals themselves, lack of transparency in the process makes accountability and enforcing land regulations increasingly difficult.[34] For ethnic minorities and indigenous people living in rural areas, the land grabs continue to drive them off arable farmland without adequate consultation or compensation. The UNDP has found that mortality rates rise up to 30 per cent for these rural poor who have been forced to abandon their traditional livelihoods and move to urban areas. Furthermore, faced with the impossibility of traditional framing practices, lack of other work skills and inadequate health and education facilities, the resettled communities are driven into deeper poverty. The problem is exacerbated by the loose enforcement of existing land regulations to compensate displaced populations. As a Communist country, Laos retains the right to forcibly seize or redistribute land without prior consent. Although a 2005 decree requires investors to compensate resettled villagers affected in full or in part at replacement cost, implementation has often been piecemeal or non-existent, with little negotiation taking place between the villagers and the government. This unlawful deprivation of land shows how the country's natural resources have been "captured by an elite growing spectacularly rich while one third of the population lives on less than $0.61 a day".[35]

Land seizures for rubber plantations by Vietnam's largest companies, Hoang Anh Gia Lai (HAGL) and the Vietnam Rubber Group (VRG), have been particularly problematic. Put together, the two rubber giants have rights to more than 200,000 hectares of land concessions in Laos. These deals have been financed by international investors, with International Finance Corporation (IFC) — the private lending arm of the World Bank — primarily investing in HAGL and the Deutsche Bank investing in both companies.[36] The non-transparent nature of investments resulted in a legal vacuum fuelling a land-grabbing crisis.[37] The companies were also accused of turning a blind eye to the deforestation and human rights abuses of the indigenous people. These abuses include depleted fish levels in waterways, encroachment and destruction of sacred land, deaths of hundreds of livestock, and even sexual abuse by company employees.[38] On 10 February 2014, indigenous communities filed an official complaint to the Compliance Advisor Ombudsman (CAO) of the IFC on the unlawful abuses. International agencies aided in lodging this complaint, and in Cambodia, such complaints have culminated in the halting of HAGL's rubber plantation constructions from 28 April to 30 November 2014.[39] There are hopes for similar outcomes in Laos, with VRG's announcements this year, that citizens will be allowed to submit formal complaints directly to the company, and of a community consultation and scheme across all twenty-one plantations in Cambodia and Laos.[40]

Meanwhile, as pointed out by Danielle Tan, Chinese investment in the natural resources of Laos, whether in mining, hydropower, or agriculture, as well as in casino tourism, may have spurred Laos' economic growth, "but the transformation has come at a high price for both local communities and the environment".[41] China has replaced Thailand as the major source of foreign direct investment (FDI) in Lao PDR. The introduction of new cash crops as a result of Chinese engagement and the North-South Economic Corridor initiative have contributed to poverty reduction and the modernisation of agricultural practices, but have also widened the income inequality of households within the village and among villages. In addition, it appears that the profit distribution of contract farming has benefitted Chinese companies more than Lao farmers, who have become dependent on the Chinese-dominated agricultural production and distribution networks due to asymmetric power relations. "Exacerbating the situation in the case of rubber production, those who could not afford to wait the seven to eight years until the plant reaches harvesting age had to give up their land rights and became agricultural labourers to sustain their daily livelihoods".[42]

As a result of such domestic policies and international engagement, while at an aggregate or macro level, Lao development can be seen to be making very satisfactory progress, at the level of individual human security and human development, governance performance leaves a lot to be desired. These policies can be seen as obstacles to achieving the Millennium Development Goals (MDGs), where there has been moderate but uneven progress in 2014. Currently, 44 per cent of children under five remain stunted and 27 per cent are severely underweight. The 2013–14 fiscal year observed a slightly narrower fiscal deficit compared to 2012–13, but only as a result of cutbacks in public sector wages and benefits.[43]

In 2014 the Asian Development Bank (ADB), the World Bank (WB) and the International Monetary Fund (IMF) have each proposed remedies based on their involvement in the region. ADB has called for further economic diversification to expand opportunities, provide jobs for youth, and enable inclusive growth, as well as for improvements in governance and better natural resource and environmental management.[44] The WB notes that Laos is at a critical juncture to harness its economic growth to address the fiscal deficit problem and the barriers it poses to human development. Fiscal consolidation measures are expected to narrow the fiscal deficit to around 4.2 per cent by 2015. The WB notes, however, that to enable structural transformation in an economy geared towards subsistence farming and low-productivity agriculture, the government must solve labour and skilled labour shortages through investments in education. Thus the WB's sector focus this year has been on school-based management — raising the level of non-wage, public recurrent expenditure, to improve education quality.[45] Investment in education is expected to promote development of the labour market, and reduce risks of macroeconomic instability.[46] Taking a more neo-liberal perspective, the IMF states that natural resource exports and post-WTO expansion in non-resource sectors have contributed to favourable economic prospects. To guard against the negative effects of expansionist macroeconomic policy, it recommends tightening fiscal and monetary policies as well as building up fiscal buffers and replenishing international reserves. Fiscal tightening policies should be accompanied by a non-mining fiscal deficit of no more than 5 per cent GDP and continued improvements in tax collection, to ensure the necessary fiscal space for human development and capital spending.[47]

The government response, on the other hand, has been to further focus on economic efficiency rather than on distributive concerns. It announced in October of 2014 that it would focus on enhancing efficiency and encouraging private investment, in order to mobilize resources into production. It promised improvements in the areas of public investment, social development, and economic integration. For public investment, the government will focus on improving public financial management, particularly building a strong database on tax collection and revenue administration. For social development, the government aims to invest in education and healthcare and strengthen economic foundations to resist external shocks and respond to natural disaster. For economic integration, significant reforms will be undertaken to improve trade and investment regulations, so as to satisfy commitments towards joining the ASEAN Economic

Community at the end of 2015. Combined with monetary and fiscal initiatives to maintain a stable exchange rate and inflation at a single-digit level, the government hopes that progress in the three identified areas will help the country meet its economic growth targets.[48]

The reality of these international organizations' and the government's efforts at development, however, is that they have not prioritized needs of the most vulnerable, to guard such people against the negative consequences of development. It is important to note here that the Government of Laos has not been a passive victim of Chinese, or Vietnamese, or Thai neo-colonialism and exploitation. Its focus on development has caused it to seek out such international partnerships which have had little regard for the impact on the most vulnerable. The government, to an extent, is able to get away with sacrificing vulnerable groups for "the collective good", due to the authoritarian nature of its governance structure, which is also a hallmark of East Asian developmentalism. The oppressive nature of the Lao PDR state is further explored in the final section on domestic governance and human rights.

Domestic Governance and Human Rights in Lao PDR

Laos remains a single-party Communist state dominated by the Lao People's Revolutionary Party (LPRP) which came into rule in 1975. Since the establishment of LPRP, Laos has ratified more than a hundred international conventions, including seven out of nine international conventions associated with human rights.[49] Most recently in September 2012, it ratified the UN Convention against Torture and in November of the same year, it adopted the ASEAN Human Rights Declaration.[50] The number of human rights treaties to which Laos is party would seem to be a testament of its willingness to engage with the international community, by conforming to international standards. Yet the government has not made tangible progress in its human rights commitments, made during the first Universal Periodic Review (UPR) in 2010.[51] As observed in the second UPR held in October 2014 at the United Nations Human Rights Council in Geneva, Laos continues to restrict fundamental rights in four core areas: enforced disappearances; freedom of speech, association, and assembly; the treatment of detainees in drug detention centres; and labour rights.[52]

The December 2012 disappearance from a police station of prominent civil society leader Sombath Somphone, who had helped to organize the Asia-Europe People's Forum the previous October, is seen as emblematic of the human rights challenges in Laos. The government has been accused of failing to conduct serious investigation into his disappearance. It has continually rejected offers to analyse the original CCTV footage to determine the identities of abductors and gather data on the vehicles that were at the scene.[53] Human Rights Watch and Amnesty International have both noted that Sombath's disappearance to date shows the blatant lack of progress in human rights, despite international legal obligations.[54] Civil society groups in fellow ASEAN countries have condemned the actions, or inactions of the Lao Government in this case, but the organization itself has been relatively quiet due to its doctrine of non-interference in the internal governance matters of member states.

As party to the International Convention on Civil and Political Rights (ICCPR), Laos accepted recommendations at the 2010 UPR to comply with international human rights standards and "allow media and civil society organizations to undertake education, advocacy, monitoring and reporting on human rights issues".[55] Since 2010, however, it has failed to protect the right to freedom of speech, press and assembly, using its power as a one-party state to suppress political expression. Indeed, the state has been criticized as being the most repressive in the region.[56] To free itself from such criticism, Laos needs to address the following issues: harassment and arbitrary arrest of human rights defenders, government control over civil society and the media, and unlawful detention of people facing criminal prosecution.[57]

Instead, this year Laos followed the Chinese example in curbing NGOs, placing them under supervision of the Ministry of Foreign Affairs (MOFA) and limiting them to the fields of agriculture, education, public health, sport, science, and humanitarians. NGOs are banned from receiving overseas funding and must report any donation greater than 50 million kip (US$6,250).[58] International NGOs (INGOs) were further restricted in their activity, with all project proposals, foreign staff, and the establishment of offices subject to approval by MOFA. INGOs were also required to submit financial reports at regular intervals.[59] The government censors all TV, radio, and printed publications in the country based on Article 23 of the Constitution, which states that all "mass media activities" contrary to "national interests" or "traditional culture and dignity" are prohibited.[60] The government started regulating online social media in late 2013, and in 2014, an official decree was signed prohibiting online criticism of the ruling party. The decree made it a criminal offence for Internet service providers to disperse information deemed threatening to society and national security.[61] Amnesty International reports that three prisoners of conscience remain in prison, and although two ethnic Hmong had nine months deducted from their sentences, they face twelve and twenty years respectively, for obstruction of justice and weapon possession.[62]

Suspected drug users are arbitrarily arrested, denied a fair trial and subjected to cruel and inhumane treatment in the drug centres. Detainees are held for periods of three months to more than a year, in barbed-wire compounds, punished by being tied up without adequate food or water or beaten for trying to escape. The conditions are so brutal that many detainees attempt suicide by ingesting glass or hanging. There are at least eight such drug detention centres across the country, with the Somsanga detention centre in Vientiane being the oldest and the largest. Laos recognized that its treatment of detainees violate international human rights standards at the 2010 UPR review, but has not investigated reports of abuse or taken up measures to close drug rehabilitation centres since then.[63] In fact, the Somsanga Rehabilitation Centre this year will receive six billion kip to construct additional facilities.[64]

Based on the Trade Union Law of 2008 and the Labour Law of 2007, workers are restricted from forming unions of their own choosing and exercising the right to strike. The only legal trade union remains the government-controlled Lao Federation of Trade Unions (LFTU). Critics note that the LFTU violates Article 22 of the ICCPR and Article 8 of the International Covenant on Economic, Social, and Cultural Rights (ICESCR).[65] The 2007 Labour Law states that any person or organization causing or inciting verbal calls for work stoppage are subject to prosecution, between one and five years of imprisonment. The International Labour Organization (ILO) notes that this restriction on strikes goes against ILO Convention Number 87 and 98 on the right to organize and collectively bargain, which Laos has signed but not ratified.[66] It is clear therefore, that Lao PDR's labour rights law falls short of international legal standards. For the country, however, such labour rights are seen as critical to boosting productivity (in line with the developmental agenda), as stated in the 7th National Socio-economic Development Plan (NSEDP) for 2011–15. The ILO, for its part, has provided a programmed basis for the NSEDP by offering a Decent Work Country Programme (DWCP) 2011–15. Whereas the NSEDP merely envisions the importance of realizing the Millennium Development Goals (MDGs) through economic growth and social development, the DWCP stresses the crucial link between labour and development, highlighting issues such as training and skills formation, employment generation, social protection, industrial relations and labour market governance.[67]

Conclusion

Lao PDR is a country with tremendous growth potential, the success of which depends on utilizing its natural resource wealth. In extracting wealth from the country's natural resources, Lao PDR has followed the centralized developmental state model, focusing on macro-economic growth, aggregate measurements of success, and the sacrifice of vulnerable individuals and groups to the pursuit of "collective good". By these measurements the performance of Lao PDR in 2014 can be seen as a qualified success. Unfortunately, as a result of the negative impacts of developmentalism, the same cannot be said of governance performance if measured by human-centric and distributive criteria.

At the level of international affairs, Laos continued to expand its networking and cooperation with neighbours, international organizations, and the wider international community. Again, however, the focus of the pursuit of these international partnerships was macroeconomic development, neglecting both the impact of policies on vulnerable individuals and groups, and criticism of such by members of the international community. The "strong-state" mentality of the Lao PDR has consistently seen national development and security pursued to the detriment of human development, human security, and human rights.

2014 was a year of qualified progress and consolidation in terms of development, but also a year in which criticism of the regime at both the national and international level reached new heights. The Government of Laos needs to address the human-centred shortcomings of its governance policies if it is to maintain the support of its people and the international community.

Notes

The authors would like to acknowledge the support of the BK21 Plus Program for Global Networking Leadership Development and Education, the Graduate School of International Studies, Ewha Womans University, and Korean Studies Department of the Freie Universität Berlin.

1. Barry Buzan and Gerald Segal, "Rethinking East Asian Security", in *World Security: Challenges for a New Century*, edited by Michael T. Klare and Yogesh Chandrani (New York: St. Martin's Press, 1998), p. 107.
2. Kenneth Christie and Denny Roy, *The Politics of Human Rights in East Asia* (London: Pluto Press, 2001), p. 5.

3. Lao PDR Overview, available at <http://www.worldbank.org/en/country/lao/overview#3>.

4. "Govt Plans 7.5 percent Growth in 2014–2015", *Tai Viet Corporation*, 7 August 2014, available at <http://en.vietstock.vn/2014/07/govt-plans-75-percent-growth-in-2014-2015-71-180154.htm>.

5. Vanthana Nolintha, S. Sengaloun, and D. Siyotha, "Economic Outlook in 2014 and Medium-Term", *Macroeconomy in 2014 and the Outlook in 2014* (Laos: National Economic Research Institute, 2014), pp. 27–28.

6. "Lao PDR: Economy", available at <http://www.adb.org/countries/lao-pdr/economy>.

7. "Lao PDR Economic Monitor January 2014: Managing Risks for Macroeconomic Stability", available at <http://www.worldbank.org/en/country/lao/publication/lao-pdr-economic-monitor-january-2014-managing-risks-for-macroeconomic-stability>.

8. Somphao Phaysith, "Statement by the Hon. Dr. Somphao Phaysith, Governor of the Fund for the Lao People's Democratic Republic", 2014 Annual Meeting of IMF and WBG, Washington, D.C., 10–12 October 2014, pp. 2–3.

9. "Lao Economic Growth Expected to Moderate: World Bank", *Shanghai Daily*, 6 October 2014, available at <http://shanghaidaily.com/article/article_xinhua.aspx?id=245140>.

10. "Lao PDR Economic Monitor January 2014", op. cit.

11. "Revenue Collection Misses Target", *Vientiane Times*, 31 October 2014, available at <http://www.vientianetimes.org.la/FreeContent/FreeConten_Revenue.htm>.

12. "Lao PDR Economic Monitor January 2014", op. cit.

13. Statement by His Excellency Mr Thongloun Sisoulith, Deputy Prime Minister, Minister of Foreign Affairs of the Lao PDR, at the 68th session of the United Nations General Assembly, New York, 28 September 2013, available at <http://www.mofa.gov.la/en/the-ministry/the-deputy-prime-minister-minister-of-ministry-of-foreign-affairs/308-unga2013>.

14. Prashanth Parameswaran, "What Will WTO Membership Mean for Laos?" *The Diplomat*, 7 February 2013, available at <http://thediplomat.com/2013/02/what-will-wto-membership-mean-for-laos/>.

15. Lao People's Democratic Republic and ADB, available at <http://www.adb.org/countries/lao-pdr/main>.

16. ADB Supports Public-Private Hydropower Project in Lao PDR, available at <http://www.adb.org/news/adb-supports-public-private-hydropower-project-lao-pdr?ref=countries/lao-pdr/news>.

17. Asian Development Bank (ADB), "46293-003: Greater Mekong Subregion Tourism Infrastructure for Inclusive Growth Project", *Project Data Sheet* (Manila: ADB, 8 September 2014), available at <http://adb.org/projects/details?page=details&proj_id=46293-003>.

18. "Maintaining human development requires reducing risks and building resilience", available at <http://www.la.one.un.org/media-center/news-and-features/98-maintaining-human-development-requires-reducing-risks-and-building-resilience>.

19. Paul Collier, *The Bottom Billion* (Oxford and New York: Oxford University Press, 2008).

20. Vatthana Pholsena and Ruth Banomyong, *Laos: From Buffer State to Crossroads?* (Bangkok: Mekong Press, 2006).

21. Jonathan Rigg, "Uneven Development and the (Re-)engagement of Laos", in *Uneven Development in South East Asia*, edited by Chris Dixon and David Drakakis-Smith (Aldershot: Ashgate, 1998).

22. Roseanne Gerin, "China Gives New Pledge on Lao Rail Project", *Radio Free Asia*, 6 October 2014, available at <http://www.rfa.org/english/news/laos/railway-project-10062014181543.html?searchterm:utf8:ustring=laos+Railway+>.

23. International Rivers, "The Xayaburi Dam: Looming Threat to the Mekong River", International River's factsheet, Berkeley, 2011, p. 2.

24. Shane Worrell, "Xayaburi dam 30% Finished, says Laos", *Phnom Penh Post*, 25 March 2014, available at <http://www.phnompenhpost.com/national/xayaburi-dam-30-finished-says-laos>.

25. Don Sahong Dam, available at <http://www.internationalrivers.org/campaigns/don-sahong-dam>.

26. Martin Stuart-Fox, "Laos: The Chinese Connection", in *Southeast Asian Affairs 2009*, edited by Daljit Singh (Singapore: Institute of Southeast Asian Studies, 2009), pp. 141–69.

27. Andreas Heinimann and Peter Messerli, "Coping with a Land-grab World: Lessons from Laos", *Global Change* 80 (Sweden: International Geosphere-Biosphere Programme, 12 June 2013), available at <http://www.igbp.net/news/features/features/copingwithalandgrabworldlessonsfromlaos>.

28. International Rivers, op. cit., pp. 2–3.

29. Rachel Vandenbrink, "Assistance for Villagers Resettled by Xayaburi Dam to Last One Year", *Radio Free Asia*, 18 June 2013, available at <http://www.rfa.org/english/news/laos/xayaburi-06182013164824.html>.

30. International Rivers and the Rivers Coalition in Cambodia, "Don Sahong Dam Fact Sheet", International River's factsheet, Berkeley, 2008, p. 4.

31. Ibid.

32. "New Dam on Mekong River Could Doom Irrawaddy Dolphins", available at <http://www.worldwildlife.org/stories/new-dam-on-mekong-river-could-doom-irrawaddy-dolphins>.

33. "Laos to Undergo Prior Consultation, but Continue Building Don Sahong Dam", available at <http://www.internationalrivers.org/resources/8351>.

34. Dana MacLean, "Laos 'land grabs' Drive Subsistence Farmers into Deeper Poverty", 22 May 2014, available at <http://www.irinnews.org/report/100116/laos-land-grabs-drive-subsistence-farmers-into-deeper-poverty>.

35. "Can REDD stop the land grabbing crisis in Laos and Cambodia?", available at <http://www.redd-monitor.org/2013/05/15/can-redd-stop-the-land-grabbing-crisis-in-laos-and-cambodia/>.

36. "Rubber Barons: How Vietnamese Companies and International Financiers are Driving a Land Grabbing Crisis in Cambodia and Laos", available at <http://www.globalwitness.org/rubberbarons/>.

37. Megan MacInnes, "Vietnam Rubber Group Says Its Doors are Now Open to People Affected by Plantations in Cambodia and Laos", *Global Witness*, 20 August 2014, available at <http://www.globalwitness.org/library/vietnam-rubber-group-says-its-doors-are-now-open-people-affected-plantations-cambodia-and>.

38. "Cambodia and Laos: IFC-backed Rubber Land Grabs", available at <http://www.inclusivedevelopment.net/cambodia-and-laos-hagl-rubber-plantations/>.

39. Daniel De Carteret, "Rubber Projects on Hold", *Phnom Penh Post*, 8 May 2014, available at <http://www.phnompenhpost.com/business/rubber-projects-hold>.

40. MacInnes, op. cit.

41. Danielle Tan, "China in Laos: Is There Cause For Worry?", *ISEAS Perspective* 31 (Singapore: Institute of Southeast Asian Studies, 2014), p. 1.

42. Ibid., pp. 10–11.

43. Lao PDR Overview, available at <http://www.worldbank.org/en/country/lao/overview#3>.

44. Lao People's Democratic Republic and ADB.

45. "Lao PDR Economic Monitor", op. cit.

46. "Lao Economic Growth Expected to Moderate: World Bank", *Shanghai Daily*, 6 October 2014, available at <http://shanghaidaily.com/article/article_xinhua.aspx?id=245140>.

47. "IMF Lauds Laos for Economic Growth, Urges Caution", *Global Times*, 28 November 2014, available at <http://www.globaltimes.cn/content/828358.shtml>.

48. Somphao Phaysith, "Statement by the Hon. Dr Somphao Phaysith, Governor of the Fund for the Lao People's Democratic Republic", 2014 Annual Meeting of IMF and WBG, Washington, D.C., 10–12 October 2014, p. 3.

49. "Laos Ratifies Three Un Conventions", *Vientiane Times*, 28 September 2012, available at <http://www.vientianetimes.org.la/FreeContent/FreeConten_Laos_ratifies.htm>.

50. Amnesty International, "Annual Report 2013: Laos", *Amnesty International Annual Reports* (UK: Amnesty International, 2013), available at <http://www.amnesty.org/en/region/laos/report-2013>.

51. Human Rights Watch, "Laos: No Progress on Rights", *Human Rights Watch*, 10 June 2014, available at <http://www.hrw.org/news/2014/06/10/laos-no-progress-rights>.

52. "Laos: Universal Periodic Review Submission", available at <http://www.hrw.org/news/2014/06/10/laos-universal-periodic-review-submission>.

53. Ibid.

54. Joshua Lipes, "Laos Accused of Shirking Human Rights Commitments", *Radio Free Asia*, 10 June 2014, available at <http://www.rfa.org/english/news/laos/review-06102014124629.html>.

55. "Laos: Universal Periodic Review Submission", op. cit.

56. Richard Finney, "Laos Human Rights Abuses 'Serious,' But Mostly Hidden From View", *Radio Free Asia*, 19 February 2014, available at <http://www.rfa.org/english/news/laos/abuses-02192014164829.html?searchterm:utf8:ustring=sombath+somphone>.

57. "Laos: Universal Periodic Review Submission", op. cit.

58. "Laos Follows China's Example to Curb NGOs", *Asia News.it*, 17 September 2014, available at <http://www.asianews.it/news-en/Laos-follows-China's-example-to-curb-NGOs-32179.html>.

59. Joshua Lipes, "NGOs Say Proposed Guidelines Would Hamstring Lao Civil Society", *Radio Free Asia*, 2 October 2014, available at <http://www.rfa.org/english/news/laos/decrees-09232014172406.html?searchterm:utf8:ustring=sombath+somphone>.

60. "Laos: Universal Periodic Review Submission", op. cit.

61. Lipes, op. cit., 2 October 2014.

62. Amnesty International, op. cit.

63. "Laos: Universal Periodic Review Submission", op. cit.

64. "Somsanga Rehabilitation Centre in Vientiane Seeks More Funding", available at <http://article.wn.com/view/2014/04/20/Funding_for_US_startups_hits_highest_level_since_2nd_quarter/>.

65. Both Article 22 of the ICCPR and Article 8 of the ICESCR protect the right of labour workers to form and join trade unions of their choice and organize strikes.

66. "Laos: Universal Periodic Review Submission", op. cit.

67. International Labor Organization (ILO), "Decent Work Country Programme Lao PDR (2011–2015)", *Decent Work Country Programme* (Geneva, Switzerland: ILO, 2011).

Malaysia

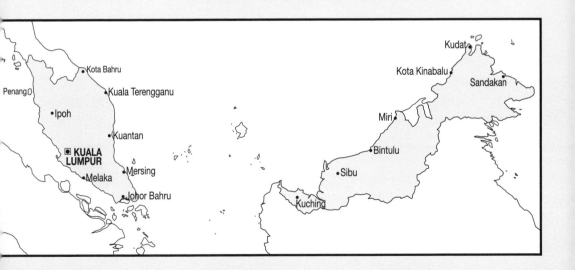

Southeast Asian Affairs 2015

MALAYSIA IN 2014
A Year of Political and
Social Ferment

Faisal S. Hazis

Introduction

The year 2014 saw an intense conflict between liberalism and narrow conservatism in Malaysia. The push for democracy and inclusive policies by the opposition and civil groups opened up a call from the right-wing Malays to "reclaim" their special rights and position as the "indigenous" people of the land. The right-wing Malays even raised the ghost of May 13, the bloody racial riot that brought at least 200 civilian deaths with ethnic Chinese making up the biggest number. The Malay-dominated ruling government remained tight-lipped over the right-wing groups' antics, hence implying its support for them which helped to perpetuate the spread of racial politics. The conflict became more complex with the internal schisms in the two main parties, Barisan Nasional (National Front or BN), and opposition coalition, Pakatan Rakyat (People's Alliance or PR) which led to further division and discord among the general public.

The political and social ferment continued to persist despite a long list of tragedies that hit Malaysia in 2014. From the mysterious disappearance of Malaysia Airlines MH370 on 8 March to MH17 that was shot out of the sky on 17 July to the tragic crash of AirAsia Indonesian flight QZ8501 on 28 December, the majority of Malaysians were divided along party lines over the way the authorities handled these calamities. As the year was drawing to a close,

FAISAL S. HAZIS is a Senior Lecturer at the Department of Politics and International Relations, Universiti Malaysia Sarawak.

Malaysia was hit with the worst floods in three decades. More than 150,000 had to be evacuated with infrastructure losses amounting to RM2 billion (US$0.58 billion).[1] The unprecedented disaster, however, failed to heal the political divisions.

On the economic front, Malaysia continued to record higher growth even though it faced multiple challenges in keeping its economy competitive and strong in its push to be a developed economy by 2020. Global forces such as the declining oil prices along with its own archaic economic policies had impeded Malaysia's potential to grow and expand. One of the indications of a troubling domestic economy was the steep increase in household debt over the years, turning Malaysia into a country with the highest household debt in Southeast Asia. Some analysts even argued that Malaysia was going through the middle income trap where it would be facing great difficulty in leaping forward to become a developed nation.

Despite tensions at home, Malaysia continued to play an important role on the regional and international stage with a projected image of a moderate and progressive Muslim country. However, the involvement of some Malaysians with Islamic State of Iraq and Syria (ISIS)[2] and the increasingly worrying problem of human trafficking[3] had somewhat tainted this image. Worse, the Malaysian Government's repressive moves in quelling dissent at home was criticized by international human rights groups[4] and several Western countries including the United States of America (U.S.).[5]

2014 was a challenging year for Malaysia. This chapter traces the political and social ferment that poses a serious challenge to Malaysian ethnic harmony and political stability that had long been its major strength. The chapter also looks at Malaysia's struggle to pursue economic growth against a background of rising oil prices, weakening currency and archaic domestic policies and practices. It is argued that the ruling government's continued insecurity over its ability to hold on to power led to an increase in authoritarianism and racial politics. Although this has yet to evolve into something more serious like a full blown racial riot, it could lead to that if left unchecked, impeding the realization of Malaysia's goal of becoming a developed and progressive Islamic nation.

Political and Social Ferment

In 2008, the strong electoral challenge mounted by the opposition and the desire for change among a significant part of the electorate had resulted in the biggest defeat of the ruling BN after more than five decades of dominating Malaysian politics. Led by then premier Abdullah Badawi, the BN lost its traditional two-thirds parliamentary majority and five state governments. The shocking defeat forced Abdullah to vacant his seat, thus elevating his deputy Najib Razak. To win back the people's support, Najib introduced a flurry of transformative policies and projected a more inclusive image of the government. The opposition, on the other hand, continued to push for more democratic space, end of corruption and cronyism, respect for human rights and more inclusive economic policies. This set the scene for the defining elections in 2013 that saw the battle between BN's transformation agenda versus PR's promise of change.

Despite Najib's reform promises and an unprecedented number of pre-election handouts (estimated to be about RM57.7 billion (US$16.7 billion)),[6] BN performed much worse than 2008. Not only did it fail to regain two-thirds parliamentary majority, the ruling party lost seven more seats and recorded below 50 per cent popular vote. After the 2013 elections, the battle between BN and PR continued to divide Malaysians. This was further compounded by Najib's desperate move to hold on to power after a strong attempt to topple him by his detractors within UMNO. These two factors became the source of political and social ferment that marred Malaysia in 2014.

Najib survived the attempt to unseat him but he was back under serious attack in 2014. As a result, he had to accommodate his critics within UMNO who wanted the premier to stop making concessions to non-Malays and reward the Malays who had ensured the continuity of BN rule. There were also calls for Najib to tighten political control, hence rolling back his transformation agenda leading to the 2013 elections. This allowed the right-wing Malay groups such as Pertubuhan Pribumi Perkasa Malaysia (PERKASA) and Ikatan Muslimin Malaysia (ISMA) to gain prominence. When several PR leaders and Christian groups called for the return of Bibles seized by the Selangor Islamic Department (JAIS), PERKASA issued threats against these groups by saying "if you don't shut your mouth from continuing to belittle Islam, we will shut your mouth for you and if you betray the Sultan (of Selangor), we will chop your heads off."[7] The right-wing Malay group even called some UMNO leaders including Youth and Sports Minister Khairy Jamaluddin and Public Accounts Committee (PAC) chairman Datuk Nur Jazlan *bangsat*[8] (despicable) for criticizing PERKASA over their aggressive antics.

ISMA stepped up the attack against the non-Malays especially Chinese by labelling them "intruders and trespassers who, along with the colonial British, bullied the Malays".[9] The non-Malays bashing did not stop there. When the non-Muslims raised their concerns over the plan to implement *hudud*, ISMA chided them by telling them not to poke their nose into the affairs of the Malays. Worst, they labelled those critical of the government as "anti-Malay" and "anti-Islam".[10] Najib's silence over the right-wing Malay groups' antics raised doubts over his 1Malaysia and *wasatiyyah* (moderation) rhetoric. Federal Islamic authority, JAKIM, also played the ethno-religious card. Faced with the issues of *murtad* (apostasy), declining support for the UMNO-led government and increased fragmentation among the Malays, JAKIM blamed Christians for this sorry state of affairs. The government agency through its Friday sermon reminded Muslims that

> our religion is under attack. Our faith is being threatened. Our pride is being challenged. Remember, if believers are easily carried away without realising that the cancer was spreading among its victims, then the mind will be damaged, self-worth would be lost, and this would eventually bury power and self-respect.[11]

JAIS also stirred ethno-religious feelings by seizing Malay and Iban-language Bibles on the second day of 2014, saying it could not be used in Selangor, the country's wealthiest state. This heavy-handed action was motivated by the long-standing battle over the rights to use "Allah" by Christians especially those from Sabah and Sarawak. Even when the Attorney-General advised JAIS to return the Bibles, the state Islamic body brushed it aside and stood firm. It took a change of chief minister and eleven months for the seized Bibles to be returned. All the Bibles were stamped with a warning that they could not be used in Selangor — reflecting Malaysia's shrinking space for religious freedom and tolerance. This episode shows why Najib's moderate and inclusive messages in the 2013 elections failed to capture middle Malaysia — because of the lack of political will and flip-flopping decisions.

Although religious extremism dominated public discourse in 2014, there were many moderate voices that attempted to challenge it. Comprising twenty-five prominent Malay leaders, Group 25 (G25) spoke strongly against ISMA, JAKIM and other groups that had resorted to using ethno-religious sentiments to divide Malaysians. The group openly called for the Prime Minister to end the unresolved disputes over the position and application of Islamic laws in this country. Scores of groups and other prominent individuals rallied in support of the G25.[12] The group's bold move had paved the way for more moderate voices to speak out against the right-wing groups that claimed to represent the Malay community.

Apart from rising ethno-religious nationalism, strong regional consciousness also re-emerged in 2014. In Borneo, the call for more autonomy and rights for Sabah and Sarawak had been a staple issue among marginalized groups ever since the two states had lost their special rights in the late 1960s. The call for autonomy, however, became louder after the 2013 elections due to the weakening of BN's federal power and the increased importance of Sabah and Sarawak as king-makers of national politics. In 2014, some groups even went further by calling for the secession of the two states from Malaysia. Through their blogspot and Facebook page, the group that called themselves "Sabah Sarawak Keluar Malaysia" (Sabah Sarawak Secession from Malaysia) openly promoted the idea of secession. In response, the authorities threatened to charge its leader, Doris Jones, who operated from outside of Malaysia, under the Sedition Act. Issues of autonomy had enough support such that even the BN state governments of Sabah and Sarawak openly echoed this sentiment. In May 2014, the Sarawak State Assembly passed a resolution demanding an increase of oil royalty from 5 per cent to 20 per cent from the federal government, one of the issues constantly raised by the proponents of Sabah and Sarawak autonomy.

When Najib Razak took over from Abdullah Badawi after the 2008 elections, he introduced a flurry of transformative policies and programmes which included the push for more democratic space. Among the measures taken were to repeal the highly criticized Internal Security Act (ISA), amend other repressive laws (Sedition Act, Emergency Ordinance, Banishment Act), reform outdated censorship laws, review the electoral system, and introduce a peaceful assembly bill. These reforms were introduced not out of Najib's pro-liberal stance but as a strategy to win over middle Malaysia in the 2013 elections. However, when Najib failed to perform better than Abdullah Badawi in 2013, his nemesis in UMNO, Mahathir Mohamad, called for his ouster. Najib's critics argued that his transformation agenda and accommodative policies had failed to capture the middle ground, especially the non-Malay voters. Instead, they argued, BN and UMNO should strengthen their support base (Malays and Bumiputera Sabah and Sarawak) and ignore the non-Malay voters. They further opined that Najib's political reform had threatened the special position and rights of the Malays. To pacify his critics and secure his position, Najib rolled back his democratic push. This led to an increase of authoritarianism, reminiscent of the Mahathir era.

The first sign that the ruling government was rolling back on its democratic push was its decision not to abolish the Sedition Act. In fact, the draconian law was being used extensively to silence the opposition and to instil fear among government critics. According to Amnesty International, at least forty-four people had been charged under the Sedition Act between 2013 and November 2014.[13] Among them were academics, students, opposition leaders, human rights activists and journalists. Initially Najib stood firm against the call by many parties to retain the Sedition Act, giving public assurance of his commitment to political reform. But the premier eventually succumbed to pressure especially from within his own party. During the UMNO General Assembly in November 2014, Najib declared that "having consulted with party leaders, including my deputy, vice-presidents, NGOs and the grassroots, as the Prime Minister, I have taken the decision to retain the Sedition Act".[14]

Political clampdown was also expanded to the increasingly vocal university students. Despite the amendment to the Universities and University-Colleges Act (UUCA) 1971 which allowed students to be active in politics, the ruling government imposed strong restrictions on student activism in 2014. This was in direct contrast to the spirit of the amendment. A total of twenty-five students were reported to face disciplinary actions under the UUCA for the first half of 2014 for allegedly tarnishing the university's image through their involvement in various political, economic and social issues.[15] In a highly publicized event by the University of Malaya campus Student's Union in October 2014 which featured UM alumnus Anwar Ibrahim, the University Student Affairs Division took stern action by suspending two and fining four student leaders who were behind the organization of the event. On 9 November 2014, ten students from different universities were harassed by Sabah police officers for giving a speech at Jalan Gaya, Kota Kinabalu, Sabah. And again on the same the day, the students were ejected from the University Malaysia Sabah (UMS) campus, preventing them from attending a scheduled talk on student autonomy. This action is damaging to academic freedom and image of the country's public universities.

To further halt the progress of democracy, government-backed groups such as ISMA attacked liberalism by labelling it a "manifestation of Satan's struggle to mislead mankind".[16] They warned that Malaysia should not be heading towards liberal democracy; instead it should be based on a "system that is dominated by the Malays with Islam having a superior position".[17] Even Najib joined in the attack against liberalism by saying that

> they call it humanrightism, where the core beliefs are based on humanism and secularism as well as liberalism. It's deviationist in that it glorifies the desires of man alone and rejects any value system that encompasses religious norms and etiquette. They do this on the premise of championing human rights.[18]

Paradoxically, the Federal Constitution is based on liberal and democratic principles while the country is embracing a *laissez faire* economy.

Another manifestation of political ferment was the near collapse of the opposition coalition, PR. Due to its young life and the lack of a binding ideology, PR is susceptible to infighting and split. Its vulnerability was made worse by the actions of self-serving and weak leaders who could not see beyond petty politics and short-term pay-offs. In 2014, the fragile coalition was tested by the "Kajang Move", which was a plan to change Selangor Chief Minister, Khalid Ibrahim, who was deemed not fit to lead the opposition coalition in the state.[19] Initiated by Parti Keadilan Rakyat (PKR), the move was intended to allow opposition leader, Anwar Ibrahim, to contest in the state seat of Kajang and subsequently take over from Khalid. The move, however, was thwarted bythe ruling BN. Anwar was convicted of sodomy, thus making him ineligible to contest. Instead, PKR nominated Wan Azizah, Anwar's wife, to contest the by-election which she won easily. It was subsequently proposed that she takes over from Khalid. PKR, however, failed to achieve this because of opposition from its own ally, Parti Islam SeMalaysia (PAS), and the Sultan of Selangor. Although the PKR and Democratic Action Party (DAP) stood firm on their choice of candidate, the palace defied parliamentary convention by appointing another PKR assemblyman, Azmin Ali as Chief Minister. Despite its resentment against the palace's decision, PKR and later DAP endorsed Azmin's appointment, thus sacrificing their principles and surrendering their power to choose the state's chief executive. The "Palace Move" not only went against democratic convention but it also called into question the role of constitutional monarchy in Malaysia's shrinking democracy.

The Selangor crisis had not only deepened factional fights in PKR and PAS but it also amplified inter-party schism within PR. Worst, the crisis exposed PAS's true colours (that is, its long-standing obsession with the Islamic state agenda, non-democratic culture via *ulama* control, feudal state of mind and its lack of commitment in upholding the spirit of the opposition coalition). PAS basically abandoned its welfare state and centrist agenda which the Islamic party had been staunchly promoting in the last four general elections. Instead, it went for UMNO's bait to break up PR by taking up the ruling government's offer to introduce *hudud* in Kelantan. It is a known fact that DAP would strongly oppose the introduction of the highly controversial Islamic laws by PAS. Thus, PAS's *hudud* plan would either force PR to expel the Islamic party or lead to the exit of DAP from the coalition. Either way, the opposition coalition would collapse. To further weaken the opposition, there were numerous calls for PAS to join the ruling party for the sake of Malay unity and Islamic solidarity. These developments put great strain on the future of the opposition coalition. Even if the opposition survives these tests, voters would have serious doubt over their commitment to take over federal power.

PR, however, has some breathing space because BN is equally fragmented and lacks leadership. The ruling party still failed to understand the demand for change that the majority of Malaysian voters had expressed in the 2013 elections. The opposition's chance to capture federal power in the next general elections would come to waste if they cannot resolve their differences and show strong commitment towards change.

The political and social ferment that clouded Malaysia in 2014 is not expected to subside anytime soon. In fact, it would be getting worse especially closer to the next general elections. This is certainly not the direction that the country which is pushing to be a developed nation would want to take.

Middle Income Trap?

Amidst growing political and social tension, Malaysia continued to show strong economic growth even when faced with many global and domestic challenges. The Malaysian economy expanded at its fastest rate in four years in 2014, with a Gross Domestic Product (GDP) growth of 6 per cent, outpacing economists' estimates of 5.8 per cent.[20] Overall, growth was supported by higher exports and continued strength in private domestic demand. Private sector activity remained the key driver of growth during the second quarter of 2014 amid strong investment and consumption. Public sector spending declined during the corresponding period, due to lower public investment and consumption.[21] Among the major Southeast Asian economies, Malaysia recorded far better growth than Singapore, Indonesia and Thailand while the Philippines continued to record the highest growth rate at 6.9 per cent.

TABLE 1
GDP Growth in Selected Southeast Asian Countries
(in percentage terms)

	2010	2011	2012	2013	2014
Singapore	15.1	6.0	1.9	4.1	2.8***
Thailand	7.8	0.1	6.5	2.9	n.a.
Phillipines	7.6	3.6	6.8	7.2	6.9**
Indonesia	6.2	6.5	6.3	5.8	5.1*
Malaysia	7.4	5.2	5.6	4.7	6.0

Note: *Third Quarter of 2014,
       **Fourth Quarter of 2014,
       ***Estimates
Source: Malaysia (2014: iv),[22] Badan Pusat Statistik (2015),[23] Philippine Statistics Authority (2015),[24] Ministry of Trade and Industry (2015).[25]

During 2014, the Malaysian economy retained a strong appeal for overseas investors despite the political and social ferment that the country was facing. According to the International Trade and Industry Ministry, Foreign Direct Investment (FDI) inflows totalled RM52.5 billion (US$15 billion) in the first three quarters, representing a 30.5 per cent increase and exceeding the 2013 total of RM45 billion (US$13 billion).[26]

Although the Malaysian economy continued to perform better than the previous year, its ballooning budget deficit became a serious concern. Based on a Bloomberg report, the Malaysian Government's debt-to-GDP ratio (54.6 per cent) was jointly ranked with Pakistan's as the second highest among thirteen emerging Asian markets after Sri Lanka.[27] This prompted rating agency, Fitch, to downgrade Malaysia's sovereign debt to "A minus" in August 2014, which is the last rung of the upper-medium grade ratings.[28] Malaysia continued to accumulate public debt despite trimming the headline deficit number due to the liabilities amassed primarily through government-linked firms and investments. A government-investment arm, 1Malaysia Development Berhad (1MDB), received severe criticism after it accumulated an astronomical RM42 billion (US$12.2 billion) debt and a negative cash flow of RM2.25 billion (US$0.6 billion) for its financial year ended 31 March 2014.[29] The 1MDB scandal was just another manifestation of poor decisions by Malaysian policymakers, driven more by political considerations than sound economic judgment. Another troubled government-linked firm, Malaysian Airlines, was pushed close to bankruptcy in 2014. The airline's majority shareholder, the state investment fund, Khazanah Nasional Bhd, began preparations to privatize the loss-making national carrier after it received approval from minority shareholders.[30]

Another cause of concern for Malaysia is its high household debt. Malaysian household borrowings hit 86.3 per cent of GDP in 2013 when it had been just 60.4 per cent in 2007, surpassing even the United State's 80.6 per cent registered in the first three months of 2014.[31] A major contributor to local household debt in Malaysia is the people's affinity to cars, which are among the world's highest priced. This, along with spiralling home prices, reduced consumers' spending power, despite growing debt levels.[32] Worse, the government is planning to introduce the Goods and Sales Tax (GST) in April 2015 which would surely place further strain on household expenditure. In the chapter titled *Lessons not Learned*, the McKinsey Global Institute (MGI) in its report warned that

> untenable household debt in some of the world's largest economies, such as the U.S., had been at the core of the 2008 financial crisis. These figures suggest potential risk but do not signal imminent crises. Nonetheless, these countries should, at a minimum, be monitoring the situation very carefully," said MGI in the report.[33]

Like many oil producing nations, Malaysia's economy was hit by plummeting global energy prices. At the end of November 2014, state-owned oil company, Petronas, said its contributions to the government next year could be 37 per cent lower if oil traded in the US$70 to US$75 band.[34] The pressure from falling oil prices would be slightly offset by the reductions in fuel subsidies in 2014, as well as the lower cost of imported fuels and related products. In recent years, Malaysia had protected its citizens from the impact of surging crude oil prices with fuel subsidies, but this measure had worsened the budget deficit. Thus, by cutting oil subsidies, the government was expected to save up to RM20 billion (US$5.8 billion) a year.[35] However, many analysts said that the 40 per cent drop in oil prices in 2014 would more than wipe out the effect of the subsidy cut.[36] Several opposition leaders criticized the government's reduction of oil subsidies when it continued to offer other subsidies such as Bantuan Rakyat 1Malaysia (1Malaysia People Assistance) as a measure to win over the electorate, especially the rural poor.

With continued declining global oil prices, the Malaysian currency, ringgit (RM), could experience accelerated weakening. As of 8 December 2014, the value of the ringgit dropped against the U.S. dollar (USD) to a five-year low of RM3.4955/USD, being the weakest since the 2008 global financial crisis.[37] Due to the fluctuating oil price and weakening ringgit, Malaysia now expects GDP to grow in a range of 4.5 per cent to 5.5 per cent in 2015, down from a previous range of 5 per cent to 6 per cent.[38] It also expects its 2015 budget deficit to widen to 3.2 per cent of GDP, from a previous estimate of 3 per cent.

Despite the gloomy outlook, the Malaysian Government was confident that the country would continue to record positive growth due to its strong fundamentals. This optimism, however, failed to convince some analysts[39] who think that Malaysia might be experiencing the middle income trap, a stage where a middle income country loses its competitive edge and fails to push forward to become a developed economy. The cynics argued that Malaysia's progress would not only be determined by strong economic fundamentals but more importantly, its commitment towards democracy and inclusive policies. Unfortunately, Malaysia is digressing from these important fundamentals.

Foreign Affairs: Two-Faced Policy

2014 marks an important milestone for Malaysia's foreign policy. It successfully secured a non-permanent seat in the fifteen-member United Nations Security Council (UNSC). In welcoming the success, Prime Minister Najib Razak said "Malaysia planned to expand the moderation agenda at the global level, now that the country had been given a say in the most powerful body."[40] He said in addition, "Malaysia intended to encourage negotiations as a solution to conflicts, support UN peacekeeping and aid in the process of bringing peace to nations in conflict zones."[41] This is the fourth time Malaysia has won a seat in the UNSC. The first time was in 1965, before being elected again in 1989/1990 and 1999/2000. Five permanent members of the UNSC (China, France, Russia, the United Kingdom and the United States) have veto power, making it the most powerful body in the United Nations.

Within the region, Malaysia also achieved a very important milestone when it took up the ASEAN chairmanship. Taking over from Myanmar, Malaysia pledged to establish a people-centred ASEAN Community, develop the region's ten-year-post integration plan and guide ASEAN's continued growth from 2016 to 2025.[42] Apart from that, Malaysia also aspires to lead ASEAN in becoming a modern regional block, similar to the European Union (EU) and the North American Free Trade Area (NAFTA).[43] This would definitely be a challenging and daunting task for Malaysia especially when the ten-member organization has been constantly criticized for its inability to steer regional economic integration and address human rights violation among its members.[44]

Another highlight for Malaysia's international relations in 2014 was the maiden visit by U.S. President Barack Obama in April, the second by a U.S. president to Malaysia, after Lyndon Johnsons' in 1966. Malaysia also intensified engagement with key global and regional players, with high-level visits from China, Australia, Netherlands, Thailand and Banglandesh among others. Najib also visited China, South Korea, the U.S., the Netherlands, Myanmar, Azerbaijan, Milan, Australia and Kazakhstan among others. These diplomatic ties have contributed to further boosting political relations and strengthening economic diplomacy.

Unfortunately, the moderate and soft image that Malaysia portrayed internationally ran contrary to its approach in dealing with its critics at home. At the same time, Najib's silence over the right-wing Malay groups' attacks on the non-Malays was perceived to be the government's way of sub-contracting racialism to other parties. The different approach that the ruling BN took in dealing with domestic and international issues exposed Najib's two-faced policy. This approach, however, is not something that Najib started. It could be traced back to Mahathir's era in which the powerful leader had masterfully portrayed a liberal progressive image abroad but kept a strong authoritarian approach in dealing with domestic issues.

Malaysia's foreign affairs in 2014 did not end without any crises and controversies. With the disappearance of the Malaysia airline Flight MH370, the close ties between Malaysia and China were tested. Despite strong criticisms by netizens from both countries, government leaders from Malaysia and China were able to handle the crisis without any untoward incidence albeit the lingering mystery over the disappearance of the ill-fated aircraft. In less than four months after the MH370 tragedy, Malaysia was again tested with another air disaster involving MAS Flight MH17. Showing a stronger leadership in handling the crisis, Najib spoke to rebel leader Alexander Borodai in Ukraine to retrieve the bodies and black boxes from the downed aircraft. The Malaysian Government's handling of the MH17 crisis was more commendable compared to the MH370 tragedy. Yet, a different sort of crisis struck Malaysia again in July 2014 when its diplomat in New Zealand was sent back under diplomatic immunity due to a sexual case against him. The diplomat, however, was asked to return to New Zealand as the family of the victim put pressure on its government to take legal action against the Malaysian diplomat. The case was a big embarrassment to Malaysia.

Conclusion

2014 was a trying time for Malaysia. The political and social ferment would continue to haunt the country as the battle to capture federal power intensifies. This fierce battle ultimately might impede the country's progress towards achieving the developed nation status in year 2020. Malaysia's important position at international arena would mean nothing if its most treasured assets, political stability and racial harmony, slipped through its grip.

Notes

1. "Infrastructure Losses Due to Floods Estimated ar RM2 billion", *Malaysian Insider*, 8 January 2015, available at <http://www.themalaysianinsider.com/malaysia/article/infrastructure-losses-due-to-floods-estimated-at-rm2-billion> (accessed 5 March 2015).
2. "Wisma Putra: 15 Malaysians ISIS Militants Allegedly Killed in Syria", *Malay Mail Online*, 24 June 2014, available at <http://www.themalaymailonline.com/malaysia/article/wisma-putra-15-malaysian-isis-militants-killed-in-syria> (accessed 5 March 2015).
3. "Malaysia Drops to Tier 3, Lowest Ranking in US Human Trafficking Report", *Malaysian Insider*, 20 June 2014, available at <http://www.themalaysianinsider.com/malaysia/article/malaysia-drops-to-tier-3-lowest-ranking-in-us-human-trafficking-report> (accessed 5 March 2015).
4. "Malaysia: Increasing Use of the Sedition Act Fosters a Climate of Repression", *Amnesty International*, 4 September 2014, available at <http://aimalaysia.org/malaysia-increasing-use-sedition-act-fosters-climate-repression> (accessed 5 March 2015).
5. "Biden's Criticism Apt, Putrajaya Should Feel Ashamed, Pakatan Rep Says", *Malay Mail Online*, 6 December 2014, available at <http://www.themalaymailonline.com/malaysia/article/bidens-criticism-apt-putrajaya-should-feel-ashamed-pakatan-reps-say> (accessed 5 March 2015).
6. "Buying Support — Najib's Commercialisation of GE13", *Malaysiakini*, 23 April 2013, available at <http://www.malaysiakini.com/news/227713/> (accessed 5 March 2015).
7. "Perkasa's Beheading Threat Would Constitute a Hate Crime, Says Unity Council", *Malay Mail Online*, 24 June 2014, available at <http://www.themalaymailonline.com/malaysia/article/perkasas-beheading-threat-would-be-a-hate-crime-says-unity-council>.
8. "Khairy: Ibrahim's Remarks not Vital", *The Star*, 16 December 2014, available at <http://www.thestar.com.my/News/Nation/2014/12/16/Unfazed-by-criticism/> (accessed 5 March 2015).

9. "Isma Stands by Statements on Chinese as 'Trespassers', Refuses to Apologize", *Malaysian Insider*, 9 May 2014, available at <http://www.themalaysianinsider. com/malaysia/article/isma-stands-by-statements-on-chinese-as-trespassers-refuses-to-apologize/> (accessed 5 March 2015).

10. "Negara-ku Just Another Anti-Islam, Anti-Malay Body, Says Isma", *Malaysian Insider*, 10 July 2014, available at <http://www.themalaysianinsider.com/malaysia/ article/negara-ku-just-another-anti-islam-anti-malay-body-says-isma/> (accessed 5 March 2015).

11. "Jakim Reminds Muslims to Protect Supremacy of Islam", *Malaysian Insider*, 17 January 2014, available at <http://www.themalaysianinsider.com/malaysia/article/ jakim-reminds-muslims-to-protect-supremacy-of-Islam/> (accessed 5 March 2015).

12. "G25 Gets Bigger with 11 More Prominent Malays", *Malay Mail Online*, 2 January 2015, available at <http://www.themalaymailonline.com/malaysia/article/g25-gets-bigger-with-11-more-prominent-malays> (accessed 5 March 2015).

13. "Open Letter: Use of the Sedition Act to Restrict Freedom of Expression in Malaysia", Amnesty International, 2014, available at <http://www.amnesty.org/ download/Documents/.../asa280112014en.pdf/> (accessed 5 March 2015).

14. "Najib: Sedition Act to Stay", *The Star*, 27 November 2014, available at <http:// www.thestar.com.my/News/Nation/2014/11/27/umno-sedition-act-to-be-retained-strengthened/> (accessed 5 March 2015).

15. "Memorandum Mansuhkan Auku dan Akta 174 — 5 Jun 2014", Suara Rakyat Malaysia, available at <http://www.suaram.net/?p+6039/> (accessed 5 March 2015).

16. "Isma Preacher Labels Liberalism a Manifestation of 'Satan's Agenda'", *Malay Mail Online*, 8 April 2014, available at <http://www.themalaymailonline.com/ malaysia/article/isma-preacher-labels-liberalism-a-manifestation-of-satans-agenda/> (accessed 5 March 2015).

17. "Isma Preacher Labels Liberalism a Manifestation of 'Satan's Agenda'", *Malay Mail Online*, available at <http://www.themalaymailonline.com/malaysia/article/ isma-preacher-labels-liberalism-a-manifestation-of-satans-agenda/> (accessed 5 March 2015).

18. "Muslims Threatened by Liberalism, Secularism and LGBT, Says Najib — Bernama", *Malaysian Insider*, 14 May 2014, available at <http://www.themalaysianinsider.com/ malaysia/article/muslims-threatened-by-liberalism-secularism-and-lgbt-says-najib/> (accessed 5 March 2015).

19. "Six Reasons Why Khalid Must Go, According to PKR", *Malay Mail Online*, 5 August 2014, available at <http://www.themalaymailonline.com/malaysia/article/ six-reasons-why-pkr-wants-khalid-out/> (accessed 5 March 2015).

20. "Malaysia's GDP Grew 6pc in 2014: BNM", *New Straits Times*, 12 February 2014, available at <http://www.nst.com.my/node/72681/> (accessed 5 March 2015).

21. Bank Negara Malaysia, "Developments in the Malaysian Economy", *Quarterly Bulletin, First Quarter 2014* (Kuala Lumpur: Bank Negara Malaysia, 2014).

22. Malaysia, *Annual Gross Domestic Product, 2005–2013* (Kuala Lumpur: Statistics Department Malaysia, 2014).

23. Badan Pusat Statistik, "Gross Domestic Product at 2000 Constant Market Prices by Industrial Origin (Billion Rupiahs), 2000–2013", available at <http://www.bps. go.id/eng/tab_sub/view.php?kat=2&tabel=1&daftar=1&id_subyek=11&notab=3> (accessed 13 February 2015).

24. Philippine Statistics Authority, "GDP", available at <http://www.nscb.gov.ph/stats/ statwatch.asp> (accessed 13 February 2015).

25. Ministry of Trade and Industry, "Singapore's GDP Grew by 1.5 per cent in Fourth Quarter of 2014", available at <http://www.singstat.gov.sg/docs/default-source/ default-document-library/news/press_releases/press02012015.pdf> (accessed 14 February 2015).

26. Bank Negara Malaysia, "Developments in the Malaysian Economy", op. cit.

27. "Amid Growing Debt Worries, EPU Minister Says Malaysia Deserves Better Ratings Outlook", *Malay Mail Online*, 4 September 2014, available at <http://www. themalaymailonline.com/malaysia/article/amid-growing-debt-worries-epu-minister- says-malaysia-deserves-better-rating> (accessed 6 March 2015).

28. "Fitch Maintains Negative Outlook on Malaysia Sovereigns", *The Star*, 12 January 2015, available at <http://www.thestar.com.my/Business/Business-News/2015/01/12/ Fitch-Ratings-maintains-negative-outlook-on-Malaysia-sovereigns/?style=biz> (accessed 6 March 2015).

29. "Bank Negara Grills Top Executives as 1MDB Fails to Settle RM2 Billion Debt", *Malaysian Insider*, 2 January 2015, available at <http://www.themalaysianinsider. com/malaysia/article/bank-negara-grills-top-executives-as-1mdb-fails-to-settle-rm2- billion-debt> (accessed 6 March 2015).

30. "MAS Privatisation is Done Deal, says Maybank Investment", *Malay Mail Online*, 7 November 2014, available at <http://www.themalaymailonline.com/money/article/ mas-privatisation-is-done-deal-says-maybank-investment-banking-research> (accessed 6 March 2015).

31. "Malaysia's Soaring Household Debt Feared Unsustainable, May Trigger Crisis", *Malay Mail Online*, 7 February 2015, available at <http://www.themalaymailonline. com/malaysia/article/malaysias-soaring-household-debt-feared-unsustainable-may- trigger-crisis> (accessed 6 March 2015).

32. "Mortgages, Car Loans Driving Up Malaysia's Household Debt", *Straits Times*, 15 April 2014, available at <http://www.stasiareport.com/the-big-story/asia-report/ malaysia/story/mortgages-car-loans-driving-malaysias-household-debt-201404> (accessed 6 March 2015).

33. McKinsey Global Institute (MGI), *Debt and (not much) Deleveraging* (London: MGI, 2015).

34. "Petronas' Dividend Contribution Slightly Lower This Year", *Borneo Post*, 21 January 2015.

35. Oxford Business Group, "Malaysia Year in Review 2014", 31 December 2014, available at <http://www.oxfordbusinessgroup.com/news/malaysia-year-review-2014> (accessed 6 March 2015).

36. Ibid.

37. "Ringgit Near Five-Year Low as Oil Prices Dip", *Malay Mail Online*, 28 November 2014, available at <http://www.themalaymailonline.com/money/article/ringgit-near-five-year-low-as-oil-prices-dip> (accessed 6 March 2015).

38. Malaysian Institute of Economic Research, "Malaysian Economic Outlook", 28 January 2015, available at <http://www.mier.org.my/outlook/> (accessed 6 March 2015).

39. The Asia Foundation, "Malaysia's Middle Income Trap", 2015, available at <http://asiafoundation.org/in-asia/2011/01/26/malaysia%E2%80%99s-middle-income-trap/> (accessed 5 March 2015).

40. "2014: UNSC Membership, Asean Chairmanship, Highlights of Malaysia's Successful Foreign Policy", *The Sun*, 18 December 2014, available at <http://www.thesundaily.my/news/1271164> (accessed 6 March 2015).

41. Ibid.

42. "Malaysia Assumes 2015 Chairmanship", *The Star*, 14 November 2014, available at <http://www.thestar.com.my/News/Nation/2014/11/14/Malaysia-assumes-2015-chairmanship-PM-pledges-for-an-integrated-Asean-Community/> (accessed 6 March 2015).

43. ASEAN, "Malaysia's Chairmanship of ASEAN 2015 to be Challenging and Interesting", 8 April 2014, available at <http://asean2015.bernama.com/newsdetail.php?id=1028752> (accessed 6 March 2015).

44. Vinod K. Aggarwal and Jonathan T. Chow, "The Perils of Consensus: How ASEAN's Meta-Regime Undermines Economic and Environmental Cooperation", *Review of International Political Economy* 17, no. 2 (May 2010): 262–90.

THE *HUDUD* CONTROVERSY IN MALAYSIA
Religious Probity or Political Expediency?

Ahmad Fauzi Abdul Hamid

Introduction

2014 will be remembered as a year in which the whole Malaysian nation came together in the wake of the double tragedy involving the national carrier Malaysian Airlines, namely the disappearance of MH370 from Kuala Lumpur to Beijing on 8 March, and the shooting down of MH17 over Ukrainian airspace on 17 July, killing all 298 passengers. The two mishaps, while bringing politics to a temporary halt, were not devoid of uncanny political circumstances. The MH370 mystery, in particular, took place on exactly the sixth anniversary of the 12th General Elections (GE12) on 8 March 2008, which changed the course of Malaysian politics when the Anwar Ibrahim-led People's Pact (PR: Pakatan Rakyat) opposition alliance denied the ruling National Front (BN: Barisan Nasional) its coveted two-thirds parliamentary majority and added Penang, Selangor, Kedah and Perak to the list of states it controlled; Kelantan having already been under an Islamic Party of Malaysia (PAS: Parti Islam SeMalaysia)-led government since 1990. The loss of flight MH370 also came immediately following the Court of Appeal's verdict finding Anwar Ibrahim guilty of the charge of sodomizing his former aide Mohd. Saiful Bukhari Azlan. This momentous ruling overturned Anwar's acquittal by the High Court in January 2012, and has had significant implications for Anwar's and PR's political plans for the rest of the year.

Ahmad Fauzi Abdul Hamid is a Professor of Political Science and chairs the Political Science section, School of Distance Education, Universiti Sains Malaysia, Penang, Malaysia.

The fractious bickering among politicians over the role of Islam, which has been constitutionally designated as the "religion of the Federation" or as many put it, the country's "official religion", has continued to dominate the political scene since the end of Malaysia's 13th General Elections (GE13) in May 2013. GE13 had witnessed the ruling National Front (BN) coalition losing further ground to PR. Although BN managed to recapture the state of Kedah and legitimize its hold on Perak which it snatched from PR through defections in February 2009, BN's share of parliamentary seats declined from 140 to 133, besides losing the popular vote tally with only 47 per cent of votes as compared to PR's 51 per cent.[1]

Results of GE13 propelled Islam to the forefront of national politics in more ways than one. On the one hand, as a major signifier of Malay ethnicity as formalized in the Federal Constitution, Islam held symbolic value for United Malays National Organization (UMNO), the archetypal party of Malay nationalism. Under pressure from its rank and file to recover loss of support from the Malay masses in two successive general elections, UMNO leaders played along with ethnocentric sentiments of its divisional and branch level figures which sought to portray the Malay nation as being under threat of being overwhelmed by non-Malay forces, acting in cahoots with "renegade" Malays from Anwar's People's Justice Party (PKR: *Parti Keadilan Rakyat*) and PAS. Islam emerged as a rallying cry for such party-based conservative voices, which were supported by the Malay language mainstream media and Malay-Muslim non-governmental organizations (NGOs). They together made up a loosely bound conservative Islamist civil society, which were becoming infamous by the day for their inclination to issue incendiary remarks on ethno-religious matters.[2]

On the other hand, the outcome of GE13 was not a necessarily happy one for PAS either. While its participation in PR has enabled it to make inroads in states outside its traditional strongholds of northern and northeastern Peninsular Malaysia, PAS was understandably worried that its apparent moderation in ethno-religious issues had alienated rural Malay-Muslim voters, who have now turned to UMNO as their protector against a perceived non-Malay onslaught. Among PR constituent partners, PAS was the biggest loser, winning merely 21 out of 66 parliamentary seats contested. In comparison, the social democratic and Chinese-dominated DAP bagged 38 out of the 51 parliamentary constituencies it contested. PAS's foray into urban areas was more than offset by the setback it was feeling in the hardcore Malay countryside. Alarmed by what was potentially a more than temporary reversal of support, PAS's powerful *ulama* elite was increasingly calling for a rethink of the nature of its cooperative framework within PR. Some puritans among the party leadership felt that PAS's membership of PR, though strategically beneficial, was in danger of compromising its avowed objectives, chief among which are the erection of a judirical Islamic state and the accompanying implementation of *Syariah* (Islamic law), of which the *hudud* (Penal Code) is an indispensable component.[3]

Hence, as they ushered in the year 2014, both sides of the Malay-Muslim political divide were bracing themselves for a battle of identities that would inevitably centre around Islam, its proper public role, and ultimately, *hudud*. In Islamic jurisprudence, *hudud* penalties are by definition criminal punishments instituted by the Quran and *Sunnah* (oral and behavioural traditions of the Prophet Muhammad) after going through the due process of law, and are therefore not subject to change by human agency. Examples often given are the amputation of hands and limbs for theft and robbery, stoning to death for adultery, and floggings of one hundred lashes for fornication and eighty lashes for slandering an innocent person of illicit sex. In terms of language, *hudud* is the plural of *hadd*, which means "limits" or "regulations" and is transliterated into Malay as *had*.[4]

Hudud Issue in Malaysia: Old Wine in New Bottle?

Two political issues dominated Malaysian politics in 2014: disputations surrounding the position of the Chief Minister or *Menteri Besar* (MB) of the state of Selangor, and the brouhaha over the Kelantan state government's intention to table two Private Members' Bills to pave the way for the implementation of *hudud* laws. Both issues tested the survival instincts of the opposition PR, within hardly a year of its denying BN not only the two-thirds parliamentary majority but also the popular vote majority in GE13.

The Selangor MB crisis began in January 2014 with the abrupt resignation of the sitting assemblyman for the state constituency of Kajang, Lee Chin Cheh. This so-called "Kajang Move" was purportedly a strategic plan to install Anwar Ibrahim as Selangor MB, amidst growing dissatisfaction with the incumbent MB from PKR, Khalid Ibrahim. The original plan, however, went awry in March when Anwar's position as the PR candidate for the Kajang by-election was rendered untenable by his conviction for engaging in homosexual activity. PR eventually nominated Anwar's wife-cum-PKR President Wan Azizah Wan Ismail as Kajang assemblyman and upon her election, PKR thrust her forward in an attempt to replace the beleaguered Khalid. When Khalid refused to relinquish his post, PKR sacked him. Now partyless, Khalid's days as MB were numbered but he managed to hold on to power for over two months upon the Sultan of Selangor's confidence. Unhappy at the prospect of having in Wan Azizah, a MB "remote-controlled" by Anwar, the Sultan eventually settled for PKR Deputy President Mohamed Azmin Ali as the new MB by late September, but not before chiding PKR and DAP for insisting on Wan Azizah as their choice for MB.[5]

The Selangor MB saga exposed internal rifts within PR. To PKR and DAP, PAS was going against the spirit of cooperation in PR in continually backing Khalid Ibrahim as MB. Two of PAS's assemblymen, Saari Sungib and Hasnul Baharuddin, who broke ranks with their party to demonstrate support for Wan Azizah, were later condemned during the PAS General Assembly and later suspended.[6] PAS's lack of *esprit de corps* with respect to PR was further illustrated in a leaked chat among central committee members over the WhatsApp social messaging application in late July. In the conversation, PAS Research Operations Director Dr Mohd. Zuhdi Marzuki criticized Anwar Ibrahim's dictatorial tendencies and floated the idea of a new PAS-UMNO alliance in an effort to restore Malay-Muslim dominance in Selangor.[7]

So what had apparently warmed some influential PAS figures to UMNO as the year progressed? UMNO strategists' knew all along that PAS, especially conservatives who form the bulk of its *ulama* wing, have a perennial weakness for *hudud*. The temptation of being offered the opportunity to implement *hudud*, touted as "the highest peak in the study and learning of Islamic law" in a foreword to a simple guidebook on *hudud* written by one of PAS's top religious scholars, is simply too great for them to resist.[8] As indicated above, the post-GE13 scenario saw a convergence of interests among conservatives from both UMNO and PAS. If both sides combined forces, they would easily make the largest voting bloc not only among Malay-Muslims but also as a national constituency. UMNO has been under constant pressure from its conservative old guard to re-assert its self-proclaimed position as defender of Malay-Muslim rights, in the wake of what they see as UMNO's recent compromises with non-Malays and middle-class Malays whose support for BN has been steadily dwindling. For example, Zainuddin Maidin, former Information Minister and ex-editor-in-chief of arch-conservative Malay daily *Utusan Malaysia*, recently praised vice-chief of Johore UMNO Youth Khairul Anwar Rahmat for asserting the right of Muslims to live in accordance with the *Syariah*. Suggesting that voices defending the Islamic faith and Malay dignity now emanate from NGOs such as the Organization for Empowered Indigenous Peoples of Malaysia (PERKASA: *Pertubuhan Pribumi Perkasa Malaysia*) rather than from UMNO's national leadership, Zainuddin boldly called for — in apparent contradiction to Prime Minister Najib Razak's stance — the principle of *wasatiyyah* (moderation) to be shelved in religious matters.[9]

With the rise in UMNO of cohorts of *ulama* trained in the Wahhabi-Salafi puritanical strand of Islam,[10] pro-*Syariah* sentiments within UMNO has been growing. The more radical voices however, are sub-contracted to the slew of right-wing NGOs that have proliferated to make up for Najib's balancing act in stemming the drift of non-Malays away from BN. PERKASA, for instance, has admitted receiving assistance from government agencies for its programmes.[11] The interests of UMNO's Islamists and nationalist conservatives have aligned to uphold a *Syariah*-oriented Islam increasingly emerging as an expedient political tool.[12] *Hudud* — an agenda which has all along been identified as PAS's pet project — emerged as their rallying cry for an UMNO version of *Pax Islamica* (Islamic order), which Najib until today has failed to showcase. Stopping short of endorsing PAS's brand of *hudud*, they nevertheless wrested the initiative to raise the possibility of implementing *hudud*. In concluding his parliamentary debate on 27 March, Minister in the Prime Minister's Department Jamil Khir Baharom offered the federal government's help to enable Kelantan to practise *hudud* laws via its *Enakmen Kanun Jenayah Syariah (II) 1993* (hereafter KJS 1993). KJS 1993, despite being passed twenty years ago by the Kelantan State Legislative Assembly, had been held in abeyance since the state government received an official letter from then Prime Minister Dr Mahathir Mohamad warning it against implementing *hudud*.[13] Mahathir's reasoning was then based on unfavourable constitutional and judicial factors, so this time round, the Kelantan government through MB Ahmad Yakob declared that its MPs would table two Private Member's Bills in Parliament in order to effect the legal changes necessary to enable it to enforce *hudud* among Muslims in Kelantan. The bills would amend relevant clauses of Article 76 of the Federal Constitution, expanding the powers of the *Syariah* courts to encompass hard crimes that have previously been dealt with by the Penal Code. They would also enable the state government to enlist the support of federal enforcement agencies such as the police and prison administration in handling offenders under *hudud*.[14]

Throughout the first *hudud* saga in 1993–94, bad blood prevailed between the Kelantan government and the federal administration. Nik Aziz Nik Mat,

Kelantan MB from 1990 till 2013, testified that he feared that Kelantan would be put under the emergency rule of the National Operations Council (MAGERAN: *Majlis Gerakan Negara*) should it proceed to implement *hudud* without the federal government's consent in 1994.[15] Nik Aziz's fear was not without basis, for there exists a precedence in Kelantan's brief rule under MAGERAN during its MB crisis in 1977–78.[16] In 2014, however, statements delivered by PAS notables indicated that they earnestly believed in the sincerity of UMNO leaders in its willingness to allow *hudud* to be practised in a PAS-ruled Kelantan. PAS President Haji Abdul Hadi Awang even went to the extent of claiming that UMNO leaders' acceptance of *hudud* of late was a testimony to the effectiveness of PAS's *dakwah* (propagation) efforts at all levels of society.[17] Nik Aziz, who remained PAS's *Mursyid al-'Aam* (General Spiritual Guide) till his death, admitted that conditions today had changed and he was happy with the current state of affairs pertaining to the roadmap for the realization of *hudud* laws in Kelantan. In Kelantan Deputy MB Mohd. Amar Abdullah's view, it was unwise for PAS leaders to forego the opportunity laid out to them towards achieving one of the major goals of their struggle. In other words, since UMNO had given the green light, PAS might as well go for it.[18] PAS leaders' confidence was driven by the fact that the number of Muslim parliamentarians exceeded the 112 figure required to obtain a simple majority to pass the *hudud* bills.[19] Taking into account UMNO's present right-wing trajectory, voting against the bills would render their members of Parliament vulnerable to accusations of being anti-Muslim and anti-Malay.

Indeed, UMNO leaders have undeniably issued public statements which are enough to convince a neutral observer that UMNO is serious in wanting to see *hudud* practised in Kelantan and perhaps eventually Malaysia. Chief opposition leader in the Kelantan state assembly, Mohd. Alwi Che Ahmad, for example, was on record for saying that he would no longer be in UMNO if UMNO leaders had become stumbling blocks against the implementation of *hudud*.[20] Kelantan UMNO chief-cum-Minister of International Trade and Industry Mustapa Mohamed also declared that *hudud* posed no problems for UMNO as far as he was concerned.[21] In April, the venerable Nik Aziz happily welcomed courtesy visits by Dr Asyraf Wajdi Dusuki, head of the state-funded Islamic *Dakwah* Foundation of Malaysia (YADIM: *Yayasan Dakwah Islamiah Malaysia*) and UMNO Supreme Council member, and Deputy Prime Minister Muhyiddin Yassin to his office and home respectively.[22] It was after this visit and a separate meeting with Deputy MB Mohd. Amar, that Muhyiddin proposed the formation of a national-level technical committee on *hudud* that would work hand-in-hand with its state-level counterpart chaired by Mohd. Amar. The precise words used by Muhyiddin in coming up with the idea were unthinkable for an UMNO leader of the Mahathir era: "The committee will look at *hudud* from all angles and how it could be implemented in Malaysia, especially in Kelantan. ..."[23]

Muhyiddin's statement was in tandem with Prime Minister Najib's assurance that the federal government had never rejected the implementation of *hudud* per se, but it had to look meticulously into related "loopholes and shortcomings" before proceeding to apply it.[24] PAS was encouraged further by developments in the neighbouring sultanate of Brunei, which had promulgated the commencement of *hudud* laws from 1 May. PAS delegations visited Brunei, but its spokesmen were quick to point out that KJS 1993 as slated for operationalization in Kelantan was different from Brunei's version of *Syariah* in exempting non-Muslims from *hudud*.[25] By the end of October, the Kelantan government claimed to have enlisted the cooperation of the federal police and prison departments to implement *hudud* by 2015, to which it had allocated a budget of RM1 million (US$277,000).[26] The situation was looking good for PAS's plans as the end of the year 2014 approached, so much so that investigative journalist Joceline Tan could remark, "Kelantanese have been slowly but surely inching towards an Islamic state."[27]

Hudud in 2015? Between Politics and Religious Uprightness

PAS's original timeline for tabling its Private Member's bills in Parliament by June 2014 was pushed back in order to give all sides more time to get prepared. PAS denied that the delay was due to pressure from other parties, either PR or BN; instead, it was actively ironing out pertinent issues in the *hudud* technical committees on a "state government to federal government" basis.[28] PAS vehemently rejected the suggestion by MCA that the postponement was intended to boost the chances of DAP candidates at the forthcoming parliamentary by-elections for Bukit Gelugor and Teluk Intan on 25 May and 31 May respectively.[29] Both constituencies were DAP seats which fell vacant after the elected representatives died. Formerly held by renowned lawyer Karpal Singh, the outcome for Bukit Gelugor was for many a foregone conclusion. Karpal's son Ramkarpal Singh's destiny to replace his father was never in doubt, and Karpal's well-known opposition to *hudud* and an Islamic state would disfavour PR by bringing out its policy incoherence into the open. Teluk Intan was more contentious, as DAP put forward rookie female politician Dyana Sofya Mohd. Daud as PR's candidate. When Dyana's defeat to GERAKAN President Mah Siew Kong by a slim margin was attributed by DAP Puchong MP Gobind Singh Deo, another son of Karpal Singh, to the *hudud* controversy, it became clear that the BN component parties' tactic of driving a wedge among PR component parties by manipulating the *hudud* issue was bearing fruit.[30]

In attempting to recoup its electoral losses, UMNO looks as if it is prepared to go so far as to renege on its own promises. One could recall Najib Razak's assurances in September 2011 that *hudud* laws were not part of the federal government's agenda.[31] Such a drastic turnabout within the space of two years could not have come about if not for UMNO's desperation to reclaim the undisputed status of champion of Islam and therefore of the allegedly besieged Malay-Muslims. UMNO and BN have known all along that breaking up PR is the only possible way to stem the tide of support that has been ebbing away from the ruling coalition. Just as PR's predecessor, the Alternative Front (BA: Barisan Alternatif) had been broken up in 2001 over the Islamic state issue, *hudud* in 2014 serves as a most convenient bait to create fissures within PR, knowing its irresistible appeal to the PAS old guard.[32] While there has been convergence of interests between UMNO strategists and PAS conservatives in wishing *hudud* to be realized in Kelantan, their motivations cannot be more different. UMNO is driven by politics, but faith in God's law is what goads PAS's purists.

PAS's coalition partners realize this looming danger and have sought to warn PAS of the unfortunate consequences for Malaysian democracy should PR break up. Liew Chin Tong, DAP MP for Kluang, Johore, for instance, recalled how MCA manipulated the *hudud* issue to defeat DAP candidates in non-Malay-majority areas, and lamented DAP's years out of BA for delivering a walkover to BN in the 2004 elections.[33] In a similar vein, DAP MP for Bukit Mertajam, Penang, Steven Sim Chee Keong, surmised that through the resurrection of the *hudud* faultline, UMNO was also offering a lifeline to MCA to upstage DAP in its effort to regain the trust of the Chinese community.[34] Indeed, since the *hudud* issue resurfaced, MCA has been fond of issuing anti-*hudud* diatribes in the mainstream media, arguing that DAP could not be relied on to defend non-Malay interests on account of its alleged kow-towing to PAS's demands and Islamic state programme.[35] PR supremo Anwar Ibrahim, himself embattled over renewed sodomy allegations, has been visibly perturbed by the difficulties that *hudud* was causing to unity among PR component parties. Not wanting to offend the sensibilities of both DAP and PAS, he regularly vacillates between appeasing the sensibilities of the former and accommodating the idealisms of the latter.[36]

To be fair to PAS, some leading figures within the party did realize that UMNO and BN were out to exploit the hullabaloo over *hudud* to maximize political gains.[37] But such voices of caution, coming mostly from members of the "professionals" or "Erdogan" faction with purported links to Anwar Ibrahim, were drowned out during the PAS General Assembly in Johore in September 2014. They were furthermore put on the defensive when they were perceived to be siding with PKR and DAP, against PAS's official stand, in the Selangor MB crisis. This led observers to wonder whether the break-up of PR was imminent.[38]

As 2014 drew to a close, it looked as though PAS was ever more resolute to see *hudud* laws implemented in Kelantan in one year's time. PAS is encouraged by UMNO's apparent backing for its proposal to introduce Private Member's bills in Parliament towards achieving that purpose. PAS's *ulama* wing does not appear to suspect that UMNO strategists might harbour ulterior motives in allowing PAS to proceed with its plan. That UMNO's religious sincerity is questionable is reflected in its reluctance to propose similar laws in states under its control. In fact, the UMNO-controlled state legislative assembly in Terengganu, which under PAS's rule in July 2002 had passed the *Enakmen Kesalahan Jenayah Syariah (Hudud dan Qisas)* comparable to KJS 1993, even rejected a PAS assemblyman's motion to debate the proposals.[39]

Religious probity is furthest from UMNO's thought in provisionally agreeing to permit PAS to attempt to turn its *hudud* draft proposals, stalled for over twenty years, into reality. In BN's slick political calculation, it would gain political benefit from UMNO's message to the Malay masses that it supports Islamic laws, but at the same time not obstructing its non-Malay component parties from issuing statements that Malaysia is and will always be a secular state in which the implementation of *hudud* laws can only lead to injustice arising from inequality of citizens before the law in a dual legal system. In subscribing to such an argument, interestingly, MCA's position falls in line not only with MIC but also with DAP and Dr Mahathir Mohamad, the UMNO arch-conservative who remains stoutly anti-*hudud*.[40] In fact, in June 2014, MCA and DAP were involved in a heated spat with Minister in the Prime Minister's Department Jamil Khir Baharom over Malaysia's status as a secular state, which the latter denied.[41]

Conclusion and Future Scenario

The author is of the view that UMNO and BN's antics in this whole *hudud* saga are part of a grand design to outflank PAS where it matters most, that is, at the next general elections. Double-speak has been UMNO's political game for many years. It secures Malay-Muslim sympathy by appearing pro-Islam on the one hand, but uses its partners to make sure that non-Malays are not repelled by BN altogether. As perception rules in politics, the façade of UMNO politicians getting together with their PAS Muslim brothers, as bandied about in the mainstream Malay language media, is all too important for UMNO's image as a party that gives importance to Islamic unity more than anything else.

Several factors militate against a favourable outcome to PAS's plans for the erection of a *hudud*-based *Pax Islamica* in Kelantan, at least in the near future. The principled opposition to *hudud* by Dr Mahathir, who remains godfather of UMNO conservatives, in particular PERKASA, will be vital in determining UMNO's move on the *hudud* front in 2015.[42] Najib will not want to risk alienating the UMNO conservatives, whose clout engineered the downfall of his predecessor Abdullah Ahmad Badawi and continually casts a dark shadow over the image of UMNO reformists such as Saifuddin Abdullah, former MP for Temerloh, and Nur Jazlan Rahmat, MP for Pulai.[43] Worst comes to the worst, UMNO might allow PAS to table the Private Member's bills but will make sure they are defeated by lack of time or during voting by instructing an adequate number of its MPs of the reformist-liberal strand to vote against them. In such an eventuality, ironically, both UMNO and PAS will derive political advantages. UMNO will be able to retain the bulk of its conservative-based support while faulting its maverick liberal MPs for voting against *hudud*, thus persuading the Malay-Muslim masses that the party vanguard is not out to weaken the position of Islam or dismantle Malay-Muslim privileges. As for PAS, it can placate its diehard Islamist members by blaming UMNO for scuttling the *hudud* bills, while at the same time hope to remain in PR and thus retain the trust of many moderate-minded Malays and Malaysians.[44]

Reduced to a political tool at the hands of both UMNO and PAS, Islamic law unfortunately continues to be interpreted via conservative lenses, at variance with the many revisionist and reformist interpretations that have been offered by contemporary *ulama* who have done extensive research on the applicability of *Syariah* — understood widely as encompassing not just *hudud*, in the modern age.[45] The portrayal of *Syariah* in Malaysia at the moment, with undue emphasis on *hudud*, has had the deleterious effect of showcasing only the punitive side of the law, unduly neglecting its compassionate side. As budding DAP politician Liew Chin Tong has also argued, discourse on *Syariah* in Malaysia is still constricted within the boundaries of a colonial worldview which conceives Islamic law in the context of solely personal laws, hence sidelining issues of national importance such as corruption, transparency, social justice and socio-economic rights.[46]

Notes

The author wishes to acknowledge financial support from USM's short-term research grant (no.: 304/PJJAUH/6313110) for making research possible for this chapter.

1. Several edited volumes analysing the results and implications of GE13 have been published. See for example, James Chin (guest editor), "Special issue: Malaysian General Elections 2013", *The Round Table: The Commonwealth Journal of International Affairs* 102, no. 2 (2013); Ahmad Fauzi Abdul Hamid and Muhamad Takiyuddin Ismail (guest editors), "Special issue: Malaysia's 13th General Election: Reform, Change and Conservatism", *Kajian Malaysia: Journal of Malaysian Studies* 32, supplement 2 (2014); Mohamed Nawab Mohamed Osman, ed., *The 13th Malaysia Elections: Issues, Trends and Future Trajectories*, RSIS Monograph no. 30 (Singapore: S. Rajaratnam School of International Studies, 2014).

2. Ahmad Fauzi Abdul Hamid and Muhamad Takiyuddin Ismail, "Islamist Conservatism and the Demise of Islam Hadhari in Malaysia", *Islam and Christian-Muslim Relations* 25, no. 2 (2014): 159–80.

3. Abdillah Noh, "Malaysia's Dilemma: Economic Reforms but Politics Stays the Same", *Southeast Asian Affairs 2014*, edited by Daljit Singh (Singapore: Institute of Southesat Asian Studies, 2014), p. 198.

4. Tuan Guru Dato' Dr Haron Din al-Hafiz, *Jom! Kenali Hudud* [Come! Let's Know Hudud] (Shah Alam: PSN Publications, 2014), pp. xvii, 1–16.

5. T. Avineshwaran, "Selangor Palace: PKR, DAP's Refusal to Submit more than Two Names Complicated Situation", *The Star Online*, 23 September 2014.

6. "Hadi Slams 'Brokers and Pimp'", "Selangor MB crisis: Saari to Hadi — 'Show Proof I was Bought Over'", *The Star Online*, 21 September 2014.

7. "Make It Clear if You Want to Ditch Pakatan, PAS told", *The Star Online*, 30 July 2014.

8. Ustaz Mohammad Subki Abdul Rahman al-Hafiz, *"Kata Penerbit"* [Publisher's Foreword], in Haron Din al-Hafiz, *Jom! Kenali Hudud*, p. xiv.

9. Sofian Baharom, *"Zam puji keberanian Khairul Anwar"* [Zam lauds Khairul Anwar's courage], *Utusan Malaysia*, 8 November 2014.

10. Mohamed Nawab Mohamed Osman, "Salafi Ulama in UMNO: Political Convergence or Expediency?", *Contemporary Southeast Asia* 36, no. 2 (2014): 206–31.

11. "Perkasa Admits Getting Aid from Putrajaya", *The Malaysian Insider*, 25 December 2013.

12. Boo Su-Lyn, "In 'Islamist' Umno, Analysts See a Nation Torn by Religion", *The Malay Mail Online*, 10 December 2013.

13. Ahmad Fauzi Abdul Hamid, "Implementing Islamic Law Within a Modern Constitutional Framework: Challenges and Problems in Contemporary Malaysia", *Islamic Studies* 48, no. 2 (2009): 174.

14. Aziz Muda, *"Kelantan akan kemuka* 'private bill' *hudud ke Parlimen"* [Kelantan will propose private bills on *hudud* to Parliament], *Harakah*, 7–10 April 2014; "PAS to Move for Private Bill on Hudud in Kelantan", *The Star Online*, 10 April 2014.

15. Mohd Nor Yahya, *"Dulu PM hantar surat amaran halang buat hudud"* [Previously it was the PM who sent a warning letter against the implementation of *hudud*], *Harakah*, 2–4 May 2014.

16. Dr Syed Iskandar Syed Jaafar Al Mahdzar, *"Menoleh semula di sebalik Mageran Kelantan 1977"* [Reflections on Mageran Kelantan 1977], *Harakahdaily*, 21 March 2013.

17. Khairul Azlam Mohamad, *"Kesan dakwah PAS, akhirnya Umno terima hudud"* [As a result of PAS's *dakwah*, Umno finally accepts *hudud*], *Harakah*, 25–27 April 2014.

18. Lanjusoh, *"Hudud: Benarkah pemimpin Melayu senada?"* [*Hudud*: Is it true that Malay leaders are on the same wavelength?], *Harakah*, 5–8 May 2014.

19. Aslani M, *"Sokongan 112 ahli Parlimen bolehkan hudud dilaksana"* [Support of 112 Members of Parliament will allow *hudud* to be implemented], *Harakah*, 18–20 April 2014.

20. *"Nik Aziz hargai sokongan Alwi"* [Nik Aziz appreciates Alwi's support], *Harakah*, 10–13 March 2014.

21. "Mustapa to PAS: Explain Hudud to Muslim and Non-Muslim MPs", *The Star Online*, 13 April 2014.

22. Lanjusoh, *"Hudud: Benarkah pemimpin Melayu senada?"*; "PAS not Working with Umno, says Nik Aziz", *The Star Online*, 8 May 2014.

23. "Umno Proposes National-Level Hudud Technical Committee", *The Star Online*, 27 April 2014.

24. Kiatisak Chua, "Government Never Rejected Hudud, says Najib", *The Star Online*, 24 April 2014; "PM on Hudud: Not Now We're Not Ready", *The Star Online*, 25 April 2014.

25. Batu Syahadah, *"Rahmat pelaksanaan hudud di Brunei"* [Bounties from the implementation of *hudud* in Brunei], *Harakah*, 3–5 January 2014; Mat Zain Mat

Isa, *"Hudud Terengganu rujukan Brunei?"* [Terengganu's *hudud* the reference for Brunei?], *Harakah*, 7–9 March 2014; Arif Atan and Nyza Ayob, *"Takzir untuk bukan Islam, tak ikut Brunei"* [*Takzir* for non-Muslims, we don't follow Brunei], *Harakah*, 12–15 May 2014.

26. Syed Azhar, "Kelantan Govt Fine Tuning Bill on Hudud", *The Star Online*, 21 October 2014; Syed Azhar, "Kelantan MB: RM1mil for Hudud Implementation Next Year", *The Star Online*, 22 October 2014.

27. Joceline Tan, "Pushing for 'God's Law'", *The Star Online*, 2 November 2014.

28. "Hadi Postpones Plan to Table Hudud Bill", *The Star Online*, 12 May 2014; Nyza Ayob, *"Tangguh hudud bukan tekanan mana-mana pihak"* [Deferring *hudud* is not due to pressure from any side], *Harakah*, 16–18 May 2014.

29. "Rocket Party Powerless to Stop Coalition Partner's Hudud Agenda, says Wee", *The Star Online*, 13 May 2014; "MCA: PAS Delaying Hudud Bid to Boost DAP's Chances in Polls', *The Star Online*, 14 May 2014.

30. "Gobind: Hudud Issue Contributed to DAP's Loss", "PAS' Hudud did not Lead to Dyana's Defeat in Teluk Intan By-election", *The Star Online*, 4 June 2014.

31. "Najib: No Hudud in M'sia", *The Star*, 25 September 2011.

32. On this point of political expediency, see for example analyses by President of human rights NGO *Aliran Kesedaran Negara* (ALIRAN) Francis Loh in "Hudud (Part 1): Is Umno Goading Pas?", *Aliran Online*, 6 May 2014, and "Hudud (Part 2): Umno Restrategises — Back to Old Politics", *Aliran Online*, 7 May 2014. Loh was formerly Professor of Political Science at Universiti Sains Malaysia (USM), Penang.

33. Liew Chin Tong, *"Hudud: Politik siapa lebih jantan"* [*Hudud*: Politics of who is more masculine?], *Harakah*, 5–8 May 2014.

34. Steven Sim Chee Keong, *"Hudud: Talian hayat kepada PAS…atau?"* [*Hudud*: Lifeline for PAS…or?], *Harakah*, 9–11 May 2014.

35. See for example, "Liow: DAP will be Held Responsible if Hudud is Implemented", *The Star Online*, 26 April 2014; "MCA Questions Pakatan's Hesitation to Make a Stand on Hudud Issue", *The Star Online*, 27 April 2014; Yuen Meikeng, "MCA: We are Firmly against Hudud", *The Star Online*, 27 April 2014; "Chew: Hudud Laws will Infringe on Rights of Non-Muslims", *The Star Online*, 7 May 2014; "We have been Steadfast over Hudud Issue, says MCA", *The Star Online*, 1 July 2014; Martin Carvalho, "MCA: DAP Making Umno Conservatives Push for Hudud too", *The Star Online*, 6 October 2014; "MCA: Hudud may spark Kelantan exodus", *The Star Online*, 29 October 2014.

36. Rahmah Ghazali and Martin Carvalho, "PAS has Every Right to Push for Hudud Law, says Anwar", *The Star Online*, 16 April 2014; Rahmah Ghazali, "Anwar: Pakatan Partners Need More Time to Discuss Hudud Implemention", *The Star Online*, 29 April 2014.

37. See for example, Dr Dzulkefly Ahmad, "Rantings yet Again over the Great Hudud Debate — An Open Letter to Malaysians", *Harakah*, 12–15 May 2014; Mohamed Hanipa Maidin, *"Hudud: Antara jalan lurus, berliku"* [*Hudud*: Between a straight and winding path], *Harakah*, 16–18 May 2014.

38. Baradan Kuppusamy, "Doubts on Pakatan Coalition", *The Star Online*, 20 September 2014; "Hanipa Booed for Going with Pakatan's Stand", *The Star Online*, 21 September 2014; "PKR Censures Hadi for 'Pimp and Broker' Statement"; Baradan Kuppusamy, "PAS' Open Display of Defiance", *The Star Online*, 22 September 2014; T.K. Chua, "Pakatan as Good as Dead", *Free Malaysia Today*, 17 November 2014.

39. *"Kesal hipokrasi Umno-BN tolak hudud"* [Umno-BN's hypocrisy in rejecting *hudud* in Terengganu is regretted], *Harakah*, 21–24 April 2014.

40. "No Justice if Hudud is Practised", *The Star Online*, 1 May 2014.

41. Hemananthani Sivanandam, Yuen Meiking and Martin Carvalho, "Malaysia is Not a Secular State, Jamil Khir Tells Parliament", *The Star Online*, 16 June 2014; Yuen Meiking, "DAP Requests Clarification over Secular State Issue", *The Star Online*, 16 June 2014; "MCA Calls for Action against Jamil over Remark", *The Star Online*, 18 June 2014.

42. On Dr Mahathir's continual influence in UMNO and BN beyond his prime ministerial tenure, see Ahmad Fauzi Abdul Hamid and Muhamad Takiyuddin Ismail, "Malaysia's General Elections Amidst the Shadow of Re-Mahathirisation", *Kajian Malaysia* 32, supplement 2 (2014), special issue "Malaysia's 13th General Election: Reform, Change and Conservatism", edited by Ahmad Fauzi Abdul Hamid and Muhamad Takiyuddin Ismail, pp. 1–24.

43. For Saifuddin's and Nur Jazlan's critical views on UMNO, see for instance, Ram Anand, "For Saifuddin Abdullah, Integrity Doesn't Pay", *Malaysiakini*, 21 October 2013; and Shahanaaz Habib, "Rebel with a Cause", *The Star Online*, 9 November 2014.

44. For recent calls from both non-Malays and Malays for the government to check the rise of religious bigotry, see for example Tan Sri Ramon Navaratnam, "Moderates a Boon for Posterity", letter to the editor, *New Straits Times*, 4 November 2014; and "Group of Prominent Malays Calls for Rational Dialogue on Position of Islam in Malaysia", *The Star Online*, 7 December 2014.

45. For critical assessments of KJS 1993, see Ustaz Ashaari Muhammad, *Falsafah Perlaksanaan Hukum Hudud Dalam Masyarakat* [The Philosophy of Implementation of *Hudud* Laws in Society] (Kuala Lumpur: Penerbitan Hikmah, 1992), and Mohammad Hashim Kamali, "Punishment in Islamic Law: A Critique of The Hudud Bill of Kelantan, Malaysia", *Arab Law Quarterly* 13, no. 3 (1998): 203–34. *Falsafah Perlaksanaan Hukum Hudud Dalam Masyarakat*, written by the late leader of the controversial Darul Arqam movement Ashaari Muhammad, was banned, but not

before being secretly used by officials in the government's Islamic bureaucracy to counter PAS's KJS 1993 when the first *hudud* saga erupted in 1993–94. In personal communication with the present author, Khadijah Aam, Ashaari's wife who accompanied her husband during a face-to-face meeting with Dr Mahathir Mohamad in June 2001, related how Haji Dusuki Ahmad, a top religious officer who was together with Dr Mahathir in the meeting, had grudgingly acknowledged the author of *Falsafah Perlaksanaan Hukum Hudud Dalam Masyarakat* as a "big ulama".

46. Liew Chin Tong, *"Hudud di Malaysia: Strategi atau perangkap?"* [*Hudud* in Malaysia: Strategy or trap?], *Harakah*, 12–15 May 2014.

Myanmar

Myitkyina●

● Mandalay

● Taunggyi

⊡ **NAYPYITAW**
●
Pyinmana

Yangon
●
● Pathein

MYANMAR IN 2014
'Tacking Against the Wind'

Morten B. Pedersen

Introduction

Having garnered widespread acclaim for its reform efforts during the first three years in office, Myanmar's transitional government in 2014 found itself increasingly under attack from critics, both at home and abroad. Opposition leader Daw Aung San Suu Kyi whose approval of President Thein Sein's reform agenda in 2011 had done much to convince sceptics that Myanmar was truly turning a new leaf now publically complained that reforms had stalled. Over the course of the year, talk of backsliding became an increasingly common refrain among human rights groups and the media. Particular concern centred on the failure of the government to revise the Constitution, crackdowns on the media and social protesters, armed clashes in ceasefire areas, growing anti-Muslim ferment, and major problems of land grabbing.

The critics did not have it all their own way. In a press conference in Yangon in November, U.S. President Barack Obama explicitly backed President Thein Sein, whom he had received in the White House during better days in 2012, arguing "Myanmar's democratisation process is real".[1] Echoing this sentiment, the International Crisis Group later the same week warned against overstating the significance of recent difficulties:

> Myanmar is four years into a transition from 50 years of authoritarian rule and chronic, grinding civil conflicts... We should not be surprised that certain areas remain problematic or new difficulties arise... Bad-news stories about Myanmar's transition are easy to find. But the good-news stories reflect a broader trend.[2]

This more pragmatic view seemed to be reflected also in a number of

MORTEN B. PEDERSEN is a Senior Lecturer in International and Political Studies at the University of New South Wales, Canberra and a former Senior Analyst for the International Crisis Group in Myanmar.

opinion surveys conducted by Myanmar Egress,[3] the International Republican Institute[4] and the Asia Foundation[5] in 2014, which all indicated that a majority of Myanmar people were positive about the country's political and economic prospects (although this was more apparent in the Burman heartland than in the ethnic states).

Yet, when it comes to shaping international perceptions, the media invariably have the upper hand and over the course of 2014, pressure grew on Western governments in particular, to reconsider their support of the Thein Sein government; some Western activists and parliamentarians even called for reintroducing sanctions,[6] although Aung San Suu Kyi explicitly rejected such a dramatic step.[7]

Given the potency of this question of the state of the reform process and the implications of the answer for the country's future, it provides a useful focal point for the present review of developments in 2014, which focuses on four key areas: democratization, peace-building, socio-economic development, and international engagement.

Democratization

Myanmar is not a democracy yet. The president and other key government leaders were effectively appointed by the head of the previous military junta, Senior General Than Shwe, after the military-aligned Union Solidarity and Development Party (USDP) secured a landslide victory in multi-party, but flawed, elections in November 2010. Moreover, the 2008 Constitution, which came into force with the inauguration of the new government in March 2011, formally reserves major areas of power for unelected military officers. Yet, the current government has shown a clear commitment, in both words and deeds, to promote democratic institutions and values, and developments in 2014 remained broadly positive. While the military indicated that it would veto any effort to amend the Constitution to reduce its political role at this point, existing democratic institutions continued to perform robustly and the prospects for a freely elected government emerging in 2015 looked good.

Constitutional Amendments

The democratic deficits of the 2008 Constitution go to the heart of Myanmar's transition process and have been the main target of Aung San Suu Kyi and her National League for Democracy (NLD) since they joined Parliament in 2012. The urgency of this issue is rooted in article 59(f) of the Constitution, which disqualifies anyone with foreign family ties from becoming president and thus would block the opposition leader, whose children are British nationals, from assuming the highest office even if the NLD wins the 2015 elections. However, other, arguably more fundamental, issues concern the role of the military in politics, including article 436 which effectively gives the *Tatmadaw* (Myanmar armed forces) a veto over constitutional change, and the distribution of power between the central government and the fourteen states and divisions.

The Constitutional Review Committee established by Parliament in 2013 to elicit views on constitutional amendments delivered its report in January, having received thousands of letters from the public (as well as ninety-four suggestions for amendments from the ruling USDP and 168 from the NLD). This was followed by further discussions in another, smaller parliamentary committee, the Constitutional Amendment Implementing Committee, which was charged with making official recommendations to the Parliament, and, finally, in the full *Pyidaungsu Hluttaw* (Union Parliament), which spent four days during its last session of the year in November debating the Constitution.

President Thein Sein, in a speech on the third anniversary of his government in March, expressed support for constitutional amendments, but urged parliament to be careful not to upset the country's delicate political stability and underscored the continued need for the military to "be present at the political roundtable where political problems are solved by political means".[8] Chairman of the USDP and Speaker of the *Pyithu Hluttaw* (People's Parliament) Shwe Mann went further and explicitly threw his support behind changes to key articles, including 436 and 59(f). Other USDP members also generally expressed support for efforts to expand the powers of elected bodies. Ultimately, however, even the ruling party could do little without the support of the military, and statements by military representatives throughout the year strongly indicated that the *Tatmadaw* would not accept any dilution of its role at this point,[9] nor any revision of the existing criteria for presidential candidates. On the contrary, they proposed strengthening the authority of the unelected National Security and Defence Council by extending its authority to take over state power if Parliament proved unable to handle its responsibilities.

Aung San Suu Kyi, who in late 2013 had suggested that the NLD might boycott the next elections if the Constitution were not changed,[10] pushed hard to break the deadlock, particularly targeting Article 436 which she described as the "master key" to the Constitution. When her calls for high-level talks between President Thein Sein, Speaker Shwe Mann, Commander-in-Chief Min Aung Hlaing and herself to negotiate a way forward were rebuffed, the NLD took the debate into the streets. Joining forces with 88 Student Generation leaders, the main opposition party organized a series of public rallies in late 2013 and early 2014, followed by a nationwide petition campaign that over a period of two months from May to July collected five million signatures in support of changing Article 436. Although the NLD was reportedly warned by election officials that its extra-parliamentary activities put it in violation of the oath taken by Members of Parliament to "uphold and abide" by the Constitution,[11] the authorities largely tolerated the campaign. However, at times the confrontational tone of Aung San Suu Kyi who, among other things, denounced the political role of the *Tatmadaw* as "a violation of Buddhist principles",[12] angered senior military officials and as such may have backfired. The Catch-22 for the NLD is that any overt attempt to weaken the role of the military as the self-prescribed guarantor of the country's stability simply reinforces the argument by hardliners that the *Tatmadaw* must continue to "hold the ring". This dilemma is probably only resolvable over time through confidence-building between long-standing antagonists in Myanmar's deeply fractured society and the gradual evolution of a new military vision for its role in the country.

With no easy compromises in sight, Shwe Mann in November instructed the Implementing Committee to prepare a bill on constitutional amendments for the first session of Parliament in 2015 and suggested that a referendum could be held in May.[13] It remained unclear, however, what potential amendments would be put to the public and whether it would indeed be feasible to organize such a time-demanding and expensive event just six months before the general elections. At the same time, the Speaker declared that no changes to the Constitution could take effect until they were ratified by the next Parliament, although the rationale and implications of this, too, remained unclear.[14] At the end of 2014, the prospect for constitutional change thus remained manifestly uncertain.

Democracy in Action

While negotiations over constitutional change ensued, Myanmar's nascent democratic institutions continued to perform robustly, although not without some significant problems. Parliament, which has been one of the positive surprises of the post-2011 regime, had another busy year. The two Houses of the *Pyidaungsu Hluttaw* sat for a total of thirty weeks in 2014, divided over three sessions (January–March, May–July and September–November), and passed a slew of new laws aimed primarily at reversing the repressive legacy of five decades of military rule and jumpstarting the economy. This included two new media laws, an amended law on peaceful assembly, a new law for registration of civil society associations, the country's first ever Human Rights Commission law, a major new education law, and several laws concerning tax and financial sector reform. Members of Parliament also continued to vigorously exercise their mandate to oversee the executive branch, regularly rejecting or revising legislative proposals from the President, questioning Ministers about executive actions, and reviewing complaints from the public about land grabs, corruption and other issues involving other state agencies.

The outcome of these new parliamentary processes was not always positive. A thinly disguised rivalry between the legislature and the executive at times got in the way of effective policymaking and slowed down the pace of reform. On a number of economic issues, including tax, banking and land, Parliament played a conservative, if not regressive, role, reflecting the strong influence of business interests in its ranks and on key committees. However, one very positive aspect of Myanmar's new parliamentary politics, which continued to play out in 2014, was the emphasis placed on "national" or "consensus" politics. Although the USDP had a clear majority in both houses, it rarely behaved like a ruling party. Shwe Mann maintained a close working relationship with opposition leader Aung San Suu Kyi and bills initiated by smaller parties stood a fair chance of being passed. Indeed, Members of Parliament often voted along committee lines rather than party lines.[15] This is perhaps unsurprising given the highly personalized nature of Myanmar politics and institutional weaknesses of the country's fledgling political parties. However, there is also a sense among many Members that Parliament as a new institution is "on trial" and that they need to prove themselves to the military, which has historically considered politicians to be selfish and unruly. To the extent that this has served to constrain the kind of highly confrontational party politics that has been so damaging to some of Myanmar's neighbours, the country's home-grown system of "disciplined democracy" perhaps has a silver lining, at least for a transitional period.

If Parliament flourished in 2014, the situation for another critical institution for democracy — the (free) media — was more mixed. For the first time under the current government, several local journalists were arrested and imprisoned on charges ranging from harassment and defamation to — in the two most serious cases — breaches of the country's opaque security laws. The government also reduced the duration of visas for foreign journalists from three months to one, and some publications reported an increase in other, more subtle forms of official interference.[16] Critics saw in all of this a resurgent pattern of intimidation and divide-and-rule familiar from the previous era of military rule, which they believed was intended to force the new media to "toe the line".

The press, however, remained vibrant throughout 2014 (not least in exposing any perceived attacks on itself), and even if some government officials clearly still view the free media as a general nuisance and potential threat, the government's press policy continued to evolve in a positive direction. The new News Media Law, which was drafted in constructive tension between the Ministry of Information and domestic and international media groups, explicitly accords journalists a range of rights, including the right to freely criticize the government, and mostly limits potential punishment for breaches of an associated code of conduct to relatively small fines (a notable exception is "writing that inflames ethnic or religious conflict", which remains subject to other, much harsher applicable laws). The formal establishment of a semi-independent Press Council further promised to significantly improve the ability of the private media to bring problems to the attention of the relevant authorities and negotiate the inevitable tensions arising during a time of major institutional transformation. In a meeting with the Press Council in August, President Thein Sein reportedly acknowledged the need to deal with media-related conflicts through mediation rather than persecution. He also committed to help improve access to information and later took an important step in that direction by setting up a new presidential press corps with members of the private media. Meanwhile, the general expectation among members of the media industry was that those journalists sentenced under a harsher regime would be amnestied by the President once the judicial process had run its course.[17]

One case, in particular, captured the ambiguous, but generally hopeful, state of media freedom in the country. The shooting death of freelance journalist Aung Kyaw Naing in Mon State in early October while he was detained by an army battalion echoed the worst of the old era, yet also provided a more optimistic glimpse of a new. After the army first sought to cover up the killing, the President ordered an official investigation into the case, including the exhumation and medical examination of the body. The subsequent report by the National Human Rights

Commission rejected the army's claims that Aung Kyaw Naing was a member of a rebel army and recommended that the case be brought before a civilian court. Although it remained uncertain at the end of 2014 whether anyone would be held responsible, the actions of the government put local army battalions on notice that they could no longer act with impunity. Commander-in-Chief Min Aung Hlaing subsequently met with the Press Council to discuss what could be done to ensure the safety of journalists working in conflict areas.[18]

Overall, the problems of the press in 2014 were perhaps less a result of government backsliding than of the increasing vigour and boldness of the press itself, coupled with a clash of values between relatively conservative, often older, government officials and a new generation of, often younger, journalists who in many cases earned their stars as political activists and were eager to "speak truth to power".[19] Importantly, when conflicts did occur, senior government officials and media representatives generally made a genuine effort to resolve them rather than allow relations to spiral further downwards.

Tensions similar to those in the media sector were evident in the government's handling of social protests. Hundreds of people were arrested all around the country in connection with protests over issues ranging from constitutional amendments, to workers' rights, land grabbing and the new education law. Human rights organizations were quick to condemn what was described as an increase in the number of "political prisoners", which they argued had reversed the positive trend from the early years of the new government.[20] Yet, the unprecedented number of protests in 2014 could equally be seen as evidence of growing civil space. People were demanding rights provided to them under the more liberal post-2011 regime and promoted by a new generation of local activists and civil society organizations who had themselves been greatly empowered by recent reforms. Most of those arrested did in fact break the law — mostly by protesting without permission — and the laws in question were generally no longer the vague, all-encompassing security laws of the past, which had been easily manipulated to serve nefarious purposes, but rather new, more liberal and more specific laws regulating public order and carrying more lenient punishments. Indeed, the Parliament in June 2014 passed a further amendment to the recent Right to Peaceful Assembly and Peaceful Procession Law, which both made it easier to get permission to protest and significantly reduced the penalties for illegal demonstrations. Although interpretation of the new laws varied from location to location, the dark days of the previous regime when critics were routinely jailed for ten to twenty years for minor transgressions — if not on entirely trumped up charges — are far gone. The majority of those arrested in 2014 were eventually released without jail terms.

Clearly, the struggle for civil and political rights is not over. Many of the new laws could, and need to, be further improved. But the main concern in 2014 was less about government ill-will than weak state capacity, specifically the inability of the central government to control local authorities, including township administrators, judges and police. While the NLD was able to conduct a nationwide petition challenging core military prerogatives without noticeable incidents and student demonstrators were invited to sit down with Ministry of Education officials to discuss their grievances about the new education law, it was decidedly more dangerous for local farmers who were fighting to keep their land. This reflected weaknesses of the rule of law, including pervasive problems with judicial corruption and collusion between local political and economic power holders, and is probably outside the ability of any government in Myanmar to fix, at least in the short- to medium-term. Farmers are more vulnerable essentially because they fall below the radar not only of the government, but also of many of its international critics who remains preoccupied with elections, constitutional amendments and political rights more generally, to the exclusion of social and economic rights.

The 2015 Elections

Given the mixed outlook for democracy under the current government, the focus of many observers naturally converged on the next general elections scheduled for the end of 2015 and, in particular, the prospect of a new, NLD-led government coming to power. To many Myanmar people, it remained almost inconceivable that the government would allow free and fair elections, which would most probably result in an embarrassing defeat of the USDP. Yet, every indication in 2014 was that this is in fact what it intends to do.

Senior government officials in numerous public statements over the course of the year effectively staked the legacy of their administration on holding free and fair elections. As President Thein Sein emphasized, "In order to make sure that the democratic transition endures, the 2015 elections must be held in a free and fair manner.... We also must not restrict the political activities of any organizations."[21] Chairman of the Union Election Commission (UEC), Tin Aye, raised some eyebrows during a trip to Pathein in April when he criticized the 2012 by-elections campaign for resembling the 1988 Uprising, and vowed to ensure that such "unruly behaviour" would not be repeated in 2015.[22] Yet, an early draft of the new election rules, which among other things limited the campaign period to thirty days and prohibited party leaders from campaigning on behalf of other candidates in their local constituencies, was later revised to accommodate concerns raised by opposition parties. Meanwhile, the UEC was working closely throughout the year with a range of international agencies to put in place a credible framework for the poll itself, including accurate voter lists, full transparency around advanced voting (which was the major source of vote rigging in 2010), and effective election monitoring.

Another critical electoral issue was, similarly, decided in a manner that seemed to allay fears that the authorities are scheming to extend the rule of the USDP through unfair means. After months of heated debate over a proposed change from Myanmar's traditional first-past-the-post electoral system to some form of proportional representation (PR), Shwe Mann in November informed the *Pyithu Hluttaw* that PR could not be introduced before the 2015 elections because it would require constitutional change.[23] This decision was greatly detrimental to the ruling USDP, which, while expected to get a significant number of votes across the country, is unlikely to secure a majority in any but perhaps a few remote constituencies in the Burman heartland (and maybe not even that). Not surprisingly, it was warmly welcomed by the NLD and a number of ethnic political parties, which had been strongly against a change of the electoral system. The *Amyotha Hluttaw* (Nationalities Parliament) in a separate vote later decided in favour of changing to PR. However, it remained unclear what kind of PR system it wanted and by the end of 2014, the UEC had yet to start preparing for any such change and time seemed to be running out. Even if it was somehow possible to develop and implement a different electoral system for the Upper House, it would have only limited implications for the overall election result since this House has only about one-fourth of the number of seats of the full Parliament.

While much of this remained to be clarified — and, of course, tested — most indications in 2014 were that the 2015 elections would by (largely) free and fair. As Myanmar headed into another election year, the probability of a change of government seemed high. Indeed, this may, in part, explain why the military leadership was so adamant to keep its existing constitutional prerogatives in place. If it is going to allow its long-standing opponent, the NLD, to take government office, all the more reason to ensure that the *Tatmadaw* keeps a hand on the main levers of power.

Peace- and Nation-Building

While one set of critical negotiations in 2014 concerned the expansion of popular participation in political life, another and, arguably, even more critical one for the future of the country concerned the place of ethnic and religious minorities in Myanmar's diverse society. The militarization of Myanmar politics over the previous half-a-century has been due in large part to the persistence of ethnic and, to a lesser degree, religious conflict, and the future of democracy depends critically on developing and sustaining peaceful relations between different groups. Unsurprisingly, however, given the duration and intensity of past and present conflicts, they remained stubbornly resistant to resolution.

Armed Conflict

The peace talks between the government and about two dozen ethnic minority groups, which since Independence have fought for increased local autonomy, several times seemed on the verge of a breakthrough, but ultimately under-delivered. Having already negotiated bilateral ceasefires with most of the ethnic armed groups, the government worked on reaching a National Ceasefire Agreement (NCA), which would formally mark the end of sixty-five years of civil war and create momentum for a broader National Political Dialogue to help resolve the underlying causes of conflict. Between November 2013 and September 2014, the government's Union Peacemaking Working Group held six rounds of formal talks with a Nationwide Ceasefire Coordination Team representing sixteen ethnic armed groups to try to agree on a single text, including a code of conduct between the *Tatmadaw* and ethnic armed groups, as well as a number of broader commitments regarding later steps in the peace process. According to both sides, much progress was made.[24] Yet, the devil clearly was in the details and as the year progressed without any final agreement, what in late 2013 had seemed like a sensible strategy increasingly looked like the death knell for the government's hope of reaching a peace settlement during its term in office. Although some negotiators remained hopeful at the end of the year that an agreement could still be signed in 2015,[25] time had clearly run out for further political dialogue to make much progress before the elections.

The government, which from the outset had made peace one of its two top priorities (along with reviving the economy), was clearly keen to make a breakthrough and made significant concessions on the key demand of ethnic groups for "genuine" federalism. It struggled, however, to bring the *Tatmadaw* into line.

While senior military leaders, too, seemed committed to peace, they were perhaps less disposed to engage in the give-and-take of political negotiations, especially since many felt that they had effectively won the war. Over time, it also became clear that not all ethnic armed groups were necessarily interested in reaching a NCA with the current government. Some ethnic leaders reportedly felt that signing a NCA and starting a political dialogue with the Thein Sein government would be like voting for the USDP; and that it would be better to wait and have a political dialogue with the NLD after the 2015 elections.[26] In the second half of the year, a clear difference over strategy developed between the Karen National Union (KNU, which was keen to get the NCA signed as soon as possible) and the Kachin Independence Organization (KIO, which was seemingly in no hurry to do so). Meanwhile, the strongest of the ethnic armed groups, the United Wa State Army (UWSA), stayed outside of the NCA negotiations altogether. Wa chiefs, who have ruled their remote mountainous region on the Chinese border largely undisturbed by the *Tatmadaw* since the first ceasefire in 1989, argued that their concerns were different from other ethnic groups and should more appropriately be dealt with at the political dialogue stage.[27]

On the ground in ethnic areas, a similarly problematic and decidedly "mixed" situation persisted. Many former conflict-affected communities, especially in the country's southeast, benefited from much improved security and livelihood opportunities.[28] Yet, armed clashes continued throughout the year, mainly in Kachin State and nearby parts of northern Shan State where tens of thousands of internally displaced persons remained in limbo. Although most of these clashes seemingly had more to do with local military and economic dynamics than the political strategies of the main groups involved, they invariably impacted the peace talks, which ultimately hinged on building new trust among long-standing enemies. At no time was this more evident than after the *Tatmadaw* in November shelled a Kachin Independence Army training camp, killing twenty-three members of several different ethnic armies and causing a crisis in the peace talks.

Whatever the reasons for the various delays and setbacks (and there was enough blame to go around, or maybe none), the increasingly remote possibility of reaching a substantive peace settlement before the elections made for a perilous outlook at the end of the year. With key actors refocusing on the electoral contest in 2015, the risk of further armed clashes is likely to increase; and in the absence of peace, ethnic communities risked being denied the opportunity to participate in the elections, thus potentially creating a vicious circle. Under such circumstances, it is uncertain whether the fragile spirit of cooperation that had prevailed during the first four years of the Thein Sein government can be maintained.

Communal Violence

While the negotiations between Myanmar's armed groups left uncertain the prospects of formally ending the country's long-standing civil war, the conflict between the country's Buddhist and Muslim communities, which erupted in Rakhine State in 2012 and later spread to other parts of the country, was in some respects equally worrisome. Although 2014 did not see any major outbreaks of communal violence on par with those in 2012 and 2013, overall developments were deeply troubling.

In Rakhine State, the forced segregation of Rakhine and Rohingya communities kept the violence in check, but at huge expense to both communities and the hostility between them showed no signs of abating. In southern parts of the state, tens of thousands of Rohingya continued to languish in camps for the internally displaced established in the aftermath of the 2012 violence, which experts described as some of the worst in the world, and with no immediate prospects of being able to leave. In Northern Rakhine State, where the Rohingya are in a majority, a new border security force divided its efforts between keeping Rohingya and Rakhine villagers apart and building a new fence along the border with Bangladesh to keep illegal migrants out (ironically, the Bangladeshi Government was considering a similar measure on its side of the border to keep the Rohingya from fleeing to Bangladesh).

The explosiveness (and hopelessness) of the situation was vividly illustrated, although in different ways, by the attack in March by Rakhine mobs on the offices of international aid agencies in Sittwe,[29] which forced many aid workers to evacuate and severely disrupted health and other services in the Rohingya camps — and by the growing exodus of Rohingyas, many of whom risked their lives on perilous boat journeys to Malaysia and beyond rather than face a bleak future in Myanmar.[30] Much of the suffering was shared by Rohingya and Rakhine communities who were all among the poorest in the country even before the violence broke out — and many young Rakhines, too, left in search for jobs overseas. But there was one crucial difference: The Rakhines maintained their citizenship and associated civil rights, including the all-important freedom of movement.

Elsewhere in the country, 2014 will be remembered as the year when extremist Buddhist nationalism became a mainstream political force with potentially major negative implications for future community relations. The 969 Movement, which rose to prominence in 2012 and 2013 with its "Buy Buddhist" boycott of Muslim businesses, was eclipsed during the year by another monk-led group, the Organization for the Protection of Race and Religion, or MaBaTha. The two groups have overlapping membership, but with a more centralized structure and explicitly legal-political strategy MaBaTha has the potential to become a much more influential political force. This was particularly evident in its concerted, and seemingly successful, effort to push a package of four "race and religion protection" bills through Parliament, clearly targeted at Muslims including new regulations for religious conversions, interfaith marriages, polygamy and population control. MaBaTha not only drafted the original bills, but also organized a series of mass rallies to pressure Parliament to pass them. In a public statement in May, the new organization dismissed opponents of the bills, which included a significant number of women's and other human rights groups, as "traitors". The statement condemned "those critics who are backed by foreign groups for raising human rights issues and [not working for] the benefit of the public and not [being] loyal to the state".[31] At the end of the year, the bills had made their way through the legislative process and were due to be voted on in Parliament in the first session in 2015.

While the agendas of Rakhine and Burman Buddhist nationalists are different (and indeed for centuries have often been violently opposed), they have found common cause in the fear of Muslim "encroachment" on Myanmar soil. The sources of this fear are clearly more compelling in Rakhine State where the high number of Rohingyas do present a potential threat to Rakhine political and economic interests, than they are in the country at large where Muslims constitute a tiny minority. However, fear is of course no less real for being irrational and, by presenting themselves as defenders of the country's "Western door", Rakhine nationalists have been able to generate widespread sympathy and support from Buddhists elsewhere in the country. This was evident, for example, in May when Parliament passed into law a bill originally proposed by the Rakhine National Party prohibiting temporary citizens or "white card" holders (that is, mainly Rohingya) from forming political parties; a second bill was pending at the end of the year that would also deny them voting rights and thus entirely disenfranchise them politically.

The government's reaction to the growing ethno-religious tensions was mixed. Clearly concerned by the potential for further violence in Rakhine State to undermine the broader reform process, President Thein Sein took several steps to assert central authority in the state, most notably by removing the Rakhine State Chief Minister and replacing him with the then-Deputy Minister for Border Affairs, a senior active duty military officer. The government, however, remained unbending in the face of growing international demands that it revise the 1982 Citizenship Law, which provides the legal basis for strictly limiting the access of Rohingya to citizenship. Instead, it mooted plans in its draft Rakhine State Action Plan to move all Muslims who could not prove citizenship into camps in preparation for deportation. Meanwhile, the authorities everywhere remained manifestly reluctant to challenge senior monks, including some who in patent breach of the country's new laws openly engaged in anti-Muslim "hate speech" in clear breach of the country's new laws.

It is evident that many senior government officials share the view that the Rohingya are foreigners and do not belong in Myanmar.[32] Yet, aside from individual prejudices, the underlying political calculations behind the government's reticence are as clear as they are worrying. The potential costs to any Myanmar government of upsetting Buddhist, or even Rakhine, nationalist sensitivities are far greater than those of ignoring the rights of a small Muslim minority (or minorities). This was nowhere more evident in 2014 than in the continued silence of opposition leader Aung San Suu Kyi on the issue, which spoke volumes about the political risks, even for a popular icon, of siding with a widely unpopular minority and left a serious stain on her otherwise irreproachable reputation as an advocate of international universal rights.

Many Myanmar activists are concerned that the rise in Buddhist nationalism is part of a deliberate government strategy to use religion to undercut the legitimacy of the NLD among lay Buddhist voters (monks cannot vote in Myanmar, but potentially have a major influence on the views, and by extension voting behaviour, of their communities). While the risk of further politicization of religion in the lead up to the 2015 elections are obvious given the potential for mobilizing votes among the country's deeply devout Buddhist population, such conspiracy theories have not been supported by any concrete evidence, however, nor are they particularly persuasive. Many monks, including prominent leaders of the 969 Movement and MaBaTha, have a long history of opposition to the military government and the USDP as evident in the leading role they played in the 1988 uprising, the 2007 Saffron Revolution and recent protests against the Letpadaung copper mine. In this respect, the real concern is probably less that the rise of Buddhist nationalism can somehow help the USDP snatch the expected election victory away from the NLD, and more that it will force all the major political parties, including the NLD and ethnic parties representing Buddhist constituencies, to adopt openly discriminatory policies. In this area at least, it is far from assured that democracy in Myanmar would be consonant with international human rights.

Socio-economic Development

Myanmar's general economic performance and outlook remained positive in 2014, reflecting continued strong government commitment to reform. New figures from the World Bank, however, indicated that poverty was much more entrenched than official figures showed, thus underscoring the extent of the social challenges the country faces. Moreover, serious concerns remained about the balance between economic growth and social justice in the government's development strategy.

Real GDP growth for financial year 2013/14 (April–March) was 8.7 per cent, up from 7.3 per cent in 2012/13 and projected to increase to 9.1 per cent in 2014/15.[33] Despite the pressure from fairly large inflows of foreign investment and a weakening kyat, consumer price inflation remained stable at a manageable 5.7 per cent for 2013/14, projected to increase slightly to 6.6 per cent in 2014/15. Longer-term IMF projections suggested that both growth and inflation would remain stable for the next several years. Exports, meanwhile, grew from US$10.3 billion in 2012/13 to US$12.2 billion in 2013/14, an increase of 18 per cent, and were projected to grow further to US$15 billion in 2014/15. Imports increased even faster, generating a substantial and growing current account deficit, up from –4.3 per cent in 2012/13 to –5.4 per cent in 2013/14. However, this was covered by resurgent foreign direct investment, which hovered around US$3 billion per year.

While Myanmar's new economy thus performed robustly, supported by the country's opening to the world, there was bad news on the poverty front, although this was in some respect purely academic. Based largely on a recalculation of existing data from the 2009/10 Household Survey intended to bring them into line with current international practice, the World Bank concluded that the country's real poverty incidence at the time might have been 37 per cent rather than 26 per cent as originally found.[34] No more recent figures are available. However, since neither agricultural productivity nor industrial employment opportunities appears to have grown significantly in the meantime, despite strong economic growth, it is unlikely that the situation has improved significantly for the poorest strata.

One of the big economic stories of the year was rice exports, which were expected to total more than 1.5 million tonnes in 2014/15, the largest quantity since the 1960s.[35] Two other major developments were the roll-out of the new telecommunications networks by Norwegian Telenor and Doha-based Ooredoo, and the much anticipated award of twenty new blocks for offshore oil and gas exploration, which attracted major interest from many of the big players in the industry. By contrast, government efforts to attract more foreign direct investment, especially, in export manufacturing through the establishment of three new Special Economic Zones, showed less promise. While there was significant progress in Thilawa, near Yangon, due in large part to strong Japanese interest and support, investors continued to shy away from Dawei on the Myanmar/Thai peninsula and Kyaukphyu on Myanmar's west coast. In the latter case, the future of the project seemed particularly dim due to major uncertainties about the planned road and rail links to the Chinese border, which would be key to its success. This was not necessarily a bad thing as each of the three zones had become mired in controversy, with major concerns about corruption, land grabs and the environmental impact. Some also questioned whether Dawei and Kyaukphyu, in particular, were as economically sound as generally assumed.[36] Given the huge costs involved, both financially, socially and environmentally, this is an area where Myanmar might benefit from further careful analysis before proceeding. Nonetheless, the lack of progress in these zones weakens the country's prospects for export-driven growth, and especially the diversification away from natural resources.

From a policy perspective, 2014 lacked the highlights of the first couple of years of the reform process, but the commitment to improvement remained unwavering. Having taken the easy steps to liberalize the economy, the government in 2014 focused on improving the legal and regulatory environment in key areas, including tax, banking and foreign investment. The year saw significant financial sector reform which is key to future growth in Myanmar's capital-starved economy, including continued efforts to strengthen the capacity of the newly independent Central Bank, improve the operational environment for domestic banks and facilitate the entry of foreign banks on terms that would bolster the overall banking sector without undermining the domestic segment. The government also took an important step in developing the country's capital market by signing an agreement with two Japanese companies, Japan Exchange Group and Daiwa

Institute of Research to establish a long-awaited stock exchange in Yangon. This was all done in close cooperation with international agencies, and generally seemed to be guided by international best practice.

Key initiatives to further bolster foreign trade and investment included a new Special Economic Zones Law enacted in January 2014 and work on a new investment law which would amalgamate, and further refine, the existing foreign and domestic investment laws passed in 2012 and 2013 respectively. The new law, like so many others, was due to be brought before Parliament in the first session in 2015.

The government's stated ambition to halve poverty by 2015 was less evident in 2014. However, it did continue its efforts to increase the availability of credit to farmers and micro-enterprises through a much expanded micro-credit scheme. It also took some small but important steps to improve the conditions for workers, for example, by establishing a minimum wage and enhancing existing social security schemes.

Economists complained (perhaps a bit unfairly) that the government lacked a plan for economic reform, and (more reasonably) that more needed to be done to revitalize agriculture, accelerate industrialization and thus broaden the spread of the new growth, including through employment creation. The government, however, clearly recognized these challenges and the problem was perhaps more that it lacked the capacity to do everything at once — and to do it well — and less that it was not trying.

The more cogent criticisms perhaps came from social activists who worried that economic reforms are actually moving too fast, before adequate safeguards have been put in place to ensure that economic growth does not happen at the expense of social justice. Concerns centred especially around the push to open the country up to foreign investment and the inadequacies of the new foreign investment and land laws, which many argued favoured foreign (and domestic) investors at the expense of local communities. These issues, too, were very much on the government's radar in 2014. The application for membership of the Extractive Industries Transparency Initiative (EITI),[37] a global Standard to promote openness and accountable management of natural resources, in July confirmed what had already become evident from the government's dealings with individual investors the previous couple of years, that it was intent on ensuring that Myanmar and its people in the future would benefit more from foreign investment in the country's rich natural resources. Moreover, work underway on a Land Use Policy, which would guide the implementation of two new land laws from 2012, showed at least some recognition of the potential pitfalls of the latter for local communities and, especially, upland farmers. Importantly, the processes involved in both the EITI application and the drafting of the Land Use Policy showed, for Myanmar, unprecedented willingness on part of the government to consult with and facilitate the participation of civil society, including advocacy organisations as well as local beneficiaries.

Having said that, critics were right to be concerned. The government's instinctive approach to development is still very much top-down, with an emphasis on large-scale development projects (a bias which is perhaps not so different from that of the international financial institutions and other donors with whom the government is working closely in most areas of reform). Moreover, as already indicated, even if appropriate legal safeguards were put in place, implementation would likely remain a major problem in a country where rule of law has long meant "rule of power".

International Engagement

Despite some "tiffs" with Western parliamentarians and Chinese companies, Myanmar's relations with the outside world, and vice versa, continued to strengthen in 2014 as the country's diplomacy flourished, technical cooperation with international organizations deepened, and international economic exchanges expanded. Indeed, Myanmar's international relations, which for so long has been a negative influence on its development, were confirmed both as an important driver of change and a key protection against future reversals of the reform process.

Judging from the media headlines at the end of 2013, one might have expected Myanmar's chairmanship of ASEAN to become one of the big stories of 2014. As it turned out, this was not to be the case, at least not from a media perspective. However, this in itself is an important story. Contrary to widespread speculation that Myanmar was unprepared for this responsibility, the government pulled it off with hardly a glitch. The chairmanship became a non-story because the logistics worked. Myanmar proved able to handle the hot-button South China Sea issue; and because ASEAN critics of the country's handling of its "internal affairs" (that is, the treatment of Muslims) remained largely silent. Myanmar was helped by the fact that it was in the interest of all member states to make the chairmanship a success and thus justify the faith the organization had put in Myanmar in appointing it chair. It also helped that other member states had their own serious internal problems in 2014 and were not inclined to open that particular can of worms. None of this should distract from the fact that Myanmar performed above expectations, proving to its neighbours and critics alike that it is fast becoming a full-fledged and constructive member of the regional community. This will have increased the confidence of the country's leadership in taking further steps out onto the international stage and thus decisively closing a long and sad chapter of the country's post-independence history.

A step down from the lofty heights of international diplomacy, Myanmar in 2014 also continued to deepen its engagement with foreign donors and international organizations. This included, among many other initiatives close cooperation with the Internal Foundation of Electoral Systems and International Institute for Democracy and Electoral Assistance on elections preparations, with the European Union (EU) on police training, with the United States Agency of International Development on worker's rights, with the International Financial Institutions on economic reform and institution-building, and with Japan International Cooperation Agency (JICA) on a Yangon city Master Development Plan, as well as the establishment of embryonic military-to-military relations with the United States, the United Kingdom and Australia. Much of this was probably driven mainly by a desire to attract foreign trade and investment. However, for a country that has so long suffered from isolation, including from international standards, this new willingness to work closely with foreigners on important and often sensitive national issues is a very important marker of the commitment to reform. Together with the growing reliance on foreign economic exchanges, it also greatly decreases the risk that any group or institution in the future would risk reversing the reforms of the past four years and losing new development opportunities.

None of this is to suggest that Myanmar is abandoning its long and proud tradition of independence and non-alignment in international relations and "rolling over" for the great powers or anyone else, quite the contrary. The government made it clear on several occasions that it would brook no foreign (read: American) interference in its "internal affairs", including questions of constitutional amendments and criteria for citizenship. It also continued its efforts to renegotiate existing natural resource contracts with Chinese companies, in particular, to ensure that Myanmar receives a fairer share of the benefits, and rejected several offers of loans which were seen not to be in the national interest. This all reflected a positive strain of Myanmar nationalism, which promises to serve the country well in the rough and tumble of international geo-politics in the future. What has clearly changed though, are the knee-jerk, isolationist reactions of the past to any perceived foreign slight or threat. While elements of xenophobia persist in some circles, the current leadership understands the importance of being part of the world and the added value that international advice and support can bring to its reform efforts. Indeed, it seems that reformers have increasingly been embracing "international standards" in a range of areas as a way of empowering themselves in the struggle against more conservative groups and vested interests. This is exactly how such standards can be most useful — not as foreign values imposed through shaming or sanctions, but as frameworks voluntarily adopted to bolster locally-driven reform efforts — and, as such, it represents another positive trend with clear benefits for the reform process.

Conclusion

The sheer complexity of Myanmar's multi-stranded transition makes it extremely difficult to pass simple judgements on the performance of those who are driving it — or for that matter to identify exactly who that is. Yet, while President Obama may have had domestic political reasons for bucking the trend and insisting that the reforms are real, any objective assessment of developments in 2014 would have to conclude that many of them certainly are. There may have been some worrying events — and even a few worrying trends — but as the International Crisis Group concluded and several opinion surveys confirmed, the overall impression was that reforms continued to move forward across a broad range of areas.

To further unpack the implications of developments in 2014, it is worthwhile considering who was responsible for particular successes and failures and what the causes were of the latter. The Myanmar Government is no longer the hierarchical, and therefore largely monolithic, institution it used to be — at the very least one needs to distinguish between the Executive, the Parliament and the *Tatmadaw*. Moreover, given the nature of the reforms underway, the government is no longer as autonomous as it used to be. Many non-government actors now have significant influence over the outcome of government initiatives. President Thein Sein and key ministers and officials around him clearly remained committed to both political and economic liberalization, even if at times this may have gone against their natural inclinations. The Parliament, too, continued in many ways to play the part it is assigned in democratic theory, even if this at times meant protecting the vested interest of powerful constituencies. The *Tatmadaw* remained an obstacle to full democratization, but this was to be expected given the roadmap for change that it had laid out before 2011 and the concerns that informed that roadmap, notably about political stability. Meanwhile, the new generation of generals seemed largely content to let their former superiors, now "civilian" government leaders lead, and to exercise their own constitutional powers relatively sparingly. The most serious problems in 2014, including the failure to close the peace deal, the continuing rise of extremist Burman Buddhist nationalism, and the exploitation of new economic opportunities by the strong at the expense of the weak, all implicated a broad range of actors, both inside and outside of government, but there were also hopeful development in each of these areas, often from within an empowered civil society. It was true in 2014, as it had been in the earlier phases of the reform process that good — or at least "not too bad" — government policy often suffered from a failure of execution and therefore did not have the benefits for the general population that were intended. Yet, this too, was to be expected given the enormous task the government has set itself and the acute lack of state capacity in many areas. There is a lot of goodwill and support for reform in Myanmar today. Some of the changes that are underway may seem unbelievable in light of the country's past, but as an astute observer of Myanmar politics recently commented: "How many times do we have to see the unbelievable before it becomes believable?"[38]

2015 will be a dangerous year in Myanmar. It remains unclear if the country can face a genuine political contest without dividing further. Certainly, the current government could have used more time to bring to fruition many of the reforms it has started. However, if the main political groups manage to keep their eye on the price and avoid harmful confrontation and instability, 2015 could also become the start of a new era, both politically and economically — and then the transitional government would have truly proven itself.

Notes

1. Quoted in "Obama's Second Visit Fall Flat", 14 November 2014, available at <www.irrawaddy.org>.
2. Jean-Marie Guéhenno and Richard Horsey, "Despite the Headlines, Progress in Myanmar isn't Slipping Away", 19 November 2014, available at <www.crisisgroup.org>.
3. Marie Lall, "Hearing New Voices in the Debate on Citizenship", 10 February 2014, available at <www.mmtimes.com>.
4. International Republican Institute, "Survey of Burma Public Opinion: 24 December 2013–1 February 2014", n.d., available at <www.iri.org>.
5. Asia Foundation, "Myanmar 2014: Civic Knowledge and Values in a Changing Society", 12 November 2014, available at <www.asiafoundation.org>.

6. See for example, Burma Campaign U.K., "Parliament Committee: Re-Impose Burma Sanctions if No Improvement in Human Rights", 27 November 2014, available at <burmacampaign.org.uk>.

7. "Myanmar's Suu Kyi Says Wants West to Spur Reform not Reimpose Sanctions", 26 December 2014, available at <www.reuters.com>.

8. "President Backs Constitutional Reform in Anniversary Speech", 26 March 2014, available at <www.mizzima.com>.

9. According to senior military officers, Myanmar's stability remains fragile and therefore still requires the "strong hand" of the military. Interview by author, Deputy Minister of Defence, Brigadier General Aung Thaw, Naypyitaw, November 2013.

10. "Suu Kyi Warns Against Taking Part in 2015 Vote Without Charter Reform", 16 December 2013, available at <www.irrawaddy.org>.

11. "Three Million in Myanmar Sign Petition Seeking Military Veto Removal", 30 June 2014, available at <www.rfa.org>.

12. "Tatmadaw's Parliamentary Role in Violation of Buddhist Principles, Says NLD Leader", 19 May 2014, available at <www.mizzima.com>.

13. "No Constitutional Amendments Before Election: Shwe Mann", 18 November 2014, available at <www.dvb.no>.

14. A requirement that any constitutional amendments be ratified by the new Parliament before taking effect would seem to rule out any changes in the number of military seats in Parliament for the next government term (2016–20), but not necessarily that Aung San Suu Kyi could be elected President by that Parliament or that the selection procedures for other government officials could be changed before the relevant appointments were made.

15. Interview by author, Chit Win, Australian National University, 10 December 2014.

16. See, for example, Aung Zaw, "New Hurdles for An Already Hobbled Press", 9 March 2014, available at <www.irrawaddy.org>.

17. Interview by author, Thomas Kean, *Myanmar Times*, Yangon, December 2014.

18. "Myanmar's Military Chief Meets Journalists over Coverage Constraints", 14 October 2014, available at <www.rfa.org>.

19. Some experienced journalists, while condemning the harsh sentences meted out in a few cases in 2014, acknowledged that part of the problem was the weak professional standards of the industry itself. Interviews by author, Yangon, December 2014; see also Rhys Thompson, "Myanmar: Media Freedom and the Unity Journal Case", 30 July 2014, available at <www.lowyinterpreter.org>.

20. "Myanmar Jails Still Hold 70 Political Prisoners: AAPP", 15 December 2014, available at <www.mmtimes.com/>.

21. President Thein Sein, "Remarks at the High-Level Political Meeting", Naypyitaw, 31 October 2014 (translation in author's possession).

22. "UECs — Neutral Mediator or Ruling Party Stooge?", 19 May 2014, available at <eleven.mm.com>.

23. "Lower House Chairman Rejects PR System Proposal", 14 November 2014, available at <www.irrawaddy.org>.

24. Interviews by author, Yangon, May 2014. See also, "Another Round of Ceasefire Talks Set for September", 18 August 2014, available at <www.irrawaddy.org>; "Ceasefire Negotiators Target Union Day Signing", 24 December 2014, available at <www.mmtimes.org>.

25. "Compromises Reached on Most Ceasefire Issues", 24 December 2014, available at <www.dvb.no>.

26. Euro-Burma Office Briefing, "KNU and UNFC", September 2014.

27. "Myanmar's Wa Rebels to Join Peace Process When Time is Ripe", 30 January 2014, available at <www.rfa.org>.

28. Myanmar Peace Support Initiative, "Lessons Learned from MPSI's Work: Supporting the Peace Process in Myanmar", March 2014.

29. This followed the expulsion of Médecins Sans Frontières a month earlier after it was accused by the government of stirring up communal conflict by reporting claims of a deadly attack on a local Rohingya village.

30. The U.N. estimated that 53,000 people, mostly Rohingya, fled from Rakhine State and Bangladesh by boat in 2014 bound for Thailand and Malaysia. This was an increase of 37 per cent from the year before.

31. "Nationalist Monks Call NGOs 'Traitors' for Opposing Interfaith Marriage Bill", 14 May 2014, available at <www.irrawaddy.org>.

32. See, for example, U.S. Commission on International Religious Freedom, "Burma: Religious Freedom and Related Human Rights Violations are Hindering Broader Reforms", a field visit report, September 2014.

33. Unless otherwise stated, figures in this section are from IMF. "Myanmar: 2014 Article IV Consultation — Staff Report", October 2014.

34. World Bank, "Ending Poverty and Boosting Shared Prosperity in Myanmar", December 2014.

35. "Rice Exports to Top 1.5 Million Tonnes", 22 December 2014, available at <www.mmtimes.com>.

36. See, for example, Josh Wood, "Myanmar's Special Economic Zones, Part I–III", 23–25 October 2014, available at <asiapacific.anu.edu.au/newmandala>.

37. The EITI is a global Standard to promote openness and accountable management of natural resources, including full disclosure of taxes and other payments made by oil, gas and mining companies to governments.

38. Interview by author, Don Higgins, Myanmar Peace Centre, Yangon, December 2014.

ONGOING CONFLICT IN THE KACHIN STATE

Mandy Sadan

Background to the Conflict

Even casual observers of the Myanmar political scene will be aware that one of the most difficult and enduring problems that continues to challenge the country's political transition is the need to find a resolution to the manifold conflicts that have taken place in the so-called "ethnic" states.[1] One of the longest of these conflicts has been in the Kachin State, in the north of the country. The Kachin Independence Army was founded in 1961 and entered into armed conflict with the central military regime following General Ne Win's takeover of power in 1962. Although there were some attempts to broker ceasefires during the following decades, the fighting continued more or less without cessation until 1994, when an agreement to retain arms but refrain from violence was eventually signed. In June 2011, this ceasefire in turn collapsed after being in place for seventeen years and the conflict has since then remained stubbornly impervious to resolution. It is proving as difficult as ever it was in the past to find a way forward through negotiation, and the national peace process, centred upon the conclusion of a nationwide ceasefire with all principal ethnic armed groups as promoted by the national government, is floundering once more.[2]

It is a convention in almost any policy document or analysis of the Kachin conflict to begin with a longer history of the Kachin region, often invoking, too, a pseudo-anthropological interpretation of kinship and lineage as perennial markers of "Kachin" identity and a means of explaining the nature of this enduring resistance. Typically, too, such analysis will describe the Kachin experience under colonial rule as a decisive factor in explaining the continuation

MANDY SADAN is Reader in the History of South East Asia and Associate Dean (Research), Faculty of Arts & Humanities, SOAS, University of London.

of problems down to the present. This includes the political separation of the Frontier Areas from the rest, the military privileging of ethnic recruits into the colonial army and then the failure and ongoing symbolism of the Panglong Agreement of 1947.[3] The agreement was signed by General Aung San and a number of elite representatives of "ethnic minority" communities with the intention of facilitating the speedy withdrawal of British imperial power on the basis of a future commitment by the Burmese nationalist government to introducing a federal system.[4] This over-arching historical narrative, which is used to explain the emergence and rationale of the Kachin conflict down to the present, is so well-rehearsed that it has become almost impossible to resist.

Yet there is a case for saying that the continued repetition of the same historical narrative to explain the Kachin conflict, and others, has served mainly to naturalize, even to normalize the prevalence of conflict in this region. As a result, more penetrating analysis of the present re-emergence of conflict in the Kachin region is often lacking because the causes are already felt to be known and understood. One outcome of this tendency to normalize conflict rather than subject its longevity and resilience to a careful critical questioning is that there is a tendency also to believe that it will only be fully resolved when there is capitulation of the weaker to the stronger political impetus, of the "traditional" to the "modern" — in this case, the innate drive of the unitary state must inevitably win out over that of the federal with its implicit attachments to perennial loyalties.[5] The sense of frustration with "the Kachin" is palpable among those Myanmar and foreign policymakers and observers who seem mainly to wish that they would stop fighting a battle that they are bound to lose, and which they consider currently as producing a great impediment to political progress nationally.

From the perspective of central government concerns, this seems to be a not unreasonable line of analysis. However, if we are to understand why in 2014 we are in many respects as far from an agreement to end the conflict than we were in 2013, closer attention needs to be paid to understanding a more contemporary history rather than relying on convention within a narrative about a more distant past. While this longer history is threaded through the present situation, not least in the symbolic justifications of resistance and in a prevailing social memory of injustices borne, developments since the signing of the ceasefire in 1994 also require our attention.[6] These developments have created a newly politicized movement in urban areas of the Kachin region that have been vitally important in creating social support for the resumption of conflict, and which has gone a long way to reversing the decline of the Kachin Independence Army's (KIA's) and Kachin Indepdendence Organization's (KIO's) civil support base in the years between

1994 and 2008. These developments have brought in newly active nationalist inspired groups of young Kachin people, who have become energized in the cause of Kachin ethno-nationalism in a digital age. Understanding the dynamics of this rapidly changing Kachin society is as important for understanding the intransigent nature of the current conflict and the failure to bring resolution to it in 2014 as is that of the longer view.

The Signing and Breaking of Ceasefires

The ceasefire between the KIA and the *Tatmadaw* (Myanmar Armed Forces) in 1994 was one of many that were enabled from the late 1980s onwards between the Burma Army and the country's many non-national armed groups.[7] The changing geo-politics of the region at this time helped the Myanmar military government to reposition itself favourably in relation to these developments. These changes in the wider political arena also made the conclusion of ceasefire agreements a more attractive proposition to many non-national armed groups than it had been previously. Two external factors were particularly important in this respect, and both seemed to weaken the position of "ethnic" armed groups to resist pressures to conclude ceasefires.[8] The first of these was the collapse of the Communist bloc, which saw also the collapse of the Communist Party of Burma or CPB. The CPB had long played a critical role in many of the conflict zones, especially along the eastern and northeastern borders of the country. The second factor was the changed orientation of Thailand and China in particular to negotiating with the Myanmar regime. Both nations increasingly sought to engage directly with the Myanmar Government to build political relations and to facilitate access to natural resources within the country. Previously, their concerns had been more with local security control in border areas, which had been effected through relying on ethnic nationality and opposition groups in the borderlands to contain local conflict zones. Most non-national armed groups agreed to ceasefires following these changes, relinquishing some territory while keeping other areas ostensibly under their control. This was the pattern that also influenced the KIA in 1994 to conclude a ceasefire agreement. However, because the early ceasefires were arranged without clear agreements about how to implement a proper process of political reform beyond the cessation of violence, they amounted mainly just to the absence of fighting and not the establishment of genuine peace in many cases. The promise that political discussions would follow in due course was taken largely in good faith and on the back of the weakened position of many groups to insist on this later process, as noted.[9]

Yet this notwithstanding, many ceasefire groups, including the KIA/KIO, for their part agreed to halt armed conflict whilst having a range of objectives in mind of their own should the hoped for political progress not materialize, which was for many a highly probable outcome. For the KIA/KIO, the ceasefire also represented an opportunity to re-group after so many decades of conflict and to reconnect with the civilian populations from which they had become increasingly isolated. The nature of these conflicts, which saw the troops of non-national armed groups ensconced in the hills and mountains away from the towns, meant that armed groups had become increasingly isolated over time from the civil and especially urban constituencies from whom they needed to draw support. Following the ceasefire, the KIO leadership hoped that they would be able to reconnect with Kachin people in areas from which the KIO and KIA had been excluded for many years. These concerns about rebuilding the social, political and economic base of their movement also influenced their desire to conclude a ceasefire for some of the Kachin politico-military elites responsible for making the critical decision.[10]

The Kachin ceasefire was considered at the time something of a coup for the national military regime. It was hoped that the Kachin agreement would become an example for how armed militias could be brought back within the national fold and "tamed" towards a common political purpose of national unitary government. From the outset, therefore, the intentions and perspectives of what the ceasefire might bring for both sides were at best uncertain and taken on trust and at worst, potentially highly contradictory between the various signatories. The key issue, however, was that the agreements were made without any clear political framework for developing lines of further communication around substantive issues of political grievance.

The local developments leading to the collapse of the ceasefire in June 2011 have been fairly well documented.[11] The breakdown centred upon government attacks upon KIA troops close to the Ta-pein hydropower plant and subsequent retaliations by the KIA, with progressive escalation of attacks on both sides through the summer of 2011. However, the lead time to the breakdown was much longer than this local problem in June 2011 suggests. Indeed, the fact that the conflict was sparked in territory adjacent to a Chinese-owned hydropower plant also reflects that developments during the ceasefire had created a range of new issues in the region that influenced local perceptions of the ceasefire and its outcomes.[12] The response to these, not least of which was a perception of the progressive exclusion of local to foreign economic interests in the exploitation of the region's natural resources, continued to undermine the notion that the ceasefire and current processes of political reform were capable of delivering substantive, positive economic and political change.

By 2011, the Myanmar state was probably stronger than it had ever been due to the economic gains it had made through oil and gas and other natural resource exploitation.[13] It was also bolstered by increasing engagement with the international community following the re-emergence of Daw Aung San Suu Kyi into national political life. Initially, all opposition forces raised questions about the future direction of political progress, given the continued strengthening of the Myanmar Armed Forces and the extension of state and military influence in the Kachin region and elsewhere. When combined with the limited capacity of the political reforms to remove the dominance of the military, there was some credence to the accusation that foreign governments had perhaps responded too enthusiastically to what were, in essence, quite limited signs of real change. The lack of attention to ethnic nationality concerns by these foreign powers, at least initially, may have even inadvertently weakened the capacity of ethnic interest groups to have their concerns addressed. Not least of these concerns was whether the constitutional mechanisms in place to defend against future institutional violence were genuine and viable. While even Burmese opposition politicians raised concerns about many problematic features embedded in the constitutional proposals, a primary concern especially for non-Burman political interest groups, who felt that control over their economic resource base was slipping out of their hands, was intense uncertainty about how much reform would be allowed by a government and political system that continued to be dominated by the Myanmar Armed Forces.

The inevitable conclusion many drew from this situation was that the new arrangements being proposed for a national ceasefire and the reconfiguration of large non-national armies as small Border Guard Forces were not focused enough towards "genuine peace": they aimed mainly at the cessation of fighting rather than being directed towards substantive forward movement politically. By June 2011, therefore, the decision to continue with the escalation of conflict rather than withdraw and pursue its containment reflected very strongly that the cessation of fighting during the 1990s was now understood as being a juncture that had allowed the Myanmar Army to penetrate new areas that had previously resisted that penetration, while also enabling them to engage in the preferential exploitation of natural resources, which is often referred to as a process of "ceasefire capitalism".[14]

These developments, however, also created new forms of social opposition prior to June 2011. This is reflected across the country in protests objecting to hydroelectric Dam projects, for example. Protests over copper mines and the Myitsone Dam as seen in the years building up to the collapse of the ceasefire reflected underlying and significant processes of social transformation that were felt in the urban areas of Kachin State as much as in central Myanmar.[15] This has resulted in a newly politicized social domain within Kachin society in recent years, especially among urban youth and diaspora Kachin groups, that draws on new forms of communication and has sharpened expectations in relation to the nature of political progress that they are prepared to consider "genuine". These developments have created new challenges for elite leadership of the Kachin nationalist movement, too. They have also had to modify their modes of interaction with the political-civil constituency of modern, urban Kachin society to reflect this more broad-ranging politicization. In this respect, the desire to use the ceasefire of 1994 to build a strong civil political culture had clearly been realized, although perhaps not entirely in ways that were anticipated by the nationalist leadership who concluded the ceasefire in 1994.

The experience of the ceasefire 1994–2011, therefore, has in many ways become a marker of the antithesis of real political progress that highlights instead the limitations of engaging in such agreements unless the political terrain is made more stable. This has, again, progressively made a return to a ceasefire agreement harder to implement, even though 2013 seemed to suggest that there was some progress in this regard.[16] These newly politicized demographic groups were able to ally themselves increasingly to more focused demands from within the KIA/KIO leadership following 2011, that an end to the present conflict could not now be a matter of hope over experience: agreements would have to be managed and responded to on a political level if "genuine" peace was to be achieved. It is this internal dynamic within Kachin society that has also made the resolution of conflict throughout 2014 more difficult to facilitate, given the way in which support for continuing the conflict has coalesced.[17]

Ending the Year on a Low Note?

It would be preferable to begin a review of events relating to the ongoing conflict in the Kachin State during 2014 with a statement that some of the optimism that had been demonstrated at the end of 2013 had continued to bear fruit. Since the violence of June 2011, there had been numerous low-level incidents but there were also repeated efforts to try to find a basis upon which substantive discussions could take place to halt the fighting. 2013 ended on a somewhat optimistic note in this respect and things boded well for events in 2014 to be more positive.

The tensions that were starting to build between those groups who were now engaged in recent ceasefire agreements and those who were not were one major issue of concern for KIA/KIO elites. 2013 ended with a significant meeting taking place in Laiza, the border town which some refer to as "the real Kachin capital", between leaders of many ethnic armed groups facilitated by the KIA. The meeting hoped to develop a coherent multi-group strategy that would prevent too great a divide being created between current ceasefire and non-ceasefire groups. This reflected some challenge to the government's push towards a national ceasefire, which many observers now felt was to be an almost inevitable outcome of the current political trajectory. The light that the continuing conflict shone on government attitudes to genuine reform towards greater autonomy of "ethnic" states within a unified Myanmar in many ways began to empower the KIA/KIO at this time, enabling them to progress their desire to build coalitions with other groups to counteract the fragmentation that the recent ceasefires and peace negotiations seemed to generate. The KIA/KIO has long been at the forefront of such strategies of multi-group cooperation,[18] and it maps also onto internal models of allegiance-building that have, overall, served the Kachin ethno-nationalist cause well.[19]

In October 2013, therefore, the "ethnic" conference in Laiza saw a wide range of groups with ethnic nationality allegiances meet to discuss how to develop a more united strategy. The absence of such a strategy has long been the stumbling block of ethnic resistance, as well as being a cause of frustration for those who might wish to support them. Clarifying the diverse agendas and orientations of multiple groups locked in what might appear superficially to be highly local interests has been a persistent challenge. The eighteen groups who attended preliminary discussions at Laiza also wanted to put forward an alternative to the national ceasefire proposals that had been promoted by the government and in different form by the United Nationalities Federal Council (UNFC)[20] and Working Group on Ethnic Coordination (WGEC) respectively. The alternative they tried to develop focused on the higher political objectives desired by these long-term resistance movements: the need for substantive political dialogue and changes to the Constitution to ensure democratic governance, as well as respect for claims for greater autonomy and the higher values of human rights. Despite the fundamental and huge differences in the pathways to national ceasefire that these various documents proposed, the difficulty in the detail was considered by some observers, who longed for the blocks to a national ceasefire to be removed, as largely a circumstantial issue of lesser importance than the fact that some negotiations or discussions were being resumed. This is what made the development seem hopeful at the end of 2013.

Following the ethnic conference, the government peace negotiating team met with the KIA/KIO. The delegation was led by U Aung Min and his expressed intention was to pursue a political process through an agreed framework. Monthly meetings were then held between a KIO Technical Advisory Team and government representatives to develop constructive lines of engagement. The United Nations Special Adviser on Myanmar, Vijay Nambiar, also expressed his hope and expectation that a breakthrough might be found. In short, at the end of 2013 it was felt by many observers and analysts that a national ceasefire was still a viable outcome during the next few months and that resist or not, the Kachin politico-military elites would be drawn into this process almost as an inevitability.

Yet there was a counter-analysis to this optimism from the start. On the Kachin side, the Myitkyina meetings saw a massive local outpouring of support for the KIA leadership as they rode in convoy through the town to discuss the pathways to agreement.[21] This local outpouring reflected the widespread anger at the displacement of many thousands of people to border refugee camps over the previous two years. The United Nations estimates that as many as 100,000 civilians have been displaced during this time.[22] The local sense is that there is disinterest in this human suffering among all political groups in mainstream political life and a general unwillingness to engage substantially with the political issues of concern in this region. Increasingly this has included a sense of distrust of Daw Aung San Suu Kyi herself, further widening the gulf between the local and the national.[23] Yet the likelihood of success in the talks was diminished by the insistence by Lt Gen Myit Soe of the Ministry of Defence that ethnic groups would have to trust the government to act on their behalf. This has been the sticking point since the collapse of the quasi-federal state in Burma over decades: how can trust be built in the national political system when it seems to be enshrined in policies and practices determined to undermine the federal autonomy that so many see as a viable way ahead? Trust must surely be earned following so many years of mistrust is the not unreasonable retort; it is in this regard that the history of the recent ceasefire is so critical to understanding present difficulties. The Laiza agreement signed by seventeen of the eighteen ethnic armed group representatives present was a new testing ground for working out the orientation of political negotiations to follow in 2014. That it ultimately shone a light on the impossibility of moving forward negotiations along anything other than government-defined lines of least resistance led, throughout 2014, to the gradual unravelling in this year of the national ceasefire accord as a whole.[24]

The gulf between expectations that substantive talks about political change should form a basis for developing further talks has remained too difficult to bridge. Regrettably, therefore, as noted, 2014 has seen few positive developments towards ending the conflict in Kachin State. Indeed, in many respects, the two sides seem as far apart as ever. As 2014 has passed, the recurring violence between the KIA and the *Tatmadaw* has continued to influence perceptions that the desire of the civil-military Myanmar Government to bring about true political transformation, which respected the interests of "ethnic" communities, was less than genuine. Perhaps even more significantly, the ongoing antagonism created around the situation in the Kachin region seems now to be drawing into its orbit increasing numbers of representatives from other ethnic groups who were initially inclined favourably towards signing a national ceasefire agreement, making this cornerstone of the government's peace plan seem more out of reach than ever it was at the end of 2013.

The recurrent, low-level violence that continued to surface in many parts of the country throughout the year, including increasingly a return to low-level violence in the northern Shan states, has had a corrosive effect upon attempts at trust-building.[25] In addition, the ongoing actions of radical Burmese Buddhist groups and anti-Islamic violence has sharpened the sense among many of the country's non-Burman communities that the same prejudices and chauvinism of Burmese nationalism that has long undermined attempts to have their grievances addressed at a national political level are simply being manifested in another way.[26] The gap between many of the ethnic constituencies and the government seems to widen as time goes by and in the absence of substantial progress around key political issues and the roller-coaster continues. The year 2014, therefore, drew to a close on a sombre note that merely highlights the incredible difficulties that inhibit Myanmar as a whole moving towards a stable political future based on democratic institutions, which might be capable of resolving finally these entrenched hostilities.

The year in Kachin State has drawn to a close marked by events on 19 November, when shells were fired by the Burma Army Light Infantry

Battalion 390 from their position on Hka Ya Bum, a mountain just outside Laiza. Hka Ya Bum has particular relevance in local expressions of Kachin nationalist anger at recent events as it was taken by the *Tatmadaw* following a series of unprecedented air strikes around Laiza at the end of 2012 and continuing into 2013.[27] Howitzer shells of 105-mm landed on the parade ground of the Officer Training School of the Kachin Independence Army, which is located on Woi Chyai Bum, another mountain close to the border town. Initial reports following the shelling of the Officer Training School stated that twenty-three young officer cadets had been killed, many of whom were not Kachin but came from a number of different ethnic armed groups, while a similar number had been wounded. Unsurprisingly, the attacks were immediately followed by claims and counter claims from both sides: it was an "accident", said a Burma Army spokesman initially;[28] it was a deliberate provocation, claimed the KIA; it was a "warning shot" to force the KIA to cease from its attacks upon columns of the Burma Army patrolling nearby roads and routes.[29] One thing that seems to have been generally agreed, however, was that the shelling was yet another blow to trust-building and to the peace talks that had failed to move forward as part of the country's reform programme following a year of skirmishes, attacks and low-level violence.[30]

Yet shells continued to be fired from the Burma Army post over the following week, suggesting that "accident" was certainly not a viable explanation of the initial action. Some of these shells landed perilously close to civilian areas and the tragic human settlements that have sprung up close to the border to house the many thousands of internally displaced people forced to flee their homes since the collapse of the ceasefire in June 2011. Indeed, incidents such as these have prompted even some of the most experienced, long-term analysts of the country's ethnic politics, who are often highly sceptical of conspiracy theorists and projections of grand schemes of targeted persecution, to suspect that the Kachin movement may justifiably see itself as being subject to a special form of discrimination and punishment to finally force it to buckle and become compliant with government demands in the absence of openings for imposing a ceasefire. In this respect, the use of air strikes upon KIA strongholds and close to the civilian areas of Laiza, which was a previously unseen strategy in *Tatmadaw* engagements with ethnic armed groups, seems to ring true.

For any outside observer who remains perplexed at the ongoing, apparently intransigent resistance of the KIO to acquiesce to pressures for a renewed ceasefire throughout 2014, the recent shelling of the Officer Training School therefore raises more issues for consideration than just simply the pointlessness of the bloodshed. While the creation of the Officer Training School reflected outwardly the ongoing, entrenched militarized ethno-nationalism that had marked the post-colonial history of the Kachin State, the creation of the Training School in 2007 also reflected other issues. It represented the integration of yet another generation of young Kachin men into the formal military structures of the movement, and a specifically contingent set of concerns around the pressures being placed then on the KIA to disband and form a Border Guard Force and for its political representatives to blend themselves into the backdrop of political reforms around the National Convention and the Constitution. In this sense, it represented yet another new phase of developments and not just the repetitive cycling of perennial, even archaic ones.[31] While these new orientations inevitably drew strength from a narrative of the past, the officer cadets were clearly a new demographic group choosing to sign up to a variety of armed groups that were concurrently being pressured to disarm.

In April 2014, KIA Deputy Commander in Chief, General Gun Maw, visited the United States.[32] Increasingly it seems clear that what happens next to resolve the conflict in the region will be influenced significantly by international affairs, and most specifically by the degree to which China and the United States use this region as a proxy or testing ground for their own regional rivalries.[33] This wider geo-political rivalry may have unforeseen consequences as it is played out. However, the Chinese influence may be the one factor capable of promoting a renewed ceasefire in the short term, as authorities in China, who have also worked hard at building strong relations with the Jingpo national minority elites on the China side of the border, seem to be more interested in a cessation of violence than either, apparently, the Myanmar Army or the KIO/KIA. However, the particular cross-border concerns with China and issues of resource extraction and economic development in the region create an overarching, highly complex geo-political situation that is generally unstable and unpredictable. It is undoubtedly difficult for the KIO to manage these broader influences in their own interests, whatever their capacity to generate linkages across borderlines.

The relationship with and involvement of China, therefore, remain critical in this process. While the Chinese authorities do not actively support the KIO, neither do they entirely trust the Myanmar Government, which many in China see as unreliable.[34] At the same time as top-level meetings between Burmese and Chinese officials have been taking place, therefore, increased unofficial engagements between the KIO and authorities in China have also been seen. The Kachin politico-military elites have tried to take advantage of this in producing a language of negotiation, emphasizing longer term historical connections between the region and China, through the jade trade, for example. Some Kachin elites have tried to emphasize their closer ethnic/historical ties to the Han as opposed to the Burmese in this respect, as a means of negotiating preferential or sympathetic relations with local authorities in Yunnan. However, negotiation meetings have been challenging as the Kachin have also found the Chinese to be overbearing; some Chinese negotiators find the Kachin elites politically shrewd but lacking insight or power to negotiate a better deal for themselves, making the relationship between the two unstable and fraught as the stakes become higher for both sides. Chinese perceptions of the Burmese state are also marked by suspicion and there is a fear of contemporary Myanmar being "used" by the USA. It seems clear to many observers, too, that the Myanmar state itself is not ready for big Chinese investment and the overt extension of their economic and political ambitions through the Kachin region which, again, may result in unintended or unanticipated consequences of a renewed ceasefire without solid foundations for political progress. This is especially likely given the current emphasis on the cessation of fighting rather than substantive political forward movement. The lessons of the recent past are that this leads mainly to unfulfilled aspirations and an ever-sharpening sense of frustration with a possible descent to further forms of violence in the future. As the focus of attention at the end of 2014 now shifts to concerns about the general election in 2015, the terrain seems just as unstable.

Notes

1. Martin T. Smith, *Burma: Insurgency and the Politics of Ethnicity* (London: Zed Books, 1999); Ashley South, *Ethnic Politics in Burma: States of Conflict* (Abingdon: Routledge, 2008).

2. Aung Naing Oo, "The nationwide ceasefire agreement at a glance", *Myanmar Times*, 30 July 2014, available at <http://www.mmtimes.com/index.php/national-news/11219-the-nationwide-ceasefire-agreement-at-a-glance.html>.

3. Smith, *Burma: Insurgency and the Politics of Ethnicity* gives the best overview of this period affecting ethnic politics down to the 1990s. For a detailed historical account that seeks to challenge some of the historical simplifications that prevails, see also Mandy Sadan, *Being and Becoming Kachin: Histories Beyond the State in the Borderworlds of Burma* (Oxford: The British Academy and Oxford University Press, 2013).

4. Matthew Walton, "Ethnicity, Conflict and History in Burma: The Myths of Panglong", *Asian Survey* 48, no. 6 (2008).

5. Robert H. Taylor, "Perceptions of Ethnicity in the Politics of Burma", *Southeast Asian Journal of Social Sciences* 10, no. 1 (1982).

6. See also "Ceasefire: Reflections on community politics and social change in the Kachin region of Burma (Myanmar), 1994 to the present", SOAS, University of London, 12 October 2013, available at <http://soasceasefireseminar.weebly.com/seminar-reportsummary.html>.

7. Mary P. Callahan, *Political Authority in Burma's Ethnic Minority States: Devolution, Occupation and Coexistence* (Washington, D.C.: East-West Center, 2007).

8. See Lee Jones, "Understanding Myanmar's Ceasefires: Geopolitics, Political Economy and Statebuilding", in *Kachin Ceasefire: Reflections on Community, Politics and Social Change in the Kachin Region of Burma (Myanmar), 1994 to the Present*, edited by Mandy Sadan (NIAS Press, forthcoming 2015).

9. Ibid.

10. See Martin Smith, "Reflections on the Kachin Ceasefire: A Cycle of Hope and Disappointment", in Sadan, ed., forthcoming 2015.

11. For a good survey of news coverage since the re-emergence of conflict in June 2011, see <http://www.networkmyanmar.org/index.php/kachin-state>.

12. Kevin Woods, "Community Forestry in Cease-Fire Zones in Kachin State, Northern Burma: Formalizing Collective Property in Contested Ethnic Areas", paper presented at the CAPRi Workshop on Collective Action, Property Rights and Conflict in Natural Resources Management, Siem Reap, Cambodia, 2010; Kevin Woods, "Ceasefire Capitalism: Military-Private Partnerships, Resource Concessions and Military State Building in the Burma-China Borderlands", *Journal of Peasant Studies* 38, no. 4 (2011).

13. Lee Jones, in Sadan, ed., forthcoming 2015.

14. Woods, "Ceasefire Capitalism: Military-Private Partnerships, Resource Concessions and Military State Building in the Burma-China Borderlands".

15. See also "Ceasefire: Reflections on community politics and social change in the Kachin region of Burma (Myanmar), 1994 to the present", op. cit.

16. Mizzima, "The Conflict in Kachin State", 1 April 2015, available at <http://www.networkmyanmar.org/index.php/kachin-state>.

17. See also "Ceasefire: Reflections on community politics and social change in the Kachin region of Burma (Myanmar), 1994 to the present", op. cit. and Sadan, ed., forthcoming 2015.

18. Smith, *Burma: Insurgency and the Politics of Ethnicity*.

19. Sadan, *Being and Becoming Kachin: Histories Beyond the State in the Borderworlds of Burma*.

20. Myanmar Peace Monitor, "United Nationalities Federal Council", available at <http://www.mmpeacemonitor.org/stakeholders/unfc>. The KIO had been important in the early development of the UNFC and these divergences were now a consequence of divisions between those groups prepared to engage in ceasefires and those that were not.

21. Saw Yan Naing, "Thousands Greet Convoy of Ethnic Leaders in Myitkyina", *The Irrawaddy*, 3 November 2013, available at <http://www.irrawaddy.org/burma/thousands-greet-convoy-ethnic-leaders-myitkyina.html>.

22. Joseph Lipes, "Nearly Two Dozen Kachin Rebels Killed in Myanmar Military Attack", Radio Free Asia, 19 November 2014, available at <http://www.rfa.org/english/news/myanmar/attack-11192014161203.html>.

23. "Suu Kyi claims no need to speak out on Kachin conflict", Kachin News Group, 29 November 2013, available at <http://www.kachinnews.com/news/2602-suu-kyi-claims-no-need-to-speak-out-on-kachin-conflict.html>.

24. Murray Hiebert and Phuong Nguyen, "High Stakes in Myanmar's Peace Process", *Asia Sentinel*, 22 August 2014, available at <http://www.asiasentinel.com/politics/high-stakes-myanmar-peace-process>.

25. Shan Human Rights Foundation, available at <http://www.shanhumanrights.org>.

26. Matthew Walton, "The 'Wages of Burman-Ness': Ethnicity and Burman Privilege in Contemporary Myanmar", *Journal of Contemporary Asia* 43, no. 1 (2013). See also the many useful articles in the international media written by Matthew Walton on this issue collated at <http://oxford.academia.edu/MatthewWalton>.

27. "UN Warns Burma on Airstakes in Kachin", *VOA News*, 2 January 2013, available at <http://www.voanews.com/content/un-warns-burma-on-airstrikes-in-kachin/1576741.html>.

28. Hnin Yadana Zaw and Nyein Nyein, "Burma Army Says Deadly Shelling of Rebels Was 'Unintentional'", *The Irrawaddy*, 20 November 2014, available at <http://www.irrawaddy.org/burma/burma-army-says-deadly-shelling-rebels-unintentional.html>.

29. Aung Hla Tun and Jared Ferrie, "Myanmar army says deadly strike against rebels meant only as 'warning'", Reuters, 21 November 2004, available at <http://www.reuters.com/article/2014/11/21/us-myanmar-kachin-idUSKCN0J50J920141121>.

30. Thomas Fuller, "Burmese Rebels' Deaths Hurt Peace Talks", *New York Times*, 20 November 2014, available at <http://www.nytimes.com/2014/11/21/world/asia/peace-talks-in-myanmar-jeopardized-by-killing-of-rebels.html?emc=edit_tnt_20141120&nlid=21134157&tntemail0=y&_r=1>.

31. See Sadan, ed., forthcoming 2015.

32. "Kachin Rebel General Makes US Visit Amid Fighting at Home", Radio Free Asia, 14 April 2014, available at <http://www.rfa.org/english/news/myanmar/gun-maw-04142014174506.html>.

33. See Lee Jones, op. cit., forthcoming 2015 and Enze Han, "Changing Sino-Myanmar Relations and Its Implications for Ethnic Politics along the Border", in Sadan, ed., forthcoming 2015.

34. "Ceasefire: Reflections on community politics and social change in the Kachin region of Burma (Myanmar), 1994 to the present", op. cit.

Philippines

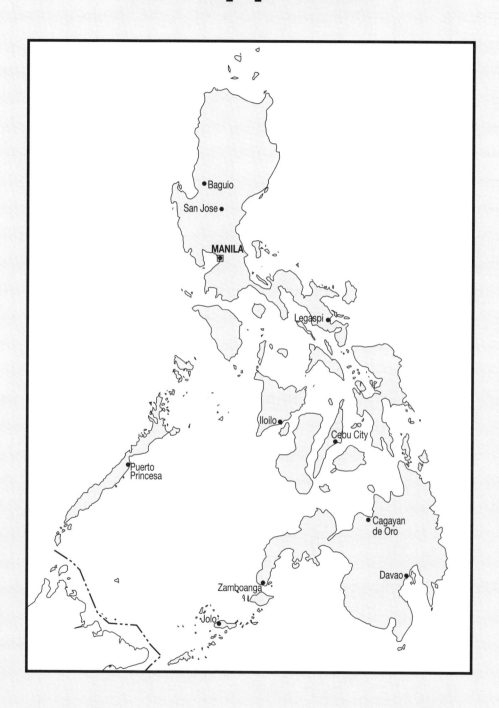

THE PHILIPPINES IN 2014
The More Things Stay the Same

Malcolm Cook

The year 2014 reaffirmed the strongest underlying assumption of resilient continuity in Philippine political studies and by all early indicators 2015 will as well. This idea of resilient continuity is at the core of most academic and journalistic analysis of the Philippines. David Timberman referred to the Philippines as "changeless land", while the last two *Southeast Asian Affairs'* Philippines chapters also were organized around this prevalent idea.[1] Structure determines agency.

The preponderant view is that this powerful, resilient continuity is bad for Philippine society and is deeply rooted in the nature of the Philippine political system (cacique democracy), domestic economy (booty capitalism) and controversially a damaged post-colonial culture.[2] This sobering often defeatist image of the country heavily affects many Filipinos' own views of their state and nation. A minority of local scholars have challenged this dominant narrative on both nationalist and analytical grounds while noting that most of its seminal works are by American scholars. These repeated challenges have had little effect.[3]

The single six-year term of Benigno Aquino III, which in 2014 moved from its mid-term to late-term phase, acts as a good test of this resilient and negative continuity assumption. President Benigno 'PNoy' Aquino III personally reaffirms political elite continuity being the son of the Philippines' first post-Marcos president, Corazon Aquino, and the leading anti-Marcos politician, Benigno Aquino Jr., as well as the present scion of one of the most powerful Philippine political dynasties.

MALCOLM COOK is a Senior Fellow at the Institute of Southeast Asian Studies (ISEAS), Singapore. He was the Dean, School of International Studies, Flinders University from 2011 to 2014.

His popularity in the 2010 elections, when he won the largest plurality of all post-Marcos presidential elections, was derived much more from the popular attraction of his family name and enhanced by sympathy from the death of his mother in August 2009 than by his unimpressive twelve-year record as a legislator.

Yet by 2010, the Philippine economy was already the strongest performer in maritime Southeast Asia and had sailed through the global financial crisis largely unperturbed. It belied the country's "sick man of Asia" moniker and the assumption that political continuity in the Philippines predetermines economic stasis especially in comparison to its previously higher-performing Southeast Asian neighbours.

This chapter argues that the economic and political year of 2014 reinforces the dominant assumption about political continuity and its bad social outcomes while showing that the economy as a whole and even the economic reform agenda are not necessarily predetermined to stasis, elite capture and bad social outcomes. The chapter will briefly look at the developments in 2014 in four areas; national politics, the peace process with the Moro Islamic Liberation Front, the national economy and foreign policy. It will not consider the fallout and recovery from super-typhoon Haiyan (Yolanda in the Philippines) as this is the subject of the following chapter.

National Politics

Two structural continuities of Philippine politics, corruption scandals, the early creeping onset of the president's late-term lame duck status and the reallocation of political energy and focus to the next presidential and congressional elections, largely consumed national politics in 2014. On the corruption front, as expected, President Aquino's 2010 campaign emphasized his anti-corruption commitment, criticized with justification the previous Macapagal-Arroyo administration's impressive corruption (not anti-corruption) record and promised a "straight and narrow path" (*tuwid na daan*) administration not deterred or diverted by corruption. The fact that the President came from one of the wealthiest and most established political dynasties and boasts a political career yet to be sullied by corruption claims supported many Filipinos' faith that this President and his administration may actually walk this less-travelled path.

Until mid-2014, Philippine voters across the archipelago and economic classes were steadfast in this faith. According to Social Weather Stations polling, President Aquino is the only post-Marcos president to maintain positive net results for their administration's attempts to eradicate graft and corruption. All

Aquino's predecessors including his mother started their administrations with positive ratings on this issue before quickly plummeting into negative territory where they stayed for the remainder of their terms. Yet from mid-2014 onwards, Aquino's net ratings in the Social Weather Stations' quarterly polls, while still positive, began to slide. In corroboration, a September 2014 Pulse Asia survey recorded 36 per cent of respondents disagreeing with the statement that the President has "fulfilled his promise to follow a straight path" and only 29 per cent agreeing with it.[4]

A trio of ongoing corruption scandals from mid-2013 are behind the erosion of popular faith in Aquino's anti-corruption credentials. As Renato Cruz de Castro noted, the "mother of all scams" linked to the illegal use of public funds by politicians through the unconstitutional Priority Development Assistance Fund (PDAF) dominated national media coverage from July 2013.[5] In 2014, this rolling scandal led to the filing of graft charges against and incarceration of three leading opposition senators, Juan Ponce Enrile, 'Jinggoy' Estrada and Ramon 'Bong' Revilla Jr. The fact that only three opposition leaders have been arrested despite the majority of senators and representatives benefiting from this dismantled pork barrel scheme led to widespread accusations of selective justice favouring the administration and hurting the opposition led by Vice-President Jejomar Binay, the country's most popular and trusted politician.[6]

This scam in 2013 was overtaken in 2014 by the Disbursement Acceleration Programme (DAP) scandal that saw the Supreme Court rule as unconstitutional the Aquino administration budget reallocation scheme masterminded by Budget Secretary Florencio 'Butch' Abad. In its two years of existence, the programme was responsible for the reallocation of close to 180 billion pesos (US$4.08 billion) of government funds without congressional approval, much of which government employee bodies claimed came from funds for their benefits and pensions.[7]

Rather than accept the Supreme Court ruling and calls for Abad to step down, Aquino mounted a full-scale defence of his long-time friend and 2010 campaign manager Abad and publicly attacked the Supreme Court and called for constitutional amendments to weaken the power of the judiciary. While not a corruption scandal per se, the peak of the DAP scandal and Aquino's attack on the Supreme Court coincided with the sharpest drop in his administration's popularity and anti-corruption ratings. While the PDAF scandal suggested to many the selective justice against opposition, the DAP one and Abad's continuation as Budget Secretary suggest selective justice in favour of the administration and a presidential predilection to attack the judiciary in defence of political and personal peers.

National politics in the second half of 2014 was diverted by the re-opening of long-known and previously investigated graft charges against Vice-President Binay and his wife, Elenita Binay, relating to their periods as Mayor of Makati City.[8] The National Bureau of Investigations was to hand down its initial report on the charges against the Vice-President at the end of 2014. The re-opening of these charges by a Senate Blue Ribbon committee led by two Aquino supporters, Senator Antonio Trillanes IV and Senator Alan Peter Cayetano, is the clearest sign that the fight for the 2016 presidential elections has started early and could well be one of the most bitterly contested. Senator Cayetano reported receiving death threats tied to his leading role in the Senate investigation.[9] Senator Trillanes publicly expressed fears that he may be assassinated if, as the polls suggest, Binay wins the 2016 presidential election.[10]

The early and explosive start to the unofficial 2016 presidential campaign in mid-2014 means that the last two years of President Aquino's single six-year term will be dominated by manoeuvrings to replace him. The re-opening of these charges and the blanket national coverage of the Senate hearings has caused Binay's sizable early lead over other 2016 presidential hopefuls to drop significantly from 29 per cent in July 2014 to 8 per cent by year end.[11] In comparison, Grace Poe, another presidential hopeful, has seen the 18 per cent gap between her and Binay in July 2014 shrink to only 12 per cent by the end of the year. Binay has not helped himself by refusing to appear in front of the Senate commission to defend himself and challenging Senator Trillanes to a public debate on the issue and then cancelling it at the last minute, thereby reducing his credibility.

The early and explosive start to the campaign also is a sign of the entrenched weakness of the likely Liberal Party candidate, its president Manuel 'Mar' Roxas, who narrowly lost the 2010 vice-presidential election to Binay. Roxas, scion of another powerful political dynasty, consistently lags far behind Binay in polls and is struggling to achieve double-digit support despite the strong belief that the still popular Aquino will support Roxas' bid. Roxas' claim to the Liberal Party nomination in 2016 is being undermined by his consistent lack of popularity aggravated by his bad handling of super-typhoon Yolanda in late 2013 as the Secretary of the Interior and Local Government. Roxas, in a sign of recognition of his own weakness, was the lead spokesperson for a brief flirtation with the idea of seeking a constitutional amendment to allow Aquino to run for a second term. There was no public support for this trial balloon just as there was none when President Ramos supporters floated the same idea at the end of his term a decade and a half ago.[12] Neophyte senator and daughter of movie megastar Fernando Poe Jr., Grace Poe, is now the clear second favourite for the presidential campaign in 2016 despite her repeated demurring from the idea of running.

The switch in political focus in the second half of 2014 to the 2016 presidential election carries two political costs for the Aquino administration already apparent by the end of 2014 and only likely to grow in 2015 and 2016. The first is the changing political status of the President himself from a personally popular leader with clear majorities in both legislative houses to a lame-duck president less and less able to gain the political attention and support of legislators who are positioning themselves behind likely presidential candidates for 2016. The single-term presidency in the Philippines is a strong institutional disincentive, as it is in South Korea, to the development of strong parties and strong party loyalty. One clear sign of the President's waning hold over the legislature was the fact that Congress had not provided the president by year's end the emergency powers that he sought in September although this was permitted under the 2001 Electric Power Industry Reform Act so as to deal with a looming power crisis in 2015. This was despite Liberal Party-led coalitions holding majorities in both houses.

The second, mutually aggravating cost is the further slowing down of an already slow legislative process. House Majority Leader Neptali Gonzalez complained in November that the mounting number of probes into members being undertaken by the two houses of Congress was reducing the amount of time available for passing legislation.[13] The Bangsamoro Basic Law, submitted to Congress in September and the decades-delayed competition law appear to be two of the main victims of this second cost among the twenty-nine priority bills for passage identified by the President.

Moro Peace Deal

Overseeing a successful peace deal that would end the centuries-old Moro Islamic insurgency could be President Aquino's greatest achievement. The beginning of 2014 saw seventeen years of peace negotiations between the Government of the Philippines and the Moro Islamic Liberation Front (by far the largest and best organized Moro Islamic insurgent group) culminate in the signing of the Comprehensive Agreement on the *Bangsamoro*.[14] Three key differences between this Agreement and the 1996 one struck by the Ramos administration and the Moro National Liberation Front that largely failed to deliver a workable political solution mean that the 2014 Agreement has a better chance of success:[15]

- By 1996, the Moro Islamic Liberation Front was the largest and most formidable insurgent group. Yet, it was excluded from the peace negotiations and rejected the 1996 agreement. The excluded insurgent groups from the 2014 deal are much weaker and less able to play an effective spoiler role.

- The 2014 deal provides the Moro Islamic community a much greater degree of regional autonomy than the 1996 deal.

- There is greater international engagement and support for the present deal.

After the euphoria and heightened expectations of the signing ceremony on 27 March, the hard grind of turning the Agreement into a draft Bangsamoro Basic Law and having the law passed and ratified have begun to quell the euphoria and turn expectations into concerns. The decades-long search for a peace deal to end peace deals has had many false dawns — the 1973 Tripoli Agreement under Marcos, the 1989 establishment of the Autonomous Region of Muslim Mindanao under Corazon Aquino, the 1996 peace deal under Ramos and the 2008 Memorandum of Agreement on Ancestral Domain under Macapagal-Arroyo — followed by a return to low-intensity conflict and a more complicated, less peace deal-friendly situation.

As expected but not planned for, the process of translating the Agreement reached between the negotiating parties into a Bangsamoro Basic Law hit delays. President Aquino set out an infeasible timeline tied to his own rapidly shortening time in office. The draft law was to be submitted to Congress a short six weeks after the signing ceremony, the draft bill signed into law by year end with the referendum for areas presently outside the Autonomous Region of Muslim Mindanao but able to join the new expanded Bangsamoro regional government by mid-2015 and the first elections for this new regional government to be held simultaneously with the 2016 presidential elections.

Fearful of successful constitutional challenges by opponents to the Bangsamoro Basic Law, President Aquino submitted the draft bill to Congress a full five months later than scheduled after significant legal scrubbing that led to accusations from the Moro Islamic Liberation Front that Aquino was walking away from the Agreement.[16] The 2008 Memorandum of Agreement on Ancestral Domain agreed upon by the two negotiating parties was quickly ruled unconstitutional ending the hope for a peace deal under President Macapagal-Arroyo. Even before the draft Bangsamoro Basic Law was tabled in September, congressional leaders ruled out being able to pass it by year-end, with the House of Representatives choosing to launch a long process of public consultations only ended in December 2014.[17]

The Commission on Elections noted it had no allocated budget for the required Bangsamoro membership plebiscites in 2015 and would need at least six months, once funds were provided, to organize them.[18]

Concerns that powerful interests will oppose the Agreement and aim to quash the Bangsamoro Basic Law in Congress or through the courts that were behind the delayed submission seem justified. The Philippine national broadsheets, all based in Manila, have run an ever growing number of opinion pieces and features or citing legal luminaries and national politicians concluding that the Agreement and draft law are unconstitutional as they give too much sovereign power to the yet-to-be established Bangsamoro political entity.[19] Further complicating the situation, senior government officials appointed by President Aquino and from local Mindanao dynasties long opposed to Moro autonomy have voiced similar concerns about a loss of national powers.[20] Political leaders from the long-restive Cordillera region are eyeing an enhancement of their own regional autonomy arrangement in line with the draft Bangsamoro Basic Law.[21] The Moro National Liberation Front also appears to be overcoming its internecine factionalism to reject the deal. With the support of the Organization of Islamic Cooperation, in which the Moro National Liberation Front is the only observer organization, it is demanding that the new Bangsamoro Basic Law be integrated with the existing law that codified the 1996 peace deal it struck with Manila.[22]

The Comprehensive Agreement on the Bangsamoro still is the best chance for a successful political solution to the Moro Islamic insurgency. However the slow process of the draft Bangsamoro Basic Law in 2014 symbolizes how difficult a chance it still is.

National Economy

The Philippine economy in 2014 benefited from three strong and important positive continuities from 2013 and years before: strong GDP growth, a stable macroeconomic situation and the introduction of new significant economic reforms. In 2013, international and regional credit rating agencies recognized these benefits so at odds with the historically-based expectations of Philippine economic performance and elevated the credit rating for the Philippines to investment grade. In 2014, these same firms raised the Philippine rating one notch higher. The more upbeat even expressed the belief that the present economic reform and macroeconomic management momentum is so strong and institutionalized that it will endure whoever becomes president in 2016.[23] Praise for the Aquino administration's economic policy record was not limited to the risk raters of sovereign debt. The 2014 World Economic Forum Global Competitiveness Report, using 2013 statistics, rated the Philippines the most improved country overall among 144, moving seven places from 59th in 2013 to 52nd.[24] Transparency International's 2014 Corruption Perception Index also delivered good news with the Philippines improving from 94th place in 2013 (and 105th in 2012) to 85th place in 2014.[25]

Sustained high levels of real Gross Domestic Product (GDP) growth has been a feature of the Aquino administration's term and a positive contrast to that of his two predecessors. The latest International Monetary Fund (IMF) estimates for 2014 and 2015, again have the Philippine growth rate as the fastest among Southeast Asia's six main economies (Indonesia, Malaysia, the Philippines, Singapore, Thailand and Vietnam) and well above the average for the ten ASEAN economies. In 2011, the Philippines was the second slowest growing major Southeast Asian economy well behind the regional average. In 2014, the national economy is expected to grow at 6.2 per cent compared with the Southeast Asian average of 5.5 per cent. In 2015, the Philippines is predicted to grow at a ruddy 6.3 per cent compared with the predicted regional average of 5.6 per cent. According to the *Bangko Sentral ng Pilipinas*, the growth in remittances inflows in 2014 matched real GDP growth with almost US$20 billion flowing into the Philippines in the first nine months of 2014, up 6.2 per cent. Remittance flows equate to roughly 10 per cent of total gross national income. As of the end of October, growth in goods exports at 11.9 per cent and services exports at 9.2 per cent outstripped real GDP growth in another positive sign for the economy.

2014 also saw the first sign that two key lagging economic indicators, Foreign Direct Investment (FDI) inflows and employment, finally may be improving in the wake of real GDP, remittances and export growth. Net FDI is estimated to have risen sharply in 2014 by 61.3 per cent after growing by 12.7 per cent in 2013. Net direct investment flows from the United States, the largest holder of foreign direct investment in the Philippines, saw an impressive turnaround of over US$1.4 billion from 2013 to 2014. Total net foreign direct investment is estimated at US$4.9 billion for 2014. According to the International Labour Organization, in 2013, the Philippines had the highest unemployment rate among Southeast Asian economies at 7.3 per cent. Indonesia came second at only 6 per cent.[26] The Philippines also has a relatively low labour force participation rate further aggravating the true employment situation. While green shoots often do not turn into sturdy plants, the employment situation showed some signs of improvement through 2014. By the end of October, the unemployment rate had fallen according to Philippine Government statistics to 6.0 per cent, the lowest rate in a decade, down from 7.0 per cent in January while the labour force participation rate actually increased.[27]

The latest government statistics show a similar positive trend in poverty levels. From mid-2012 to mid-2013 the poverty rate fell from 27.9 per cent in the first semester of 2012 to 24.9 per cent in the first semester 2013.[28] However, Filipinos' perception of themselves as poor continues to remain stubbornly high despite three years of above average real GDP growth and government poverty statistics. According to the Social Weather Stations' quarterly polling on self-rated poverty, over half of Filipinos rated themselves as poor (*mahirap*), with this already high percentage inching up over the term of President Aquino.

The 2014 economic reform story was a very similar one of benefits being reaped from previous difficult reforms and new ones undertaken. After more than two decades of stalemate in Congress, in 2012 the Aquino administration did what many thought would never happen and passed the "sin tax" on alcohol and cigarettes despite very powerful vested interests. San Miguel, the largest local alcohol producer, is the Philippines largest private sector firm. In 2014, sin tax receipts well overshot revenue estimates. For the first three quarters of 2014 total sin tax revenue was 45.5 per cent higher than budget estimates, bringing in an extra 11.6 billion pesos to the public coffers.[29] The sin tax has helped broaden the traditionally narrow and porous tax base and increase the comparatively meagre ratio of taxation revenues to GDP. Since the passage of the sin tax, the tax take has risen from 12.9 per cent of GDP at the end of 2012 to 13.7 per cent in 2013 and an estimated 14.1 per cent in 2014 (a full 2 per cent higher than in 2010). The improving tax take and credit ratings is contributing to recent declines in the government's consolidated public sector borrowing requirement and the country's external debt to GDP ratio.

The Philippine banking sector was the focus of the most significant economic policy reform in 2014. In July, the President signed into law Republic Act 10641 permitting full and free access for foreign banks to the long-protected banking market, as long as 60 per cent of total banking assets remain in banks with majority Philippine ownership. At the moment, local banks control about 85 per cent of total banking assets, meaning that this aggregate limit on foreign penetration will not act as a true barrier for years to come. All branching limitations on foreign banks have also been removed. In October, the central bank redefined and raised the minimum paid-up capital requirements for all banking licences, leading to a six-fold increase for some universal banks and eight-fold for some thrift banks. This pincer movement on local banks of greater foreign competition and higher paid-up capital minimums, as were similar less drastic actions two decades ago, are aimed at forcing local bank consolidation and an improvement in consumer banking practices and products. Local banks, most tied to the leading diversified conglomerates that rule the Makati skyline, complained about the speed and scope of the reforms to little avail.[30] Today, the Philippines has the most liberal entry policies to its domestic commercial banking sector in Southeast Asia.

Foreign Policy

The Philippines' territorial dispute with the People's Republic of China in the West Philippine Sea was the focus of Philippine foreign policy in 2014 as it has been for the whole term of this president.[31] Manila's decision in early 2013 to seek a ruling on its maritime boundary dispute with China at the International Tribunal on the Law of Sea has added a new international legal dimension to the long-running dispute. In 2014, the Philippine policy on the dispute gained greater international interest and support just as the filing of the case did in 2013. However, as in 2013, China's assertive actions in these disputed waters grew establishing greater Chinese control over a growing number of land features in the disputed waters.

Over the last two decades, the Philippines has been the strongest proponent for regional and international actions to counter Chinese unilateral assertion in the disputed waters of the South China Sea. For most of the time, the Philippines has been alone in ASEAN circles in the strength of its focus on this issue and demands for action. ASEAN-wide attention on this issue was sparked by the unannounced positioning of a very large Chinese oil rig in disputed waters between Vietnam and China the week before the first annual ASEAN Summit. This led to ASEAN foreign ministers releasing a joint statement using the firmest diplomatic language on the disputes in the South China Sea in two decades. The Philippines was no longer the distant outlier in ASEAN circles on the South China Sea disputes.

Vietnam's public position on its South China Sea dispute with China moved closer to the Philippines' firm stance focused on international law adopted by President Aquino. Philippine and Vietnamese leaders met repeatedly in 2014 and voiced their shared concerns over Chinese actions and the need for the two claimants to work more closely together. In late November, Vietnam sent its two most capable warships on the first-ever port call by the Vietnam Navy to the Philippines despite the Philippines and Vietnam also being split by competing territorial claims in the South China Sea.[32] In December, Hanoi requested that the International Tribunal on the Law of the Sea take into consideration Vietnam's legal rights in their arbitration of the Philippine case while supporting the tribunal's right to hear the case and rejecting China's nine-dash line claim to the majority of the South China Sea.[33]

The Philippines' use of its rights under the United Nations Conference of the Law of the Sea (UNCLOS) to seek arbitration gained wider support in 2014 from a range of countries and international organizations that share the Philippine stance that international law should be the basis for addressing disputes in the South China Sea (and beyond) and concerns about China's growing assertiveness. In May, South Korea, which faces its own territorial dispute with China in the East China Sea, announced it would donate a corvette to the Philippine Navy following steps in 2013 by Japan to provide up to ten maritime patrol vessels to the Philippines and the arrival of decommissioned U.S. vessels provided on concessionary terms.[34] In an unprecedented move, the Atlanticist G7 grouping, in its annual joint statement, supported the Philippines' right to seek arbitration in its dispute with China.[35] President Aquino's trip to Europe in September brought similar support for the Philippine position from the European Commission.[36] However, despite having five of its ten member-states facing maritime boundary disputes with China in the South China Sea, ASEAN has not come out in public support of the Philippines' right to seek arbitration.

Conclusion

Not only was 2014 quite similar to 2013 in terms of national politics, the national economy and foreign policy, signs are strong that the same may well be repeated in 2015. Under President Aquino, the Philippine strong macroeconomic performance and firm line on the territorial dispute has remained constant to the benefit of the country's economic and geopolitical position. Since 2013 though, national politics has slowly fallen back into its regular pattern of scandal and in-fighting. The 2016 presidential elections could well act as a break to this pattern of national continuity. Yet as this pattern under Aquino has largely been beneficial to the Philippines, change may not necessarily be better than continuity, even in the case of today's Philippines.

Notes

1. David G. Timberman, *A Changeless Land: Continuity and Change in Philippine Politics* (Singapore: Institute of Southeast Asian Studies, 1991). Timberman acknowledges taking his title from the work of renowned Philippine writer F. Sionel Jose. Patricio N. Abinales, "The Philippines under Aquino III, Year 2: A Ponderous Slog Continues", *Southeast Asian Affairs 2013*, edited by Daljit Singh (Singapore: Institute of Southeast Asian Studies, 2013); Renato Cruz De Castro, "The Philippines in 2013: Popular President Confronts Daunting Challenges", *Southeast Asian Affairs 2014*, edited by Daljit Singh (Singapore: Institute of Southeast Asian Studies, 2014).

2. For more on the concept of cacique democracy, see Benedict Anderson, "Cacique Democracy in the Philippines: Origins and Dreams", *New Left Review* I/169 (May–June 1988): 3–33. For more on the concept of booty capitalism, see Paul D. Hutchcroft, *Booty Capitalism: The Politics of Banking in the Philippines* (Ithaca, NY: Cornell University Press, 1998). For more on the idea of a damaged culture, see James Fallows, "A Damaged Culture: A New Philippines?" *The Atlantic*, 1 November 1987.

3. Some examples of this counter-narrative include Bernardo M. Villegas, *The Philippine Advantage* (Manila: University of Asia and the Pacific Foundation in cooperation with Shell Companies in the Philippines, 2001; and Mahar Mangahas, "The Philippine Social Climate", *Philippine Studies* 44, no. 2 (Second Quarter 1996): 270–79.

4. Natashya Gutierrez, "Nearly 4 out of 10 Filipinos Feel Aquino Strayed from 'Straight Path'", *Rappler*, 13 October 2014.

5. Cruz De Castro, op. cit., pp. 245–47.

6. Joel E. Zurbano, "IBP: Selective Justice in Pork", *Manila Standard*, 12 June 2014.

7. Rhodina Villanueva, "Workers to Noy: Account for P178 Billion", *The Philippine Star*, 14 July 2014.

8. The Binay family have controlled the politics of Makati City, the main municipality in Metro Manila, since President Corazon Aquino first appointed Jejomar Binay as officer-in-charge of the city in 1987. Binay's only son, Jejomar Jr., is presently Mayor having succeeded his mother who succeeded her husband. Jejomar Binay's daughter, Nancy, is a first-term senator for the United Nationalist Alliance coalition led by her father.

9. T.J. Burgonio and Leila Salaverria, "Alan Cayetano Gets Death Threat", *Philippine Daily Inquirer*, 13 November 2014.

10. Maila Ager, "Trillanes: I Might Be Killed or Jailed if Binay Becomes President", *Philippine Daily Inquirer*, 13 November 2014.

11. Leila Salaverria, "Pulse Asia Survey: Binay Falling, Poe Surging", *Philippine Daily Inquirer*, 10 December 2014.

12. Natashya Gutierrez, "Palace Not Giving Up On Aquino Second Term Amid Poll Results", *Rappler*, 2 October 2014.

13. Gil. C. Cabacungan, "Too Many Probes, Hardly Any Time for Making Laws — House Leader", *Philippine Daily Inquirer*, 17 November 2014.

14. *Bangsamoro* roughly translates as the Moro nation.

15. For more information about the Comprehensive Agreement on the *Bangsamoro* and the Moro Islamic insurgency, see Malcolm Cook, "Peace's Best Chance in Muslim Mindanao", *ISEAS Perspective*, no. 16 (Singapore: Institute of Southeast Asian Studies, 17 March 2014).

16. Manuel Mogato, "Peace Deal in Jeopardy as Moro Rebels Cry Foul", *Luwaran*, 8 August, 2014. The draft law can be viewed at http://www.scribd.com/doc/239243742/Draft-Bangsamoro-Basic-Law (accessed 15 December 2014).

17. T.J. Burgonio, "Drilon Sees Bangsamoro Law Passed Early Next Year", *Philippine Daily Inquirer*, 12 August 2014.

18. John Carlo Cahinhinan, "P500M Needed for Bangsamoro Plebiscite", *Sun Star Manila*, 8 October 2014.

19. Examples include Paolo Romero, "Ex-SC Justice: BBL Unconstitutional", *The Philippine Star*, 29 October 2014; Jemy Gatdula, "Bangsamoro Agreement More Problem than Solution", *Business World*, 7 August 2014; and Ayee Macaraig, "Miriam: Bangsamoro Deal Illegal, Creates Substate", *Rappler*, 2 April 2014.

20. Edwin Espejo, "Bangsamoro Powers Alarm Cabinet Exec", *Rappler*, 2 September 2014.

21. Jess Diaz, "Cordillera Also Eyes Autonomy", *The Philippine Star*, 22 September 2014.

22. Kimberly Jane Tan, "OIC Wants Peace Pacts with MILF, MNLF Linked", *GMA News*, 20 June 2014.

23. Clarissa Batino and Cecilia Yap, "Philippines wins S&P Upgrade as Aquino's Changes Seen Enduring", *Bloomberg News*, 9 May 2014.

24. Leandro Tan, "WEF Declares Philippines Most Improved Country in Global Competitiveness", *In Asia* (Asia Foundation weblog), 10 September 2014.

25. Angela Casauay, "PH Perceived to be Less Corrupt — 2014 Global Survey", *Rappler*, 3 December 2014.

26. Tina G. Santos, "PH Tops Asean List of Jobless, Says ILO", *Philippine Daily Inquirer*, 2 May 2014.

27. Edu Lopez, "Unemployment Rate Dips to 6% in October", *Manila Bulletin*, 10 December 2014.

28. "Philippine Poverty Incidence on Downward Trend — NEDA", *Rappler*, 29 April 2014.

29. "'Sin Tax' Take Exceeds Target", *Philippine Daily Inquirer*, 23 October 2014.

30. Bernie Magkilat, "Business Raises Concern over Full Foreign Bank Ownership", *Manila Bulletin*, 27 July 2014.

31. Just as the Vietnamese refer to the South China Sea as the East Sea, the Philippines refers to the waters where it is in dispute with China as the West Philippine Sea.

32. Manuel Mogato, "Vietnam Warships Visit Philippines amid South China Sea Dispute", *Reuters*, 25 November 2014.

33. Jay L. Batongbacal, "Vietnam's Impact on the Philippines/China Arbitration — A Closer Look", *Cogitasia*, 18 December 2014.

34. Alexis Romero, "Seoul to Donate Corvette Warship to Phl Navy", *The Philippine Star*, 5 June 2014.

35. Camille Diola, "G7 Backs Legal Solution, Opposes Coercion in South China Sea", *The Philippine Star*, 5 June 2014.

36. Aurea Calica, "Phl Gets EC Backing for Arbitration", *The Philippines Star*, 17 September 2014.

TYPHOON YOLANDA
The Politics of Disaster Response and Management

Lorraine Carlos Salazar

Introduction

On 8 November 2013, typhoon Yolanda (internationally referred to as Haiyan), the strongest recorded typhoon ever to make landfall hit central Philippines, with wind speeds of more than 300 km/hour and storm surges of over four metres. Yolanda's impact was massive. It passed through 171 cities and municipalities in fourteen provinces in the country leading to an estimated 6,300 deaths, over a thousand people missing, around 1.5 million families (around 7.5 million individuals) displaced, and in all affecting 3.4 million families (about 16 million people) and damaging or destroying a million homes.[1]

Experts opine that in some ways the impact of Yolanda was greater than the Haiti earthquake in terms of shelter damage (affecting about 475,000 people in 95,000 households) or the 2004 tsunami in terms of total number of people affected (about 2.3 million).[2] Yolanda's total economic impact, estimated to reach US$10 billion in damages, was considered one of the top two most destructive disasters in the world during 2013.[3]

The enormity of the disaster overwhelmed the administration of President Benigno Aquino whose response during the first few days of the crisis was widely criticized. The local governments of most of the affected areas, particularly Tacloban City, which suffered the most devastation, were caught

LORRAINE CARLOS SALAZAR is a Knowledge Expert with a global management consulting firm based in Singapore. She was a Visiting Fellow at the Institute of Southeast Asian Studies (ISEAS), Singapore from 2005 to 2007.

unaware and took some time to get back on their feet and start organizing relief response. Meanwhile, haunting images broadcast internationally by the global media galvanized an unprecedented international response for relief and aid. However, due to logistical challenges, aid items took time to reach the ground. The Philippine Government, in partnership with national and international humanitarian actors, led the massive efforts to clear the roads, re-establish power systems and provide a range of life-saving humanitarian support to millions of people.[4]

While progress could be seen and the focus had shifted from relief to recovery and rehabilitation a year after the typhoon, much remained to be done in terms of infrastructure, social services, resettlement and livelihood. In fact as of November 2014, many of the affected still lived in temporary shelters as only about 2,000 of the 205,000 permanent homes needed had been built. Meanwhile, replanting of the 33 million coconut trees could not be done immediately because of the huge task of clearing debris. In short, the level of recovery and reconstruction tasks ahead is enormous.

In this chapter, the effect of Typhoon Yolanda is reviewed by looking at what progress has been achieved so far. In particular, we look at the initial responses to the typhoon by both the national and local governments. We then focus on the Office of the Presidential Adviser of Rehabilitation and Recovery (OPARR), formed in December 2013 to unify the rehabilitation and recovery efforts. Finally, the chapter examines the outpouring of private and international support for aid and rehabilitation of the affected areas.

The second section looks at how familial politics has hampered the relief and recovery response in Tacloban City due to political animosity between President Benigno Aquino and Tacloban's Mayor, Alfred Romualdez.

Thirdly, since the Philippines is one of the most disaster-prone countries in the world, being located in the Pacific Ring of Fire and facing an average of twenty typhoons annually, the chapter looks at the capabilities of the Philippine state to respond to natural disasters which have been increasing due to global warming and climate change. The chapter further examines how the Philippines legislated a "world class" national disaster risk reduction and management law in 2010. However, the law's institutionalization and implementation is lacking. Of particular interest is the law's provisions, the complicated composition of the national disaster body, the role of the local government units and their capabilities to deliver. The chapter argues that an independent, empowered, national disaster management agency is needed to replace the current body.

This section also showcases an example of "pockets of efficiency"[5] in the Philippine state, highlighting the best practices to understand what are the key lessons that can be gleaned, from the example of Albay Province where under the leadership of Governor Joey Salceda, there were zero casualties from the typhoon.

Finally, the chapter concludes by outlining the key steps the Aquino administration should consider with regard to disaster risk reduction and management during its last eighteen months in office.

The Impact of Yolanda

Two days before Typhoon Yolanda hit land, the Philippine weather bureau, PAGASA (Philippines Atmospheric, Geophysical and Astronomical Services Administration) warned the public of a "storm signal number 4 (the highest category of warning there is) with heavy rains and very strong winds of more than 185 kilometers per hour for at least 12 hours." In a footnote on its forecast report, the agency warned that "those living in coastal areas are alerted against storm surges which may reach up to 7-meter wave height."[6] About 800,000 people were evacuated. However, many people who have lived through typhoons in the past chose to stay in their homes to weather the storm. Still, others who live near coastal areas including Tacloban Mayor Alfred Romualdez, admitted that they did not understand what a "storm surge" meant.[7] If PAGASA had used the term "mini-tsunami", perhaps more people would have understood, prepared or evacuated. The government is now correcting this, with PAGASA working with linguists to arrive at clearer and more understandable terms for rain, flood and storm surge warnings.[8]

Meanwhile, the National Disaster Risk Reduction and Management Council (NDRRMC), the country's lead agency for disaster preparedness and response, was already on red alert forty-eight hours before the typhoon, providing its regional and local counterparts with information bulletins and advising them to take preventive action. In response, various national government agencies started the mobilization of people and resources in anticipation of a huge natural calamity. Also, the heads of the Departments of Social Welfare and Development and of Interior and Local Government were in Tacloban with prepared relief packages, which were later washed away by the force of the rain, wind and waves from Typhoon Yolanda.[9] As Department of Social Welfare and Development (DSWD) Secretary Corazon Soliman put it, "the preparation of the local and the national government agencies was not equal to the strength of the typhoon."[10]

Homes, business establishments, government buildings, roads, airports and telecoms towers were all destroyed. Before Typhoon Yolanda struck, many of the areas in eastern Visayas were already vulnerable, with poverty rates estimated at around 40 per cent and over 30 per cent of the population considered landless and living in constant threat of eviction in the hazard prone coastal areas. In one affected province, Eastern Samar, the poverty rate was at a high of 63 per cent.[11] Yolanda left the Philippine population that was already living in poverty much poorer and vulnerable.

Establishment of OPARR

To coordinate the national government's response to Typhoon Yolanda, President Aquino established the Office of the Presidential Assistant for Rehabilitation and Recovery (OPARR) in December 2013 through Memorandum Order No. 62. All government agencies were directed to render full cooperation with the OPARR to carry out its functions.

The OPARR was tasked to act as the overall manager and coordinator of the rehabilitation, recovery and reconstruction effort; coordinate with the NDRMMC and its member agencies, consult with local government units (LGUs) in the formulation of plans and programmes which would be submitted to the President for approval; and call upon any department, or agency of the government, and request NGOs, the private sector and other entities for assistance.[12]

President Aquino appointed former Chief of the Philippine National Police and two-term Senator, Panfilo Lacson, to head the OPARR. In carrying out its mandate, the OPARR produced an 8,000 page document called the Comprehensive Rehabilitation and Recovery Plan (CRRP) that puts together the:

- reconstruction Assistance on Yolanda Plan, the government's framework for planning and implementation of recovery and reconstruction programmes in the affected areas developed by the National Economic and Development Agency (NEDA);
- the Post Disaster Needs Assessment (PDNA) report of the NDRRMC, based on on-the ground verified information assessing the impact of the disaster and prioritizing recovery and reconstruction needs;
- the Local Government Rehabilitation and Recovery Plans (LRRPs), which were developed bottoms-up from each barangay, municipality and province and

- the cluster action plans on resettlement, infrastructure, livelihood and social services developed by respective government departments.

Given the number of national and local actors involved and the expanse of area affected by Typhoon Yolanda, the Plan took about ten months to complete and was submitted to President Aquino for approval on 1 August 2014. The CRRP articulates the overall strategic and integrated short-, medium- and long-term plans for the 171 affected cities and municipalities with four key goals:

- to restore, rehabilitate or reconstruct damaged infrastructure necessary to sustain economic and social activities;
- to repair the houses or rebuild settlements and basic community facilities and services that are more resilient to natural calamities;
- to restore the people's means of livelihood and continuity of economic activities and businesses, and
- to increase resilience and capacities of communities in coping with future disasters.

The CRRP required a total budget of PhP170.92 billion (US$3.948 billion)[13] to fund over 25,000 projects in infrastructure, social services, resettlement and livelihood (see Table 1).

The proposed infrastructure budget totalled PhP35.148 billion, comprising 20 per cent of the total budget, and was aimed at building better and more disaster resilient roads, bridges, airports, seaports, power lines, and other infrastructure.

Social services comprised 15 per cent of the budget (PhP26.4 billion), covering delivery of basic services such as health, education and social protection to affected communities through projects such as basic and higher education support, health and nutrition and distribution of food and subsidy to vulnerable groups.

Resettlement, given the damage to homes and buildings, comprised PhP75.7 billion or 44 per cent of the total budget. The aims were: constructing disaster resilient houses that can withstand wind speeds of up to 250 km/hour; development of new settlement sites away from disaster prone zones; and capacity building programmes for affected communities such as community management and self-help training programmes.

Finally, livelihood plans which aimed to promote sustainable businesses and jobs in affected areas was allotted PhP33.8 billion or 20 per cent of the total budget for projects to support agriculture, fisheries and aquaculture, industry and

TABLE 1
Proposed Budget Breakdown for the Comprehensive Rehabilitation and Recovery Plan (CRRP) in Philippines Pesos

Cluster	Proposed 2014–16 Budget	in USD	Funded	% Funded	Balance	% Balance	in USD	Approved Plan (as of 29 October 2014)
Infrastructure	35,148,634,708	811,934,274	23,213,888,217	66%	10,853,664,191	34%	250,719,894	35,148,634,708
Social services	26,406,233,815	609,984,611	2,844,529,077	11%	23,561,704,738	89%	544,275,924	26,406,233,815
Resettlement	75,678,680,000	1,748,179,256.18	2,438,638,000	3%	73,240,042,000	97%	1,691,846,662	75,678,680,000
Livelihood	33,682,884,442	778,075,408.69	8,923,114,258	26%	24,759,770,184	74%	571,951,263	30,600,000,000
TOTAL	170,916,432,965	3,948,173,550	37,420,169,553	22%	133,496,263,412	78%	3,058,793,742	167,833,548,523

services, emergency and livelihood assistance, science and technology support to medium and SMEs, vocational and technical skills training and capacity development programmes.

The CRRP provides for the rehabilitation of the following key provinces with their respective allocations: Leyte (PhP39.5 billion), Iloilo (PhP22.8 billion), Tacloban City (PhP15.7 billion), Cebu (PhP14.5 billion), Eastern Samar (PhP11.3 billion) and Samar (PhP8.8 billion).[14]

While the CRRP is large, Oxfam points to a few critical missing elements. First, the design of livelihood and resettlement programmes fails to integrate disaster risk reduction principles with new resettlement sites, lacking specific provisions for the establishment of safe and durable evacuation centres and a stable food supply with linkages to markets and transport systems. Secondly, coordination mechanisms between government offices and their Non-Governmental Organizations (NGOs) and local communities are yet to be fully operationalized.

Thirdly, support for the effective implementation of recovery processes to LGUs is missing. Due to the decentralized nature of governance in the Philippines, LGUs are given the primary responsibility for the implementation of local disaster risk reduction and management plans, including post disaster recovery. However, many LGUs have limited technical and financial capacity for drawing up up-to-date local land-use plans and disaster risk reduction and management plans. In addition, after the typhoon, the majority of the LGUs struggled to resume their core operations. Furthermore, many of the government officials and employees were themselves victims of the typhoon, taking time to regroup and go back to work. Thus, many struggled to develop the required recovery plans and to perform related tasks such as developing the beneficiary lists for shelter and livelihood assistance. The OPARR is looking at international development partners to fill the gap of providing capacity building trainings at local levels. However, instead of relying on partners, investing in capacity building should be an integral part of the overall CRRP. Ad hoc initiatives could result in municipalities falling further behind in the recovery efforts.[15]

On 29 October 2014, a week before the first anniversary of Yolanda and two months after OPARR submitted the plan, President Aquino signed the CRRP with a slightly revised budget of PhP167.9 billion. With the exception of livelihood, which saw a cut of about PhP3 billion from the proposed budget, OPARR's recommended plan for infrastructure, social services and resettlement was fully endorsed by the President. The approval came after many delays, bureaucratic infighting and haggling. Some local government officials as well as Secretary Lacson himself expressed impatience with the slowness of the process and even expressed disappointment with "3 Cabinet members who are foot dragging". In fact, Lacson observed that his post was "set up to fail" because he was not given the appropriate powers and authority commensurate to the work that he was tasked to accomplish. Existing government department and line agencies retained control over their funds and disbursements, which essentially relegated the OPARR to coordination.[16]

Reportedly, of the PhP169 billion budget allotment for the plan, 85 per cent will be coursed through government agencies while 15 per cent will be disbursed through NGOs. About PhP52 billion has already been released.[17] Lacson stated that the government aims to complete 80 per cent of the CRRP projects before the end of President Aquino's term in 2016, although long-term projects would need the support of the next administration for completion.[18]

However, many are unhappy with the pace of rehabilitation. A group called People Surge, an alliance of Yolanda survivors, staged a protest rally in Tacloban to commemorate the anniversary of the Typhoon and called for Aquino's ouster for his "betrayal of the Yolanda survivors and the Filipino people as a whole, and his anti-poor, anti-environment, pro-big business and pro-foreign policies".[19] Earlier in May, they also sent delegates to Malacanang to demand that the Aquino administration give each affected family PhP40,000 in financial support. The President however dismissed their demands as unreasonable.[20] Secretary Lacson dismissed the protest group as "communist pawns out to agitate the people and discredit the government".[21]

The Role of the International Community

A noticeable aspect of the relief and recovery efforts was the unprecedented level of support from the international community. Many foreign countries also deployed their Armed Forces, rescue personnel and cargo planes and ships to bring in much needed aid.

As of November 2014, the Department of Finance reported that the country received pledges amounting to PhP199.48 billion (US$4.6 billion) in total assistance from the international community. Of this, PhP73 billion (US$1.68 billion or 37 per cent) was aid donated to communities while PhP126.18 billion (US$2.9 billion or 63 per cent) were loans. Key contributors include the Asian Development Bank (ADB), the World Bank (WB), Japan International Cooperation Agency (JICA), the European Union, Germany's KfW and GIZ, USAID, Korea International Cooperation Agency (KOICA), the Embassy of the UAE, the United Kingdom's Department for International Development (DFID), the International Fund for Agricultural Development (IFAD), the Embassy of China, Australia's Department of Foreign Affairs and Trade (DFAT), IsraAid and Swiss Humanitarian Aid, among others. In addition, ASEAN member states were quick to arrive at the scene to help the country recover.[22]

However, the office of the President clarified that pledged and received amounts differed and sometimes it was challenging to get a follow-through on pledges as there was no legal commitment by the foreign countries or organizations. The experience of Indonesia after the Aceh Tsunami is instructive, where it was able to collect 93 per cent of all international pledges because it hired an "ambassador" that knocked at the doors of the international community to follow up on their commitments.[23]

Local and international private sector and non-governmental organizations were also proactive in their support, working with the OPARR as well as the national and local governments in building transitional and permanent housing, classrooms, health units and providing new fishing vessels to fishermen.[24]

Status of Rebuilding Efforts as of November 2014

In November, the OPARR announced what had been accomplished by then:[25]

- **Infrastructure:** the government has undertaken a major task of repairing or building roads, bridges, classrooms, hospitals and other infrastructure facilities.[26] It also plans to build a 27-square kilometre dike connecting Tacloban, Palo and Tanauan that can act as protection from storm surges. The dike has an initial funding of PhP4.4 billion and is expected to be completed by end 2016.[27]
- **Power:** as early as March 2014, the government had restored power in 155 out of 196 *barangays* in the municipalities of Palo, Babatngon and Tacloban.
- **Resettlement:** 1,252 housing units had been built, and a total of 7,377 units are to be completed by March 2015 out of a target of 205,128 by 2016. The government also provided ongoing emergency shelter assistance to 14,096 families whose houses were destroyed and 24,111 for damaged houses. It expects to finish around 117,000 housing units by the end of 2015 and the remaining 88,000 by the end of 2016.[28]
- **Social Services:** the government extended food assistance, healthcare, skills training and educational assistance to affected families.

- **Livelihood:** around 4981 families out of the targeted 517,214 families with partially damaged houses have been provided with cash for work assistance. Cash help has also been extended to 236,916 families for building livelihood assets, surpassing the target of 187,385 families.
- Project Nationwide Operational Assessment Hazard (NOAH) has completed the high resolution 3D mapping of the topography of Tacloban City and its adjacent areas ready for use by December 2014. Project NOAH will also provide up-to-date and accurate information on weather predictions, flood forecasts, rain water levels and landslide warnings.

Finally to ensure transparency and prevent corruption in the rehabilitation efforts, OPARR launched the Electronic Monitoring Platform Accountability and Transparency Hub for Yolanda (EMPATHY). The website is an online platform accessible to the public to track ongoing projects, to ensure everything is monitored and accounted for. LGUs and people in local communities are also encouraged to provide feedback and photographs of ongoing projects.[29]

Familial Politics, Red Tape and Rehabilitation

> " You have to remember that you are a Romualdez and the President is an Aquino"…
>
> DILG Secretary Mar Roxas to Mayor Alfred Romualdez a few days after Yolanda devastates Tacloban City.

While the typhoon first hit land at a small town called Guian in Eastern Samar, Tacloban City, Eastern Visayas' economic capital became the face of the impact of Yolanda with about half of the total deaths (3,200 with 600 others classified as missing) taking place in Tacloban.

Unfortunately, the city is the political enclave of the Romualdez family. Its current Mayor, Alfred Romualdez, is the nephew of former First Lady Imelda Romualdez Marcos. The Marcoses are the political arch-enemy of the family of President Benigno Aquino III, whose father Benigno Senior, was a key member of the opposition against President Ferdinand Marcos in the 1970s. Benigno Senior was imprisoned and was assassinated in 1983, allegedly by hired guns of the Marcos regime.[30]

Days after the typhoon, President Aquino visited Tacloban City and criticized Mayor Romualdez for "not preparing enough". Romualdez responded that Aquino's comments were hurtful and insulted the dead and called for the national government to revamp its disaster policies instead of pointing blame.

According to the law, the national government should declare a state of emergency when certain conditions were met.[31] However, it took President Aquino three days before declaring so for Tacloban. A tearful Romualdez said the national government refused to help Tacloban City unless he signed an ordinance to allow it to take over. The discussion which involved DILG Secretary Mar Roxas, a staunch ally of President Aquino where he was quoted on record saying to Romualdez: "You have to remember, we have to be careful, you are a Romualdez and the President is an Aquino." Roxas claimed that the video which was widely circulated on social media was edited and taken out of context.[32] However, the damage had been done.

In a public forum in March 2014, President Aquino again took a swipe at Tacloban's lack of preparation and coordination as the reason behind the huge damage to the city. Aquino stated "everybody was reporting very minimal casualties and up to the conclusion, very few, but in this particular portion of the country, something very different happened." Aquino questioned the city's overall lack of preparedness and detailed how Tacloban did not follow through with his instructions when he visited after the storm hit, expressing disappointment with its local government's leadership.[33]

In May 2014, during a Senate hearing that his cousin, Senator Ferdinand 'Bong-Bong' Romualdez Marcos called, Mayor Romualdez cried and accused the national government of a slow and inadequate response. He also questioned the need for a signed legal document before the national government could step in to help Tacloban… stating "why is it illegal (that is, the national government stepping in to help Tacloban without a signed paper from the Mayor and the City Council)? As far as I know the President of the Philippines is also the president of Tacloban City…"[34] Romualdez also questioned how the funds that many foreign donors gave did not reach their intended beneficiaries because the national government had established unnecessary conditions for towns and cities to avail of these resources. Romualdez claimed that incompetence and red tape in the national government was delaying the rehabilitation.[35]

Various aid agencies made a similar observation stating "money is not reaching local government units so even if capacity is there, money hasn't come down to the field level. Thus, LGUs are turning to NGOs, the Red Cross, and the private sector."[36] In an interview with the British *Guardian* newspaper, Oxfam's Sabyte Paguio states that

> for people who know how governments should be working, how resources should be used for recovery, it's been slow... According to the law, when a disaster is this huge, the national government has to come in. The fact that Manila failed to act in time says something profound. They weren't prepared at all.[37]

A year after the typhoon, Mayor Romualdez claimed that they have not received a single cent from the national government for the rehabilitation of Tacloban City. In a radio interview, Romualdez stated that he had only received PhP251 million (US$5.8 million) from the DILG-RAY funds for its city hall, public market and civic centre repairs but not for bunk houses and city rehabilitation. He also declared no knowledge of some alleged PhP6 billion (US$138.6 million) funds that OPARR Secretary Lacson claimed had been given to the city government. "If we had P6 billion, we could have done a lot of things."[38] Instead, a lot of people are still living in tents and only 1,422 households have been relocated to permanent shelters.[39]

During a press conference, OPARR Secretary Lacson disputed Mayor Romualdez's claims that Tacloban City did not receive any funds from the national government and insisted the city had already received a total of PhP6.1 billion in terms of projects, programmes and activities.[40] Lacson criticized Tacloban for planning to commemorate the Yolanda anniversary with a protest rally, calling the city a "class of its own" and said it was unfair for foreign and local observers to base their judgment of the government handling of Typhoon Yolanda just on Tacloban... because in other places like Samar, Guiuan and Tanauan, local governments were not rallying."[41] He claimed Romualdez had been "hijacking (the) rehabilitation efforts" and that his attitude was unlike those of other mayors who despite being in the opposition were able to achieve significant accomplishments.

Yet, media reports show that while Romualdez was being singled out for "telling lies and for performing below par a year after the disaster", other mayors in affected areas share the Tacloban mayor's disappointment. For instance, Mayor Lesmes Lumen of La Paz, a 5th-class municipality in Leyte states that "the (national government) are not doing anything to begin with. We are recovering on our own and have not received a centavo from the PhP50-million recovery plan."[42] In particular, LGUs complain that to get access to the national government's Calamity Fund Assistance, they need to submit at least ten documents, including a programme of work and a financial plan required by the Commission on Audit (CoA). LGU officials like Mayor Lumen criticize these rules as a "huge drag on the recovery process" and have instead requested for a "direct downloading of rehabilitation funds to local government units.[43]

However, Budget Secretary Florencio Abad argues that "the closer you are to the ground, the value is more speed... but the farther you are, the value is do(ing) the right thing."[44] In particular, under the "build back better" principle, proposals for rehabilitation need to be translated into engineering designs that will reduce risks. However, many LGUs lack technical skills such as geo-hazard assessment, land use planners or structural engineers to come up with the necessary designs. Thus, the government cannot release the necessary funds even after the disaster.

The environment of being overly cautious despite the magnitude of the disaster can only be understood in the broader political climate surrounding the Priority Development Assistance Fund (PDAF) or the President's pork barrel fund which the Supreme Court declared unconstitutional in November 2013. Despite this, the government should have been able to distinguish between real emergency and normal governmental procedures, which do not work during times of calamity. Haoling Xu, U.N. Development Programme Regional Director for Asia and the Pacific, pointed out that the U.N., World Bank and the ADB activate special procedures during disaster response which alter normal recruitment or procurement procedures and policies to adapt to emergency situations.[45]

On 7 November 2014, a year after Yolanda, President Aquino chose to visit Guiuan in Eastern Samar and skipped Tacloban City because "he has limited time".[46] Aquino stated, "I would hope we can move even faster and I will push everybody to move on even faster but the sad reality is the scope of work we need to do can really not be done overnight, I want to do it correctly so that benefits are permanent."[47]

Meanwhile in Tacloban, Mayor Romualdez led the commemorations with a remembrance mass, flanked by Senator Bong Bong Marcos and former First Lady Imelda Marcos. Romualdez was quiet on Aquino's decision to skip Tacloban and stated that "we have announcements that this (CRRP) plan is approved but I don't know what's going on in the national government and it's difficult to explain to the people... It's been all talk and announcements. People are really tired and they want to see something happen...."[48]

People Surge chair Efleda Bautista argued that the people of Tacloban did not see or feel any form of assistance from the national government and most likely the money was used for patronage. She criticized Lacson "for reducing their grievances to a political feud between the Aquino and Romualdez families and for misrepresenting their anger over the slow pace of rebuilding efforts." She argued that Lacson failed to comprehend that the protesters were the voices of discontent which both he and the President did not want to hear, thus they were reducing the protests to an extension of local politics and the conflict between Romualdez and Aquino.[49]

Clearly, familial politics had gotten in the way of rehabilitation progress in Tacloban, which is fuelling movements like the People Surge. While it is understandable that familial history weighs heavily on the shoulders of President Aquino, it is a shame that he and most of his Cabinet members involved have dealt with Tacloban in this way, to the detriment of the poor and vulnerable survivors.

Philippines Government's Capacity for Disaster Preparedness

According to the Annual Disaster Statistical Review of the Centre for Research on the Epidemiology of Disasters, there were around 330 natural disasters that took place in 2013. Of these, only two killed more than a thousand people — one of which was Yolanda which killed 7,354 people.[50] This is not surprising as Philippines is ranked among the top five countries worldwide which has the most frequent natural hazards.[51]

In response to the frequency of natural and man-made disasters in the country, in February 2010 Congress passed Republic Act 10121 (RA 10121) which aimed to strengthen the Philippine Disaster Risk Reduction and Management System. The new law is important in that it signalled a paradigm shift from emphasizing disaster response to risk reduction, a principle which experts unanimously agree to be the best way to prepare for disaster and reduce its impact. Instead of just responding to one crisis after another, disaster risk reduction should emphasize advance preparation to reduce risk. Disaster mitigation and prevention should be seen not as a cost but as a worthwhile investment. In fact, the World Bank has estimated that every dollar invested in prevention yields between US$7–14 saved in response cost.[52] With the law's passage, the U.N. lauded the Philippines as having one of the best disaster risk reduction legislations in the world.[53]

Secondly, the law recognizes the need to strengthen the capacities of local government units (LGUs) and communities in mitigating and recovering from disasters on the basis of principle of subsidiarity. That is, decisions and actions must be made at the level that is closest to the problem or situation.[54]

The law created the National Disaster Risk Reduction and Management Council (NDRRMC) replacing the Marcos-era body, National Disaster Coordinating Council. The NDRRMC is tasked to develop strategies to mitigate the impact of disasters and increase the capacities of the national and LGUs to face disasters.

RA 10121 enumerates seventeen key responsibilities for the NDRRMC, including:

- Development of a comprehensive, multi-sectoral, inter-agency and community-based approach to national disaster risk reduction and management.
- Ensuring a multi-stakeholder participation in the development, updating and sharing of a Disaster Risk Reduction and Management Information System.
- Establishing a national early warning and emergency alert system to provide accurate and timely advice to national and local emergency response organizations.
- Monitoring the development and enforcement by agencies and organization of various laws, guidelines, codes, or technical standards as required by RA 10121.
- Developing vertical and horizontal coordination mechanisms for a more coherent implementation of disaster risk reduction and management policies and programmes by sectoral agencies and LGUs.

The NDRRMC was created as an attached agency under the Department of National Defence (DND) and will be headed by the Secretary of National Defence as Chairperson, supported by four clusters to be headed by the respective cabinet secretaries, namely Disaster Preparedness (Department of Interior and Local Government, DILG), Disaster Response (Department of Social Welfare and Development, DSWD), Disaster Prevention and Mitigation (Department of Science and Technology, DOST) and Disaster Rehabilitation and Recovery (Director-General of the National Economic and Development Authority, NEDA). These, as well as, about twenty secretaries of various functions in the Cabinet, eight national level offices, four national level representatives of local government units, four representatives from civil society organizations, a private sector representative and the head of the Office of Civil Defence comprise the full membership of the NDRRMC.[55]

While the NDRRMC is the national body, local government units are expected to be at the frontline of emergency response in the aftermath of a disaster. Every LGU is required to create a Local Disaster Risk Reduction and Management Plan (LDRRMP) covering four aspects namely: disaster preparedness, disaster response, prevention and mitigation and rehabilitation and recovery. The LDRRMPs should be consistent with the National DRRM plan and be implemented by the local Disaster Risk Reduction and management office in every province, city and town in the country.[56] RA10121 mandates that no less than 5 per cent of an LGU's internal revenues allotment should be set aside for its LDRRMP. It is, however, unclear how many local government units follow this legal provision or have already set up a functioning LDRRM office.

Even though there were earlier natural disasters where the capacity of the NDRRMC and the intentions of RA 10121 were tested, it was Typhoon Yolanda that finally exposed its limitations and the overall institutional failure of the Philippine state to respond to a massive disaster.

When Typhoon Yolanda struck, it was the DILG and DSWD Secretaries in their lead roles for disaster preparedness and response that were seen on the ground in Tacloban. The Defence Secretary, who was head of NDRMMC, was nowhere to be seen.[57] During a press conference where the media asked who was in control on the ground, DILG Secretary Mar Roxas answered that the NDRRMC had no such thing as a ground commander. He explained that the process was consultative and based on a team effort. Given this, it was not surprising that in the early days the national government's response was slow and uncoordinated, with aid workers expressing frustration.[58]

While it is commendable that national legislation is in place, the absence of a fully functional disaster management structure and plans at both the national and local levels reflect the broader weakness in the capacity of both the national and local governments to translate laws into a more concrete reality. Two key institutional lessons can be learnt from Typhoon Yolanda—first the need for a strengthened, independent national disaster body at the national level, and second, the need to develop capacities at the local government level.

On the need for a national disaster body, Antonio La Viña, Dean of Ateneo School of Governance and former Under-Secretary of the Department of Environment under the Ramos administration has summed up the case aptly:

> We need to create a single, permanent organization with the mandate, powers and budget to oversee a singular comprehensive, coordinated strategy for addressing natural and man-made disasters. An independent agency would have the mandate to assist and train local governments with disaster risk reduction and be empowered under certain circumstances to set procedures, to preempt local government primacy for disaster response when it is likely that the expected or actual disaster is too big for a particular LGU to handle.... A stand-alone agency will not have to compete with the bureaucratic priorities of the bureaucracy or other cabinet secretaries that make up the NDRRMC. It can be given authority to manage the national funds and budgets allocated under RA10121 and international assistance to ensure effective and accountable disbursements.
>
> This national disaster agency must be staffed by world-class disaster professionals... and headed by a manager with powerful political skills, strong crisis leadership, extensive experience in managing disaster response and high credibility who can work closely with local officials, have the respect of his peers in cabinet and the trust of the president. Such a person must know how to command and control and become the ground commander during emergencies. Creating such an independent body to reduce our vulnerability and lower disaster risks is a necessary step forward.[59]

Secondly, given the decentralized structure of the Philippine state in terms of governance, it is critical that local government units are enabled to develop capabilities to put in place a fully functional disaster management structure and plans. As Oxfam points out,

> capacity building at the local level, including local authorities, civil society organizations and communities themselves is a critical foundation for a more operational and inclusive disaster management system. Recovery efforts must not only rebuild physical infrastructure but also strengthen the ability of communities to deal with future hazards.[60]

A 'Pocket of Efficiency' in the Local Government: The Case of Albay, Sorsogon

While the spotlight has been on the dramatic story of devastation in Tacloban City, a smaller share of the limelight was cast on Albay Province, where under the leadership of Governor Joey Salceda, there were minimal human casualties during Typhoon Yolanda. Even before the typhoon, Salceda was a champion of disaster risk reduction and was elected co-Chair of the U.N. Green Fund in October 2013.[61] A former banker and economic adviser to former President Gloria Arroyo before running for the governorship of Albay, Salceda argues that "zero casualty during disasters is not merely a statistic. It is a body of commitments that ensures nobody falls by the wayside due to poverty, exposure or even stubbornness".[62] So, it is interesting to find out how Albay did it.

In various public discussions, Salceda highlights a few important accomplishments:

First, the province started institution and capacity building over twenty years ago, beginning with the establishment of a permanent disaster management office. This can be understood in the context of Albay being the location of one of the most active volcanos in the Philippines, volcano Mayon, as well as being in the pathway of typhoons every year.

Second, while "zero casualties" is a difficult goal, Salceda argues that it is achievable if the goal is incorporated into people's way of life and involves the entire community in the preparations and response to a disaster. It is critical to clarify and know one's policy objectives and communicate them clearly.

Third, the Albay provincial administration allocates at least 5 per cent of the province's revenues towards disaster mitigation and preparedness as RA10121 mandates. Salceda argues that it is important for local government units to allocate necessary resources and prioritize risk reduction and mitigation because local government units need to be appropriately trained to respond to disasters. Also, it is very difficult to source for international funds for disaster mitigation and climate change adaptation. Ironically, humanitarian aid only comes when people die but "international agencies will not help you mitigate... they'll help you if there are dead on the street."[63]

Fourth, reducing uncertainly and identifying risks require a lot of research and fact-based plans and decisions. A key aspect is having in-depth and up to date hazard preparation which can be the basis of plans of action.

Fifth, creating real incentives is useful in convincing people to act, especially in the context of evacuations. The Albay provincial government evacuates communities at risk up to three days before a storm. Evacuees are requested to stay for at least two more days after the storm to ensure safety. To convince people to move to evacuation centres, the provincial government ensures the centres are clean and safe and as a bonus, they provide families five kilos of rice.

Sixth, ensuring communities are made aware and understand the risks they face is important. The provincial government conducted household risk mapping in all *barangays* and informed citizens of what sort of hazards they face during a natural calamity and where to go for safety. Also, they have initiated risk education classes starting at primary schools.

Seventh, keeping communication lines with community leaders and other government agencies open is crucial. Salceda points out that interestingly, in Albay, disseminating information has changed from being traditional media centric to one dominated by the social media, with 56 per cent of people preferring the Internet and social media for disaster information compared to 32 per cent for television, 24 per cent for radio and 12 per cent for newspapers.[64]

Finally, it is critical to create local capacity for disaster response so people understand and can identify risks and mitigate them appropriately. Coordinating locally means remote areas can handle situations themselves after being given proper information.[65]

Albay shows that preparing well before a disaster pays off in terms of lives saved and costs of rehabilitation.

The Broader Context of the Debate: the Global Response to Climate Change

At the same time that Yolanda was tearing through the Philippines in November 2013, the two-week U.N. Conference of Parties (COP) on Climate Change started in Warsaw, Poland. In an emotional speech that brought tears to the eyes of many delegates and a standing ovation, Yeb Sano, head of the Philippine delegation argued that there is a clear link between climate change and the devastation brought by Typhoon Yolanda in the Philippines. Sano said he was speaking for all Filipinos, especially those who lost their lives in the storm and declared that he will fast until "we stop this madness". Sano's family was from Tacloban City and spoke first-hand about the agonizing wait to hear words about the safety of his family and relatives.[66]

Yeb Sano's intervention made him an instant and unlikely "climate star".[67] However, the long route towards arriving at a globally agreed and accepted way to cut carbon emission and slow down global warming still lies ahead. Climate talks just concluded in Peru arrived at some form of agreement on a format for national pledges on curbing greenhouse gases, with pledges expected to be submitted by the first quarter of 2015 for countries that are ready to do so. The pledges will be self-determined and the U.N. will then assess the pledges' aggregate effect on the goal of reducing global temperatures by 2 degrees Celsius. The meeting is in preparation for the 2015 Paris Summit where a binding deal among nations is expected to be signed.[68] While this is positive development, operationalization of commitment will remain a challenge.

Conclusion

Typhoon Yolanda has been the most devastating typhoon that has ever hit a country, testing the capacity of the Philippine national and local governments in responding to disaster. While theoretically the Philippines has a good legislative framework to guide disaster risk reduction and management, the key implementing body does not have enough capacity and independence to fully execute its mandate. Also, its front-line responders, the local government units, need greater help in capacity building to be able to effectively do their part for disaster response and management. Yet, instead of beefing up the capacity of the current disaster body, the NDRRMC, the President created a new body, the Office of the Presidential Adviser on Rehabilitation and Recovery to coordinate efforts across different national and local government bodies as well as with the domestic and international governments, agencies and organization.

While the magnitude of the impact of the typhoon means that rehabilitation will take time, progress was particularly slow in Tacloban City, which bore the brunt of the typhoon because of political differences between the President and the city's Mayor. It is clear that the national government has tried to bypass the local government which has unfortunately affected the survivors who need help.

However, as Antonio La Vina argues, it is a mistake to put the blame on political differences among leaders and miss out on the institutional flaws of the Philippine state's disaster risk reduction and management system as well as the lack of a clear command and leadership at the time of a massive disaster.[69] In particular, it is crucial that an independent disaster agency be created that is fully empowered with people and resources to prepare a country that will most likely see more typhoons like Yolanda in the future. Two bills in the Senate have been filed to update RA 10121, which the Aquino administration can target as priorities for delivery before his term's end in June 2016.

The recent response to Typhoon Hagupit (internationally known as Typhoon Ruby) in December was a good start. Over 1.4 million people were evacuated and loss of lives was minimized to less than thirty people. Ad-hoc, unplanned responses should be replaced with systematic institutional and capacity building for national and local disaster risk reduction and management. The "pocket of efficiency" example from Albay shows that zero casualties is achievable if the government plans, prepares and engages respective communities in the process.

NOTES

1. The typhoon also destroyed 33 million coconut trees, 600,000 hectares of agricultural land, 248 transmission towers, 305 kilometres of farm-to-market roads, 20,000 classrooms, over 1,200 public structures (such as roads, markets and government halls) and around 400 hospitals and rural health stations. See Diana Mendoza, "Philippines: One Year after Typhoon, Tacloban Calls Recovery Below Par", *Inter Press Service*, 10 November 2014.
2. "In the Shadow of the Storm: Getting Recovery Right One Year after Typhoon Haiyan", *Oxfam Briefing Paper*, 6 November 2014, p. 9. Hereafter cited as *Oxfam Briefing Paper*.
3. See Loren Legarda, "Disaster Risk Reduction is Everybody's Business", *Philippine Daily Inquirer*, 16 November 2014. The other was the flood in east and south Germany that caused US$12.9 billion in damages.
4. See *Oxfam Briefing Paper*.
5. Here we borrow from Peter Evans the concept of "pocket of efficiencies" in which sometimes, a certain organization or agency exhibits capabilities that are not seen in general in the rest of the state body. See Peter Evans, *Embedded Autonomy: States and Industrial Transformations* (New Jersey: Princeton University Press, 1995).
6. See PAGASA's 7 November 2013 forecast as reported in "Storm Surge Not Explained Enough — Pagasa Official", *Rappler*.
7. Yoly Villanueva-Ong, "The Yolanda Effect", *Rappler*, 17 November 2014.
8. "Storm Surge, Other Terms to be Made Simple", *Philippine Daily Inquirer*, 27 November 2014.
9. Michael Lim Ubac, "Why Paralysis, Systems Collapse, Chaos Happened", *Philippine Daily Inquirer*, 15 November 2014.
10. Kate Hodal, "Tacloban Suffers Typhoon's Long Tail", *Guardian Weekly*, 21 November 2014.
11. See *Oxfam Briefing Paper*.

12. Presidential Memorandum Order no. 62, "Providing for the Functions of the Presidential Assistant for Rehabilitation and Recovery", 6 December 2013.

13. Based on an exchange rate of US$1 = PhP43.29 as of 16 July 2014.

14. "OPARR seeks LGUs wider role in Yolanda Rehab", *Philippine News Agency*, 18 August 2014.

15. See *Oxfam Briefing Paper*, pp. 11–12.

16. Joyce Panares and Mel Caspe, "Palace Admits Shortcomings in Rehab Program", *Philippine Daily Inquirer*, 5 November 2014.

17. "P199.48 B Available for Yolanda Rehab", *Manila Bulletin*, 13 November 2014.

18. Genalyn Kabiling, "Ping Submits P170.9 B Yolanda Rehab Plan", *Manila Bulletin*, 2 August 2014.

19. Panares and Caspe, op. cit.

20. Many survivors express disappointment at how slow the government's rehabilitation response has been. The *Guardian* reports that in November 2014, an NGO called the Green Mindanao Foundation distributed US$175 (for people whose homes were fully destroyed) and US$110 (for those whose homes were partially destroyed) to a few hundred people in Tacloban City. Charlie Reyes of the Green Mindanao Foundation claims that "while the amount is not much, it is the first real aid many people have seen. People feel abandoned by the government". See Kate Hodal, "Tacloban Suffers Typhoon's Long Tail", *Guardian Weekly*, 21 November 2014.

21. Villanueva-Ong, op. cit.

22. "P199.48 Available for Yolanda Rehab", *Manila Bulletin*, 13 November 2014.

23. Esmaquel II Paterno, "Philippines Gets 135% of Yolanda Cash Pledges", *Rappler*, 13 May 2014.

24. In total, as of July 2014, about 1,289 private sector and NGO projects have been tracked by the OPARR, with support and pledges totalling PhP11.8 billion (US$272 million).

25. Transcript: "Q&A of the Press Briefing on Yolanda Rehab and Recovery Efforts", 10 November 2014, available at <http://www.gov.ph/2014/11/10/transcript-q-and-a-of-the-press-briefing-on-yolanda-rehab-and-recovery-efforts-november-10-2014/> (accessed 18 November 2014).

26. The government has repaired or built 26km of national roads, 57.7km of farm to market roads, 158.5km of bridges, two flood control structures, 101 newly constructed classrooms, 833 renovated classrooms, 79,245 pieces of school furniture, 370 irrigation facilities, five national irrigation systems, two potable water systems, 14 rehabilitated seaports, 28 airports, 29 public markets, 33 cooperatives with power fully restored, three health facilities in government hospitals, 25 health facilities in regional health units and 96 health facilities in *barangay* health stations.

27. "117,000 Housing Units in Yolanda-hit Areas to be Completed by 2015", *Philippine News Agency*, 10 November 2014.

28. Ibid.

29. See <http://empathy.oparr.gov.ph/>.

30. Benigno Aquino Senior's assassination was a turning point which started the downfall of the Marcos regime and led to the election to the presidency of his widow, Corazon Aquino in 1986. Benigno Aquino III, the current president was elected in 2010, based on the groundswell of support for him after his mother, former President Corazon Aquino passed away in August 2009.

31. See Section 16 of Congress of the Philippines, *Republic Act 10121, "An act strengthening the Philippine disaster risk reduction and management system, providing for the national disaster risk reduction management framework and institutionalizing the national disaster risk reduction and management plan, appropriating funds therefor and for other purposes"*, 1 February 2010. Hereafter cited as RA 10121.

32. For the YouTube clip of the exchange, see "Yolanda MAR ROXAS Telling off Tacloban Mayor Alfred Romualdez", available at <https://www.youtube.com/watch?v=g_oxV8ylgOI>.

33. Natashya Gutierrez, "Aquino: Yolanda Delays the Fault of Tacloban City Gov't", *Rappler*, 13 March 2014.

34. Esmaquel II Paterno, "Romualdez: Cabinet Red Tape behind Yolanda Delay", *Rappler*, 12 May 2014.

35. Esmaquel II Paterno, "Philippines gets 135% of Yolanda Cash Pledges", *Rappler*, 13 May 2014.

36. Paterno, "Romualdez: Cabinet Red Tape", op. cit.

37. Hodal, op. cit.

38. "Ping Slams Tacloban Mayor over Rehab Protests", *Philippine Star*, 11 November 2014.

39. Diana Mendoza, "Philippines: One Year after Typhoon, Tacloban Calls Recovery Below Par", *Inter Press Service*, 10 November 2014.

40. Transcript: "Q&A of the Press Briefing on Yolanda Rehab and Recovery Efforts", op. cit.

41. "Ping Slams Tacloban Mayor", op. cit.

42. Voltaire Tupaz, "Malacanang's Yolanda Aid Dilemma:speed or Procedure?", *Rappler*, 11 November 2014.

43. Ibid.

44. Ibid.

45. Transcript: "Q&A of the Press Briefing on Yolanda Rehab and Recovery Efforts", op. cit.

46. Guiuan was where the typhoon first hit land and had a death toll of 107 people compared to Tacloban which lost 2,678 lives according to the NDRRMC. Pope Francis

is scheduled to visit Tacloban City in January 2015. It will be interesting to see whether President Aquino will be able to look beyond political differences and accompany the Pontiff in his visit to the affected communities.

47. Mendoza, op. cit.

48. Fritzie Rodriguez, "Tacloban Mayor to National Government: Build Back Better for Us", *Rappler*, 8 November 2014.

49. "Declare Ping Unwelcome in Tacloban", *Manila Standard*, 12 November 2014.

50. Totals vary but essentially the official statistic from the government is over 6,300 died and over 1,000 were missing totalling to the 7,354 figure of people killed by Yolanda.

51. Legarda, op. cit.

52. Lim Ubac, op. cit.

53. Along with RA 10121, the Philippines has also legislated Republic Act 9729 or the Climate Change Act, which sees climate change adaptation and disaster risk reduction and preparedness as interlinked. See Michael Ubac, "UN lauds Philippines' climate change laws 'world's best'", *Philippine Daily Inquirer*, 4 May 2012.

54. See RA 10121. See also Dean Tony La Vina and Jed Alegado, "Recovering from Yolanda: Gains, Missed Chances, Opportunities", *Rappler*, 8 November 2014.

55. See Section 5 of RA 10121.

56. See Sections 10–12 of RA 10121.

57. Aries Rufo, "NDRRMC: Too Many Cooks Spoilt the Broth", *Rappler*, 30 November 2013.

58. "Who is Calling the Shots after Haiyan", *Rappler*, 20 November 2013.

59. See Tony La Vina, "Urgently Needed, a New Disaster Agency", *Rappler*, 23 November 2013. See also La Vina and Alegado, "Recovering from Yolanda", op. cit.

60. See *Oxfam Briefing Paper.*

61. The U.N. Green Fund is a US$100 billion fund set up to help developing nations adapt to climate change. The bulk of the funding is supposed to come from developed nations who have committed to fully fund the U.N. Green Fund by 2020. See Zak Yuson, "Salceda Elected as UN Green Climate Fund Co-chair", *Rappler*, 14 October 2014.

62. Jee Geronimo, "Zero Casualty during Disasters Not Just about the Numbers", *Rappler*, 8 October 2014

63. Jodesz Gavilan, "Salceda: Funds for Climate Mitigation Hard to Get", *Rappler*, 5 August 2014.

64. "Abay's Sir Chief on Social Media", *Rappler*, 23 September 2013.

65. Bea Cupin, "When Disaster Hits: Salceda's Advice to Local Execs", *Rappler*, 30 January 2014.

66. See the full text of Yeb Sano's speech at <http://www.rtcc.org/2013/11/11/its-time-to-stop-this-madness-philippines-plea-at-un-climate-talks/#sthash.az9SsGGw.dpuf>. See also Matt McGrath, "Typhoon Prompts 'fast' by Philippines Climate Delegate", *BBC* news, 11 November 2013.

67. John Vidal, "Yeb Sano: Unlikely Climate Justice Star", *The Guardian*, 1 April 2014.

68. "Nations Agree on Format for Global Climate Deal", *Straits Times*, 15 December 2014.

69. Tony La Viña, "Urgently Needed, a New Disaster Agency", *Rappler*, 23 November 2013.

Singapore

SINGAPORE IN 2014:
Managing Domestic and Regional Concerns and Signalling a New Regional Role

N. Ganesan

In 2014 the government made a number of new political appointments and signalled that it was preparing the country for the fourth generation political leadership. It also acted on concerns about the cost of housing and medical fees, especially for the older pioneer generation that had helped build Singapore. In regional relations there were a few hiccups with Malaysia over toll charges for vehicles crossing the common causeway and unhappiness with the Indonesian decision to name a warship after two Indonesian marines who were tried and executed in Singapore for a terrorist act during Indonesia's Confrontation against Malaysia. Singapore also initiated a number of ventures that appear to signal a greater leadership role in arbitration and disaster management.

Political and Legal Developments

In domestic politics the most significant development was the PAP government's announcement in April that two members of the Cabinet had been made full ministers. They are Tan Chuan Jin who was made Manpower Minister, and Lawrence Wong who was made Minister for Culture, Community and Youth. The government announced that together with two other earlier appointees — Education Minister Heng Swee Keat and Social and Family Development Minister Chan Chun Sing, the appointments also reflected future priorities for the government during an important period of transition that will require emphasis on social

N. GANESAN is Professor at the Hiroshima Peace Institute in Japan.

and manpower issues.[1] These appointments appear to have consolidated a group of younger ministers who are likely to be identified with a fourth generation leadership. Importantly, Tan Chuan Jin and Chan Chun Sing's appointments are well in line with having a core pool of Singapore Armed Forces (SAF) scholars within the Cabinet. The current pool also includes Prime Minister Lee Hsien Loong, Deputy Prime Minister Teo Chee Hean and Trade and Industry Minister Lim Hng Kiang.

In other political news, former presidential candidate Tan Jee Say announced the formation of a new political party called "Singaporeans First".[2] It is likely that this development is closely related to seemingly high levels of dissatisfaction among locals with the high percentage of foreigners in the domestic population. There are constant complaints among locals that infrastructure facilities and services are being stretched on account of the new arrivals. Additionally, there is also a segment within the population that regards foreigners as responsible for taking away jobs from the locals. The government is aware of the disquiet at the ground level and has been trying to address the shortage of medical and transport facilities in particular. It has also agreed to slow down the recruitment of foreign workers, much to the chagrin of small and medium enterprises that complain about a shortage of workers in the services sector. In any event, it remains to be seen if this new party will fare well in the elections that are scheduled to be held by January 2017 and challenge the seeming strength of the Workers' Party in representing the political opposition. The Workers' Party has already been subjected to criticisms by the PAP-led government of incompetence in the running of the Aljunied Group Representation Constituency (GRC). Additionally, in December it was fined S$800 (US$590) for running a Chinese New Year fair without a permit from the National Environment Agency (NEA) in Hougang Central.[3]

In November 2014, blogger Roy Ngerng was found guilty of defaming Prime Minister Lee Hsien Loong with his blog posts. The damages are yet to be assessed. The charges relate to claims by Roy that amounted to Lee having criminally misappropriated contributions into the local equivalent of the national pension fund — the Central Provident Fund (CPF). An earlier offer of an apology and payment for damages came to naught when Ngerng's offer of S$5,000 was rejected as "derisory" by Lee.[4] Earlier on in October, Ngerng had been charged with five others for public nuisance when taking part in a protest in Hong Lim Park in September and disrupting a charity carnival for the Young Men's Christians Association (YMCA). Additionally, Ngerng, and another speaker, Han Hui Hui were also charged with organizing a demonstration without prior approval.[5]

In the course of the year, a number of court cases relating to the 2013 riot in Little India were heard and several of those who took part in them were sentenced. The sentences ranged from a few months' imprisonment to much longer terms of up to thirty-three months and three strokes of the cane for those who were charged with throwing projectiles at police officers and setting police vehicles on fire. The Commission of Inquiry (COI) that was established by the government to look into the causes of the riots also released its findings. The COI attributed the cause of the riot to a number of misunderstandings about the accident that killed a foreign worker.[6] These misunderstandings included the perception that police were shielding the driver and bus time-keeper from culpability and arrest, and the belief that the accident victim died only because he was not attended to. Subsequent findings proved that the victim had died immediately and that the anger of the workers was misplaced. The report also noted an attempt to mete out "retributive justice" on the spot to those who were assumed to be guilty.

A total of eight recommendations were made by the COI and the government accepted all of them.[7] The first five of the recommendations pertained to police and civil defence personnel and procedures including proper training, coordination, command and control. It also emphasized the need to respond in a timely and concerted manner. Other recommendations included improving lighting, safety and surveillance devices and making available more services and facilities for foreign workers outside areas where such workers tended to congregate. And finally, the report also noted the role of alcohol in triggering the riot and suggested restrictions on the sale of alcohol to lessen the incidence of public drunkenness and to preserve public order. In response to the riot, Parliament had earlier passed the Public Order (Additional Temporary Measures) Act (POATM) on 18 February in order to "continue to allow the police to take calibrated measures to maintain public order in Little India...". [8] Precautions contained in the measures included the restricted sale of alcohol in parts of Little India.

Another riot broke out in March 2014 which involved fighting between foreign workers from Bangladesh and India.[9] The fight broke out between dormitory residents when they were watching a live cricket match between Bangladesh and the West Indies. A total of thirty-five workers were arrested and the situation was quickly brought under control by the police. In an unrelated development, the Attorney General's Chambers (AGC) announced that it was looking at ways to speed up court cases involving abused foreign workers.[10] Additionally, it is specifically looking at ways to procure compensation for such workers, including maids, as a result of criminal offences committed against them.

The Singapore Government also announced a series of initiatives to strengthen the country's contributions to regional peace and development. In April it announced the setting up of a Regional Humanitarian and Disaster Relief (HADR) coordination centre to be based at the Changi Command and Control Centre. The offer was made during an ASEAN-U.S. Defence Ministers' informal meeting.[11] The government's hope is that the new centre will allow for a coordinated regional military response to natural disasters in particular. The government also announced the launch of an International Mediation Centre in November to provide "world class commercial mediation services".[12] The centre hopes to provide an avenue to deal with transnational commercial disputes that arise from the marked increase in trade and commercial activities in the region.

In October, sovereign investment fund Temasek Holdings announced a S$100 million endowment to "strengthen international friendships and promote regional cooperation". The endowment fund that was named after the country's first Foreign Minister, S. Rajaratnam, is meant to partner civil society organizations and think-tanks as well as the private sector in a bid to encourage regional peace, stability and development.[13] Finally, it was also announced that the Singapore Government would contribute personnel and equipment to the multinational coalition against the Islamic State in Iraq and Syria (ISIS).[14] Singapore, which has traditionally taken the threat of religiously inspired terrorism seriously, has in the past provided similar support to multinational coalitions in Iraq and Afghanistan. It was also involved in maritime operations against the threat of piracy off the coast of Somalia.

Economic and Social Issues

The government began the budget year with a number of initiatives targeted to offer financial and start-up assistance to small and medium enterprises (SMEs). The Production and Innovative Credit (PIC) scheme has been extended by three years until 2018. Additional schemes were announced for SMEs that utilize Information and Communications Technology (ICT)-based solutions and an extension of the Micro-loan Programme for new and young companies. Additional allocations were made under the existing Co-investment Programme and the Internationalization Finance Programme to help companies expand their reach outside Singapore.

At the individual level, the government announced the usual Goods and Services Tax (GST) rebates and an additional grant for the same reason to those living in Housing and Development Board (HDB) flats ranging from $90 to $260 depending on flat type. And again, as with previous years, Service and Conservancy Charges for HDB households were waived from one to three months depending on flat type. Provisions were also made for enhanced services in education and transport for those with special needs and the tax waiver for those looking after handicapped relatives was raised by an additional $2,000.

The most significant announcement for elderly citizens was the Pioneer Generation Package that is meant to provide affordable healthcare to senior citizens beginning from September 2014. The government expects this scheme to benefit some 400,000 Singaporeans. This package is part of a broader ongoing initiative to tweak the local national medical insurance scheme (Medishield). From 2015, citizens will pay a monthly premium to access universal healthcare throughout their lives without exclusions for pre-existing conditions. Both of these developments have come a long way from the previous exclusions for existing conditions, maximum age limits as well as much smaller withdrawal limits and restrictions on claims. The truth of the matter is that healthcare has become expensive, especially for those who retired in the 1980s and 1990s.

The Medishield Review Committee that was formed to advise the government offered a number of suggestions that was taken up in its entirety by the government. These included a lifting of the lifetime claim limit of $300,000 and increasing the annual claim limit from $70,000 to $100,000. Claims for limits on in-patient ward charges, surgical procedures and out-patient charges for cancer-related treatments were also significantly enhanced.[15] The government announced a S$4 billion subsidy package in order to cover subsidies for those above the age of 80 who will be exempted from premiums and lesser offsets for the needy. The employer's contribution to the Medisave accounts of workers will be increased by 1 percentage point from 2015 and the new scheme will kick in from the end of 2015. As with all schemes, it remains to be seen how the implementation of this scheme is effected. Previous means testing measures and exclusions for procedures had led to significant negative feedback. Also, as if in response to a pent-up demand for subsidized medical treatment for the elderly, it was reported in the local media that nearly 50,000 citizens had used their Pioneer Generation cards within the first week of the implementation of the new scheme.[16] It remains to be seen if the evolution of this scheme will provide some form of coverage for school-going children as well, which is an established practice in most developed countries.

Apart from trying to make medical care more affordable for all, the government has also been looking for ways to allow owners of public housing flats to draw down against the value of their flats in order to provide them an income during old age. Depending on the age of the home owner and expected remaining life expectancy, the balance of the lease can be sold back to the government to help realize the value of the flat when its occupants are still alive.[17] However, the owners will first have to top up their Central Provident Fund (CPF) Retirement Accounts prior to receiving the remainder in cash. The scheme has now been extended to four-room flats as well. Previously, only flats with up to three rooms were part of the scheme. It is hoped that this scheme will also allow the government to repossess sold flats after their return for reoccupation.

In other economic news, Singapore was listed as the fourth priciest city in the world for expatriates by research firm Mercer.[18] Echoing similar sentiments for the local population, another report indicated that living expenses in Singapore are higher than comparable rates in Seoul and Hong Kong.[19] Such comparisons and relative cost-of-living data indicates Singapore as a rather expensive city to live in. For the country as a whole, the employment rate for the year remained high and growth is expected to average at 3 per cent. The government appears to have succeeded in raising the average household incomes of low wage workers at the 20th percentile from $1,500 in 2009 to $1,972 in 2014, up 31 per cent as reported by the Ministry of Manpower.[20] The rising cost of living had placed a disproportionate burden on the bottom 20 per cent of the work force and the government has been consciously raising their wages through a Wage Credit Scheme given to employers and mandating a higher bonus payment for such workers as well. The real local median monthly income, however, grew by a much lesser 0.4 per cent after taking inflation into consideration, at a median monthly income of $3,770.

In social news, the government is clearly trying to keep the price of housing affordable and indicated that it will not lift the newly imposed restrictions on mortgage limits and loan quantums to deter excessive speculation. It has also significantly ramped up the sale and release of public housing flats to meet the current shortfall. In May, the Housing and Development Board (HDB) announced the launch of 6,454 flats for sale, combining both Build-To-Order units and remaining units from previous sales.[21] In November, the HDB announced a similar exercise launching a total of 7,568 flats for sale.[22] There tends to be a waiting period of up to three to four years for Build-To-Order flats so the lag time for construction is often unable to stem immediate need in the demand side of the equation. In this regard, policy planning for infrastructural development that is time consuming often leads to choke points like those that now exist for housing, medical and transport facilities. It is no secret that much of the unhappiness against the recent increase in the domestic population has led to such inconveniences and this is one of the reasons for anger against the People's Action Party (PAP) government. Whereas the government is aware of this development and has acknowledged its fault in not being better prepared, the lag time in making up for the shortfall in services means that this source of unhappiness will remain for some time to come.

2014 also witnessed an outbreak of measles in Singapore, some of which was imported from the Philippines.[23] The remainder of the cases involved young children who had not been vaccinated. Singapore's Ministry of Health has in place a vaccination programme against measles, mumps and rubella and large-scale outbreaks are generally rare although the disease itself is infectious. This outbreak is therefore at odds with recent developments where it is far more common to have the outbreak of hand, foot and mouth disease for young children. Dengue fever continued to be a major health issue in 2014 as well and at the time of writing, had claimed five lives in Singapore.[24] The Communicable Diseases Department of the Ministry of Health recorded an all-time high of 842 cases of the disease on the twenty-eighth week of the year in August. Changes in the weather including higher than usual levels of rainfall has led the disease to become a major regional concern, including in neighbouring Indonesia, Malaysia and Thailand.

Foreign Policy

Singapore's relations with the major powers was reaffirmed through a series of reciprocal visits by heads of state and high-ranking officials albeit relations with neighbouring Indonesia and Malaysia underwent some strain 2014. In June, Prime Minister Lee Hsien Loong visited the United States where he marked the 10th Anniversary of the United States-Singapore Free Trade Agreement that was inked in January 2004 and noted how the Agreement had significantly enhanced trade relations between the two countries, and that Singapore remains the premier destination for United States (U.S.) investments in Asia.[25] Apart from reaffirming bilateral ties, Lee is reported to have encouraged U.S.

politicians to support President Obama's initiative for enhanced trade through the Trans Pacific Partnership (TPP). The visit also allowed Lee to open an office for the Singapore sovereign investment firm Temasek Holdings in Washington D.C.. Earlier in May, Foreign Affairs Minister S. Shanmugam had already visited the U.S. and met with State Department Secretary John Kerry. During that visit, it was reported that Shanmugam had conferred with his counterpart on tensions between China and Vietnam over the Paracel Islands, and China and the Philippines over the Spratly Islands.[26] Singapore and the U.S. share a strong strategic and bilateral security relationship that was formalized with the signing of the Memorandum of Understanding (MOU) between the two countries in 1990 that led in turn to Singapore hosting the Command and Logistics Headquarters of the Seventh Fleet (COMLOG WESTPAC) in Singapore, together with rotational deployment of military hardware. Separately, the Singapore Parliament has endorsed an U.S.-led coalition fighting against the Islamic State of Iraq and Syria (ISIS). It offered to send a contingent of between fifty and sixty personnel from the Singapore Armed Forces (SAF) for assistance in imagery analysis operating from nearby countries, as well as a KC135 tanker aircraft for air-to-air refuelling.[27]

Relations with China and Japan were also kept at an even keel. Prime Minister Lee disclosed that Singapore is keen on initiating a third joint venture project with the Chinese Government after the first Suzhou Industrial Park project twenty years ago and the second Tianjin Eco-city project that was launched in 2008.[28] The Chinese Government reportedly requested Singapore to consider the western parts of China for the third project. While in China, Lee also reaffirmed bilateral ties and expressed support for China's version of a Maritime Silk Road that would link China with the ASEAN countries through the South China Sea. Relations with Japan were strengthened when its Prime Minister Shinzo Abe visited Singapore in May and delivered the keynote address at the annual Shangri-La Dialogue — a high-profile multilateral security dialogue. While in Singapore he toured the country's casinos and expressed interest in similar developments in Japan to tap the regional gaming market. In October, Singapore's Foreign Minister K. Shanmugam reciprocated with a visit to Japan where he agreed to speedily review the Japan-Singapore New-Age Economic Partnership Agreement (JSEPA) and expressed support for Abe's "proactive contribution to peace" policy that was announced at the Shangri-La Dialogue earlier.[29] In December 2013, Singapore's Foreign Ministry had issued a statement that it regretted Abe's visit to the Yasukuni Shrine that contains the remains of convicted war criminals. The Singapore Government has consistently maintained that it can forgive but cannot forget Japan's aggression and atrocities during World War Two.

In October 2014, Singapore signed a Free Trade Agreement (FTA) with Turkey when Prime Minister Lee paid a visit to the country. Trade and relations between the two countries have steadily progressed in recent years and there appears to be sufficient synergy and willingness for both countries to move the relationship to a higher plane.[30]

Among relations with regional countries, the bilateral relationship with Indonesia underwent the most strain. Notwithstanding bilateral hiccups, Prime Minster Lee travelled to Malaysia to confer with Prime Minister Najib as part of an annual retreat in April and also attended Indonesian President Joko Widodo's inauguration ceremony. The development that triggered the strain with Indonesia was the decision to name a newly commissioned British-built naval frigate Usman Harun, drawing on the names of the two Indonesian marines, Osman Haji Mohamed Ali and Harun Said, who were executed in Singapore for bombing MacDonald House in Orchard Road in March 1965 during the Indonesian Confrontation. The bombing led to the deaths of three civilians and thirty-three persons more were injured. The naming of the frigate was clearly viewed in Singapore as an unnecessary provocation and it was reported that Singapore's Foreign Minister K. Shanmugam spoke with then Indonesian Foreign Minister Dr Marty Natalegawa to register Singapore's unhappiness.[31] Singapore's Defence Minister Ng Eng Hen and Deputy Prime Minister Teo Chee Hean were also reported to have contacted their Indonesian counterparts to urge a reconsideration of the naming. Indonesia, however, defended the action, saying that it was in line with the national policy of naming warships after those regarded as national heroes and adhered to its decision. However, the Commander-in-Chief of the *Tentera Nasional Indonesia* (TNI — Indonesian Armed Forces), General Moeldoko, expressed regret over the incident saying that the country bore no ill-will towards Singapore and that the decision had been a considered one that was made in December 2012 and in line with existing practices.[32] In March, Singapore withdrew from the Jakarta International Defence Dialogue when two marines dressed as Usman and Harun took part in the event. Jakarta subsequently tried to calm bilateral relations with Singapore by inviting Singapore to take part in the multilateral Komodo Exercise that involved military personnel from seventeen countries. Additionally, Indonesian Coordinating Minister for Political, Legal and Security Affairs, Air Chief Marshal (Ret.) Djoko Suyanto and Indonesian Defence Minister Purnomo

Yusgiantoro also expressed regret over the incident.[33] At the height of tensions between the two countries over the incident, Indonesia's top army officials decided not to attend the Singapore Airshow that was held in February 2014.[34]

On a more positive note, Singapore offered assistance in the international search-and-recovery operations for the Air Asia flight QZ8501 that crashed while flying from Surabaya in Indonesia to Singapore. The Singapore Government's offer of assistance came in the form of C-130 aircraft at the outset to help locate the missing plane. Subsequently, the Singapore Navy offered a frigate, a Landing Ship Tank (LST), a corvette and the specialized rescue vessel MV Swift Rescue.[35] These assets were deployed until salvage attempts were well underway after the missing aircraft was detected on the seabed of Karimata Strait. These maritime assets were only recalled back to Singapore after large parts of the aircraft and the remains of some fifty passengers were recovered. The Changi Airport Group also assisted Air Asia by setting up a Relative Holding Area to deal with the next-of-kin of those who were on board the ill-fated flight.

Singapore's attempts to deal with the haze situation arising from Indonesian forest fires also received support from Indonesia. Singapore introduced a bill in the country's Parliament to penalize persons and companies listed in the Singapore Stock Exchange if they were found responsible for such forest fires.[36] The local government of Indonesia's Riau Province expressed support for the bill. And more importantly, on 16 September Indonesia ratified the ASEAN Agreement on Transboundary Haze Pollution. This was done in the last days of President Susilo Bambang Yudhoyono's presidency and came twelve years after the signing of the Agreement. Incumbent President Joko Widodo has indicated that the problem can be dealt with if greater focus and willingness is brought to bear on dealing with it.[37] Indonesia's earlier refusal to ratify it for so long meant that very little could be done to deal with those responsible for the forest fires that led to the haze. In that sense, this change of heart is a positive development for countries like Malaysia and Singapore that bear a disproportionate impact from the unregulated and illegal forest fires.

Two other issues affected bilateral relations between the two countries in 2014. The first was the revelation by the Indonesian Attorney General's Office (AGO) that a raid by the police on the assets of Gayus H. Tambunan, a tax official convicted of corruption, yielded a haul of S$9.98 million in cash, among other assets.[38] This development then led to the Indonesian call for Singapore to impose expiration dates on the S$10,000-denominated bills since large amounts can be carried with little difficulty. The Singapore Government in turn responded by noting that from 1 October 2014, it would stop issuing such notes.[39] The second development was the outbreak of violence between the Indonesian Police's Mobile Brigade (Brimob) and marines from the TNI's Tuah Sakti 134 Battalion based in Batam which is proximate to Singapore and where many Singapore companies have investments.[40] The violence arose after four marines were shot by Brimob personnel who were investigating oil smuggling. The incident led in turn to a tit–for-tat marine attack on the Brimob headquarters although they had explicit orders to return to their barracks and turn in their weapons. Outbreaks of such violence between the TNI and Brimob are quite common in Indonesia although it has not happened this close to Singapore in the past. In an unrelated development, the TNI announced the establishment of the Tenth Infantry Battalion in Setotok Island in Batam with amphibious and rocket launcher capabilities.[41] This development is also likely to have been noted in Singapore which maintains a high level of interest in regional developments that could affect its security.

Singapore's bilateral relations with Malaysia started well in the year but underwent some hiccups as the year progressed. Singapore offered use of its military assets at the start of the year as part of multinational efforts to locate Malaysian Airlines System's flight MH370 that disappeared enroute to Beijing. These assets included two C-130 aircraft, a naval helicopter, a Fokker-50 maritime patrol craft, two warships and a submarine support and rescue vessel.[42] It also pledged that it was ready to provide further support if necessary.

The first hiccup was the result of seemingly tit-for-tat raises in the toll booth charges that both countries levy on traffic crossing the common Causeway between them. Singapore began the increase at least partly in order to prevent Singaporeans and Malaysians working in Singapore from being insulated from the high cost of car ownership in Singapore. Malaysia subsequently raised its own toll charges significantly in August and Singapore noted that it was prepared to reciprocate the gesture.[43] When the new Malaysian charges was announced, there was some amount of disruption to traffic since a number of buses ferrying workers were reported to have jammed the Causeway in protest against the hikes.[44] However, the situation returned to normal shortly afterwards. Then, at the end of the year in December, the Malaysian Government announced that effective from the middle of 2015, it would levy an entry fee of twenty Malaysian ringgit (US$5.50) for all vehicles entering the country via the Causeway and the Second Link from Singapore. The Singapore Government again responded that it would deal with the new situation in due course.

The second hiccup pertained to Singapore's concern about the transboundary impact of Malaysia's extensive land reclamation off the coast of the southern state of Johor. The Forest City Project mooted by Chinese developers, Country Garden Holdings, near the Second Link in the western part of the Straits of Johor is slated to involve several connected islands spanning an area of approximately 1,600 hectares.[45] Singapore protested that although the project does not cross maritime boundaries, construction work would affect the "water flows and silting" through the channel.[46] In response Malaysia's Department of Environment has set limits on the project. At the time of writing, the new limits had only been verbally informed and official confirmation had not been given yet.

In other bilateral news, an international arbitral council ruled that the Malaysian Government would not have to pay a development levy of S$1.47 billion in order to jointly develop what used to be Malayan Railway Land.[47] Singapore had sought the levy which is applied for local development works but the charge was overruled by the tribunal. The decision has since been uploaded on the website of the Permanent Court of Arbitration in The Hague. This development brings to a close one of the thorns in the bilateral relationship between the two countries. Another issue over which the countries have expressed differences are the plans to develop a high-speed rail link between Kuala Lumpur and Singapore. Malaysia has confirmed the seven stops in the network as Kuala Lumpur, Putrajaya, Seremban, Ayer Keroh, Muar, Batu Pahat, and Nusajaya. Malaysia has also indicated that such a link may not be ready by 2020 as previously expected while Singapore has not commented much on the subject apart from mentioning that a number of stops are being considered.[48] The details were revealed at the High Speed Rail Conference 2014 that was held in Tokyo to mark the 50th Anniversary of the Tokaido Shinkansen. Japan is one of the countries that has expressed interest in building the fast rail network.

Singapore's bilateral relationship with Brunei was strengthened during the year. The Brunei Sultan's state visit to Singapore in April led to the signing of a number of Memoranda of Understanding (MOU) between the two countries. These included an MOU in broadcasting and information as well as another on monetary cooperation involving "capital market development and capacity building, … and best practices on monetary management and operations, human resources, information technologies, banking supervision and payment and settlement".[49] The two countries also signed a civil aviation cooperation MOU on the sidelines of the 20th ASEAN Transport Ministers' Meeting in Mandalay, Myanmar in August.[50] One final negative development capped Singapore's regional developments for the year in review. During an anti-China riot in Vietnam in May, a Singapore Flag was burnt at the Vietnam-Singapore Industrial Park 1 in Binh Duong Province.[51] Singapore's Ministry of Foreign Affairs subsequently conveyed the country's concerns via a diplomatic note.

Conclusion

In 2014, there were a number of new appointments to the country's Cabinet and the PAP government articulated the emergence of a fourth generation of leadership for the future. The government also sought to introduce a number of safety nets for the country's pioneer generation by unveiling a new health policy and made more liberal amendments to its national health insurance scheme. The leadership also signalled a willingness to take on a larger leadership role in regional developments and set up a number of funds to undertake the task. In foreign affairs, the country's relationship with the major powers was kept on an even keel while there were some hiccups in regional relations, notably with Indonesia.

Notes

The author would like to thank Lam Peng Er and Benjamin Wong for their comments on an earlier draft of this article.

1. Thiam Yuen-C., "Cabinet Shuffle 'to See Singapore through Next Phase'", *Straits Times*, 30 April 2014.

2. Andrea Ong, "Tan Jee Say forms 'Singaporeans First' Political Party", *Straits Times*, 25 May 2014.

3. Walter Sim, "WP Town Council Fined $800 for Running Chinese New Year Fair without Permit", *Straits Times*, 24 December 2014.

4. "Roy Ngerng Found to have Defamed Prime Minister Lee", *Channel NewsAsia*, 7 November 2014.

5. Walter Sim, "Six protestors, including activist Han Hui Hui and blogger Roy Ngerng, charged with public nuisance", *Straits Times*, 27 October 2014.

6. Hoe Pei Shan, "Little India Riot: Misunderstanding about fatal Accident Sparked Violence, Says COI", *Straits Times*, 30 June 2014.

7. "Little India Riot: 8 Recommendations from Committee of Inquiry Report", *Straits Times*, 30 June 2014.

8. Lim Yan Liang, "New Public Order Law to Take Effect in Little India from Tuesday", *Straits Times*, 31 March 2014.

9. Sujin Thomas, "35 South Asian Men Arrested for Rioting in Kaki Bukit Dormitory", *Straits Times*, 27 March 2014.

10. Radha Basu, "AGC Studying Ways to Speed Up Court Cases Involving Abused Foreign Workers", *Straits Times*, 3 August 2014.

11. "S'pore Offers to Host Regional Crisis Coordination Centre", *Channel NewsAsia*, 7 April 2014.

12. Lim Yi Han, "New International Mediation Centre Launched in Singapore", *Straits Times*, 5 November 2014.

13. Walter Sim, "Temasek Launches S. Rajaratnam Endowment to Strengthen International Ties", *Straits Times*, 21 October 2014.

14. Charissa Yong, "Parliament: Singapore will Contribute Personnel and Equipment to Multinational Coalition against ISIS", *Straits Times*, 3 November 2014.

15. "Medishield Life Review Committee Unveils Recommendations" and "Medishield Life: Govt. Accepts Proposals, Will Provide almost \$4b in Subsidies", *Channel NewsAsia*, 27 June 2014.

16. Siau Ming En, "Nearly 50,000 have Used Pioneer Generation Cards: Gan", *Today Newspaper*, 8 October 2014.

17. Janice Heng, "Changes to HDB Lease Buyback Scheme: Higher Income Ceiling; More Cash Upfront for Owners", *Straits Times*, 3 September 2014.

18. Melissa Tan, "Singapore Rises to 4th Priciest City in the World for Expatriates: Mercer", *Straits Times*, 14 July 2014.

19. "Singapore More Costly for Citizens to Live in than Seoul or Hong Kong", *Channel NewsAsia*, 27 November 2014.

20. "Singapore's Employment Rate, Median Income up in 2014", *Channel NewsAsia*, 28 November 2014.

21. Janice Heng, "6,454 Flats in Combined Launch of Build-To-Order and Sale of Balance Flats", *Straits Times*, 22 May 2014.

22. Olivia Siong, "HDB Launches more than 7,500 Flats in November", *Channel NewsAsia*, 26 November 2014.

23. "Eighty Measles Cases in Singapore; 23 had Travelled to Philippines", *Channel NewsAsia*, 16 April 2014.

24. "69-year-old Man Dies From Dengue, The Fifth Person This Year", *Straits Times*, 28 November 2014.

25. "PM Lee Marks 10th Anniversary of US-Singapore FTA in Washington" and "US-Singapore FTA Paves Way for TPP Negotiation: PM Lee", *Straits Times*, 25 June 2014.

26. Jeremy Au Yong, "Shanmugam and Kerry Reaffirm Bilateral Relations", *Straits Times*, 13 May 2014.

27. Danson Cheong, "Singapore's Deployment to Combat ISIS will Number about 50 to 60: Defence Minister Ng En Hen", *Straits Times*, 1 December 2014.

28. Rachel Chang, "Singapore Wants Third Bilateral Venture with China to Fit in with Beijing's Priorities, says PM Lee", *Straits Times*, 9 November 2014.

29. "Foreign Minister Shanmugam Calls on Japanese PM Abe", *Channel NewsAsia*, 23 October 2014.

30. Wong Siew Ying, "Good Progress for Turkey-Singapore FTA Negotiations: PM Lee", *Channel NewsAsia*, 13 October 2014.

31. Zakir Hussain, "Singapore Concerned over Naming of Indonesian Navy Ship after Executed Commandos", *Straits Times*, 6 February 2014; and *Thomson Reuters*, "Singapore Angry at Indonesia Move to Name Navy Ship for Convicted Bombers", 27 March 2014.

32. Sujadi Siswo, "Indonesian Armed Forces Chief Expresses Regret over Naming of Warship", *Channel NewsAsia*; and "Singapore Welcomes Indonesia's Apology over Naming of Frigates", *Straits Times*, 16 April 2014.

33. "Two Indonesian Ministers Express Regret over Marines Posing as Bombers", *Channel NewsAsia*, 21 March 2014.

34. Bernie Moestafa and Tanya Angerer, "Indonesia Officials Skip Singapore Airshow", *Bloomberg News*, 11 February 2014.

35. "AirAsia flight QZ8501: Singapore Offers to Deploy More Vessels to Help in Search and Locate Efforts", *Straits Times*, 28 December 2014.

36. Devianti Faridz, "Singapore's Haze Bill Gets Support, but Some Question Effectiveness", *Channel NewsAsia*, 27 May 2014.

37. "Indonesian Parliament Votes to Ratify ASEAN Haze Pact", *Channel NewsAsia*, 16 September 2014; and Margaret S. Aritonang, "RI Ratifies Haze Treaty", *Jakarta Post*, 17 September 2014.

38. "Former Taxman's Cash, Gold Bars Worth Pp. 74 Billion Confiscated", *Jakarta Post*, 18 November 2014.

39. "Indonesia Urges Singapore to Impose Expiration Dates on $10,000 notes", *Jakarta Post*, 8 July 2014.

40. "Fear Grips Batam as Soldiers Attack Brimob HQ", *Jakarta Post*, 20 November 2014.

41. "Fadli, "Batam Marine Battalion Officially Ready", *Jakarta Post*, 4 November 2014.

42. "Singapore Stands Ready to Provide Further Support to Locate Missing Plane MH370: PM Lee", *Channel NewsAsia,* 15 March 2014.

43. "Singapore will Keep Matching Malaysian Toll Charges", *New Straits Times*, 10 September 2014.

44. "Malaysian Buses Stage 'Strike' at Johor Checkpoint, Says Report", *Straits Times*, 1 August 2014.

45. "We'll Work with Singapore over Land Issue, Says Anifah", *New Straits Times*, 25 June 2015; and "Vivian Balakrishnan Restates Singapore's Concerns over Johor Strait Land Reclamation Projects during KL Visit", *Straits Times*, 25 November 2014.

46. <http://blogs.ft.com/beyond-brics/2014/12/30/malaysian-150bn-mega-project-riles-singapore/>

47. Walter Sim, "Rail Land Tax: Singapore and Malaysia Wanted Win-win Deal, Says Tribunal", *Straits Times*, 2 November 2014.

48. Adrian Lim, "Malaysia Confirms Its Singapore-Kuala Lumpur High-speed Rail Stations", *Straits Times*, 23 October 2014; and "Malaysia-Singapore High Speed Rail Details to be Finalized Next Year", *New Straits Times*, 23 October 2014.

49. "Singapore, Brunei Sign MOU to Expand Cooperation in Broadcasting and Information", *Channel NewsAsia*, 22 April 2014; and "S'pore and Brunei Monetary Authorities Ink MOU on Bilateral Cooperation", *Channel NewsAsia*, 23 April 2014.

50. Pearl Lee, "Singapore Signs Civil Aviation Cooperation MOU with Brunei", *Straits Times*, 28 November 2014.

51. "Singapore Flag Burnt in Vietnam Riots: MFA", *Channel NewsAsia,* 15 May 2014.

MANAGING CYBERSPACE
State Regulation versus Self-Regulation

Carol Soon

Introduction

The traditional media in Singapore has played a supportive role in nation building since post-independence, with the print and broadcast media deployed for the purpose of communicating state policies to the populace. The government's control of the media was justified on the grounds of building social cohesion among its citizens from diverse ethnic, racial and religious backgrounds.[1] A myriad of laws was put in place to govern both print and broadcast media such as the Broadcasting Act, the Newspaper and Printing Presses Act, Undesirable Publications Act and Public Entertainment and Meetings Act. The public service monopoly of broadcasting was intended to protect and promote national culture and identity[2] and the prohibition of private ownership of the mass media as well as satellite dishes (until the 1990s) helped the government to maintain both political and social stability, critical factors that are purported to have created Singapore's economic success.

Within a short span of about forty years since its independence, Singapore's growth achieved a phenomenal rate, averaging 8 per cent per annum, an outcome that has been attributed to the government's sound economic planning and focused efforts to attract foreign investments in various industrial sectors[3]. The 1990s witnessed a shift in the policymakers' priority as they embarked on transforming the island with a population of over four million into an information hub, one that trades in ideas rather than commodities. Visible success for initiatives such as the Singapore IT2000 Masterplan and Infocomm 21 Strategy was clearly

Carol Soon is a Research Fellow at the Institute of Policy Studies, Singapore.

evident from the sharp increase of Internet penetration and broadband among the populace. By 2009, Internet access and broadband access among households reached 81 per cent and 80 per cent respectively.[4] In that same year, Singapore was ranked among the top five economies in Asia Pacific on the ICT Development Index.[5]

This chapter examines the development of the online space in Singapore, specifically the broadening of public discourse and civic engagement among citizens in recent years. While the online space has provided opportunities for marginalized voices and players to emerge, its dark side has reared up in the form of anti-social behaviour such as anti-foreigners and racist speech, trolling and witch-hunting. The latter has given rise to concerns among policymakers and the public on the polarizing effects of new media on society. However, given the emergence of pro-social speech that counters negative speech, self-regulation may be the more sustainable and effective way to regulating the online space as compared to legislative measures.

Circumvention of Media Regulation

The government's control of content when it comes to mainstream media ensures that "content stays within the unwritten parameters of political acceptability".[6] Discourse that pervades mainstream media has traditionally adhered to out-of-bounds (OB) markers such as limits to speech on race and religion. When it came to the online space, the government adopts the same philosophy. The vulnerability of the state — given its geographical location, diverse ethnic and social make-up — is the reason given by the government to curtail the expression of political opinions on the Internet. Under the Media Development Authority (MDA), the regulation of the Internet is purported to be essential, not to stop religious and political bodies from setting up websites, but to promote accountability among users by holding content providers accountable for the web content that they put up.

The Singapore Constitution guarantees freedom of speech but with caveats. Sacrosanct principles that govern public discourse include respecting the judiciary, and maintaining racial and religious harmony. A person who promotes feelings of ill-will and hostility between different races or classes of the population of Singapore can be convicted under the Sedition Act, and be fined up to S$5,000 (US$3,670) or jailed up to three years, or both.[7] In 2007, amendments were made to the Penal Code to allow greater prosecutorial discretion, and Section 298A[8] was incorporated to cover online transmissions. Besides these two laws, the 1997 Internet Code of Practice was implemented with the aim of promoting accountability and social responsibility among individuals when they communicate via the Internet. The code prohibits the publishing of material that "glorifies, incites or endorses ethnic, racial or religious hatred, strife or intolerance".[9]

More recently, the MDA on 28 May 2013 introduced a new licensing regime for websites that regularly carry local news content. News websites that have 50,000 unique visitors from Singapore each month over a period of two months and publish an average of at least one article a week on "Singapore's news and current affairs" over the same period would have to be individually licensed. Under the new scheme, sites asked to register will have to put up a performance bond of S$50,000. Failure to register will result in a fine of up to S$200,000 or a jail term of up to three years or both. Upon registration, news sites will have to renew their licence annually and remove objectionable content within twenty-four hours.

Despite these regulations which have been criticized by members of the public and free speech advocates as creating a chilling effect on speech, recent developments suggest that the Internet does play a significant and important role in broadening public discourse and enhancing civic engagement in Singapore. Approximately 85 per cent of households had home Internet access and almost all of such households connected to the Internet via broadband; although computers remain as the main equipment used to access the Internet at home, Internet-based mobile access has increased from 34 per cent in 2010 to 54 per cent in 2011.[10]

Social media tools such as blogs, online forums, and Facebook have allowed individuals to voice their opinions easily at a low cost, circumvent or ignore regulations, and experiment with new-found freedom in expressing themselves. Ericsson ConsumerLab found that using social networks, sending and receiving email, getting information and general web browsing, and reading online news were the top four activities.[11] Latest figures from the report point to an increase in smartphone penetration from 74 per cent in 2012 to 78 per cent in 2013 and from 31 per cent in 2012 to 42 per cent in 2013 for tablet penetration. These trends show that Singaporeans are increasing leveraging mobile communication for utility purposes — seeking and sharing information, and for networking.

Politically, the Internet has challenged the state's ability to regulate public discourse. George[12] argued that the inherent characteristics of the Internet and the economic benefits associated with the adoption of the technology makes it difficult for the government to regulate new media in the same way that it did with traditional media such as print and broadcast. Furthermore, the sheer volume of rapidly-transmissible packet-switched content, have resulted in the creation of loopholes that are exploited by marginalized groups and individuals. On the part of the government, some attempts have been made to regulate the Internet with a "light touch", such as rescinding the ban of political videos and posting campaign material on the Internet during the 2011 General Election and the commissioning of the Advisory Council on the Impact of New Media on Society in 2007 to explore possible approaches on how to fine-tune its "light-touch" policies on regulating Internet use.

Broadening Public Discourse and Civic Engagement

Digital technologies are playing an increasingly important role in facilitating civic engagement among ordinary citizens as they provide alternative means of assembly and organizing to those who want to advance specific causes. Prior to the Internet, individuals who wanted to form groups and organize activities to further their goals have to register with the Registrar of Societies. Under the Societies Act, the state has discretionary power to deny permit to groups and upon successful registration, civil society organizations are closely monitored by the authorities to ensure that they keep to the agenda stated in their constitution and mission. Although the same regulation exists today, digital technologies have enabled individuals to circumvent regulatory constraints.

Internet scholars have lauded the mobilizing potential of Internet technologies and how they widen the collective action repertoire. Besides creating new modalities of collective action and facilitating traditional ones, new media such as blogs, social networking sites and micro-blogging sites have given collective action an extra boost in the rapid identification and connection of like-minded stakeholders. Now on the Internet, individuals can converge with ease and advocate causes which they believe in, and the anonymity afforded by the Internet lowers risks of participation. These platforms are used to increase awareness, organize and encourage participation among their target constituencies. In addition to providing campaign details, bottom-up groups leverage the mobilization capacity of the Internet to distribute action alerts, plan and coordinate offline activities, and execute online actions.

In an earlier study by Soon and Cheong[13], issues advocated by digital bottom-up movements were categorized into three types (see Table 1). The first type focused on human-rights issues. These movements advanced the rights of marginalized communities (for example, lesbians, gays, bisexuals and transsexuals [LGBT]) as in the case of Pink Dot.sg. Others sought to restore human dignity and freedom for individuals perceived to be unjustly treated by the law, for example, the Internal Security Act (ISA) campaign and the Anti-Mandatory Death Penalty campaign. The second category of campaigns dealt with bread-and-butter issues such as rising costs of living, transportation issues and income inequality. The movements in the third category are incident-specific, organized to galvanize a collective response to specific incidents (for example, Sticker Lady Petition and Save Bukit Brown, see Table 1). These campaigns were more ad hoc and transient in nature. They also attracted a narrower segment of the population (for example, the academic community, nature lovers, and the arts community).

The target of claims for the majority of bottom-up movements in Singapore is typically the government. While some campaigns are targeted at getting the government to reconsider specific policies (Save Bukit Brown and "No to 6.9 Million People", see Table 1), most of the bottom-up campaigns advocate constitutional or legislative changes. Campaigns pushing for amendments to the Singapore Constitution include amending the death penalty for drug-related offences (Anti-Mandatory Death Penalty campaign), repealing Section 377A of the Penal Code (Repeal 377A), abolishing marital rape immunity in Sections 375(4) and 376(5) (No to Rape), and abolishing the Internal Security Act (ISA campaign).

Recently in July 2014, news of the National Library Board's (NLB) ban of two books that had homosexual themes broke in the mainstream media. NLB's move was a response to a patron's feedback that the books go against the "pro-family" ethos of our society as they dealt with same-sex partners. By noon on the same day, reactions to what NLB did spread online, with at least two individuals setting up petitions calling for the Board to resume circulation of the books. Two mothers who did not know each other connected via Facebook and organized a reading event ("Let's Read Together") that attracted 400 people from different walks of life. Organized within a space of four days, the event attracted both local and foreign media coverage. The online space was abuzz with bloggers writing on the issue and exploring different themes such as censorship, the role of the library and what "family" means. Online news sites (for example, Aljazeera, Bloomberg, Gay Star News.com, Global Post, Huffington Post, The Australian, Telegraph, Time and Washington Post) and blogs based outside Singapore also covered the ban and the backlash it has generated. A week later, the Minister for Communications and Information stepped in and announced that instead of pulping the banned books, the library would move the books to the adult section.

Such developments point to changes in political opportunity structures and a growing optimism in possibilities of the Internet in engendering political and

TABLE 1

Bottom-Up Movements in Singapore (Soon and Cheong, 2014)

Alternative *Change opinions pertaining to a specific issue among a target group*	*Redemptive* *Bring about a dramatic change to the lives of individuals belonging to a specific group*
Occupy Raffles Place Call for greater transparency and accountability for investments made by Temasek Holdings and Government of Singapore Investment Corporation **Pink Dot.sg** Eradicate prejudice against the LGBT community **Slut Walk** Raise awareness for the problem of sexual harassment of women and eradicate victim-blaming	**Lehmann Brothers and Minibonds** Seek compensation for investors who lost money in Lehmann-linked structured products **Internal Security Act (ISA) Campaign** Increase awareness for ISA detainees and their experiences; and call for the abolition of the Internal Security Act
Reformative *Change an entire community or society in a specific way*	*Revolutionary* *Eradicate an old social order and replace it with a new one*
"No to 6.9 Million People" Petition the government to reconsider population policies and curbing immigration **No to Rape** Advocate the total abolition of marital rape immunity in Sections 375(4) and 376(5) **Repeal 377A** Seek the repeal of Section 377A of the Penal Code which criminalizes sex between mutually consenting adult men **Save Bukit Brown** Petition against the government's decision to build a highway through Bukit Brown cemetery, a heritage site **Sticker Lady petition** Petition the Ministry of Home Affairs to reduce Sticker Lady's charge and recognize her work as art, not vandalism **Anti-Mandatory Death Penalty campaign** Seek legislative changes to the death penalty for drug-related offences	Nil

social change; specifically, in providing opportunities for deliberative discourse and the lobbying for policy changes. The authoritative stance adopted by the government in regulating societal discourse could have led to the burgeoning of anti-establishment voices and aggregations in the cyberspace. Anonymity and low barriers to publication and participation cultivate a conducive environment and to a large extent safe haven for the expression of dissenting views.

The 'Dark Side' of the Online Space

The advent of "web 2.0" technologies has contributed to growing personal and political expression online, and a shift from information consumption to information production.[14] Users now enjoy far greater access, participation, and reciprocity when interacting with one another in cyberspace. Although new technologies and social media give voice to the voiceless and help level the communication landscape and galvanize like-minded people for the greater good, the ugly side of the Internet rears up whenever complete lack of civility and decorum occur online. Perceived anonymity yields positive effects by lowering individuals' inhibitions when participating in online discussions and encouraging individuals in distress to come forward for help. However, it has also led to anti-social behaviours online such as astroturfing, flaming and trolling. What is more, people can be uncivil anonymously, without bearing any responsibilities that go with such actions.

Although uncivil behaviour, propelled either by sheer ignorance or a deliberate intent to provoke, is not unique to cyberspace, the ubiquity of high-tech communication devices and high-bandwidth connections have exacerbated the reach and effects of such acts on an unanticipated scale. Although new technologies and social media have brought like-minded individuals together for the greater good, they have also been used to inflict harm and distress on others. One example is the practice of "naming and shaming", where people take photos of "bad behaviour" and post these online. The subjects of such exposes run the gamut from the inappropriately dressed and cars parked illegally, to commuters not giving up reserved seats in Mass Rapid Transit trains. At its worst, such tracking down of alleged "perpetrators" by netizens has gone awry, such as a wrongly identified Filipino boy. The boy was mistaken for another person who had disturbed his neighbours with his drum-playing despite complaints, an example of naming and shaming gone wrong.

Online harassment runs a wide gamut, from impersonating someone, spreading rumours and lies about the victim, posting pictures of victims without their consent, to unrelenting verbal abuse and threats. A case of online harassment with fatal consequences is the first recorded death linked to cyber-bullying in Singapore in 2010. A student from Myanmar committed suicide after her ex-boyfriend wrote cruel insults on her Facebook page. In early 2014, a series of incidents culminated in the self-expulsion of British expatriate Anton Casey. The expatriate's online posts of what seemed like personal snapshots — his son travelling on the MRT and another of his son in his luxury car — with inappropriate captions brought him instant ignominy in cyberspace. Within hours, individuals posted information of his employment details, his supervisor's contact and his residential address, and within a week, the expatriate lost his job and left the country with his family, citing "death threats".

Social media has become complicit to the problem of corrosive speech (which is wider in scope and includes speech other than those expressed with the intention of promoting resentment and hate) because online discourse now takes on a viral effect.[15] There is also the persistence of the "coffee shop" effect where people feel that they are talking and sharing their inner feelings among a small or known group. However, unlike conversations in face-to-face settings, a "sticky" message that is attention-grabbing can be replicated and transmitted to many others instantaneously on the web.

Mobile communication devices such as smartphones and tablet computers catalyse the spread of provocative content as information consumption and sharing become integrated into people's daily lives. Two cases involving adolescents illustrate social media's viral reach. A student from Nanyang Polytechnic, a tertiary institution, posted a derogatory remark on Twitter about Indians. Originally only intended for friends in her network of followers, her post went viral when one of her friends re-tweeted it.[16] In the second case, a student from the Singapore Institute of Management was recorded on video sharing racist jokes. His friend posted the video on Facebook and the video was subsequently shared via YouTube.[17]

Such incidents suggest that there is a lack of media literacy among new media users. There is an underestimation of how the anonymity and asynchonicity which people enjoy when they go online loosens their inhibitions and result in them saying things that they normally would not say to one another face-to-face. There is also little understanding of the increasingly non-existent boundary between what is private and public, and the speed at which one's personal details can be dug up and spread online. The blurring of the boundary between private and public discourse results in un-anticipated backlash for articulating a personal opinion or sharing seemingly "private" information. The permanence of the web — the text, photographs and videos that people post online can be easily copied and reposted repeatedly, making it near impossible to wipe one's slate clean — is yet another aspect of technology that seems to be overlooked by Internet users. They are unaware of the digital footprints that they leave behind on the web and often underestimate the scale and speed of information-sharing facilitated by social media.

The negative effects of anonymity are reflected in measures considered by website owners and regulators. Video-sharing site YouTube has announced that it is looking into linking comments to users' full names and photographs used on their Google+ accounts. This is to discourage people from leaving hurtful remarks on the site.[18] In South Korea, the government is policing Internet posts because "character assassinations and suicides caused by excessive insults, the spreading of false rumours and defamation have all become social issues".[19] New York lawmakers have also proposed bills to ban anonymous online posting.[20]

In Singapore, cases of anti-foreigner and racist speech uttered by people have engendered much discussion pertaining to their causes and effects. The Sedition Act has been invoked on several occasions in recent years. In 2005, a seventeen-year-old student was put on probation for two years and ordered to perform 180 hours of community service for his racist remarks on Muslims and Malays.[21] Two other men, in their twenties, were jailed a day and a month, respectively, under the same charge during that year. In an incident linked to religion, a Christian couple was jailed eight weeks in 2009 for distributing anti-Muslim and anti-Catholic publications.[22]

However, the question lies in the adequacy and effectiveness of legislation on its own in engendering a society of tolerance and understanding. First, the law can only act as a deterrent and convict, but does not bring about attitudinal or behavioural change. Second, a reliance on the authorities to resolve unhappiness arising from corrosive speech impedes the cultivation of mutual understanding and a social immunity that is needed in an increasingly diverse society. Finally, advancements in technological development and new usage behaviours will always be ahead of regulatory changes.

Regulation by the Self and Community

Responses to incidents discussed in the preceding section suggest that the same technologies can be used to cultivate "communal vigilance". On the basic level, vigilance requires circumspection — being mindful of the consequences of our actions. On another level, it requires people, regular users of the Internet, to be watchful of disruptive behaviours that can be harmful to the community, to step out and to speak up against the perpetrators. Communal vigilance channels people's collective concerns and energies to a more productive and sustainable outcome for society. Findings from an earlier study by Soon and Tan[23] point to the emergence of a positive phenomenon where small groups of individuals come forward to condemn corrosive speech. These individuals are either bloggers or online commenters who speak out against derogatory remarks against foreigners.

While some bloggers have censured others for xenophobic reportage and for fanning animosity between Singaporeans and non-Singaporeans, a small number of individuals spoke out against other readers in comment threads found on blogs such as Temasek Times and Temasek Review Emeritus. In their posts, these individuals reminded Singaporeans to be more objective when blaming foreigners for competition for jobs as well as crowded trains and public places. They identify policies as the root of the problem, and not foreigners per se. They also castigated bloggers for being irresponsible (for example, "cutting and pasting angry remarks without investigating into the background is just lazy biasness") and provoking others. Another reader shared his concern on the negative repercussions of the "naming and shaming" tactic used by some blogs. Besides these individuals, a few others also took to setting up their own blogs to denounce corrosive speech. Some of these blogs include "Every Cloud Has a Silver Lining", <http://sgmoderateobserver. blogspot.com.au/>, and "Of Kids and Education", <http://hedgehogcomms. blogspot.sg/>.

When it came to posts containing racist speech targeted at Malay and Indian minorities, there was swift condemnation from the targeted groups and other communities. Members from various communities asserted that racism should not be tolerated in Singapore. One important aspect of the response to racist speech is the reaction of the targeted or victimized communities. While many reacted to being abused with anger or worse, others also called for reason, a sense of perspective and moderation. These included community organizations and leaders. Pertaining to the incident involving the polytechnic student who made a racist remark, a few netizens have also spoken out on her behalf and appealed to others to forgive her as she was young. A commenter on Temasek Times site suggested that everyone had made racist remarks in their private spaces before, so it is wrong for netizens to take the moral high ground and lambast her as if they had not done so.

Positive reactions similar to those combating anti-foreigner corrosive speech were observed in the case of racist corrosive speech. A Singapore Facebook page called "Stop racism in Singapore" has been created to promote the anti-racist cause. It has garnered over 11,758 "Likes" so far (as of 12 December 2014). The page posted pictures like "Racism it stops with me" and other posters spreading the word on universal humanity. Such a movement parallels the Facebook movements against racism and xenophobia in Australia. Several pages such as "1,000,000 Aussies against racism", "F-- off, xenophobes we are full" and "Australians against racism and discrimination" promote the cause of anti-racism. In its page description, the moderator states:

> United, we will make a change. We will make a stand and Racism will end! We do not condone violence or rage towards any community, race or religion in Singapore. Racism is zero tolerance. This page is only for creating an awareness which will assist in making a difference against racism by methods of which are deemed to be peaceful, healthy and legal.

The swift condemnation by some online citizens of the circulation of pictures of an accident that took place in the eastern zone of Singapore which resulted in the deaths of two young boys is yet another example of communal vigilance. Soon after the photographs were posted, prominent bloggers and forum participants questioned the motives and the need for sharing such pictures. They called on the online community to show greater respect to the family of the boys who died. In response to an article on a self-purported "site for every Singaporean to express themselves" that wrongly reported on the cement truck driver's nationality, several visitors left comments which highlighted the inaccuracy of the information and questioned the writer's motive.

Conclusion

Currently, provisions for seeking recourse for anti-social speech that deals with race and religion are provided through laws such as the Penal Code. This has led to individuals turning to law enforcers to seek recourse against corrosive speech actors. However, lodging a complaint with law enforcers whenever one finds speech offensive provides only symptomatic relief and fails to resolve underlying problems and tensions. As new social and economic challenges emerge in the society, and as technological developments continue to shape how individuals interact with one another in unforeseeable ways, corrosive speech and anti-social online behaviour will assume new and unanticipated forms. In addition, there is the issue of relativity as what is corrosive speech to some may not be corrosive speech to others.

Legal enforcement based on definitions with increasingly outdated parameters will become difficult to enforce. A three-pronged approach consisting of education, empowerment and self-regulation may be an effective alternative. First, educating the young and increasing media literacy among technology users enhance individuals' capabilities to manage and deal with corrosive speech. Education is likely to be more successful than regulation in bringing about sustainable and long-term effects. Educating users on the importance of practising responsible speech is a key focus of the Media Literacy Council (MLC). Set up on 1 August 2012, the MLC is tasked with promoting a safe, secure and civil media environment through public education and advising the government on appropriate policy responses pertaining to media and technology. Its current initiatives include the Communications Literacy Seminar and tapping the global Safer Internet Day to raise local awareness of issues discussed internationally.

Second, technology users in general need to equip themselves with coping mechanisms to deal with myriad experiences, some of which may be offensive, in an increasingly connected world. Users should realize that what they say or do online will define them to the invisible masses, who will not hesitate in unearthing personal details about them, in the name of information-sharing. While it is all so easy and tempting to share bits and bytes of our lives, the simplest yet seemingly hardest thing to do would be to pause and think of the price attached to what we share. Greater awareness of the characteristics of Internet technologies will compel users to be more circumspect when they post content online. At least, it could prevent them from becoming the next headline, in print, or in cyberspace. Finally, communal vigilance in the form of self-regulation and community regulation could ultimately be a long-term and more sustainable solution to the current conundrum concerning Internet regulation. Guided by a shared vision of the type of online culture citizens want for themselves and those they care for, and defined by users themselves, a greater clarity of what are acceptable and unacceptable online practices will emerge over time. In so doing, we may be able to strike a fine balance between upholding the sanctity of freedom of expression and preserving social harmony in society.

With continuing changes in state-citizen relations and rapid technological innovation, law-based measures will be increasingly irrelevant. Furthermore, digital natives are less accepting of censorship and regulation. A paradigmatic shift is required in the government's approach in dealing with xenophobic speech. As a nation matures and goes through a different stage of development — from an authoritarian to a more democratic regime — it will have to navigate and explore a different mode of governance, from control to empowerment.

Notes

1. Indrajit Banerjee, "The Locals Strike Back?", *Gazette: The International Journal for Communications Studies* 64, no. 6 (2002): 517–35; Chen-Yu Kuo, "The Making of a New Nation: Cultural Construction and National Identity", in *Communitarian Ideology and Democracy in Singapore*, edited by Chua Beng Huat (London: Routledge, 1995), pp. 101–23.

2. Banerjee, op. cit.

3. Winston T.H. Koh and Poh Kam Wong, "Competing at the Frontier: The Changing Role of Technology Policy in Singapore's Economic Strategy", *Technological Forecasting and Social Change* 72 (2005): 255–85.

4. Infocomm Development Authority of Singapore, *Annual Survey on Infocomm Usage — Households and by Individuals, 2009*; *Annual Survey on Infocomm Usage in Households and by Individuals for 2010*, available at <http://www.ida.gov.sg/doc/Publications/Publications_Level3/Survey2010/HH2010ES.pdf> (accessed 23 September 2012).

5. International Telecommunication Union, *The World in 2009, ICT Facts and Figures*, available at <http://www.itu.int/ITU-D/ict/material/Telecom09_flyer.pdf>.

6. Cherian George, "The Internet and the Narrow Tailoring Dilemma for 'Asian' Democracies", *The Communication Review* 6, no. 3 (2003): 247–68.

7. Sedition Act, Rev. ed. Cap 290, 1985, available at <http://statutes.agc.gov.sg/aol/search/display/view.w3p;page=0;query=CompId%3A56538838-3ea5-4de8-a5ff-d345891c6a38;rec=0>.

8. Section 298A seeks to preserve "religious and racial harmony in the new global security climate", Ministry of Home Affairs, 2007.

9. Media Development Authority, Internet Code of Practice, 1997, available at <http://www.mda.gov.sg/Documents/PDF/licences/mobj.981.Internet_Code_of_Practice.pdf>.

10. Infocomm Development Authority of Singapore, *Annual Survey on Infocomm Usage in Households and by Individuals for 2011*, available at <http://www.ida.gov.sg/~/media/Files/Infocomm%20Landscape/Facts%20and%20Figures/SurveyReport/2011/2011%20HH%20mgt%20rpt%20public%20final.pdf>.

11. Networks Asia, "Singapore Smartphone and Tablet Penetration on the Rise; App Usage Increasing", available at <http://www.networksasia.net/content/singapore-smartphone-and-tablet-penetration-rise-app-usage-increasing?page=0%2C0>, 18 June 2013.

12. George, op. cit.

13. Carol Soon and Cheong Kah Shin, "Mobile Communication and Bottom-Up Movements in Singapore", in *Interdisciplinary Mobile Media and Communications: Social, Political and Economic Implications*, edited by Xiaoge Xu (PA: IGI Global, 2014), pp. 157–78.

14. Terry Flew, *New Media: An Introduction* (Melbourne, Victoria: Oxford University Press, 2005), pp. xv–xxii.

15. Carol Soon and Tan Tarn How, "Corrosive Speech: What Can Be Done", policy paper published by the Institute of Policy Studies, Singapore, available at <http://lkyspp.nus.edu.sg/ips/wp-content/uploads/sites/2/2013/06/Report_ACM_Corrosive-Speech-Report_120613-1.pdf>.

16. Kezia Toh, "He filed police report as a 'good citizen should'", *Straits Times*, Prime News, 30 March 2012.

17. Sadat Osman, "SIM student filmed making racist jokes", inSing.com, available at <http://news.insing.com/tabloid/racist-video-sim-jokes/id-de5b3f00>, 13 August 2012.

18. Samantha Murphy Kelly, "Can Real Names on YouTube End Nasty Comments?" Mashable, available at <http://mashable.com/2012/07/24/youtube-comments-full-names/>, 24 July 2012.

19. Choe Sung-Hun, "In Korean Democracy, Policing Internet Posts", *New York Times*, World Trends, 12 August 2012.

20. Amanda Holpuch, "New York Lawmakers Propose Bill to Ban Anonymous Online Speech", *The Guardian*, available at <http://www.guardian.co.uk/technology/us-news-blog/2012/may/23/anonymous-comment-ban-new-york>, 23 May 2012.

21. Teo Cheng Wee, "Jaya: Society has Role in Checking Extremism", *Straits Times*, Asia, 20 January 2012.

22. Carolyn Quek, "Seditious Tract Duo Jailed Eight Weeks", *Straits Times*, Prime News, 11 June 2009.

23. Soon and Tan, op. cit.

Thailand

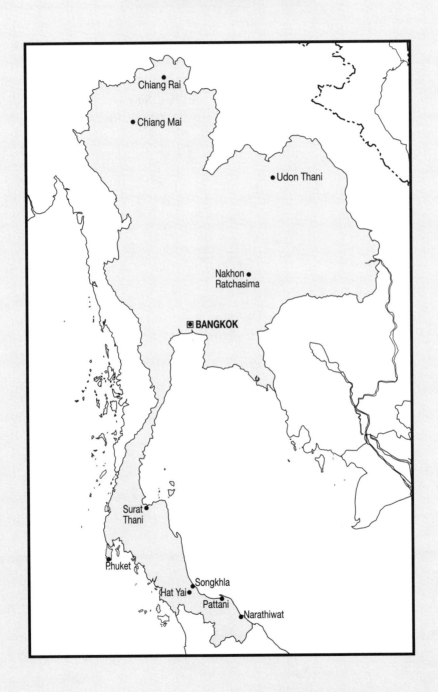

THAILAND IN 2014
The Trouble with Magic Swords

Duncan McCargo

For Thais, 2014 could be divided into two distinct periods: pre-coup, and post-coup. Before 22 May, Thailand was chaotic; after 22 May, outwardly much more orderly. However, orderly at what price? During 2014, Thailand's often contentious politics reached levels of conflict arguably not seen since the 1970s. Summarizing what happened is quite straightforward, but characterizing the conflict is more tricky. Superficially, there was a showdown between two rival power networks: the network aligned with former Prime Minister Thaksin Shinawatra (including his sister Yingluck, the Pheu Thai Party, the Red Shirt movement, elements of the business community, and the police) and the old power elite network aligned with the military (and including the palace, the Democrat Party, much of the bureaucracy, and the various "post-Yellow" movements). In this showdown, the military and their allies defeated the pro-Thaksin network by force, and then sought to consolidate their victory through lasting new political arrangements.

This interpretation assumes that the military and the Democrat Party were fast and firm friends with a common agenda. Another, and more troubling, possibility is that while Thaksin was especially disliked, the military harboured a deep distrust of all elected politicians, and has been profoundly unimpressed by the performance of the Democrats in recent years. In other words, the goal of the military is the "depoliticization" of Thai life, the creation of a public sphere in which contentious debates are permanently suppressed.[1] Since this goal was unlikely be accomplished, the junta may have been setting itself up to fail.

DUNCAN MCCARGO is Visiting Professor of Political Science at Columbia University and Professor of Political Science at the University of Leeds.

Restart Thailand?

Following a troubling attempt by her administration to push an unpopular amnesty bill through Parliament, Yingluck Shinawatra was confronted by a wave of street protests that forced her to dissolve Parliament in early December 2013.[2] The rallies peaked on 13 January 2014, when the anti-Thaksin movement attempted "Bangkok Shutdown" at eleven key locations across the city. At their height in mid-January, the protests led by the People's Democratic Reform Committee (PDRC) mobilized hundreds of thousands of people; at their nadir, by late April, they probably comprised no more than a few thousand.[3] The grouping popularly referred to as the PDRC was a repositioning or regrouping of a range of organizations that had long been discontented with Thaksin and his political machine.[4] The PDRC — whose Thai name has been more literally translated as People's Committee for Absolute Democracy with the King as Head of State[5] — was formed on 29 November 2013. It was a rebranded version of the earlier movement against the Thaksin regime, including some supporters of the Democrat Party. Other elements of the wider movement included the more hard-line Network of Students and Citizens for Reforms (NSCR), and residual elements of the old People's Alliance for Democracy (PAD).

The main PDRC rally sites all featured campsites providing accommodation for core protesters, market areas selling a range of T-shirts and other protest paraphernalia and souvenirs, food and beverage stands providing donated refreshments, large stage areas and giant plasma TV screens. During the evenings popular entertainers gave free concerts interspersed with vitriolic speeches from Suthep and other prominent movement leaders, who toured the stages in quick succession. For around six weeks, the PDRC rallies had a festive atmosphere, drawing large evening crowds, including many people there as much for the entertainment as for the political messages.[6] However, the crowds declined sharply during February following a number of fatal attacks on the rallies, apparently carried out by pro-government groups, notably three deaths (including two children) at the Ratchaprasong site on 23 February.[7] The major businesses that initially underwrote the protests became increasingly concerned about adverse effects on the economy, tourism and consumer confidence.[8] As support waned and financiers pulled the plug, Suthep was forced to wind down most PDRC rally sites, and retreated to a consolidated protest at Lumpini Park on 28 February. Following Yingluck's removal from office (along with nine cabinet ministers) by the Constitution Court on 7 May,[9] the PDRC finally withdrew from Lumpini Park on 11 May, joining remaining protestors at Government House.[10]

The Asia Foundation survey of 350 protesters conducted on 13–14 January found that 54 per cent were from Bangkok and 46 per cent from outside, mainly from adjoining provinces and the South; 40 per cent had household incomes about 60,000 baht (US$1,825) per month and another 32 per cent had monthly incomes between 30–60,000 baht — high incomes in a Thai context.[11] My own collaborative research using a small sample of interview informants identified two main kinds of protesters: people from Bangkok and adjoining provinces, many of them middle class, who joined the rallies in the evenings; and lower-income people from the upper Southern Democrat heartland provinces who spent extended periods at the protests, often camping on site.[12]

Asked why they were taking part in the protests, the top answers were:

1.   to end the Shinawatra family political dynasty (40 per cent)
2.   to protect the monarchy (15 per cent)
3.   to ensure that there will be political reform before the election (15 per cent)
4.   to prevent the government from pursuing bad policies (15 per cent)
5.   to protect democracy (7 per cent)
6.   to compel Prime Minister Yingluck Shinawatra to resign (7 per cent)
7.   to ensure that there will be political reform after the election (4 per cent)[13]

These answers could be classified into three kinds: negative, protective, and positive. Negative motivations — things demonstrators wanted to prevent (1, 4, 6) — carried by far the most weight. Protective motivations (defending the monarchy and democracy, 2, 5) also loomed quite large; while positive motivations (ensuring reforms, 3, 7), were less cited. We found a similar pattern among our own informants.

Twenty-one of our informants admitted that they had voted for the Democrat Party in the 2011 general election, while one had cast a no-vote, one did not vote at all, and several declined to give a direct answer. Nobody stated they had supported Pheu Thai, or indeed any other political party. Some informants expressed support for some of the policies pursued by Pheu Thai in the early stages of the Yingluck government, but all were very disapproving of subsequent corruption and problems in the economy, especially falling rubber prices which were an important issue in the upper south.[14] Asked whether the Democrat Party was itself in need of reform, a handful of informants disagreed, but half of them expressed differing degrees of dissatisfaction with the party.

Many were unhappy with former premier Abhisit Vejjaiva, and felt that more assertive leadership was needed. Several informants argued that the Democrats needed to change direction in order to have a broader appeal to voters, especially in pro-Thaksin regions of the country such as the north and northeast.

Our informants' responses illustrated that many PDRC protesters were far from being uncritical Democrat Party voters. Indeed, some expressed scepticism about elected politicians, saying they only supported Suthep because he had already left the Democrats. Their Democrat sympathies were often heavily qualified, hence their decision to resort to street protests to advance goals that parliamentary opposition had failed to promote. Thaksin had rendered obsolete the cautious, parliamentary-focused leadership style favoured by Abhisit and his mentor Chuan Leekpai, while Suthep met demands for a more brash and assertive leader. However, Suthep's primary appeal was not as an alternative prime minister to Thaksin or Yingluck. Rather, it was Suthep's adroit self-branding as "Lung Kamnan" [Uncle Chief Village Headman, literally Uncle Sub-district Chief] that most captivated popular attention and sympathy. In this persona of the much-loved local community leader (which bore little relation to his real career or personality), Suthep seemed to transcend politics and evoke a mythical rural past, one which had a strong appeal to urbanites in denial about the actual rural present.

The Non-Election Election

Faced with growing pressure over the amnesty bill debacle and intensive street protests, Yingluck Shinawatra had dissolved Parliament on 9 December 2013, setting the stage for a snap election scheduled for 2 February 2014 which was fraught with problems from the outset. The ruling Pheu Thai Party was singularly ill-prepared to contest it; most MPs of all parties had been counting on at least a year to refocus on constituency concerns in preparation for polls expected in 2015. The opposition Democrat Party, which had originally made vocal demands for the dissolution of Parliament, decided to boycott the election. Their boycott — coupled with the abrupt House dissolution and a climate of anti-Shinawatra sentiment in Bangkok — confirmed a widespread sense that the election would not be a game-changer for the Yingluck government.

Indeed, the 2014 election was to prove a virtual re-run of the 2006 election, which was also subsequently annulled by the courts during a series of bewildering events that culminated in a military coup. Serious problems with the election process became apparent in the closing days of 2013: there was widespread disruption of the candidate registration process, primarily in the upper south and in Bangkok, where violent clashes erupted between police and NSRC protesters at the Thai-Japanese stadium on 26 December. Twenty-eight southern constituencies had no registered candidates, and so no election took place. This disruption eventually formed the basis of the Constitutional Court's decision to annul the election, on the grounds that it had not been possible to hold polls in all constituencies on the same day.[15] The PDRC/NSRC's actions demonstrated that relatively small groups of people could completely subvert the electoral process. Yet the government was determined to press ahead with the election, hoping that it would be possible for a quorate Lower House to be formed.

The Yingluck government had a poor relationship with the Election Commission (EC), which was tasked with managing the election process. A new team of commissioners had assumed office in December 2013, and they were clearly ill-prepared for their new responsibilities. More seriously, outspoken Election Commissioner Somchai Srisuthiyakorn repeatedly made clear his personal opposition to holding the polls at all.[16] At one point the Constitutional Court was asked to rule on which body had the right to decide whether the election should go ahead or be postponed. Despite the fact that the 2007 Constitution gave full jurisdiction over the election to the EC, the Constitutional Court judges responded with a fudge, declaring that the government and the EC needed to work this out among themselves. As late as 28 January, the EC was still talking about a postponement. Finally, rather than delaying the vote, the EC pretended to hold one: the commissioners went through the legal motions without wanting a credible election to take place. Meanwhile the government clung desperately to the belief that the election would demonstrate the strength of support Yingluck still enjoyed among large swathes of Thailand's population, especially her core vote in the north and northeast. At the same time the PDRC "Bangkok Shutdown" campaign, launched on 13 January, sought to make the capital ungovernable, and to obstruct government attempts to conduct a successful election which would revalidate its legitimacy and authority.

The result was the worst of all worlds. Protesters aligned with the PDRC managed to disrupt polling on the advance voting day,[17] 26 January, in 49 out of Bangkok's 50 districts, and across the upper south. One NSRC leader was shot dead in an altercation with Red Shirt supporters at a polling station in Bang Na, in eastern Bangkok. In many other locations, would-be voters were intimidated and threatened. According to the EC, only around 5 per cent of the more than two million people who had registered for advance voting were able to cast their ballots.[18] That night, speakers at the PDRC stages celebrated their successful disruption of the advance voting process. One speaker declared that the people who had cast their ballots on that day did not truly love Thailand; indeed, he did not believe they were Thais at all, but were actually from Cambodia.[19] Thai election rules state that anyone who fails to use a pre-requested advance ballot has no subsequent right to vote on the actual election day. The advance voting disruption again left the validity of the election open to subsequent legal challenges, whatever happened on 2 February.

The day before the election, further violent clashes broke out in Lak Si, Bangkok, when attempts were made to distribute ballot boxes. A pitched gun battle was waged on the streets. Miraculously, there were no fatalities, but the resulting headlines reinforced a widespread sense that the country was spinning out of control. On 2 February, voting was disrupted in 127 of Thailand's 375 constituencies. No polling took place in nine southern provinces, all in the Democrat heartlands: Songkhla, Trang, Phattalung, Phuket, Surat Thani, Ranong, Krabi, Chumphon and Phang-nga. However, local politicians in the three Malay majority provinces of the deep south made clear that they would not tolerate any interference with the voting there, and none took place. There was no disruption in the populous north or northeast, while in 122 of the 127 constituencies in the central and eastern regions polling went off smoothly. The PDRC made only limited efforts to interfere with the polling in Bangkok, but voting was halted in three districts.[20] At Ratchatewi District Office, a group of protesters "prevented" the ballot boxes from being distributed, with the apparent collusion of local officials who themselves openly admitted they believed the election to be illegitimate.[21]

The results of the disrupted, incomplete election were difficult to assess. Turnout overall was just under 50 per cent, the lowest figure since the 1970s, down on figures of around 75 per cent for the 2007 and 2011 elections; and significantly lower than 64.77 per cent, the turnout in the parallel boycotted election of 2006, for which there was an active "no-vote" campaign.[22] There were twice as many spoilt or invalid votes as in 2011, but not as many as in 2006. Respected political blogger Bangkok Pundit estimated that of the votes cast, around 75 per cent could be seen as pro-Pheu Thai; while around 25 per cent were "anti-Pheu Thai" votes in the form of no-votes or spoilt ballot papers. Some commentators argued that the result was a disappointing one for Yingluck, reflecting poor turnout even among core pro-Thaksin voters. Certainly, election campaigning by Pheu Thai candidates during January 2014 was half-hearted at best, and even where campaign rallies were held, they were poorly attended. But while there was dissatisfaction with Pheu Thai among some voters in the northeast, for example, the peculiar conditions of the 2014 election — which was widely expected not to lead to the formation of a new government — militated against higher turnout. It was difficult to blame Yingluck and her party for the shortcomings of the polling. In previous elections, high turnout had been partly "manufactured" by local officials removing from voter lists those who were not expected to show up;[23] it is unclear how much bureaucratic effort went into such manipulations this time.

On 21 March, the Constitutional Court annulled the 2 February election on technical grounds, so drawing a line under a rather half-hearted and half-baked episode that had generated violence, intimidation and very little positive political participation. In the run-up to the coup, there was talk of fresh elections in a few months. The arguments about who was responsible for this expensive debacle rumbled on; in December the EC announced an investigation, implying that the long-ousted Yingluck government ought to be held financially responsible for the huge costs of the unwanted February polls.

By coincidence, Thailand held polls for the elected component of the Senate (77 of the 150 seats, one per province) on 29 March. Turnout for these elections was a mere 43 per cent, compared with 56 per cent for the 2008 Senate elections, and 63 per cent for the fully elected Senate in 2006. This poor turnout reflected general disillusionment with the political process and well-founded scepticism about future developments. Given these low stakes, there was no disruption of the Senate polling. Sure enough, the winning candidates scarcely had time to assume their seats before the military junta dissolved the entire Senate on 25 May.[24]

A Coup to End All Coups

For months, Army Commander General Prayut Chan-o-cha issued statements that there would not be a coup, matched by private assurances to foreign embassies and international organizations. By 15 May, 25 people had been killed in Bangkok through politically-related violence since the end of November 2013, fuelling arguments that the Army ought to "restore order".[25] Over time, Prayut's denials grew less convincing, yet they continued even after the military moved to seize control of the country on 20 May: Prayut initially insisted that this was simply a declaration of martial law, rather than a power grab.[26] The military summoned politicians and protest leaders from the two opposing sides for negotiations. On 22 May, when talks failed to produce a resolution, Prayut announced that he was arresting the negotiators and proclaiming a coup. For a moment, some of those present thought he was joking.[27]

The exact sequence of decisions leading to 22 May remains a matter of controversy. In all likelihood, the military had been gearing up for a coup for some time, but the final decision to seize power was taken at a very late stage. From the very beginning, it was apparent that the National Council for Peace and Order (NCPO) — as the junta called itself — had torn up the script of the 1991 and 2006 coups.[28] In Thailand's two most recent military putsches, very few people were arrested, a security clampdown lasted only a few days, a credible interim Prime Minister and Cabinet were quickly named, plans were rapidly drawn up to prepare a new Constitution, and elections were promised in about a year. In 2014, none of these precedents was followed. Hundreds of people were rounded up and detained for up to a week, many of them ordered to report to military facilities.[29] There was a tough crackdown on dissent of even the most moderate variety. Thailand had no parliament for more than two months, no prime minister for almost three months, and no functioning cabinet for even longer. Prayut himself became Prime Minister, instead of assigning the role to a respected civilian (as in 1991) or a retired military figure (as in 2006). While the junta talked of introducing reforms, the timetable remained rather vague, and the election date was repeatedly deferred.

Another departure from previous coups was Prayut's "one man show" style of leadership. Whereas in 1991 a group of senior military figures frequently appeared together for major public announcements, Prayut was usually the only top general to speak on behalf of the junta, even commandeering a prime time Friday night television slot for his weekly addresses to the nation.[30] In these talks, he lurched between different modes, alternately avuncular, patronizing, self-pitying, tough-talking and downright obnoxious. It soon became clear that a forty-five-year career in the military had ill-prepared him for the rough and tumble of press conferences, nor for the daily crisis management to which elected politicians are well accustomed. Prayut expected constant obsequiousness from the media, and was given to regular displays of petulance in the face of awkward questions from journalists.

Nevertheless, the personalized nature of Prayut's rule was something of an illusion. It soon became clear that he was not calling the shots single-handedly, but working as the front man of a curious triumvirate of old soldiers. His two closest associates were a pair of rather undistinguished former army commanders, Generals Anupong Paochinda and Prawit Wongsuwan. Claims that these two men had close links to the PDRC protests had been circulating for months.[31] Prawit, the oldest of the three, was the senior figure behind the coup. He had served as defence minister during the Abhisit government. More importantly, he was an architect of the backroom deal that had lured Newin Chidchob's faction of MPs out of the pro-Thaksin camp in late 2008, so paving the way for Abhisit's Democrat Party to assume power, despite having lost the 2007 general election. In other words, the 2014 military coup leadership was the same clique who had staged a parliamentary coup against a Thaksinite premier in 2008. At the same time, Prawit was no ideologue, and was rumoured to be still in close touch with Thaksin, who had originally promoted him to the position of Army chief back in 2004.

Given the anti-Thaksin history of the coup clique, the relationship between the military and the PDRC has been the subject of considerable speculation. In June 2014, PDRC leader Suthep provoked an uproar when he declared at a fund-raising event in Bangkok that he and Prayut shared common objectives and had been plotting ways to remove the Thaksin clan from power since 2010.[32] He further claimed that Prayut had told him in May that the Army planned to take over where the PDRC had left off. Prayut furiously denied these claims,[33] and Suthep was obliged to retreat to his home province of Surat Thani, where he was ordained as a monk at Suan Mok, the former temple of the late revered Buddhist thinker Buddhadasa. Nevertheless, many of the junta's moves echoed the agenda of the anti-Thaksin movement. Despite constant talk of reconciliation, the NCPO silenced all critical voices and prevented virtually any open discussion of different options for political reforms, even on university campuses. However, unlike the previous two juntas, the NCPO devoted only limited attention to investigating abuses by the government it had ousted: no special committee was put in place to examine the misdeeds of Yingluck or her fellow ministers, and Prayut made virtually no public mention of the Shinawatras. Ostensibly at least, the NCPO was firmly focused on crafting Thailand's future, rather than dredging through its recent past.

Both the 197-member National Legislative Assembly (appointed on 31 July) and the 32-member Cabinet (appointed on 31 August) proved a huge disappointment. Both were dominated by current or retired military officers, and other figures with extremely conservative credentials. Public discourse sanctioned by the junta focused on the question of how to eradicate corruption and to prevent future governments pursuing dangerously populist policies — code words for preventing the Shinawatra family from returning to power. At the same time, the NCPO was deeply mistrustful of all elected politicians, and indeed any expression of alternative opinions: their over-arching goal was the de-politicization of Thai public life. To legitimatize its intolerance for opposition, the junta engaged in a sustained information operation (IO), trying to drown out disagreements with white noise about "restoring national happiness" — ironically a goal which had originally been announced by the Yingluck government back in January. Prayut himself wrote a song promoting national happiness, which was soon playing everywhere; teams of all-singing, all-dancing "pretties" (female soldiers in scanty khaki outfits) offered free entertainment around Bangkok; and Thai TV screens were filled with pro-military propaganda emphasizing the need for unity. In a throwback to earlier decades, Prayut also announced that all school children would henceforth study twelve core Thai values which he had personally drafted,[34] including loyalty to the monarchy and deference to elders.[35]

The most striking feature of the 2014 coup was the harsh and sustained crackdown on dissent.[36] Targets including prominent academics, and particular attention was paid to student groups both in Bangkok and in the provinces. A Belgian man was arrested for buying a T-shirt saying "Peace, please"; old ladies were arrested for holding up anti-coup signs;[37] students were hauled off for using a "Hunger Games" three-fingered salute,[38] for sitting reading in small groups, and for passing out sandwiches at Thammasat University.[39] More than 300 people were detained in the two months following the coup.[40] Many of those arrested were subjected to psychological warfare techniques designed to make them love the nation, religion and King; the military viewed people holding a range of political opinions simply as threats to national security. Leading historian Nidhi Eoseewong, who was briefly detained while speaking at Thammasat University's Rangsit campus, argued that Thailand was experiencing "The end of academia".[41] Those who failed to report to the authorities soon found themselves facing charges before military courts.[42] The months that followed the coup saw the largest number of people held on *lèse majesté* charges in Thai history.[43] Some prominent critical academics and political activists who had left Thailand around the time of the coup, or who were already abroad, faced having their passports rescinded.[44] The junta also transferred large numbers of senior government officials based on their perceived loyalty to the new regime.[45] These were extraordinary developments in a country with a lively tradition of political protest and dissent, one that had consistently and regularly rejected authoritarian rule since the 1970s.

After an initial wave of anti-coup protests in late May and early June, there was relatively little overt opposition to the junta from the "red", pro-Thaksin side. Thaksin was widely believed to have stood down his supporters, while engaging in behind-the-scenes negotiations with the NCPO in the hope of securing a fresh understanding that might lead to his own political rehabilitation and return. Instead, criticism of the junta now came mainly from discontented conservatives and rival elements of the network monarchy. Publications from the *Phujatkan* stable — owned by former PAD leader Sonthi Limthongkul — relentlessly pilloried Prayut and the junta.[46] Meanwhile Privy Council President, General Prem Tinsulanond, officially cancelled his own birthday party, normally attended by the entire military top brass, on 26 August.[47] This was taken as a sign of disapproval for the NCPO, for whom General Prawit has largely usurped the "father figure" role previously played by the ageing Prem. In September the Dean of the Mahidol University Music Faculty, Sugree Charoensuk, a close associate of Prem, attended a deans' meeting wearing a tin box on his head,[48] as a personal protest against the president of Mahidol University, who had concurrently accepted an appointment as Health Minister in the Prayut Cabinet.[49] Shortly afterwards the president stepped down from his university post. Prior to his retirement from the Army on 30 September, Prayut and fellow military commanders paid a final courtesy call on General Prem.[50]

Ongoing Concerns

Many of the sources of national anxiety that continued to afflict Thailand in 2014 were long-standing concerns. Among these was collective anxiety about the royal succession: King Bhumibol turned eighty-seven in December, but a planned birthday appearance was cancelled amid continuing worries about his health, in a year when he had maintained a very low public profile, and during which the Queen was scarcely seen at all. The best-selling T-shirts at the PDRC rallies were khaki shirts bearing the Thai number "9" (for King Rama 9), and the slogan "We are the people of the King." Unusually, in the immediate aftermath of the coup, no photographs were released of the King or other members of the royal family meeting the NCPO leadership. While Princess Chulabhorn posted images of herself clad in PDRC colours on Instagram,[51] during the early months of 2014 pro-Thaksin Red Shirts had rallied in the vicinity of Crown Prince Vajiralongkorn's palace at Aksa Road, some sporting T-shirts declaring "We love the Crown Prince."[52] Whatever the Red Shirts may have hoped for from him, the Crown Prince was away in England during the coup.[53] He made international headlines in 2014 not for any interventions in Thai politics, but when he divorced his wife of thirteen years, Srirasmi, as well as apparently ordering a purge of senior police officers who had close family and personal ties with her.[54] Uncertainty over the Crown Prince's personal life did nothing to assuage anxieties about the prospects for a smooth succession.

The ongoing insurgency in the country's southern border provinces continued unabated.[55] Total fatalities since 2004 surpassed 6,000; the core problem remained a legitimacy deficit on the part of the Thai state. Despite high levels of popular support for the Malaysian-brokered peace process begun in 2013, these talks had stalled even before the coup.[56] After taking power, the NCPO quickly removed the pro-Thaksin figures who had helped shape government policy in the region — notably Southern Border Provinces Administrative Centre chief Tawee Sodsong, who had been well-liked by local Muslims — placing control firmly in military hands. Late in the year, General Prayut announced that the peace talks would resume. However, so long as the junta remained in power, substantive political solutions, such as some form of autonomy, were off the table.[57] For the time being, negotiations would be a form of shadow theatre, largely devoid of serious content.

Economy

Thailand's economy was badly affected by the political turbulence: growth was at a virtual standstill, and the World Bank expected Thailand to be the slowest growing Southeast Asian economy until 2016.[58] According to one study, military coups typically reduce economic growth by around 3.5 per cent in total over the following three years, and reduce incomes by around 7 per cent.[59] Tourist arrivals in Thailand dropped by 6.66 per cent compared with 2013, though there was some recovery in the final quarter of the year.[60] The stock market dropped precipitously in December, partly fuelled by rumours about the King's health.[61]

Despite widespread criticism of the Yingluck government's populist policies, and especially the former ruling party's controversial and financially ruinous rice-buying project,[62] the NCPO adopted very similar approaches to the use of public funds, throwing money at problems in a transparent attempt to purchase public support. The junta spent a remarkable US$.4.3 billion on special projects during its first two months in power alone.[63] Thai military spending surged in the wake of the 2006 coup; a comparative study suggests that the opportunity to boost military spending offers a power incentive to prospective coup-makers.[64] The apparent reluctance of the junta to delegate national budgetary decisions to well-qualified technocrats was a potential obstacle to Thailand's economic recovery.

Foreign Relations

The protests and then the coup had undermined Thailand's relations with long-standing Western allies such as the European Union. The all-important alliance with the United States was in especially poor shape, despite the fact that the Americans agreed to go ahead with a scaled-back annual Cobra Gold military exercise in 2015.[65] The NCPO ignored advice to appoint a plausible civilian foreign minister, instead putting Supreme Commander Tanasak Patimapragorn into the post. The ill-qualified Tanasak cut a poor figure at the U.N. General Assembly in September, where he tendentiously asserted that the country was still "fully committed to democracy and human rights".[66] In the weeks that followed, Thailand's bid for a seat on the U.N. Human Rights Council was rejected.[67] The Prayut government proved extremely sensitive to foreign criticism, and was quick to assume that even boilerplate Western diplomatic comments in support of human rights and democracy masked serious ill-will towards Thailand — when this was certainly not the case. When Prayut attended the ASEM Summit in Milan in October, he faced a number of protests, but was warmly received by Japanese premier Shinzo Abe.[68] Increasingly, Thailand was turning to both China and Japan for trade and investment; in December, China signed agreements to construct high-speed rail links connecting Laos with Bangkok.[69]

Constitutionalism: Disease with No Cure?

After 22 May, the 2007 Constitution drafted in the wake of the previous coup was immediately nullified. Constitutionalism remained a political disease that persistently undermined Thailand's stable functioning: as in 1991, 1997 and 2007, professional Constitution-drafters soon began lobbying for highly prized seats on various committees, and started advancing their own pet clauses and legal hobby-horses with a predictable missionary zeal. This time, the stakes were extremely high. The NCPO was dealing with the unfinished business of the 2006–07 junta: in short, Thailand's last coup had been a disaster, failing to erode support for pro-Thaksin parties, or to weaken the influence of the Shinawatra clan. Despite deploying all the resources at their disposal, including bringing General Surayud Chulanont out of the Privy Council to serve as prime minister, the previous junta had been unable permanently to restructure the country's politics: pro-Thaksin parties had won both the 2007 and 2011 elections. To compound matters, massive street protests by colour-coded groups had paralysed the centre of Bangkok in 2008, 2009, 2010, 2013 and 2014.

In mid-2011, the military reluctantly agreed a deal with Thaksin, permitting Yingluck to become prime minister, since unseating her after another decisive electoral victory could prove more trouble than it was worth. Although Yingluck was persistently under-estimated by many commentators, during her first two years in office she established an excellent rapport with key figures inside the military and the all-important monarchical network. This rapport was always based on pragmatic considerations rather than any deep affinity, and once Thaksin resumed his push for an amnesty in late 2013, the PTP-military deal was living on borrowed time. Nevertheless, Prayut and his associates could easily have staged a coup much earlier, had they chosen to do so. The long delay between December 2013 — when the level of public disorder was arguably sufficient to serve as the pretext for a military intervention — and May 2014 illustrates significant reluctance on the part of the generals. But having decided to make the move, Prayut was determined that the coup should not fail: in other words, both that the Shinawatras would not be able to return to power afterwards, and that Thailand's long spell of contentious politics and street protests (dating back at least to the first Yellow Shirt rallies in September 2005) would be permanently ended.

Unfortunately, a focus on Thai politics through the lens of the Bangkok elite occludes a number of important social and electoral realities. What has happened in recent years is the natural outcome of the evolution of parliamentary democracy in Thailand since the 1960s: the elite and its supporters are structurally outnumbered. Thailand is a deeply divided country; the capital city has long lorded it over the provinces, viewing the mass of Thai citizens as uneducated, ignorant and malleable. But if those Thais who are registered to vote in rural provinces were ever foolish or suggestible, they are certainly not so today. Pro-Thaksin parties have won every general election since 2001, largely because of their strong appeal in the populous north and northeast, where they have won considerable support. Neither the Democrat Party nor the military-backed establishment has proved able to match Thaksin's popularity among the urbanized villagers whose votes determine the outcomes of Thai elections, and only an extremely gerrymandered electoral system could suppress the views of large swathes of the country's population. In the early months of 2014, expressions of regionalist sentiment were loudly voiced by Northerners and Northeasterners who openly craved the division of Thailand into two distinct countries.[70] The military's "compulsory reconciliation" paradigm, which does not allow for any recognition or discussion of these difficult issues, has no chance of success without a broader and more inclusive national conversation about the nature of Thailand's divisions, and possible ways to overcome them. Michael Montesano has persuasively argued that the NCPO's interim constitution "was, in essence, the ideological foundation for a praetorian order, a regime of something approximating 'Army-people-mutuality' in which civilian elites might serve as subalterns at best". By folding the entire Thai population into a military-constructed notion of "the people", the NCPO was seeking to achieve wholesale depoliticization.[71]

While the NCPO's loyal band of constitution-drafters — led by the ever-serviceable law professor Bowornsak Uwanno — had no shortage of ideas, crafting a political order that would sharply curtail the voting power of urbanized villagers soon proved no mean feat.[72] Superficially attractive moves such as introducing direct elections for prime minister, or adopting either a mixed member proportional (MMP) or open list proportional representation (OLPR) voting system, all had significant likely drawbacks.[73] In parallel with the Constitution-drafting process, the NCPO continued to flirt with other options, including sponsoring a new discreetly-military-backed political party,[74] and banning large numbers of existing politicians from seeking office.

Legal academic Jade Donavanik, 42, the youngest member of the 36-strong Constitution Drafting Committee, used the language of popular empowerment, morality and magic to describe their goals:

> While most people are focused on whether the new charter will be written in such a way as to eradicate the old power clique or the Thaksin regime, Jade holds a different view: he thinks the charter should serve as a scripture to "arm" the people and make them strong.
>
> "We need to make the charter one that reflects the people's power. In that way, politicians won't dare to violate or abuse the people otherwise they will be expelled by the people," he says.[75]

While Jade himself acknowledged that such a constitution would be "too extreme", the rhetoric of empowering people against politicians echoed the anti-politician stance both of the military and of many PDRC supporters. The legalism of the Constitution-drafters offered a powerful weapon to use against Thailand's evil politicians, a weapon blessed with special moral and even magical powers. As Jade declared: "in the hands of those who know how to use it, a leaf can turn into a magic sword".

Conclusion

2014 was a terribly difficult year for Thailand. The 22 May coup could only paper over profound divisions that remained unresolved by year's end, and for which there was no obvious solution. The leaders of the NCPO were well aware that Thailand's last two military coups had ended in abject failure. Rather than accepting that it was not possible to re-engineer a political system from the top down, the NCPO leadership appeared to believe that it could impose a solution to the country's deep seated conflicts simply by repressing all dissenting voices. In other words, previous coups failed not because they were too ambitious, but because they did not go far enough. While it might just prove possible to turn the leaves of constitutional law books into magic swords with which to discipline wayward politicians, by the same token the magic swords of the Royal Thai Army could simply wither into weapons no more powerful than dead leaves. In the long term, depoliticizing the public sphere of such a vibrant country as Thailand surely lies beyond the realm of the possible.

Notes

Duncan McCargo would like to thank Chanintorn Pensute, Michael Connors, Petra Desatova, Jittip Mongkolnchaiarunya, Michael Montesano, Sutawan Chanprasert, Eastina Tan and various others for all their help and feedback.

1. See Michael J. Montesano, "Junta's Agenda Clearer after Yingluck Verdict", *Straits Times*, 29 January 2015, available at <http://www.straitstimes.com/news/opinion/eye-the-world/story/juntas-agenda-clearer-after-yingluck-verdict-20150129#sthash.gIvtoFYR.dpuf>.
2. For an excellent summary of the origins of the protests, see Michael J. Montesano, "What is to Come in Thailand", *ISEAS Perspective*, 10 February 2014, available at <http://www.iseas.edu.sg/documents/publication/ISEAS_Perspective_2014_07-What_is_to_Come_in_Thailand.pdf>.

3. On these figures, see Robert Talcoth's blog article, "A Numbers Game: Social Media and Political Legitimacy" and subsequent comments, *New Mandala*, 10 October 2014, available at <http://asiapacific.anu.edu.au/newmandala/2014/10/10/a-numbers-game-social-media-and-political-legitimacy/>.

4. For details of the three key networks behind the resurgent anti-government movement in 2013, see Aim Simpeng, "Who's Who in Thailand's Anti-government Forces?" *New Mandala*, 30 November 2013, available at <http://asiapacific.anu.edu.au/newmandala/2013/11/30/whos-who-in-the-anti-government-forces-in-thailand/>. For more discussion see Saksith Saiyasombut and Siam Voices, "Organized Chaos: Thai Anti-election Protesters' Hardline Faction", *Asian Correspondent*, 15 January 2014, available at <http://asiancorrespondent.com/118364/thai-anti-election-protests-hardliners-prone-to-volatile-chaos/>.

5. For a discussion of the merits of this alternative translation, see "Khao Sod English's Note on Name Translation of Anti-Govt Leadership", *Khao Sod English*, 24 December 2013, available at <http://www.khaosod.co.th/en/view_newsonline.php?newsid=TVRNNE56ZzNNNalUzTlE9PQ==&catid=03>. I would prefer to translate the PDRC's Thai title even more literally as: "People's Committee for Changing Thailand into a Complete Democracy with the King as Head of State".

6. For a discussion of PDRC motivations, see Nidhi Eoseewong, "Muanmahaprachachon", *Matichon,* 17 December 2013, available at <http://www.matichon.co.th/news_detail.php?newsid=1387190430>.

7. See Jonathan Head, "Thailand Crisis: Deadly Attacks on Opposition Rallies", *BBC*, 23 February 2014, available at <http://www.bbc.com/news/world-asia-26311828>.

8. For discussion of thirty-two alleged business financiers of the PDRC protests (from a list of 136 suspected donors compiled by government agencies), see "Thurakit mai ao maew" [Anti Thaksin businesses], *Thai Post*, 12 February 2014, available at <http://www.thaipost.net/news/120214/85922>. *Thai Rath* estimated that the first eighteen days of the "shutdown" rallies cost 126 million baht, or a little under US$4 million. *Thai Rath*, 30 January 2014, available at <http://www.thairath.co.th/content/399807>.

9. For a critical analysis of the issues in the Yingluck case, see Veerapat Pariwong, "Khosangkaet khiao kap khadi san rathathamanun" [Observations on the Constitutional Court Case], 5 May 2014, available at <https://www.facebook.com/verapat/posts/10201352328604367?stream_ref=10>.

10. *Profile of the "Bangkok Shutdown" Protestors: A Survey of the Anti-Government PDRC Demonstrators in Bangkok*, Asia Foundation, Bangkok, January 2014, available at <http://asiafoundation.org/publications/pdf/1314>.

11. *Profile of the "Bangkok Shutdown" Protestors*, p. 6.

12. This section draws on an unpublished paper by Duncan McCargo, Naruemon Thabchumpon and Sutawan Chanprasert. Semi-structured interviews were carried out

with twenty-nine protesters at the PDRC rallies in January and February 2014 by a team of doctoral students, led by Naruemon Thabchumpon, based on questions developed with the author. The sample size is too small to provide genuinely representative data, but the responses complement survey research done by the Asia Foundation.

13. *Profile of the "Bangkok Shutdown" Protestors*, p. 11.

14. To a large extent, rubber prices were beyond the control of the Thai Government. See Huileng Tan, "Rubber Falls to Four-Year Low on Fears of Oversupply, China Slowdown", *Wall Street Journal*, 24 April 2014, available at <http://online.wsj.com/news/articles/SB10001424052702304788404579521023985539330>.

15. The affected constituences were in Songkhla (8), Krabi (3), Phattalung (3), Surat Thani (6) Trang (4) — no candidates registered in the entire province; Phuket (1), Nakhon Sri Thammasat (2); Chumphon (1) — some constituencies affected.

16. In line with a recently-invented Thai tradition, Somchai's detractors created a fake Facebook page to mock his views, where videoclips of his statements may be found at <https://www.facebook.com/antisomchaicockroach>.

17. In Thailand, voters who expect to be away from home on the election date are permitted to vote a week early, so long as they register to do so. In practice, virtually all of these votes are cast by people living away from their home constituencies, especially urbanized villagers registered to vote in the provinces but actually reside in and around Bangkok.

18. See *ANFREL Briefing on the Thai Election of 2nd February 2014* (Bangkok: ANFREL, 3 February 2014). As this internal document makes clear, the EC claims that only 440,000 people were unable to cast advance ballots were contradicted by the Commission's own data: the real figure was far higher.

19. Author's observations near Asoke PDRC stage, 26 January 2014.

20. Duncan McCargo "The Thai Malaise", *Foreign Policy* (online), 18 February 2014.

21. Author's fieldnotes, Ratchatewi District Office, 2 February 2014.

22. IDEA gives a figure of 46.79 per cent, while respected political analyst Bangkok Pundit put turnout at 47.72 per cent. See <http://www.idea.int/vt/countryview.cfm?CountryCode=TH and http://asiancorrespondent.com/119339/ec-figures-show-turn-out-at-47-72/>, and <http://www.naewna.com/politic/89198>.

23. See Duncan McCargo, "Thailand: State of Anxiety", in *Southeast Asian Affairs 2008*, edited by Daljit Singh and Tin Maung Maung Than (Singapore: Institute of Southeast Asian Studies, 2008), p. 348.

24. Surachai Liangboonlertchai was made Senate President on 8 May 2014, but his appointment was never formally ratified by the King.

25. Statistics supplied to the author by the Erawan Emergency Center, Bangkok, 29 January 2015.

26. For the most detailed discussion of events surrounding the coup and its aftermath, see *A Coup Ordained? Thailand's Prospects for Stability*, International Crisis Group, Asia Report No. 263, 3 December 2014.

27. For more details of what happened, see *Matichon*, 23 May 2014.

28. See Duncan McCargo, "Tearing up the Script", *International New York Times*, 29 May 2014.

29. See *A Coup Ordained?*, pp. 17–19.

30. The full English texts of his weekly addresses from May to November can be found at <http://www.thaigov.go.th/en/speech-2.html?start=11>.

31. See, for example, Jason Szep and Amy Sawitta Lefevre, "Powerful Forces Revealed behind Thai Protest Movement', *Reuters*, 13 December 2013, available at <http://www.reuters.com/article/2013/12/13/us-thailand-protest-military-idUSBRE9BC0PB20131213>.

32. Available at <http://asiancorrespondent.com/124062/suthep-claims-in-talks-with-Prayut-since-2010-to-plot-thai-coup/>.

33. See Wassana Nanuam, "Prayut Denies Suthep's Coup-plotting Claim", available at <http://www.bangkokpost.com/news/politics/416913/Prayut-denies-suthep-coup-plotting-claim>.

34. The initial budget for this project was over a million US dollars. See <https://www.hereandthere.today/?p=1522>.

35. For a discussion, see "Thai Students Required to Recite Prayut's 12 Core Values Daily", *Bangkok Pundit*, 22 September 2014, available at <http://asiancorrespondent.com/126873/all-thai-students-required-to-recite-daily-Prayuts-12-core-values/>.

36. Critiques of NCPO statements and actions were posted almost daily on <https://politicalprisonersofthailand.wordpress.com/author/politicalprisonersofthailand/>. For another collection of posts on the crackdown, see <https://thaicoup2014.wordpress.com/>.

37. See Metta Wongwat, "Aunties on the Frontline Against the Coup: A Special Report", *Prachatai*, 9 June 2014, available at <http://www.prachatai.com/english/node/4105>.

38. For a defence of NCPO suppression of the salute by Jade Donavanik, a popular young law academic and member of the Constitution Drafting Committee, see *Matichon*, 22 November 2014, available at <http://www.matichon.co.th/news_detail.php?newsid=1416650461>.

39. For similar incidents, see <https://www.youtube.com/watch?v=zTd_FJbiRq0>.

40. "Thailand: Two Months Under Military Rule", *Human Rights Watch*, 21 July 2014, available at <http://www.hrw.org/news/2014/07/21/thailand-two-months-under-military-rule>.

41. Nidhi Eoseewong, "Aowsan nakwichakan", *Matichon*, 22 September 2014, available at <http://www.thairath.co.th/content/452265>.

42. According to ICG, as of 7 November 2014, at least sixty-nine civilians were facing court martials. *A Coup Ordained*, p. 18.

43. See "2014 Coup Marks the Highest Number of *Lese Majeste* Prisoners in Thai History", *Prachatai*, 15 July 2014, available at <http://www.prachatai.com/english/node/4218>.

44. For a discussion of this and related issues, see Tyrell Haberkorn, "Martial Law and the Criminalization of Thought in Thailand", *Asia-Pacific Journal* 12, issue 40, no. 5 (6 October 2014), available at <http://www.japanfocus.org/-Tyrell-Haberkorn/4199>.

45. See "Samruat 6 duan kho so cho yok bik kharatchan thang phaendin bai khi rikte" [Reviewing 6 months of the NCPO: Transfers of top officials measure how much on the Richter scale?], *Prachatai*, 2 December 2014, available at <http://www.prachatai.com/journal/2014/12/56791>. The article lists eighty-nine high-level, politically motivated transfers since the coup. Ironically, the Constitutional Court removed Yingluck from office for a similar abuse of power.

46. For a particularly savage anti-Prayut cartoon, see *ASTV-Phujatkan Online*, 26 October 2014 (which comes with a political advisory warning that people access the page at their own risk), see <http://www.manager.co.th/Pjkkuan/ViewNews.aspx?NewsID=9570000123219>.

47. See "In post-coup Thailand, what is happening with Prem?", *Bangkok Pundit*, 9 September 2014, available at <http://asiancorrespondent.com/126517/what-is-happening-with-prem/>.

48. "Dean covers head with box to protest rector holding dual posts", *Thai PBS*, 10 September 2014, available at <http://englishnews.thaipbs.or.th/dean-covers-head-box-protest-rector-holding-dual-posts>.

49. For related stories on subsequent *hip* (tin box) protests, see *Prachatai*, 23 September 2014, available at <http://www.prachatai.com/journal/2014/09/55685>; *Thai Rath*, 24 September 2014, available at <http://www.thairath.co.th/content/452265>.

50. See <http://news.sanook.com/1675733/>.

51. For a discussion, see Pavin Chachavalpongpun, "Princess Chulabhorn's politics", *New Mandala*, 14 January 2014, available at <http://asiapacific.anu.edu.au/newmandala/2014/01/14/princess-chulabhorns-politics/>.

52. For images and English statements from these redshirt rallies, see <http://thairedshirts.org/2014/05/13/pictures-from-aksa-road-11-12th-may-2014/>.

53. See "In for the long haul", *The Economist*, 31 May 2014, available at <http://www.economist.com/news/asia/21603033-crackdown-follows-coup-generals-may-stick-around-long-they-think-it-takes>.

54. See, for example, "Prince said to trigger police purge", *Asia Sentinel*, 27 November 2014, available at <http://www.asiasentinel.com/society/thailand-prince-said-to-trigger-police-purge/>.

55. For a detailed discussion, see Srisompob Jitpiromsri, "An Inconvenient Truth about the Deep South Violent Conflict: A Decade of Chaotic, Constrained Realities and Uncertain Resolution", Deep South Watch, 2 July 2014, available at <http://www.deepsouthwatch.org/node/5904#_ftn2>.

56. See Duncan McCargo, *Southern Thailand: From Conflict to Negotiations?*, Lowy Institute, April 2014, available at <http://www.lowyinstitute.org/files/mccargo_southern-thailand_0.pdf>.

57. See Don Pathan, "No progress in deep South unless Thailand drops strongman act", *The Nation*, 11 December 2014, available at <http://www.nationmultimedia.com/opinion/No-progress-in-deep-South-unless-Thailand-drops-st-30249556.html>.

58. "Thailand's Economy: The High Cost of Stability", *The Economist*, 8 October 2014, available at <http://www.economist.com/blogs/banyan/2014/10/thailands-economy?>.

59. For a relevant discussion see Andrew Flowers, "How Thailand's Coup Could Affect Its Economy", *FiveThirtyEight*, 23 May 2014, available at <http://fivethirtyeight.com/datalab/how-thailands-coup-could-affect-its-economy/>.

60. See "Growth Momentum Remains Weak in Thailand", *Deutsche Welle*, 1 December 2014, available at <http://www.dw.de/growth-momentum-remains-weak-in-thailand/a-18103869>.

61. See *Thai Rath*, 16 December 2014, available at <http://www.thairath.co.th/content/469304>.

62. For a summary, see "The Rice Mountain: An Increasingly Unpopular Government Sticks to Its Worst and Most Costly Policy", *The Economist*, 10 August 2013.

63. See "Thai Junta Spends $4.2 bn in 2 months", *Prachatai*, 31 July 2014, available at <http://prachatai3.com/english/node/4257>.

64. See Gabriel Leon, "Loyalty for Sale? Military Spending and *Coups D'etat*", *Public Choice* 159 (2014): 363–83.

65. Eric Slavin, "US, Thai Officials Planning Cobra Gold Exercise Despite May Coup", *Stars and Stripes*, 10 October 2014, available at <http://www.stripes.com/news/pacific/thailand/us-thai-officials-planning-cobra-gold-exercise-despite-may-coup-1.307643>.

66. See Thai UNGA statement, 27 September 2014, available at <http://www.un.org/en/ga/69/meetings/gadebate/pdf/TH_en.pdf>.

67. See "UN Rejects Thailand From Rights Council", *Khaosod English*, 22 October 2014, available at <http://www.khaosodenglish.com/detail.php?newsid=1413954464>.

68. "Protestors Jeer Prayuth outside Abe Talks", *Bangkok Post*, 17 October 2014, available at <http://www.bangkokpost.com/news/social/437980/protesters-jeer-prayut-outside-abe-talks>.

69. Warangkana Chomchuen, "Thailand, China Sign Railway Deal", *Wall Street Journal*, 19 December 2014, available at <http://www.wsj.com/articles/thailand-china-sign-agreement-on-rail-link-1418989207>.

70. See "You Go Your Way, I'll Go Mine", *The Economist*, 25 January 2014, available at <http://www.economist.com/news/asia/21594989-thailands-very-unity-now-under-threat-you-go-your-way-ill-go-mine>.

71. Michael J. Montesano, "Praetorianism and 'the People' in Late-Bhumibol Thailand", unpublished paper, online paper prepared for the European Union SEATIDE project on "Integration in Southeast Asia: Trajectories of Inclusion, Dynamics of Exclusion", available at <http://www.seatide.eu/?content=activitiesandresults&group=3>, forthcoming 2015, p. 12.

72. Saksith Saiyasombat and Siam Voices, "Thailand's Post-coup Constitution: Familiar Faces, Unfamiliar Territory", *Asian Correspondent*, 5 November 2014, available at <http://asiancorrespondent.com/127996/thailands-post-coup-constitution-drafting-familiar-faces-uncharted-territory/>.

73. See an excellent series of posts on these issues at <http://www.thaidatapoints.com/>, authored by Allen Hicken, some with Bangkok Pundit.

74. Informants confirmed that electable figures from other parties have been approached by figures inviting them to join a new political party, which they believed was backed by Prawit Wongsuwan. Author interviews, Thailand, August 2014.

75. Jintana Panyaarvudh, "Power to the People", *Sunday Nation*, 16 November 2014, available at <http://www.nationmultimedia.com/opinion/Power-to-the-people-30247785.html>.

WHAT WENT WRONG WITH THE THAI DEMOCRACY?

Suchit Bunbongkarn

The coup on 22 May 2014 in Thailand has, for the present, caused a break in the political divide and impasse, a problem that the previous elected government was unable to solve. Many were worried that the deeply entrenched political polarization which had existed for almost a decade would lead to bloodshed if it was allowed to continue. So many questions were asked on what went wrong with the presumed Thai democracy. Why did the coup happen? What would be the future of democracy in Thailand? How can it be consolidated? These questions reflect that Thailand is facing a serious problem of democratic consolidation.

Many scholars on democratization agree that the road to a stable democracy is not always smooth. They agree that democratic consolidation in many countries is not an easy task, and Thailand is no exception.

Democratic consolidation depends on a variety of factors which vary from one country to another. Nonetheless, one of the major causes for the instability of a democratic regime is related to political legitimacy. Any political regime which does not secure legitimacy will find it hard to survive since its legitimacy depends on its acceptance by its citizens as expressed through major political forces. There is no need at this stage to debate in detail here how to develop and fortify a democratic regime's legitimacy. However, it is accepted that the essential requirement for strengthening such legitimacy is the regime's effectiveness in meeting the needs of its people and the implementation of democratic values, practices and procedures.

Suchit Bunbongkarn is Professor Emeritus in the Faculty of Political Science, Chulalongkorn University and Senior Fellow at the Institute for Security and International Studies (ISIS), Thailand.

Political Polarization and the Crisis of Political Legitimacy

In the case of Thailand during the past decade, we have witnessed a deeply entrenched political polarization which had never reached such extreme levels in the past. This divisiveness, initially caused by a conflict between the pro- and anti-Thaksin groups, later developed into a crisis of political legitimacy. The anti-Thaksin group was formed around 2001 by a mass media tycoon, Sonthi Limthongkul, and later joined by some prominent political elites, notably Chamlong Srimuang, former Governor of Bangkok. In the beginning, the group was composed of thousands from the urban middle class and some upper-middle class who believed that Thaksin was leading the country towards one party rule. He was accused of trying to amass his family's fortunes through "policy corruption". For example, when he was the Prime Minister, the Parliament, presumably under his influence, passed a law enabling him to sell his family's telecom company, Shin Corp, to Temasek of Singapore and be tax exempt for the profits made. In addition, some of his populist policies, especially the provision of village funds (one million baht (US$31,000) per village) and medical care (thirty baht per one hospital visit), were criticized by a number of scholars. They argued that such policies would, in the long run, affect the national economy detrimentally. However, what the anti-Thaksin groups were most concerned about was the fact that Thaksin seemed to allow the left-wing elements in his party to freely criticize the monarchy even though most of the criticisms were unfounded. The anti-government protest rapidly received more popular support both in urban and rural areas. This gradually led to an erosion of the political legitimacy of Thaksin's government.

On the Thaksin side, the then Prime Minister and his political colleagues established a political movement, commonly known as the "Red Shirts" movement to counter the "Yellow Shirts" (People's Alliance for Democracy, PAD) and to strengthen Thaksin's legitimacy. The movement mobilized rural villagers mostly from the north and the northeast to rally in Bangkok to demonstrate the strength of their support. The movement also wanted to show how popular the government's populist policies were especially in rural provinces and towns in the north and the northeast. The political figures playing an important role in establishing the power bases of Thaksin in these two parts of the country were left-leaning party members, some of them being former student activists who fled into the jungle after the coup in 1976 to join the Communist Party of Thailand (CPT). In addition, Thaksin, through the use of his wealth, was able to bring in a large number of politically ambitious local leaders in these areas of the country to his side by enabling them to run for the seats in the Parliament under

Thaksin's party. At the top echelons of the party, apart from Thaksin, there were a number of wealthy businessmen whose financial contributions helped to oil Thaksin's political machine. However, it was known that Thaksin was the one who contributed the most financially.

The coup in September 2006 neither put an end to political divisiveness in the country nor did it eliminate Thaksin's influence. He was forced out of power, but his political clout remained. The coup-appointed government did not make serious efforts to uproot Thaksin's influence. It also did not attempt to educate the people on "what is right, what is wrong" in politics. Hence, the rural people in the north and the northeast continued to believe that Thaksin had done much good for them, and that he was the only political leader who had really helped them. To no one's surprise, therefore, when the new Constitution was put into effect and General Elections were held in 2007, the Thaksin-backed People's Power Party won.

From 2007 to the coup in May 2014, the political polarization remained a chronic problem in Thai politics, and there was no sign of reconciliation. Almost immediately after the People's Power Party won the elections and formed the government with Samak Sudaravej as Prime Minister, the Yellow Shirts (PAD) started campaigning against the government on the grounds that the government was only a "puppet of Thaksin". Thus, it was deemed no longer legitimate to govern. It was not long before the Constitutional Court ruled that Samak was disqualified to be prime minister because he had received money from a television show producer for performing as a cook on a cooking show. He was then succeeded by Somchai Wongsawat, Thaksin's brother-in-law in September 2008. The PAD stepped up its campaign against the government demanding that Somchai step down. Protesters argued that Somchai was Thaksin's puppet and that the government was not legitimate. The economy was almost crippled when the protest leaders, including Chamlong Srimuang, led a large crowd to seize Don Muang and Suvanaphumi international airports in Bangkok, causing all the international and domestic flights coming to Bangkok to divert their course to other airports and stop flying to Thailand. However, the government kept on insisting on its legitimacy, arguing that it came to power through elections. Nevertheless, it made no effort to regain its control of the airports.

Somchai's government did not last long. In early December 2008, the Constitutional Court ordered the People's Power Party, the major party in Somchai's coalition government, to be dissolved as one of its executive members was found guilty of breaking the election law during the General

Elections in 2007. The dissolution immediately led to the downfall of Somchai's government, and the PAD which had then occupied Bangkok's two airports in protest.

Nonetheless, the situation did not return to normal. When the Parliament voted Abhisit Vejjajiva, the leader of the Democrat Party, the main opposition, to be the next prime minister, the pro-Thaksin group rejected Abhisit's government outright. It argued that Abhisit was not a legitimate prime minister because he was not the leader of the largest party in the Parliament, although the majority of the members of the Parliament voted for him. The Red Shirts of the United Front of Democracy Against Dictatorship (UDD) attacked the vote as being unfair and illegitimate because, they believed, the vote was undertaken under the pressure of the military.

The Democrat-led government under the premiership of Abhisit was the first anti-Thaksin government since the elections in 2007. It was not unexpected, therefore, that the UDD would launch a large-scale protest against the government. The main objective of the UDD was to bring Thaksin back home without serving a jail sentence. It intended to destroy the image of the Prime Minister and his ability to run the country. A rally organized by the UDD disrupted the ASEAN Summit meeting in Pattaya in 2009, and in 2010 around some 10,000 UDD protesters, mostly from the north and northeast, occupied Ratprasong, the main shopping area of Bangkok for several months. They exerted pressure hoping to force the government to resign. Eventually, the government decided to use army troops to disperse the protesters. The army took utmost precautions to avoid violent clashes with the protesters. However, during several months of pressure and suppression, sporadic clashes occurred causing a number of deaths and injuries on both sides. Finally, the army was able to put an end to the protest but not without casualties. Some buildings were set on fire, including some department stores in Bangkok and city halls in some provinces.

The UDD's agreement to end the protest did not mean that the political polarization was about to end. On the contrary, the divisiveness was getting worse, soon resulting in profound hatred on both sides. The UDD condemned Abhisit for the loss of life on the UDD side during the army suppression. The community radio stations in the north and northeast and the red shirt television channel accused Abhisit's government of ordering the government troops to use live ammunition and lethal weapons with the intention to kill the protesters. Hate speech was often used in their broadcasts attacking the government. Freedom of speech, guaranteed in the previous Constitution, had provided opportunity for such mass media to play an effective role in instilling a belief among rural villagers in the north and northeast that Abhisit's government was illegitimate while strengthening popularity of Thaksin and his Pheu Thai Party in these two parts of the country.

The General Election in 2010 demonstrated an increasing divisiveness among the Thai electorate. Thaksin's Pheu Thai Party won a majority of seats in the Parliament while the Democrat Party came in second. As expected, Pheu Thai captured most of the seats in the north and northeast whereas all the seats in the south went to the Democrat Party except in one or two Muslim-dominated provinces. The result of the elections confirmed that the political influence of Thaksin remained very strong. Yingluck Shinawatra, Thaksin's sister, ran in his place as the Pheu Thai Party leader, although she had no political experience. She was elected by the Parliament to be the prime minister. Most people believed that she won due to her family ties with Thaksin.

Soon after Yingluck's government had assumed power, several anti-Thaksin groups became active again. However, they were not capable of organizing mass protests until 2013 when the government tried to amend the Constitution and introduce an amnesty bill. These actions were believed to be part of the government's effort to bring Thaksin back to Thailand without serving a two-year imprisonment.

On the issue of enacting an amnesty law, Yingluck's government was accused of abusing power. The fact that the government was trying to use the majority it enjoyed in the House of Representatives to pass this law despite strong protests from both inside and outside the House added fuel to the fire. In addition to a fierce debate against the bill in the House, the Democrat Party, the main opposition, took to the streets with some 10,000 people in Bangkok in protest against the bill. However, the government continued without heeding the protest, believing that the protest was just a tactical move of the opposition, and that it was supported only by a small group of people. However, a serious political crisis was triggered by the fact that the House of Representatives decided to vote on this bill at 4:00 a.m. without allowing full discussion. This was not only highly unusual, but also very arbitrary and presumptuous of the government, thus leading to a large-scale mass protest.

It was not only the amnesty bill that had eroded the government's legitimacy. There was also the rice pledging scheme[1] in which Yingluck's government failed to pay back farmers on time. Most critics and experts on rice trading believed that it was a wrong policy and that there was large-scale corruption at almost every level from the policymakers downward. The country's economy and the reputation of Thai rice were damaged. It was reported that the government had lost several hundred thousand million baht due to corruption and mismanagement of this policy. The most serious consequence was the suffering of the farmers due to the lack of government payment.

The Strengths, Base of Support and Weaknesses of the Anti-Yingluck Government Movement

The government's insistence on enacting the amnesty bill had resulted in widespread demonstrations, indicating a rapid increase in the strength of the government opponents and an expansion of the base of support for them. A huge number of people had decided to join the anti-government, anti-Thaksin movement, especially the one called the People's Democratic Reform Committee (PDRC) led by Suthep Teuksuban, former deputy leader of the Democrat Party. The government's abuse of power and large-scale corruption in the government were the issues picked up by the protesters to attack and condemn Yingluck and her brother, Thaksin. They hoped to obtain as large a number of people as possible, not only in Bangkok but in other urban towns and in the south which was the stronghold of the Democrat Party, to join in the protest against the government and thus force Yingluck, the Prime Minister, to resign. Hundreds of thousands of people in Bangkok from all walks of life joined the demonstration. They were government officials, professional and business people, private entrepreneurs, state enterprise workers, university teachers, medical doctors, nurses and public health workers. There were demonstrations in other provinces as well, including major provinces in the north and the northeast. However, the strongest and most solid support came from the south.

The strength of the PDRC did not rely only on the number of the protesters, but also on the financial contributions from the protesters and others who shared a similar belief with the protesters in rejecting the legitimacy of Yingluck's government. The way the people contributed money to Suthep and his organization was a phenomenon to behold. Wherever he held an anti-government rally, people would surround him, handing him thousands of banknotes. It was estimated that throughout the several months of protest the PDRC received contributions of millions of baht.

In addition to those contributions, the PDRC received support from the mass media. The most important one was the Blue Sky TV channel which was known to be pro-Democrat. Throughout the whole period of the protest, it switched to broadcast programmes supporting the PDRC. The Thai television medium was a very effective means to mobilize people to join the PDRC movement. It was a great success in expanding the base of support for the PDRC to bring in various groups of people to participate in political rallies and to donate money and other necessities for a prolonged protest, for example, food, drinking water, camping tents and blankets.

Another important factor contributing to the success of the PDRC in expanding and strengthening mass support was Suthep's leadership. Throughout the period of demonstration, Suthep had shown his perseverance, strong determination, and devotion to his cause. He campaigned tirelessly to overthrow PM Yingluck and the so-called "Thaksin system". Apart from such strength of character, his oratorical skill enabled him to capture the hearts and minds of millions of people.

Despite the strengths mentioned above, the PDRC still had some weaknesses. One of them was the lack of strong and effective coordination with other anti-government groups. Since the introduction of the amnesty bill to Parliament, there had been a number of anti-government groups formed in addition to the PDRC. One led by one of the most respected Buddhist monks, Buddha-issara, was very influential and gained the support of the masses. In fact, the group was part of the PDRC, but Buddha-issara wanted to be independent from Suthep. Other smaller groups led by some political activists, including the one which called itself the "People's Army to Dethrone Thaksin's System" and another called the 'Network of Students and People for National Reform', were actively campaigning for the same cause as the PDRC. However, effective coordination between them was absent.

Another weakness was the lack of a clear-cut reform plan. The PDRC had launched a campaign for a national reform before elections. They were successful in mobilizing voters to boycott the General Election on 2 February 2014, but what they failed to do was to present to the public the specific national reform programmes, both for the short term and long term. Another important issue the PDRC faced was how to overhaul the so-called "Thaksin system". They had announced that if the government failed to agree to the PDRC's demand, then they would launch a people's revolution. However, it was obvious that they did not know how.

The Yingluck Government's Legitimacy Crisis

Amidst the mass protests, Yingluck's government insisted on its legitimacy to rule, arguing that it was elected by the people. A legitimacy crisis occurred when the government failed to maintain law and order. Arrest warrants were issued by the Criminal Court at the government's request to arrest Suthep and a number of his colleagues on sedition charges, but the government failed to arrest them. The government was unable to disperse the protesters and prosecute them. These failures indicated that Yingluck's government was facing a very serious problem of eroding legitimacy. When the government sought loans from the government-owned banks to pay the farmers who joined the rice pledging scheme, quite a number of bank customers threatened to withdraw their deposits from these banks, thus forcing them to turn down the government's request. What was even worse was that the government could not provide a political environment favorable for organizing general elections within the time frame stipulated in the Constitution. Due to the protests and the Democrat Party's threat to boycott the elections, the government and the Election Commission had to organize the elections beyond the constitutional deadline, making the elections unconstitutional as ruled by the Constitutional Court. The government and the Red Shirts (the UDD) mobilized rural villagers, mostly from the north and northeast, to come to Bangkok to support the government and to counter the PDRC. However, the UDD's demonstration was politically ineffective. It could not compare with the PDRC in terms of the number of people involved, and the UDD could not afford to pay those villagers to stay in Bangkok for more than two or three days.

On the eve of the coup on 22 May 2014, Thailand was, therefore, plagued with an insurmountable conundrum over political legitimacy with no solution in sight, as there was no resolution acceptable to both the government and the opponents. It this situation it was impossible to find a way out though constitutional means.

The Military and National Reform

At present, the country is in the hands of the military or the National Council for Peace and Order (NCPO). They have agreed that extensive political, as well as other reforms, are urgently needed. It is hoped that the reforms would lead to political reconciliation as well as a stable democratic political system. The NCPO set up the Cabinet, the National Legislative Assembly, the National Reform Council (NRC) and the Constitutional Drafting Committee. These institutions have been assigned to launch national reform programmes and draft a new permanent Constitution.

The political reform, under consideration of the NRC and the CDC, is focusing on the development of political institutions and processes, including the election system and the political party system to ensure that elected governments in the future would be honest, responsible and serve public needs. It has been agreed that such a government must be able to accommodate the needs of various political and social groups. The people's liberty should be respected. Equality in all aspects should be encouraged, and law and order must be observed and maintained. The gap between the urban rich and the rural poor must be narrowed, and the wealth and economic power should not be in the hands of the very few.

Another reform issue which is of public concern is the relationship between politicians and government bureaucrats. The people want the reforms to ensure that the government bureaucracy, including the police and the armed forces do not become the political tools of politicians.

The devolution of the government administration is also a reform issue of importance. The NRC and CDC have agreed that the political and administrative authority must not be concentrated in the capital. More authority should be transferred from the national government to the local ones. There has been a proposal for direct elections of provincial governors and some local government officers. This is a very sensitive issue. How can we make sure that such devolution of authority will not end up providing opportunities for greedy local politicians who have an insatiable hunger for power and wealth as their personal interests prevail over national interests?

The next reform issue is the development of an effective system of checks-and-balances. This involves the strengthening of the authority and independence of public prosecutors, the national counter-corruption and human rights commissions and the judiciary.

It has also been agreed that the reforms should focus not only on the political institutions but also on the cultural and psychological aspects. The political ethics and morality of politicians and government officers must lead to a conviction that politics and government administration are public service. Joining politics must be to serve the people not to seek personal wealth, power and influence. A sense of citizenship needs to be instilled in the people. This sense of citizenship will encourage the people to participate more actively in their local affairs. They will learn how to stand on their own feet and rely less on the patronage offered by local leaders or politicians.

One of the most important reforms is the strengthening of the people's sector and civil society. The development of a sense of citizenship will empower the people's sector. The people are the foundation of democracy. If the people's sector is weak, the democracy will also be weak and unstable. In the past, Thailand did not pay enough attention to the development of the people's sector, hence the democratic system had been exploited by politicians for their personal benefit. To strengthen the Thai democracy, the people's sector must be strengthened.

Those reforms mentioned previously are only a few of the important ones facing the Thai body politic. There are many more reforms that need attention. All the reforms would lead to the development of a more effective system of checks-and-balances, the rule of law, and a greater opportunity for the citizenry to participate in the formulation and implementation of decisions affecting their lives. It is hoped that the reforms undertaken would ensure that a more stable, effective and responsible democratic government emerges in the not too distant future. This seems to be a very formidable task which cannot be completed easily within a few years as there are a number of obstacles to be tackled. Also, how these reforms can be achieved remains to be seen.

Note

1. The "rice pledging policy" was implemented by Yingluck Shinawatra's Pheu Thai government after it won the July 2011 Thai General Election. The Thai government purchased rice from farmers for 15,000 baht per tonne, around 50 per cent above market prices, which it then stockpiled. The rationale was that with Thailand as the world's leading rice exporter, this sudden price hike and potential market shortage would force global rice prices higher. This would then allow the government to sell its rice for a premium, causing minimal impact on the budget, and generating a bigger pay-off for Thai farmers in the government's electoral stronghold.

Timor-Leste

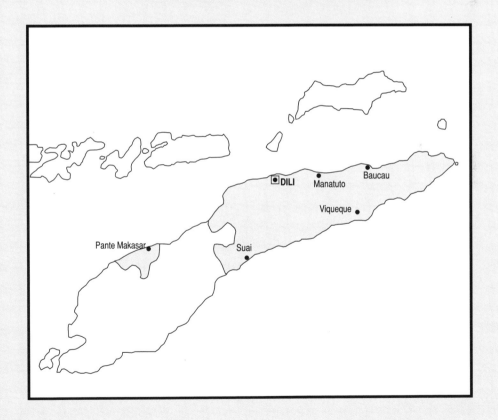

TIMOR-LESTE
The Two Sides of Success

Rui Graça Feijo

In just a year from 2013 to 2014 Dili has undergone major changes. Just outside the airport, which is to undergo a significant expansion, stands a gigantic statue of Nicolau Lobato, the guerrilla leader and sometime President of the self-proclaimed Democratic Republic of Timor-Leste, who was gunned down by the Indonesian occupiers in 1978. The statue evokes the outstanding role played by the Resistance in the struggle for national liberation, and symbolizes the contribution of deep-rooted national values (as opposed to foreign-born ideas) that have come to dominate the political discourse in the country. These ideas contributed to the victory of Taur Matan Ruak in the presidential elections two years ago and subsequent defeat of the more cosmopolitan former President, Jose Ramos-Horta. Towards the city centre there is a brand new double bridge over the Comoro River. A few yards away there are signs of new investment as exemplified by Timor Plaza, a bustling shopping mall with fancy establishments like cafés, restaurants, fashion stores, bookshops, a cinema and even an Apple Macintosh outpost. Groups of youth, using the Internet Wi-Fi facilities provided by some mobile phone operators, cram its corridors. In addition there are upmarket office facilities occupied by many international enterprises that have established themselves in the country.

On the newly paved seafront, a new building reveals a little of the motivation behind this recent surge in public works: the headquarters of the Commonwealth of Portuguese Speaking Countries (CPLP) which had its regular summit in Dili in late July, bringing several heads of state and government from Africa, Europe

Rui Graça Feijo is Associate Researcher at CES/University of Coimbra, Portugal.

and South America to the country, and promoting Timor-Leste to the chair of the organization for the next two years — a most significant achievement for its young diplomatic corps. A few blocks inland, and dominating the cityscape, another imposing building, the ten-storey iron and glass air-conditioned Ministry of Finance which cost over an estimated US$50 million, was inaugurated by the Indonesian President Susilo Bambang Yudhoyono on the occasion of his farewell visit. Indonesian building companies had taken the largest share in the construction, an example of the thriving commercial relations that bind the two countries. Several other ministries have completed building their new headquarters (Ministry of Solidarity) or are in the process of building them (Ministry of Justice). The same holds true for important official institutions, such as the National Electoral Commission, which has moved into a grandiose new building. Towards the ocean, one cannot fail to notice the presence of more than half a dozen ships waiting their turn to unload their cargo in a harbour filled with containers suggesting a growth in external trade as official figures confirm. Continuing to the east, in the pleasant seafront garden of Lecidere, which was recently expanded, youths gather by night, creating a lively atmosphere. Nearby, the Hotel Turismo completely refurbished to international standards and much changed from its original structure that was cherished by locals and generations of visitors, is another example of the sort of investment being made in order to bring Dili in line with the requirements of modern business. Major investments are not limited to the capital city, as exemplified by the inauguration of the second power station in the south coast, reinforcing the national network of electricity supply to all districts.

The scenario had changed much since 2002. Back then, the smell of smoke was still detectable, an effect of the devastation caused by the scorched earth campaign of 1999. In 2002, the Palace of the Ashes was a building in ruins, without a proper roof and makeshift windows but was the seat of the presidency of the Republic — a symbolic gesture by the then President Xanana Gusmão to call the attention of well-wishers to the dire needs of the country. Today, the very same building has been completely renovated and houses the Ministry of Health, the one governmental department that has witnessed a 100 per cent increase in its budget between 2010 and 2014. Although some figures for health show slow improvement, Timor-Leste has been declared by the World Health Organization (WHO) as polio free and the incidence of malaria is expected to fall by 75 per cent between 2000 and 2015 (intermediate figures show the country to be on the right track). Timor-Leste has also witnessed a significant rise in life expectancy, from 50 to 66 years, in the last quarter century, and ranks fifth in the world in terms of progress on this front, mainly due to much improved rates of child mortality and maternal mortality.

The health sector is not the only one to deserve such praise from international organizations. The Food and Agriculture Organization (FAO) reports an increase in the domestic agrarian production, especially grains (rice and maize). These figures have been widely publicized by the Timorese Government and constitute a rosy picture of the country and have more than a grain of truth, though do not tell the full story. Timor-Leste is marching on its own feet now, since the U.N. mission and ancillary security forces have left the country by the end of 2012. However, this march is proving to be tough.

Xanana Gusmão's 'Departure'

Early in 2014, when the National Parliament discussed the proposal for the annual budget, Prime Minister Xanana Gusmão came before the House and announced that this would be the last budget proposal under his term as leader of the government. He said that after the CPLP Summit scheduled for July, he would step down in order to pave the way for a new generation to take over. This announcement seemed to have its roots in the perceptible change of mood in the Timorese population that had elected a member of a younger generation to the presidency in 2012 — a move that was fully supported by the charismatic Gusmão.

For the best part of six months, expectations grew as fast as rumours on the true intentions of the leader, the result being a generalized idea that "big events" were lying in wait. This idea in turn fuelled a tendency in the state apparatus to withhold significant decisions. A mirror of this mood in the country can be grasped from the working agenda of the National Parliament which, with one major exception to which we shall later return, refrained from tackling contentious issues like the long overdue legislation on land rights.

Immediately after the CPLP Summit, Gusmão convened his own party, knowing that in the civil society of the country there had been no significant movement either in support of his departure or his continuation. Some political parties like Fretilin expressed the view that democratic mandates should be taken seriously and that PM Gusmão should accept the responsibility to carry out his tenure till 2017. In governmental circles, there was no clear heir apparent. Hence there was a concern that a replacement of the Prime Minister would affect the balance of power. In fact, Gusmão has structured his government in such a way that no "natural" heir would emerge easily: his Deputy Prime Minister, Fernando Lasama de Araujo, is the leader of a junior coalition party, Partido Democratico (PD), and two other figures received the rank of "State Ministers" — one from his own Conselho Nacional de Reconstrução de Timor (CNRT) Party (Agio Pereira, a devoted right hand man who does not have charisma) and the other from the third and smaller coalition partner, Frenti-Mudança (Jose Luis Guterres, also Minister for Foreign Affairs). To further complicate matters on the institutional front, the young Secretary General of Gusmão's CNRT (Dionisio Babo) has little governmental experience and is still in the process of asserting himself as a major player in local politics — although he is a powerful contender in the future.

In his party meeting, Prime Minister Gusmão accepted the need to remain at the helm, and delay his anticipated departure. He avoided committing himself to any clear schedule, although he hinted he would prefer to go before the next elections in order to groom his successor and allow him to fight the polls in a position of power.

Two fundamental reasons may explain why Gusmão decided he would step down early. First, the worst kept secret in town is that there is some sort of agreement between the members of the old guard — locally called *katuas*, or elders — that a role for them ought to be devised in the institutional mechanisms of the country, embodied in the creation of a council where Gusmão would sit alongside Jose Ramos-Horta, Mari Alkatiri and maybe some other prominent figures like Lu Olo (twice presidential candidate by Fretilin), General Lere Anan Timur (the Commander of the Armed Forces) or Mario Carrascalão (a man who sided with Indonesia and served as Governor of the 27th Province before joining the ranks of the Resistance and leading his own party). Upon the creation of such council, the way could more easily be paved for the emergence of a new generation of leadership. The big question, however, is the extent of powers to be entrusted to such a council: a mere consultative role, or executive functions that are difficult to envisage for a non-elected body? This has been the subject of much talk in Dili, but to this day no clear solution that respects the constitutional foundations (even if the Constitution is to be amended) has been found that satisfies all parties.

The second reason pertains to the realm of actual policies to be implemented. One of the hallmarks of Gusmão's tenure is the creation of generous pension schemes for "veterans" — a move that has brought with it the reduction of grievances and a basis for the establishment of peaceful relations overall. However, this policy, which has reached as many as 40,000 families and has a waiting list of almost 160,000 requests, is causing a very serious financial burden for the government. The top positions in a hierarchical scheme are stabilized and they receive the highest pensions, but the lower echelons may still see a sharp increase in their numbers, and the rules are quite generous, offering pensions and other benefits (mainly in the health and education sectors) to "veterans" and their families, extending the perception of financial assistance for a long time to come. As it stands, the veterans schemes take up a larger share of the state budget than either health or security — a clear indication of its enormous importance. Most local observers admit that the scheme must be reconsidered, and a cap imposed on spending under it, a task that probably no politician can undertake other than Xanana Gusmão himself, given his immense support among all those engaged in the Resistance. In a way, the time allocated to Gusmão to continue as Prime Minister has the implicit message that he is in the best position to devise a way to modify one of the most important policies associated with his past tenure.

Meanwhile, both supporters of the current government and senior members of the opposition have the idea that Gusmão is due to reshuffle his government — a decision he has not taken during his first term in office, and which he seemed reluctant to do. This expectation is not conducive to the efficient running of state business, as many fear they will be replaced and prefer not to risk engaging in activities that may jeopardize their chance of remaining in office. The year ended with Gusmão making an emotional Christmas address to the people in which he promised a thorough reshuffle of his government. The way in which this address was framed actually leaves the door open for Gusmão to step down from the role of Prime Minister, although he pledged to remain active in the political arena.

The Mauk Moruk Affair

The last part of 2013 was marked by the reappearance on the Timorese scene of Mauk Moruk, a former senior member of the guerrillas who attempted to overthrow Xanana Gusmão in 1984–85. He was captured by the Indonesians, paraded around the country as a significant defeat of the Resistance, and lived in exile in Holland for more than two decades. He returned, intent to challenge Gusmão once again, proposing fresh elections to replace the Constitution of 2002 by the one approved in 1975, create a new presidential regime, and return to the radical policies of that period. He managed to enlist the support of some political sectors, like the one led by his own brother who had lost his seat in Parliament in 2012, as well as the religiously inspired *Sagrada Familia* (Holy Family) group of activists. More important than this was his ability to garner support from disenchanted Timorese, and to set up a power base in the east of the country, where he is said to command a few hundred men in arms. In a way, this was made possible by the fact that the position of Fretilin in national politics evolved from open opposition to a considered collaboration with the government, expressed symbolically in the party's decision to back (after tough negotiations) the state budgets for 2013, 2014 and 2015, thus diminishing the idea that they were an opposition party in public perception.

Mauk Moruk's challenge was taken seriously by Gusmão, who suggested a public debate on television which included other relevant members of the Resistance. However, Mauk Moruk did not show up, frustrating some expectations. In March, the National Parliament passed a resolution accusing him of using military uniforms and weapons and criminal associations with a view to overthrowing the constitutional order. He was soon arrested and held in custody without having had the opportunity to appear before a court of law until a decision to release him was taken in late December.

More than the actual threat posed by what was probably an isolated case, this episode reveals the extent to which frustrations with the current state of affairs can easily extend beyond the realm of institutionalized politics, and mobilize significant numbers of people who have, for one reason or another, fallen out of grace and are disenchanted with the way the country is moving. As Anna Powles noted, this case reveals "the struggle between resistance legacies and modern government".[1] Like the martial arts groups whose activities were suspended in 2013, these forms of expression of social resentment defy the established politicians and require particular attention.

The New Media Law

Among the issues that the National Parliament tackled in the early part of the year, the new media law deserves special attention. Presentation of the proposed measures by the government was accompanied by a campaign to garner support for them. The reception in Parliament was favourable, and the bill was approved with a considerable majority of votes since Fretilin MPs joined forces with those who normally support the government (only one MP abstained and none voted against). However, the bill was vehemently opposed by influential journalists as well as by several non-governmental organizations (NGOs) — including the International Federation of Journalists — who denounced it for trying to impose severe limitations on the freedom of the press. This would be done through measures like references to the need for media instruments to be national property (which could impair the work of foreign correspondents) or the necessary "registration" of accredited journalists. In brief, they argued that what is portrayed as "regulation" may easily turn out to be some form of constriction of fundamental rights.

President Taur Matan Ruak referred the bill to the Constitutional Court for an evaluation of its content, signalling that in his view four sections were at odds with the fundamental law. The Constitutional Court ruled that three sections were indeed in breach of the Constitution, and the bill was returned to the National Parliament, which on a second reading made several alterations. However, one of the sections deemed unconstitutional was not altered. President Taur Matan Ruak this time decided to promulgate the law, but insisted on sending it once again to the Constitutional Court in view of the persistence of the contentious section, making use of an instrument called the "subsequential revision of constitutionality".

It is important to note that, while keeping a very close relationship with the government and Prime Minister Gusmão who was a critical factor in the support of his candidacy in 2012, the President of the Republic is an independent figure without party affiliation. Some of his close aides work in the media business and were vociferous opponents of the government proposal. Also, the President needs open access to the media in order to make his messages heard by the people. The risk of alienation of the support of the media community which has proved so far to be a critical ally explains the reason why the President decided to intervene in a case that had almost unanimous support in the National Parliament.

Petroleum

Petroleum is the key resource around which much of the political life of Timor-Leste revolves, given its weight in the revenue of the country. In 2014, some new facts emerged that deserve mention.

For the first time, the report of the Petroleum Fund on the third quarter of 2014 showed that the Fund had not increased from the previous quarter, keeping its level at about US$16.6 billion, which is still more than ten times the annual state budget at its current level. There are three reasons behind this negative performance: a major transfer of funds to the state budget, in accordance with existing provisions, currency exchange losses and, above all, a significant decline in oil prices in world markets. This showed that in the future, the increase in petroleum revenues would probably be slower, which may lead to a review of the transfers from the Fund to the state budget, which have been consistently above the Fund's "sustainable revenue" level, a technical index that is supposed to cap spending. However, signs emerging from the government suggest that this is being treated as an odd episode rather than a serious warning. In fact, the government approved a budget proposal for 2015 which increases spending by almost 5 per cent to US$1.57 billion, mostly supported by transfers from the Petroleum Fund. To ascertain the real importance of this fact one must consider the level of actual public spending, which in recent years has fallen way below what the generous state budget would allow, ranging between US$1.2 billion and $1.3 billion. This is due to two factors. The first is a technicality, as expenses have to be inscribed in the budget to be authorized, and delays in starting them leads to difficulties in spending the whole budgeted amount. The second is derived from the incapacity of the state administration to discharge adequately its functions due to manpower shortcomings.

Secondly, the Timorese state has initiated legal action against the major oil companies operating in the country, claiming they evaded tax payments. The taxes in question amount to about US$380 million — or a quarter of the annual state budget. However, in spite of the high expectations of the Timorese Government, the local courts have not been disposed to favour its position. From a total of 51 cases, 16 were lost (pending appeal) and 28 are now before an international arbitration court in Singapore.

On a similar count, the Timorese Government brought a case against Australia in the International Court of Justice in The Hague in 2013, regarding the seizure of confidential documents from an attorney acting on behalf of the Timorese authorities. The background to this action is the desire of Timor-Leste to challenge the terms of the agreement regarding the maritime boundaries between the two countries and their share of the Timor Sea oil. In March, before a formal trial, the judges in The Hague supported the position of Timor-Leste and ordered the Australian authorities not to use the documents they had seized. Later on, Australia and Timor-Leste agreed to a suspension of the hearings in order to resolve the case amicably, a decision that was extended to the issues pending in the Permanent Court of Arbitration regarding the settlement of their boundary disputes.

All these facts suggest that the oil issue is becoming more problematic and multi-faceted, requiring a substantial dose of realism and perhaps of some change in the current approach which seems too dependent on overly optimistic scenarios.

The Question of Portuguese Judges

Frustration over the handling of the court cases brought by the Timorese state against oil companies grew intense in the second half of the year, as the outcomes of these cases went against the expectations of the local authorities. Timorese authorities based their expectations on legal advice provided by Portuguese law experts. This sentiment merged with a deep-seated uneasiness regarding the continuing high profile role played by Portuguese and other foreign judges in the local judicial system.

During the transitional period (1999–2002), all major state functions were placed in the hands of foreign individuals. With the proclamation of independence on 20 May 2002, the executive and legislative functions were taken over by the Timorese themselves. However, the judicial system retained foreign judges in charge of the majority of courts. This odd situation in which sovereign bodies are commanded by foreigners was devised as a transitional measure allowing for the training of local judges to replace the foreign ones. More than ten years later, there has been little change, and the sentiment that expatriate judges were there to stay without any limit to their terms began to be regarded as an affront to national sovereignty. Ever since the new Minister for Justice Dionisio Babo joined the government in 2012, this issue has been on the top of the local agenda — if only to meet passive resistance from the personnel in question to face the issue as it should be faced. Dionisio Babo is supposed to have asked for a formal meeting with his Portuguese counterpart in order to discuss this matter, and one year elapsed before they could arrange such a meeting. To make things worse, the control which would normally be exercised over local judges by the Magistrates Council was widely regarded as extremely weak.

In this broad context of dissatisfaction with the underlying situation and the actual performance of several individual judges, the Timorese authorities decided to take action. First, there was a closed-door meeting of Parliament (a rare event) which took the unprecedented decision to recommend to the government that a substantial alteration of the status quo to be implemented in the very short term. Although there were some dissenting voices, namely from Fretilin, the vote in the House managed to secure wide support that extended to many members of the opposition party, thus showing that there was a widespread dissatisfaction with the judicial system. Acting upon this recommendation, the government decided to suspend the contracts of several international judges, who took offence and mostly refused to abide by the executive orders. The governmental decision met the opposition of the Magistrates Council, a critical institution in the judicial arena which supported the independence of judges, who took a stance in favour of the continuation of the status quo. Faced with outright disobedience on the part of several magistrates, the government issued expulsion orders, forcing them to leave the country within forty-eight hours.

The position of the Timorese Government has to be considered in the context of the need to have foreign magistrates participate in the organs of national sovereignty and of the frustration over the professional weaknesses in the cases that were brought against the oil companies. Due to these reasons, tough measures were implemented to deal with the issue. Portugal, the country most affected by these decisions, decided to suspend its cooperation with Timor-Leste in the judicial field, and threatened to extend such suspension to other fields.

One other aspect of this issue deserves special notice. Both in Timor-Leste and elsewhere, a strange coincidence was observed: several judges expelled from the territory were supposedly in charge of court cases referring to corruption charges against government ministers and other public officials.

Corruption is a critical feature of the Timorese political and cultural landscape and the period under Indonesian occupation has left an enduring mark. The *Transparency International Index of Corruption Perception* for 2014 signals for the third consecutive year the country's increasing corruption levels. Timor-Leste ranks 133 in a list of 175 countries — a symptom of severe problems on this count.

In the course of the year, the leader of the Anti-Corruption Commission, Adérito de Jesus, decided not to stand for another term in office. He said he was doing so for personal reasons, but it was widely believed that he was frustrated by the slow movement of processes in the judicial system. It took a long time for the government to agree to submit to the National Parliament a list of possible new leaders of the Commission before Adérito Tilman was finally chosen. For this reason, the Commission was for almost half a year without a proper leadership.

Charges have been brought against senior government members, for example, the Finance Minister, Emilia Pires, who was supposed to go to court on corruption charges a few days after the foreign judges were suspended, including the one who was to rule in her case. Most of those cases are now on hold, as the court system has been basically paralysed. In response to the allegations, PM Gusmão made a particularly controversial remark: that politicians should be judged first and foremost by the court of public opinion, that is, by the electoral processes, and ought to be given immunity while serving their terms. This view confuses political responsibility, which is undeniable, with judicial responsibility, which cannot wait until the end of a political term to act if there are grounds for suspicion. It reveals a particularly poor understanding of the evils of corruption, which he has attempted to curb in his first term as Prime Minister with the appointment of a Deputy Prime Minister in charge of the problem, an experiment that went sour with the resignation of Mario Viegas Carrascalão.

Diplomacy

In 2014, Timor-Leste had a major diplomatic success — the organization of the CPLP Summit in Dili in late July. Following the Summit, Timor-Leste will hold the Chair of the organization for two years, allowing extensive visibility in the Portuguese-speaking countries.

A note should be added though: Timor-Leste was among the leading countries supporting the membership of Equatorial Guinea, an oil-producing country with a dismal record on human rights and very feeble ties to the Portuguese language in the CPLP. Other oil-producing countries like Angola and Brazil were also active in supporting Equatorial Guinea. Portugal reluctantly accepted (and was critical of the way Timor-Leste handled the issue at the ceremonies in Dili). These actions may reduce the chances of the doors of the European Union being as widely open to Timor-Leste as some might expect given Portugal's critical role in such field.

Jose Ramos-Horta played a very high profile role in the U.N. mission in Guinea Bissau following the attempts to return the country to constitutional rule. The government of Timor-Leste decided to offer material support in the form of electoral assistance which has been widely acclaimed. It showed what was invested in the preparation of local elections in Timor Leste could be transferred to a similarly difficult situation elsewhere. This aid provided by Timor-Leste was highly visible and internationally appreciated, boosting the country's reputation as a generous giver after so many years at the receiving end of assistance.

Finally, things have been less rosy on the ASEAN front. Timor-Leste would have expected that the Indonesian Chair of the organization might move the country closer to full membership of ASEAN — but this did not materialize. Reservations exist among critical players in the ASEAN, especially Singapore, who fear that the Timorese state's fragility may open up doors to money laundering — a concern not helped by the high levels of perceived corruption in the country.

An Original Initiative

In 2014, one original initiative took place: the creation of a "Special Zones of Social Market Economies" in the enclave of Oecusse and the island of Atauro. The aim of the project is to create special conditions for sustained development in these two parts of the country through special legislation to entice private investment in a business friendly environment, with matching public funds. So far, however, actual investment has been delayed. The physical infrastructure for this project will also be used for a major event on 2015: the celebrations of the arrival of the first Portuguese Christian sailors on the island 500 years ago, a significant date which the local authorities wish to be graced by a visit of the Pope.

In the short term, however, the most remarkable feature of this initiative is that the leadership of the project was entrusted to Mari Alkatiri, the leader of the opposition party Fretilin, and sometime Prime Minister (2002–06), now said to be the "Viceroy" of Oecusse. This has been regarded as a gesture of goodwill by the government, or as an attempt to secure a very broad basis of political support. In due course, it will show whether Fretilin espouses a significantly different model of development from the one being pursued by Gusmão's government — in which case some friction might develop — or whether there is no important divergence and a prospective collaboration at central level may be devised, perhaps before the next general elections due in 2017. Whatever happens, the significance of the appointment of Alkatiri for this particular job goes beyond the "Special Zone" and indicates something with broader horizons. Perhaps the governmental reshuffle supposed to take place in early 2015, and which is rumoured to include members of Fretilin acting as technical experts rather than party representatives, will be a second step in this direction.

Note

1.   Anna Powles, "Xanana Gusmao-Mauk Moruk: Timor Struggles with Its Past and Future", *The Interpreter*, 5 December 2013.

Vietnam

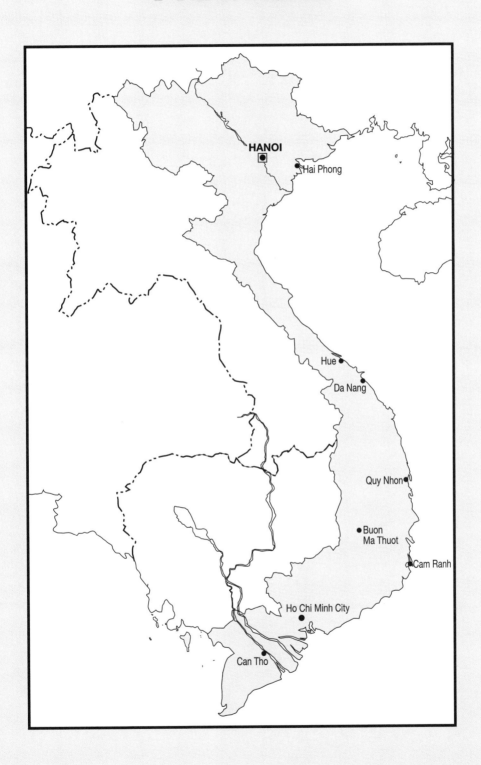

VIETNAM IN 2014
Crisis with China Makes Headlines

Ramses Amer

Introduction

The defining event of 2014 was the crisis between Vietnam and China relating to the activities of a Chinese drilling rig in areas to the west of the Paracel archipelago. The crisis and related tension lasted from early May to mid-July. Although differences relating to disputes in the South China Sea do cause periodic tension between the two countries, a crisis of this scale has not occurred since the 1990s and no previous crisis has such ramifications within Vietnam, both in terms of popular protests against China and through riots targeting foreign companies in May. This overview of Vietnam in 2014 will examine these keys developments in the context of Vietnam's domestic developments as well as its foreign relations.

Crisis with China and Its Repercussions[1]

The relationship with China continues to be of paramount importance to Vietnam in terms of both a multifaceted collaboration in various fields and the geo-strategic challenge posed by China, in particular regarding the South China Sea. The disputes with China in the South China Sea, that is, overlapping sovereignty claims to the Paracel and Spratly archipelagos as well as to maritime areas between the Vietnamese coast and the two archipelagos within the "nine-dash line" claimed by China, continued to pose a major challenge in bilateral relations in 2014. This was highlighted by the crisis and tensions caused by the dispatch of drilling rig HD-981 to areas west of the Paracel archipelago by the

RAMSES AMER is an Associate Professor in Peace and Conflict Research and an Associate Fellow at the Institute for Security and Development Policy (ISDP), Sweden.

China National Offshore Oil Corporation on 2 May. The crisis and related tension lasted until mid-July when China announced the withdrawal of the drilling rig. Prior to the crisis, there had been no tension between Vietnam and China since mid-2013. The period from mid-2013 to April 2014 was characterized by deepened bilateral cooperation and by a seemingly successful bilateral dispute management approach relating to the disputes in the South China Sea.[2]

Vietnam's and China's Viewpoints and Actions during the Crisis

Vietnam denounced the stationing of the drilling rig as illegal and demanded its withdrawal. In addition Vietnam claimed that the rig's area of operation was within Vietnam's exclusive economic zone and continental shelf as measured from its coastline; it also reasserted its claim of sovereignty to both the Paracel and Spratly archipelagos. Vietnam further accused China of using force against its ships in the waters near the Paracel archipelago and of arresting Vietnamese fishermen. It repeatedly requested negotiations and kept up diplomatic pressure on China through bilateral channels as well as by attempts to gain international support for its position not only on the issue of the drilling rig, but also more broadly relating to the status of the Paracel archipelago.[3]

China's position was that the drilling operation was carried out "totally within waters off China's Xisha islands," the Chinese name for the Paracels. China also reiterated its position that the islands are Chinese territory and that there is no dispute related to them. China accused Vietnam of trying to disrupt the drilling operations and demanded that Vietnam cease such activities and withdraws its vessels from the area. In mid-May, China sought to deflect attention to the "anti-China" riots in south and central Vietnam targeting companies operated by East Asian investors and which resulted in several Chinese casualties. In response to Vietnam's active attempts to gain international support for its position, China eventually publicized its official stand on the drilling operation and the status of the Xisha islands on 8 June.[4]

Ending the Crisis

Despite attempts to ease the tension, as highlighted by the visit to Hanoi of China's top diplomat State Councillor Yang Jiechi in connection with a meeting of the China-Vietnam Steering Committee for Bilateral Cooperation held on 18 June and his meetings with Vietnamese leaders during his visit,[5] China refused to withdraw the rig and Vietnam continued to raise objections to its presence.

Eventually the crisis was defused when China on 16 July announced the withdrawal of the drilling rig after the completion of its operation.[6] Already the week before China's official media had highlighted that the sixth round of departmental-level talks between the two countries on "low-sensitivity areas" at sea had been held in Beijing on 9–10 July.[7] Subsequently China also released Vietnamese fishermen that had earlier been detained in the waters of the Paracels.[8] Vietnam responded positively to China's announcement of the withdrawal and verified that the rig had been removed.[9] This withdrawal put an end to the incident and related tensions.

In assessing the way out of the crisis, it can be argued that it had gradually become apparent that a withdrawal of the drilling rig was the only way that could be presented as an acceptable development by both sides. Both Vietnam and China could claim that they achieved their goals, Vietnam by maintaining pressure on China until the rig was eventually withdrawn and China through the completion of the drilling operation.[10]

Political and Socio-economic Implications and Repercussions

The drilling rig crisis had political and socio-economic repercussions for Vietnam. Politically, through the many demonstrations against China and its actions in the South China Sea targeting in particular the Chinese Embassy in Hanoi and the Chinese Consulate General in Ho Chi Min City. Vietnam's tough stand against China during the crisis appeared to be in line with public sentiments in Vietnam. The "anti-China" riots in mid-May were of political, socio-economic, and international relations relevance. They made headlines as foreign owned companies operated by East Asian investors were targeted in the South and Central parts of Vietnam. Two industrial parks in Southern Vietnam were targeted, both joint ventures between Singapore and Vietnam. Although it appeared that the intended targets were factories linked to mainland China, Taiwanese, Singaporean, Malaysian, South Korean, and even Japanese factories were also affected. The riots caused casualties and some Chinese nationals were among them.[11] China made several critical statements relating to these events, bilateral talks were held, and China dispatched ships to repatriate Chinese nationals from Vietnam.[12]

Uneven trade relations characterize the economic relationship between Vietnam and China with Vietnam having a considerable trade deficit, which continues to be an issue between the two countries, in particular since the stated goal is that economic relations should be based on a 'win-win' formula. In fact Vietnam's trade deficit with China keeps increasing.[13] At the same time Vietnam would also like to see more investment by Chinese companies. In 2013 Chinese investment in Vietnam increased considerably to US$2.3 billion compared to US$345 million in 2012. This trend apparently continued in 2014 despite the riots of mid-May. According to figures from Vietnam's Ministry of Planning and Investment's Foreign Investment Agency, Chinese foreign direct investment (FDI) in Vietnam had reached US$7.94 billion as of 5 December 2014.[14]

Vietnam-China Relations after the Crisis

Following the withdrawal of the drilling rig the two countries have initiated a process aimed at rebuilding trust, normalizing the overall relationship, and addressing the territorial differences. This has been reflected in the meetings between the Vietnamese and Chinese leaders. The first step was the dispatch of a Special Envoy to China in late August by the Secretary General of the Communist Party of Vietnam (CPV).[15] Vietnam's Prime Minister Nguyen Tan Dung met with his Chinese counterpart Li Keqiang on the sidelines of the Asia-Europe Meeting (ASEM) Summit held in Italy in October.[16] Also in October Vietnam's Defence Minister Phung Quang Thanh headed a delegation to visit China for talks with his Chinese counterpart Chang Wanquan.[17] Later the same month the seventh meeting of the Steering Committee for Bilateral Cooperation was held in Hanoi. Notable in the latter case was that China's top diplomat, State Councillor Yang Jiechi headed the Chinese delegation.[18] In November, Vietnam's President Truong Tan Sang met with his Chinese counterpart Xi Jinping in Beijing. The Vietnamese President was in China to attend the Asia-Pacific Cooperation (APEC) Summit.[19] In late December a delegation from the National Committee of the Chinese People's Political Consultative Conference, headed by its Chairman Yu Zhengsheng, visited Vietnam. Yu met with Vietnam's leadership, the maritime issues and ways to manage them were discussed.[20]

This active bilateral diplomacy was aimed at re-establishing the cooperative relationship between the two countries following the drilling rig crisis. Vietnam's leadership evidently strove to build a cooperative and mutually beneficial relationship with China. However, Vietnam did not refrain from officially complaining about Chinese actions in the South China Sea including expansion of the runway construction in the Paracels, land reclamation in the Spratlys, and China's Position Paper on "the Matter of Jurisdiction in the South China Sea Arbitration initiated by the Philippines".[21]

Socio-economic Developments

The attacks on foreign companies in mid-May raised fears of possible negative repercussions in Vietnam's efforts to attract foreign investors since the owners of the companies from Taiwan, Singapore, and Malaysia, are important contributors to FDI in Vietnam's economy. As investors from Japan and South Korea were also affected, the potential damage could be even greater.[22] Attracting FDI takes place in a competitive setting and thus the ramifications could be far-reaching for Vietnam and impact negatively on Vietnam's economy at large. The revenues from the FDI sector account for two-thirds of Vietnam's total export revenue and give a significant positive contribution to Vietnam's trade balance.[23]

The General Statistics Office of Vietnam (GOSV) reported a decrease of 16.7 per cent in total registered capital of both newly and additionally financed FDI projects as of November 2014 compared to the same period in 2013. However, the number of projects increased by 21.4 per cent compared to 2013.[24] These figures indicate a tendency towards smaller projects in terms of invested capital. The downward trend in new investments started earlier during 2014, well before the riots in May, which implies that there could be some concerns over the investment climate in Vietnam in general, rather than solely related to the riots.

The Minister of Planning and Investment, Bui Quang Vinh, has given an optimistic interpretation of the developments by pointing to the fact that several large-scale FDI projects were licensed in 2013 and that a number of international corporations are now preparing major projects for the coming years, for example, Intel, Samsung, Bridgestone and LG Electrics. Thus, lower FDI figures during 2014 are not seen by Vietnam as representing a long-term trend. However, one concern is that Vietnam's important export markets in the United States and in Europe are still waiting for the full recovery of their economies. Other concerns include Vietnam's poor infrastructure, a shortage of skilled workforce, and the shortcomings in the legal and administrative systems that confront the investors.[25]

Vietnam has gone from being one of the world's poorest nations into one of Southeast Asia's most dynamic and fastest growing economies, with aspirations to be a developed nation by 2020. Since the policy of renovation and reform — "*Doi Moi*" — was launched in late 1986, Vietnam has succeeded in making an impressive shift from the dominance of low-productivity agriculture to industry and other modern trades. Vietnam has been achieving rapid economic growth and poverty reduction and is expected to keep up its growth rate at close to 6 per cent in 2014.[26] Vietnam's yearly per capita income was estimated to have reached US$1,960 in 2013.[27] Other indicators of steadily improving living conditions are the Industrial Production Index (IPI) up by 7.5 per cent, labour employed Index (LEI) up 5.1 per cent, and sales of consumer goods and services up 6.5 per cent — inflation excluded — in the year ending November 2014. [28] The consumer price index (CPI) was up 6 per cent during 2013 — the lowest in a decade[29] — and dropped to as low as 2.6 per cent during the year ending November 2014.[30]

The International Monetary Fund (IMF) compliments Vietnam for its macroeconomic stabilization and inflation containment. Furthermore, the Vietnamese Government has increased its international reserves during 2014, flexibly managed the exchange rate, and made efforts to restructure the state-owned enterprises.[31]

However, in its recent Annual Results Report on Vietnam (2013) the Resident Coordinator of the United Nations Development Program (UNDP) gives a different picture: five years of macroeconomic instability, a prolonged economic slow-down and rapid demographic changes that contribute to new forms of multi-dimensional poverty, affecting among others migrant and informal workers in urban areas and households in ethnic minority-dominated areas.[32] Already the UNDP Annual Results Report for 2012 had expressed concern over the social costs of the rapid growth and the social and economic disparities preventing certain groups from enjoying essential quality education and health services. Other problems mentioned in the report are corruption and mismanagement within the public sector.[33]

These assessments by well-placed observers indicate that business as usual with high FDI and workers leaving agriculture to fill the new factories will not be enough to meet the modern market economy. The issue of the workforce has been given special attention in the World Bank's "Vietnam Development Report 2014".[34] The World Bank states that capital investments rather than productivity have become the new source of economic growth in Vietnam and this is not a sustainable model. The youth population is shrinking and the workforce lacks the skills needed for the country to accelerate economic growth.[35]

The World Bank has done a survey among employers in Vietnam. Many of them have said that a shortage of workers with adequate skills is an obstacle to their activity. The situation is described as one where the employers are seeking workers, but they cannot find the workers that match their skills needs. These skills needs are technical, cognitive, and behavioural relating to teamwork, critical thinking and problem-solving, capabilities that are usually expected to be found in job descriptions in the developed world.[36]

Based on the survey, the World Bank made three step-by-step recommendations. First, promote school readiness through early childhood development, starting at the age group of 0–3 years — breastfeeding, child stimulation and social assistance for poor parents — followed by universal access to pre-schools. Second, build the cognitive and behavioural foundation in general education, including full-day instruction, expansion of access to secondary education, and curriculum and teaching that foster cognitive and behavioural skills. Third, build job-relevant technical skills through a more connected system between employers, students and universities, and vocational schools.[37]

The World Bank's framework for strategic skills development has its origin in a clear understanding of what human resources development requires. Expecting Vietnam to implement it can be interpreted as a sign of great confidence in the Vietnamese people and government. Many countries in the developed world are still far from achieving it. The fact that considerable parts of the Vietnamese industry have already matured to a situation where such skills are needed is in itself impressive.

Political Developments

The main political development in Vietnam during 2014 were the preparations for the Tenth Plenum of the Central Committee of the CPV which will be a major step in the preparations for the 12th National Congress of the CPV scheduled for early 2016.

The drilling rig crisis with China also had domestic political repercussions in Vietnam. There were two main repercussions. The first one, seen as positive from the perspective of the Vietnamese authorities, is the display of popular support for the tough stand taken by the Vietnamese Government against China during the crisis. The display of such support was largely peaceful and directed at China's embassy in Hanoi and its consulate in Ho Chi Minh City. The manifestation of public support for the stand taken by the Vietnamese authorities and the rejection of China's stand and actions was extensively publicized in the official Vietnamese media, for example, *Nhan Dan*, the daily newspaper of the CPV, carried numerous articles about public support for Vietnam and criticism of China during the crisis.[38]

The other more negative repercussion, from the perspective of the authorities, was that the "anti-China" riots were not only potentially harmful to Vietnam's economy which has been discussed above, but could also be seen as posing a political challenge in undermining the marketing efforts of the Vietnamese authorities to portray Vietnam as a safe and stable destination for foreign investors. It appears evident that the Vietnamese authorities were caught off-guard by the riots, and even China did not suggest that the Vietnamese authorities were behind the riots. Instead China focused its criticism on the failure to prevent and contain the riots. Thus, it is possible that anti-government and anti-CPV elements were involved in organizing the riots, which must be a cause for concern for the Vietnamese authorities even if this has not been publicly highlighted. In fact, the official media provided minimal coverage of the riots themselves and limited coverage of subsequent trials of rioters. *Nhan Dan* can again illustrate this trend and it can be contrasted to the wide coverage of the perceived positive aspects as highlighted above.[39]

In general, the socio-economic challenges outlined in the previous section also have political ramifications. Therefore the Vietnamese authorities and the ruling CPV must address them through both economic and political policies. Uneven development between different parts of the country is one of the challenges for the Vietnamese authorities in their plans for national development. The emergence of a disparity in wealth distribution among social strata in Vietnamese society is another challenge. Disparity in wealth is a sensitive issue in a socialist country like Vietnam and hence a political issue.

Foreign Relations

In 2014, Vietnam continued to pursue its foreign policy of befriending other nations through bilateral relations, regional organizations and initiatives, and multilateral organizations. Vietnam has expanded and deepened its collaboration with major powers such as India, Japan, Russia, South Korea, and the United States. Vietnam has also continued its active participation in the

Association of Southeast Asia Nations (ASEAN). Also notable is Vietnam's engagement in ASEM, and in APEC. The only relationship in which Vietnam encountered notable problems was, as noted above, the one with China.

From a geo-strategic point of view, the countries bordering Vietnam are of particular importance in Vietnam's foreign relations. This is reflected in the attention paid to relations with China and to relations with the member states of ASEAN. Well-established party-to-party relations and collaboration are particularly important with China and Laos and also of relevance in relations with Cambodia.

During the drilling rig crisis with China, Vietnam turned to ASEAN for support, but did not request or expect ASEAN to publicly criticize China. This was reflected in the official ASEAN position on the matter. This strategy ensured that ASEAN could display a unified position that was in both Vietnam's and in ASEAN's best interest.

Relations with the United States continued to expand during 2014, although U.S. criticism of Vietnam's human rights record was a source of friction.[40] During the drilling rig crisis with China, Vietnam welcomed the position taken by the United States, as it was widely understood as being critical of China's action. There has also been speculation that Vietnam might try to balance China off by moving closer to the United States. The decision by the United States to partially lift its weapons embargo against Vietnam reinforced such speculation.[41] Vietnam has thus far been reluctant to move too close to the United States *vis-à-vis* China. Vietnam's relationship with the United States attracts considerable attention domestically both in the United States and Vietnam due to the legacy of the Vietnam War and also the economic embargo imposed by the United States in response to Vietnam's military intervention in Cambodia in late December 1978. However, following normalization of relations in 1995, cooperation between the two countries has gradually been expanded with the collaboration in the military field attracting widespread attention.

Vietnam's relations with key Northeast Asian countries remain overall stable. Japan is an important counterpart not only because it is a major trading partner and an important source of FDI to Vietnam, but also because Japan is a major source of Overseas Development Assistance (ODA). In March 2014 Vietnam's President paid an official visit to Japan which expanded and elevated the strategic partnership between the two countries.[42] Also notable was that Vietnam's Prime Minister met his Japanese counterpart Shinzo Abe in connection with the ASEM Summit in October.[43] Also in October, the fifth

Vietnam-Japan Strategic Partnership Dialogue was held in Hanoi.[44] Vietnam appreciates that Japan has been critical of China on the South China Sea issues. However, this should not be interpreted as Vietnam seeking to align itself with Japan or offering public support to Japan in the Sino-Japanese dispute. [45]

Vietnam's relations with South Korea continue to be expanded through their strategic cooperation partnership. South Korea has become the second largest donor through its ODA to Vietnam. South Korea is also a major source of FDI. In early October, the Secretary General of the CPV Nguyen Phu Trong made an official visit to South Korea at the invitation of South Korean President Park Geun-hye.[46] In December, Vietnam's Prime Minister visited South Korea to attend the 25th anniversary of ASEAN-Republic of Korea (RoK) Dialogue Relations and for a working visit.[47]

Vietnam also continues to enjoy privileged relations with India. The two countries have continuously enjoyed good relations since the Cold War Era. This has created a relationship in which Vietnam considers India to be a friendly country that is not a geo-strategic challenge to Vietnam. The highlight of 2014 was the visit by Vietnam's Prime Minister to India in late October at the invitation of his Indian counterpart Narendra Modi. In connection with the visit PetroVietnam signed agreements with two of its Indian counterparts.[48]

The relationship with Russia continues to be expanded and the importance of the relationship to Vietnam was highlighted by the visit to Russia by the Secretary General of the CPV in late November 2014 at the invitation of Russian President Vladimir Putin.[49] Reportedly, during the visit the two countries signed an inter-governmental agreement easing restrictions on the entry of Russian military vessels into Cam Ranh Bay.[50]

Conclusion

During 2014 Vietnam continued to pursue its foreign policy with the aim of developing good relations with all countries on the basis of mutually beneficial cooperation. This policy continues to be successful. However, the situation remains more complex with China. China is Vietnam's major trading partner and political collaboration between the two countries is extensive. At the same time, China is Vietnam's main strategic challenge due to the disputes in the South China Sea, as illustrated by the drilling rig crisis and related tensions.

The crisis with China also had domestic repercussions: both peaceful manifestations of support of Vietnam's territorial claim and the authorities' tough response to China and more violent expressions through the so-called "anti China riots" targeting foreign companies in southern and central Vietnam.

More broadly the socio-economic developments indicate that Vietnam continues to make progress while at the same time facing challenges that have not only social and economic implications but also political ramifications. These challenges, if not properly handled, may weaken the legitimacy of the Vietnamese authorities and the ruling CPV.

Notes

1. For a broader overview of the crisis and its outcome, see Ramses Amer, "China-Vietnam Drilling Rig Incident: Reflections and Implications", *Policy Brief* no. 158 (Nacka: Institute for Security and Development Policy, 2014).

2. For studies about the bilateral approach to managing disputes, see Ramses Amer, "Sino-Vietnamese Border Disputes", in *Beijing's Power and China's Borders: Twenty Neighbors in Asia*, edited by Bruce Elleman, Stephen Kotkin and Clive Schofield (Armonk, New York and London: M.E. Sharpe, 2012), pp. 295–309; and Ramses Amer, "China, Vietnam and the South China Sea — Disputes and Dispute Management", *Ocean Development & International Law* 45, no. 1 (2014): 17–40.

3. For an extensive list of references from official Vietnamese sources, see Ramses Amer, *Dispute Management in the South China Sea*, National Institute for South China Sea Studies, 2015, available at <http://en.nanhai.org.cn/uploads/file/file/20150302_Ramses.pdf> (accessed 6 March 2015), pp. 53–54.

4. For an extensive list of references from official Chinese sources see ibid., pp. 52–53.

5. Ministry of Foreign Affairs of People's Republic of China, "Yang Jiechi Holds Heads-of-delegation Meeting of China-Viet Nam Steering Committee for Bilateral Cooperation with Deputy Prime Minister and Foreign Minister Pham Binh Minh of Viet Nam", 18 June 2014, available at <http://www.fmprc.gov.cn/mfa_eng/wjb_663304/zzjg_663340/yzs_663350/gjlb_663354/2792_663578/2794_663582/t1167408.shtml> (accessed 23 June 2014). For additional reports, see Ministry of Foreign Affairs of People's Republic of China, available at <http://www.fmprc.gov.cn/mfa_eng/wjb_663304/zzjg_663340/yzs_663350/gjlb_663354/2792_663578/2794_663582/>.

6. Ministry of Foreign Affairs of People's Republic of China, "Foreign Ministry Spokesperson Hong Lei's Remarks on the Completion of the Operation in Waters to the South of China's Zhongjian Island", 16 July 2014, available at <http://www.fmprc.gov.cn/mfa_eng/xwfw_665399/s2510_665401/2535_665405/t1174949.shtml> (accessed 17 July 2014).

7. "China, Vietnam Consult on Maritime Cooperation", *People's Daily*, 12 July 2014, available at <http://english.people.com.cn/n/2014/0712/c90883-8754552.html> (accessed 15 July 2014).

8. "China releases VN fishermen", *Viet Nam News*, 16 July 2014, available at <http://vietnamnews.vn/society/257531/china-releases-vn-fishermen.html> (accessed 15 August 2014).

9. *Nhan Dan*, "PM Affirms Resolute Measures to Protect Nations' Sacred Sovereignty", 16 July 2014, available at <http://en.nhandan.org.vn/politics/item/2651402-pm-affirms-resolute-measures-to-protect-nations'-sacred-sovereignty.html> (accessed 18 July 2014).

10. This line of argument draws on the one used in Amer, "China-Vietnam Drilling Rig Incident", p. 2.

11. On this issue see Ramses Amer, "Looting Chinese factories won't help the Vietnamese economy", *The Conversation*, 16 May 2014, available at <https://theconversation.com/looting-chinese-factories-wont-help-the-vietnamese-economy-26782> (accessed 16 May 2014).

12. Ministry of Foreign Affairs of People's Republic of China, "China Lodges Solemn Protest over Serious Violent Attacks against Chinese Enterprises in Vietnam", 15 May 2014, available at <http://www.fmprc.gov.cn/mfa_eng/wjb_663304/zzjg_663340/yzs_663350/xwlb_663352/t1156742.shtml.> (accessed 9 June 2014). For additional reports, see Ministry of Foreign Affairs of People's Republic of China, available at <http://www.fmprc.gov.cn/mfa_eng/wjb_663304/zzjg_663340/yzs_663350/gjlb_663354/2792_663578/2794_663582/>.

13. General Statistics Office of Vietnam, "Imports of Goods by Country Group, by Country and Territory", n.d., available at <http://www.gso.gov.vn/default_en.aspx?tabid=472&idmid=3&ItemID=15934> (accessed 14 December 2014); ibid., "Exports of Goods by Country Group, by Country and Territory", n.d., available at <http://www.gso.gov.vn/default_en.aspx?tabid=472&idmid=3&ItemID=15940> (accessed 14 December 2014).

14. "China Invests 7.94 bln USD in Vietnam in 2014: Ministry", *People's Daily*, 9 December 2014, available at <http://en.people.cn/n/2014/1209/c90777-8820401.html> (accessed 14 December 2014). For 2013 see Vietnamnet, "Chinese Investment in Vietnam Soars", 20 April 2014, available at <http://english.vietnamnet.vn/fms/business/100245/chinese-investment-in-vietnam-soars.html> (accessed 14 December 2014).

15. "Party Chief's Special Envoy visits China", *Nhan Dan*, 26 August 2014, available at <http://en.nhandan.org.vn/politics/external-relations/item/2750602-party-chief's-special-envoy-visits-china.html> (accessed 2 December 2014). For additional reports, see *Nhan Dan*, available at <http://en.nhandan.org.vn/>.

16. "PM Nguyen Tan Dung Meets with Chinese, Japanese Counterparts", *Nhan Dan*, 16 October 2014, available at <http://en.nhandan.org.vn/politics/external-relations/item/2871702-pm-nguyen-tan-dung-meets-with-chinese-japanese-counterparts.html> (accessed 5 December 2014).

17. "Vietnam, China Seek Stronger Military Partnership", *Nhan Dan*, 16 October 2014, available at <http://en.nhandan.org.vn/politics/external-relations/item/2870902-vietnam-china-seek-stronger-military-partnership.html> (accessed 3 December 2014). For additional reports see *Nhan Dan*, available at <http://en.nhandan.org.vn/>.

18. "Vietnam-China Committee for Bilateral Co-operation Holds 7th Meeting", *Nhan Dan*, 27 October 2014, available at <http://en.nhandan.org.vn/politics/external-relations/item/2895302-vietnam-china-committee-for-bilateral-co-operation-holds-7th-meeting.html> (accessed 2 December 2014).

19. Ministry of Foreign Affairs of People's Republic of China, "Xi Jinping Meets with President Truong Tan Sang of Viet Nam", 10 November 2014, available at <http://www.fmprc.gov.cn/mfa_eng/wjb_663304/zzjg_663340/yzs_663350/gjlb_663354/2792_663578/2794_663582/t1209896.shtml> (accessed 30 November 2014).

20. "China's Top Political Advisor Yu Zhengsheng Welcomed in Hanoi", *Nhan Dan*, 26 December 2014, available at <http://en.nhandan.org.vn/politics/item/3037902-china's-top-political-advisor-yu-zhengsheng-welcomed-in-hanoi.html> (accessed 30 December 2014).

21. On the runway, see "China's Run-way Construction in Hoang Sa is Unlawful: Spokesperson", *Nhan Dan*, 9 October 2014, available at <http://en.nhandan.org.vn/politics/external-relations/item/2855102-china's-run-way-construction-in-hoang-sa-is-unlawful-spokesperson.html> (accessed 17 October 2014). On land reclamation, see Ministry of Foreign Affairs of Vietnam, "Remarks by MOFA Spokesperson Le Hai Binh on the South China Sea Arbitration Case", 6 November 2014, available at <http://www.mofa.gov.vn/en/tt_baochi/pbnfn/ns141212143709> (accessed 30 November 2014). On China's Position Paper, see ibid., "Remarks by MOFA Spokesperson Le Hai Binh on the South China Sea Arbitration Case", 12 December 2014, available at <http://www.mofa.gov.vn/en/tt_baochi/pbnfn/ns141212143709> (accessed 14 December 2014).

22. See discussion in Amer, "Looting Chinese Factories". See also Nguyen Phuong Linh and Michael Gold, "Riots Risk Ruining Vietnam's Industrial Zones; Lynchpin of Growth", *Reuters*, 16 May 2014, available at <http://www.reuters.com/article/2014/05/16/vietnam-china-investment-idUSL3N0O14GI20140516> (accessed 30 November 2014).

23. General Statistics Office of Vietnam, "Social and Economic Situation in Eleven Months of 2014", 28 November 2014, available at <http://www.gso.gov.vn/default_en.aspx?tabid=462&idmid=2&idmid=2&ItemID=16113> (accessed 10 December 2014).

24. Ibid.

25. "Foreign Investment Concerns Addressed", *Nhan Dan*, 5 August 2014, available at <http://en.nhandan.org.vn/business/economy/item/2699302-foreign-investment-concerns-addressed.html> (accessed 5 December 2014).

26. "PM Nguyen Tan Dung Pledges Reform to Boost Growth", *Nhan Dan*, 5 December 2014, available at <http://en.nhandan.org.vn/business/economy/item/2985102-pm-nguyen-tan-dung-pledges-reform-to-boost-growth.html> (accessed 5 December 2014).

27. "Per Capita Income in Vietnam Reaches almost USD2,000", VietNamNet Bridge, 7 December 2013, available at <http://english.vietnamnet.vn/fms/business/90862/per-capita-income-in-vietnam-reaches-almost-usd2-000.html> (accessed 10 December 2014).

28. General Statistics Office of Vietnam, "Socio-economic situation in 2013", n.d., available at <http://www.gso.gov.vn/default.aspx?tabid=622&ItemID=14774> (accessed 20 November 2014).

29. General Statistics Office of Vietnam, "Social and economic situation in eleven months of 2014", op. cit.

30. Ibid.

31. International Monetary Fund, "Statement by Mr Abdul Ghaffour, Alternate Executive Director and Ms Nguyen, Advisor to the Executive Director, On Vietnam Staff Report for the 2014 Article IV Consultation", in "Vietnam: 2014 Article IV Consultation-Staff Report; Press Release; and Statement by the Executive Director for Vietnam", *IMF Country Report* No. 14/311, 16 October 2014, available at <http://www.imf.org/external/pubs/cat/longres.aspx?sk=42391.0>, <cr14311.pdf>, pp. 1–4 (accessed 11 December 2014).

32. United Nations Development Program, *Delivering as One Annual Results Report 2013*, 17 October 2014, available at <http://www.un.org.vn/en/publications/one-un-documents/doc_details/429-delivering-as-one-annual-results-report-2013.html> and <elivering results Annual Report 2013-17Oct2014small.pdf>, p. 4 (accessed 10 December 2014).

33. United Nations Development Program, *Delivering as One Annual Results Report 2012*, July 2013, available at <http://www.un.org.vn/en/publications/one-un-documents/doc_details/429-delivering-as-one-annual-results-report-2013.html> and <Delivering results Annual Report 2012 Final Web.pdf>, p. 10 (accessed 10 December 2014).

34. The World Bank, *Skilling up Vietnam: Preparing the Workforce for a Modern Market Economy, Vietnam Development Report 2014*, Vol. 2, November 2013, available at <http://www.worldbank.org/en/country/vietnam/publication/vietnam-development-report2014-skilling-up-vietnam-preparing-the-workforce-for-a-modern-market-economy> and <829400AR0P13040Box0379879B00PUBLIC0.pdf> (accessed 17 November 2014).

35. Ibid., p. 7.

36. Ibid., pp. 7–8 and 15–16.

37. Ibid., pp. 17–24 and 30.

38. Based on online searches on *Nhan Dan* Online English version, available at <http://en.nhandan.org.vn/>, both during the drilling rig crisis in May–July 2014 and again in early December 2014.

39. Ibid.

40. "US Releases Inaccurate Evaluation of Human Rights in Vietnam", *Nhan Dan*, 1 March 2014, available at <http://en.nhandan.org.vn/society/item/2338502-us-releases-inaccurate-evaluation-of-human-rights-in-vietnam.html> (accessed 5 December 2014).

41. Carl Thayer, "The US Lifts Arms Embargo: The Ball is in Vietnam's Court", *The Diplomat*, 6 October 2014, available at <http://thediplomat.com/2014/10/the-us-lifts-arms-embargo-the-ball-is-in-vietnams-court/> (accessed 7 October 2014).

42. "Promoting Friendship and Strategic Partnership between Vietnam and Japan", *Nhan Dan*, 16 March 2014, available at <http://en.nhandan.org.vn/politics/editorial/item/2369802-promoting-friendship-and-strategic-partnership-between-vietnam-and-japan.html> (accessed 5 December 2014).

43. "PM Nguyen Tan Dung Meets with Chinese, Japanese Counterparts", *Nhan Dan*, op. cit.

44. "Vietnam, Japan Hold Fifth Strategic Partnership Dialogue", *Nhan Dan*, 24 October 2014, available at <http://en.nhandan.org.vn/politics/external-relations/item/2891202-vietnam-japan-hold-fifth-strategic-partnership-dialogue.htm> (accessed 5 December 2014).

45. More broadly on Vietnam-Japan relations, see Carl Thayer, "Vietnam's Extensive Strategic Partnership with Japan", *The Diplomat*, 14 October 2014, available at <http://thediplomat.com/2014/10/vietnams-extensive-strategic-partnership-with-japan/> (accessed 14 October 2014).

46. "Comprehensively Promoting and Deepening Vietnam — RoK Strategic Co-operation", *Nhan Dan*, 1 October 2014, available at <http://en.nhandan.org.vn/politics/editorial/item/2834502-comprehensively-promoting-and-deepening-vietnam---rok-strategic-co-operation.html> (accessed 5 December 2014).

47. "PM to Attend ASEAN-RoK Commemorative Summit, Visit RoK", *Nhan Dan*, 5 December 2014, available at <http://en.nhandan.org.vn/politics/external-relations/item/2984002-pm-to-attend-asean-rok-commemorative-summit-visit-rok.html> (accessed 5 December 2014).

48. The agreements are listed as "HoA between OVL and PetroVietnam" and "MoU between ONGC and PetroVietnam". See "Joint Statement on the State Visit of Prime Minister of the Socialist Republic of Vietnam to India", *Nhan Dan*, 29 October 2014, available at <http://en.nhandan.org.vn/politics/external-relations/item/2900302-joint-statement-on-the-state-visit-of-prime-minister-of-the-socialist-republic-of-vietnam-to-india.html> (accessed 5 December 2014).

49. "Forging Vietnam-Russia Comprehensive Strategic Partnership", *Nhan Dan*, 21 November 2014, available at <http://en.nhandan.org.vn/politics/external-relations/item/2951902-forging-vietnam-russia-comprehensive-strategic-partnership.html> (accessed 5 December 2014). For additional reports, see *Nhan Dan*, available at <http://en.nhandan.org.vn/>.

50. See Carl Thayer, "Vietnam's Navy Crosses the Line", *The Diplomat*, 2 December 2014, available at <http://thediplomat.com/2014/12/vietnams-navy-crosses-the-line/> (accessed 2 December 2014).

VIETNAM'S ONLINE PETITION MOVEMENT

Jason Morris-Jung

In July 2014, sixty-one members of the Vietnamese Communist Party (VCP) posted online an open letter to the party leadership and all of its members. While decrying the Party's response to China's bullying in the South China Sea, the letter called on the Party to "leave off from the mistaken path of socialism for a definitive change to the path of the people and democracy" (Para 6). It was a bold statement for a country where public expressions of opposition to the authoritarian regime are strongly discouraged and sometimes harshly punished. Later in October, another online statement by a new generation of self-declared independent "civil society organizations" declared their support for pro-democracy demonstrators in Hong Kong and made an appeal to Vietnamese youth to take on a similar struggle at home. These initiatives were examples of a new movement in Vietnam of using online petitions to publicize social grievances while also directly or indirectly promoting liberal democratic ideas and challenging authoritarianism.

The online petition movement is a recent development in Vietnam's domestic politics. It has helped generate open and critical commentary on the most controversial topics of the moment, in contrast to the state's tendencies to hide and censor them. In doing so, it has also advocated for liberal constitutional freedoms of speech, assembly and private property, rule of law, and opposition to party dictatorship. Furthermore, the people leading the petitions have included many renowned public figures — loosely referred

JASON MORRIS-JUNG is a Visiting Fellow at the Institute of Southeast Asian Studies (ISEAS), Singapore.

to as "prominent intellectuals" (*nhân sỹ trí thức*) — and those signing onto them have come from all walks of life. While their total numbers still only reach a few thousand — with the notable exception of the 15,000 that signed the petition on constitutional reform in 2013 — they are a leading edge in a country where, traditionally, only the boldest and most radical individuals expressed their opposition to party dictatorship. This article retraces the emergence of Vietnam's online petition movement and examines its significance.

The Internet and Domestic Politics

The emergence of Vietnam's online petition movement partly reflects the rapid expansion of the Internet in Vietnam. However, the Internet should not be seen strictly as a technological miracle that automatically makes societies more democratic. Rather, it has been used both to support and resist democratization efforts. Scholarly literature on the topic has warned against unilineal assumptions on the causal relation between the Internet and democratization. As much as the Internet might facilitate access to information and enable wider political participation, governments, businesses and other powerful forces have also used it effectively to reinforce existing power relations.[1] In authoritarian regimes, state forces have made use of the Internet to spread propaganda (overtly and covertly), monitor and gather evidence against activists, and deploy highly sophisticated strategies of online censorship.[2] To understand more clearly the varying contributions of the Internet to the processes of democratization demands attention to the specific socio-historical and political contexts in which they are used. In this regard, Vietnam's online petitions have been significant as a socially and historically embedded practice that uses the Internet to challenge the ideology and political culture of state authoritarianism.

Internet technologies became widely available in Vietnam only in the early 2000s, though this was largely contained to Vietnam's major cities. Availability and use expanded from 180,000 Internet subscribers in 2001 to 5.6 million by 2008.[3] Currently, Vietnam has nearly 40 million Internet users, representing nearly 43 per cent of the national population.[4] Some 66 per cent of Vietnamese Internet users use the Internet every day and spend an average of 29 hours on it per month.[5] However, as Surborg has noted, access and usage is biased towards the wealthier and urban populations.[6] Social media has also expanded rapidly in recent years, with an estimated 8.5 million users in Vietnam today.[7] Facebook is the most popular interface, with a new Vietnamese user joining every three seconds. Increasingly, Vietnamese citizens have been using the Internet for a wide range of purposes, including social and political activism.[8] Notably, Blogging and Facebook have become increasingly important for expressing dissent and organizing campaigns that criticize government policies and challenge state authority.

Writing letters and petitions to state authorities or rulers has a much longer and storied history in Vietnam. In Vietnamese folklore, even the lowliest peasant could gain a sympathetic ear by sending a letter to the Emperor, so long as the letter never criticized the Emperor himself. Under Vietnamese socialism, critical letters and petitions also fit in with the tenets of "democratic centralism" so long as they were maintained as strictly internal matters and they clearly displayed a loyal endeavour to improve — rather than challenge — state authority. However, petitioning is also fraught with risks. A few exemplary cases of state crackdowns have been enough to serve as constant reminders, from the harsh crackdown on artists and intellectuals in the 1950s to the suppression of the pro-democracy coalition Bloc 8406 in 2006.

These two practices come together in the online petition, which simultaneously reflects a culturally and historically embedded practice for appealing to political leaders, while also challenging this tradition by making them highly visible and confrontational. The online petitions discussed here come under a range of titles, including petition or recommendation (*kiến nghị*), declaration (*tuyên bố*), appeal (*lời kêu gọi*) or open letter (*thư ngỏ*), or more straightforwardly as statements to "oppose" (*phan đối*), "demand" (*yêu cầu*) or "contribute ideas" (*góp ý*). They also address a variety of issues, for example, bauxite mining, political prisoners, Internet regulations, national development and the South China Sea conflict. However, the petitions all share a common general form. They are usually brief texts of one to three pages, initially signed by a well-known group of Vietnamese persons and then posted online for a wider public to read, comment on and, if they so choose, sign. In certain cases, the petitions are more like collective declarations, posted online for a wider audience to consult and review but without soliciting further signatures. The petitions are most commonly addressed to the nation's top leaders, though they may also be addressed to specific organizations or individuals for particular issues. Usually, the petitions address the most controversial issues of the moment. Table 1 presents a selection of some of the most popular online petitions in the past five years.

The first of these petitions to make a splash was one against bauxite mining in April 2009. This petition protested what had then become a widespread controversy on government plans for bauxite mining in the Central Highlands. The petition garnered so much attention mainly for the first 135 people that had signed it. It was the first time in the post-war era that such a well-known group of Vietnamese intellectuals from across the country and around the world had spoken out together against a major state policy.[9] The petition also collected online more than 2,700 supporters, which was also an unprecedented number in the post-war era. They cut across all categories of Vietnamese people and were spread out over an extensive geography. Critical comments on a controversial national-level issue, the leading role played by prominent intellectuals, and the widespread public response to the petition are key features that have since defined the online petition movement.

Since 2009, such high profile and controversial online petitions have emerged every year with increasing frequency and popularity. A year-and-a-half later, the group that had organized the bauxite petition posted another one online in reaction to a massive tailings spill at a bauxite processing plant in Ajka, Hungary. The second bauxite petition was significant because it connected two groups of prominent intellectuals, one that had emerged around bauxite and another group who identified themselves as former members of what had initially been touted as Vietnam's "first independent think-tank", but was then controversially disbanded — the Institute of Development Studies (IDS). This petition also collected more than 2,700 signatures. Among them was former Vice-President Nguyễn Thị Bình, who is nationally renowned for her role in negotiating the 1973 Paris Peace Accords.

Bold new strides were taken in 2011. In April, the bauxite group led another online petition to demand the release of lawyer Cù Huy Hà Vũ, who had been recently sentenced on charges of "spreading propaganda against the state". If the bauxite mining petitions had offered a degree of political cover by focusing on an "environmental" or "scientific" matter, the petition for Cù Huy Hà Vũ was explicitly political. While these petitioners were certainly not the first to speak out against human rights violations, the petition was significant because prominent intellectuals who had previously kept quiet on these divisive

TABLE 1
Selection of Online Petitions 2009–14

Full title	Year	Date	Initial Signatures (#)	Total Signatures (#)	Lead signature
Petition on the Master Plan and projects for bauxite mining in Vietnam	2009	9 April	135	2,746	Nguyễn Huệ Chi
Petition on bauxite mining in the Central Highlands, in light of the red mud spill disaster at the Ajka Timfoldgyar factory, Hungary	2010	9 October	12	2,765	Hoàng Tụy
Petition for the release of citizen Cù Huy Hà Vũ	2011	9 April	—	1,889	Nguyễn Huệ Chi
Petition to Ministry of Foreign Affairs to clarify its relations with China	2011	2 July	18	No longer available	Nguyễn Trọng Vĩnh
Petition for the protection and development of the country in the current situation	2011	10 July	20	1,219	Hồ Uy Liêm
Open Letter to the leaders of Vietnam on foreign threats and national strengths	2011	21 August	36	No longer available	Doãn Quốc Sỹ
Total reform to develop the country [note: overseas Vietnamese]	2011	8 September	14	14	Hồ Tú Bảo
Petition of the citizens [on case of Đoàn Văn Vươn]	2012	February	—	1,361	Lê Hiền Đức
Declaration on the forceful expropriation of land in Văn Giang [in Hưng Yên Province]	2012	1 May (International Labour Day)	—	3,350	Nguyễn Huệ Chi
Open letter [by the persons who signed the 7–11 and 9–11 petitions]	2012	6 August 2012	71	71	Nguyễn Quang A

Petition	Year	Date		Signatures	Representative/Leader
Declaration to oppose the Chinese authorities on printing an image of the "cow's tongue" [i.e., nine-dash line on South China Sea] in citizen passports	2012	25 November	—	359	Nguyễn Đình Đầu
Appeal to enforce human rights in accordance with the National Constitution of Vietnam	2012	25 December (Christmas Day)	82	347	Hoàng Tụy
Petition for revising the National Constitution of 1992 [Petition of 72]	2013	19 January	72	~15,000*	Nguyễn Quang A
Declaration to oppose Decree 72 of the Government	2013	29 August	108	545	Nguyễn Quang A
Letter to demand pursuit of legal action against China in international court	2014	15 May	—	3,711	Nguyễn Quang A and Lê Trung Tĩnh
Letter on the urgent situation of the country	2014	30 June	115	1,030	Phạm Xuân Yêm
Letter to the Central Committee and all Party members of the Socialist Republic of Vietnam	2014	28 July	61	61	Nguyễn Trọng Vĩnh
Declaration on the pro-democracy demonstrations in Hong Kong and Vietnam	2014	5 October	22	22	Bạch Đằng giang Foundation, Đại diện: Ths Phạm Bá Hải**
Demand for release of writer Nguyễn Quang Lập, also known as blogger Quê Choa	2014	10 December (International Human Rights Day)	35	1,548 (January 2015)	Nguyễn Ngọc

Notes: ** Signatures no longer available online. This figure is taken from Malesky (2013).
    ** This petition was led by organizations, each listed with a representative individual.

issues and now joined with other more dissident ones. Later in the summer several petitions emerged after incidents of harassment and intimidation of V ietnamese fishing and oil exploration vessels by Chinese military and non-military ones in the South China Sea. On 11 July, an online petition (dubbed as the 7–11 Petition) led by former director of the government's Vietnam Union for Science and Technology Associations (VUSTA), Hồ Uy Liêm, sounded an alarm about the current political crisis of the country and the inability of the current leadership to protect national sovereignty. This call for a critical re-assessment of Vietnam's current political situation was echoed by another online petition on 21 August by thirty-six overseas Vietnamese intellectuals and yet another on 8 September (dubbed as the 9–11 Petition) by fourteen others. Even though these latter two petitions were led by overseas Vietnamese, they were also signed by many persons in Vietnam.

These latter petitions reflected a growing uneasiness among Vietnamese about China's increasing assertiveness in the South China Sea. They also emerged during a time when mass demonstrations on the South China Sea were being regularly held every Sunday morning in the streets of Hà Nội and Hồ Chí Minh City. The online petitions both raised attention for mass demonstrations and, by their critical commentary, connected them with a stern critique of Vietnamese political leadership and organizations. In this way, they connected popular unrest with problems in the political system. Several leaders of the online petition movement joined the demonstrators in the streets and posted pictures of them together online, lending credibility and legitimacy to the demonstrations.

In 2012, online petitions emerged in response to yet another kind of conflict. One involved a farmer in Hải Phòng, Đoàn Văn Vươn, who hid out in a tree on his orchard to shoot at local police officers as they tried to evict him. The incident, which was widely reported in the domestic media, had elicited much public sympathy as reflective of growing problems of injustice in state land expropriation for private development. The other involved mass demonstrations by a few thousand farmers and residents against state expropriation of land in Văn Giang, Hưng Yên Province. The petition defended the rights of local people to demonstrate and protested the government's crackdown upon them. As with the South China Sea conflict, these petitions connected widespread grievances over land expropriation with critical discourses of the political system. They also promoted liberal constitutional rights by defending freedom of assembly, rule of law and rights to private property. They also brought more new kinds of people into the movement. Among the online signatures to the Văn Giang petition were also hundreds of farmers and residents from the Văn Giang area.

The bar was raised yet again in early 2013, when nearly 15,000 persons signed an online petition on constitutional reforms.[10] The Petition of 72, as it was dubbed after the seventy-two prominent intellectuals who initially signed it, made recommendations to the government's open consultations on constitutional revisions and provided its own draft text for the revised Constitution. The petition's recommendations boldly called for a "society based on democracy, equality and rule of law" (Para 11), protecting the "natural rights of humans" according to the criteria of the United Nations' Declaration on Human Rights (Para 18), limiting powers of the state to expropriate land (Para 24), and "protect[ing] in reality the independence of the judicial system" (Para 25). In addition, the petitioners argued that one of the basic objectives of the Constitution was to "limit abuse of power by the authorities" (Para 5) and not to spread propaganda for a particular organization (Para 7), without naming names of course. The draft text for the revised Constitution boldly omitted Article 4, which provides a constitutional basis for party dictatorship. It also proposed renaming the country from the Socialist Republic of Vietnam to the Democratic Republic of Vietnam (ironically, as North Vietnam was called prior to reunification).[11]

And then came 2014. The event that marked 2014 for Vietnam was when a Chinese oil rig moved inside Vietnam's Exclusive Economic Zone (EEZ) on the South China Sea to drill for hydrocarbons. The event led to mass demonstrations across the country, including a few that descended into violent riots, and much public debate.[12] Over the two-and-a-half months during which the Chinese rig was stationed inside Vietnam's EEZ, at least a dozen online petitions and collective statements were posted online. They condemned Chinese aggression, chastised the Vietnamese leadership for complacency and incompetence, and supported more public demonstrations while also admonishing against violence. The open letter of sixty-one Party members was a crescendo to this outpouring of public criticism, shortly after the China unilaterally withdrew its rig in mid-July. Building on the bold statements of the Petition of 72, the sixty-one Party members — twenty-five of whom had also signed the Petition of 72 — demanded an end to socialism in Vietnam and a definitive shift towards democracy. "Confronting the poor and dangerous situation of the country", they demanded all Party members to "voluntarily and proactively … leave off from the mistaken path of socialism for a definitive change to the path of the people and democracy, and most importantly change the political system from totalitarianism to democracy in a decisive but stable way" (Para 6). Although the precise nature of democracy was left vague, the petition made clear that it was something more than conventional "inner-part democracy".

Such explicit demands for democracy emerged again in October in an online declaration to support pro-democracy demonstrations in Hong Kong. While the statement's ostensible purpose was to commend and support Hong Kong protesters in their "opposition to the communist regime" of Beijing (Para 4), it also decried the current situation in Vietnam as "a thousand times more undemocratic and hostile to human rights than Hong Kong" (Para 8). It encouraged young people in Vietnam to take up the struggle for democracy by wishing them to gain a "deep awareness of democracy" (Para 8) and for parents, teachers and leaders to help "cultivate the democratic mindset in our young people" (Para 9). It also cited the general example of young people in Eastern Europe and, more recently, Northern Africa, the Middle East, Ukraine, Shinjang and Tibet as models for Vietnamese youth (Para 11) and called on the "youth of Hong Kong to be the hope of the world" (Para 13).

This petition was additionally significant because it was signed by organizations rather than individuals, though individual names representing these organizations were included alongside. It is significant because these organizations have defied government impositions on autonomy — a question that has plagued discussions on Vietnamese civil society for decades[13] — by declaring their existence online. While their activities are still restricted inside Vietnam, they have an online presence that sometimes translates into more tangible campaigns and activities.

Petitioning for Democracy

To understand how the online petition movement is contributing to the promotion of democracy in Vietnam, it is critical to understand how it specifically responds to the Vietnamese political context and its political history. As political scientist Dan Slater has argued, Vietnamese politics in the post-war era has been characterized by a "chronic absence of democratic mobilization".[14] However, the reasons for this lay deeply in Vietnam's revolutionary history and the eventual consolidation of state power by the Vietnamese Communists. Through decades of revolution and war, the VCP simultaneously eliminated potential hegemonizing forces — notably, religious groups and the imperial tradition — and established itself as the sole repository of nationalist authority. As Slater writes, nationalist authority "accrued from Ho Chi Minh to the post-colonial VCP, which was further reinforced through the Indochinese wars".[15] The result has been a symbolic advantage in relation to the VCP that has left democracy activists "chronically hamstrung".[16]

These dynamics are significant because, as Slater argues, of the three main political resources (namely, money, arms and symbolism), activists can usually only gain an advantage *vis-à-vis* the state in symbolic authority. Furthermore, his comparative study of seven Southeast Asian polities shows that the only types of symbolic authority that have led to significant democratic movements in Southeast Asia have been either religious or nationalist. In the Vietnamese case, religious authority was dissipated and dispersed through war and revolution, while the VCP maintains a monopoly on nationalist authority. The dynamics of this problem are evident whenever the VCP chooses to crack down on a high-profile dissident or groups of activists. These crackdowns are rarely carried out solely by state violence. Typically, they are accompanied by extensive propaganda campaigns in the state media. A common point of attack is to allege that dissidents or activists were being manipulated by external forces. Rekindling rhetoric from the revolutionary era, these campaigns portray activists as foreign collaborators and position them in diametric opposition to the VCP. In other words, the VCP leverages on its symbolic advantage to discredit and marginalize activists, as well as to justify harsh treatment against them.

For these reasons, it should be understood that the petitions are largely a symbolic intervention on political discourse and ideology. More than trying to influence state decision-making — which if used as a measure, the petitions have been abysmal failures — the primary significance of the petitions is to challenge mainstream thinking about the nation-state and both the people's relations to it. Their objectives are about raising awareness in the Vietnamese public and exposing abuses of state power, disregard for the common people, and the empty rhetoric of state socialism.

However, it is equally important to recognize that the petitions promote liberal democratic ideals through concrete contemporary problems with particular significance to Vietnamese political history, such as peasant rights to land, the leadership of the VCP, and struggles against foreign and especially Chinese domination. Their primary points of reference for liberal democratic ideals are not international agreements or even universal ideals, but rather culturally and historically embedded experience. The emphases the petitions have given to struggles with China in the South China Sea are especially significant because they directly challenge the nationalist authority of state leaders. They allege that state leaders are ineffective or, worse, compromised by their socialist ties with China. They flip the party-state's own rhetoric against pro-democracy activists on its head by promoting the nationalist credentials of the petitioners and generating scepticism over that of state leaders.

Who has been leading the petition is also significant. Slater argues that a key reason for the chronic absence of democratic mobilization in Vietnam has been the absence of autonomous communal elites. Communal elites are "society's primary possessors of nationalist and religious authority", which, in Vietnam, has been dominated by the Communist heroes and leaders of the anti-colonial revolution and Indochinese wars.[17] However, as Slater argues, "democratic uprisings are more likely both to emerge and succeed when communal elites ... assume an oppositional posture [to the ruling regime]."[18] Communal elites are "pivotal players" in determining the course of democratic mobilization in Southeast Asia. It can be argued that many of the persons leading the online petition movement have been these types of figures. They represent some of the VCP's brightest lights, notably in terms of their creative and intellectual contributions to science, the arts and scholarship. Many of them built their careers and reputations as Party members in service of the state. They are communal elites, who, through the petitions, have been taking increasingly oppositional stances towards the state. In Vietnamese, they are often referred to as "prominent intellectuals" (*nhan sy tri thuc*), which reflects both their intellectual achievements and revered social status. It also symbolically associates them with the fabled intellectuals who led the anti-colonial resistance movements and revolution.

Finally, the different types of people who have joined in the petitions have also been significant in a symbolic sense. As mentioned, the number of persons signing the petitions has been miniscule relative to the national population. However, they include farmers, workers, professionals, intellectuals, artists, journalists, dissidents, Buddhists, Catholics, state officials, military, NGO workers, students, and more. Furthermore, they come from every region of Vietnam and from both inside and outside the country. Their heterogeneity is especially significant in a state that has so effectively suppressed dissent by dividing and isolating forces of opposition.

In sum, the online petitions are an intervention in the Vietnamese political discourse and ideology that challenges the symbolic advantage of the VCP. And while the participants of the petitions do not yet constitute a significant portion of the domestic population, they represent an important slice of it.

Conclusion

The online petition movement that has emerged since the bauxite mining controversy in 2009 has been an important new development in Vietnam's domestic politics. The popularity of the petitions are reflective of the advance and widespread popularity of the Internet and social media in recent years. However, as this paper has argued, their relevance to domestic politics is in their particular use of the Internet to indirectly promote liberal democratic ideas in ways that respond directly to Vietnam's particular political context and history. They challenge the nationalist authority of the VCP, they give visibility to a growing force of increasingly autonomous communal elites, and they have been endorsed by a wide cross-section of Vietnamese society. Each of these developments has been important for challenging the symbolic advantage of the VCP that has for so long hamstrung pro-democracy activists in Vietnam.

While the petitions may help pro-democracy activists gain more symbolic advantage, it is certain that political leaders still maintain an enormous political advantage in terms of financial resources and brute force — two other key kinds of political resources. However, it should be noted that the petitions themselves are examples of non-violent forms of political struggle and they beckon state authorities to follow their lead. The online petition movement itself is mostly elite- and urban-based in its composition. While the petitioners may represent a vanguard group (that is, the ones taking personal and professional risks for the sake of the wider society), it remains to be seen how they might represent a more sizable proportion of the domestic population. While some will continue to believe that the online petition movement is currently too miniscule to be significant, its interventions in the political discourse and ideology may yet prove to have significant political effects over the longer term.

Notes

1. John Michael Roberts, *Digital Publics: Cultural Political Economy, Financialisation and Creative Organisational Politics* (Routledge: Taylor & Francis, 2014); Robert W. McChesney, *Digital Disconnect: How Capitalism is Turning the Internet Against Democracy* (New York: The New Press, 2013); John Bellamy Foster and Robert W. McChesney, "The Internet's Unholy Marriage to Capitalism", *Monthly Review* 62, no. 10 (2011): 3.

2. Evgeny Morozov, *The Net Delusion: The Dark Side of Internet Freedom* (New York: PublicAffairs, 2012); Shanthi Kalathil and Taylor C. Boas, *Open Networks, Closed Regimes: The Impact of the Internet on Authoritarian Rule* (Washington, D.C.: Carnegie Endowment for International Peace, 2010).

3. Björn Surborg, "Is It the 'Development of Underdevelopment' All Over Again? Internet Development in Vietnam", *Globalizations* 6, no. 2 (2009): 225–47, doi:10.1080/14747730902854182.

4. See <http://www.internetlivestats.com/internet-users/vietnam/>, and <http://wearesocial.net/tag/vietnam/>. Vietnam ranks 14th worldwide in total number of Internet users, though only 111th in terms of Internet penetration.

5. "Vietnam", available at <http://wearesocial.net/tag/vietnam/> (accessed 12 November 2014). Data collected by We Are Social show that some 95 per cent of the population aged between 15 and 24 have access to the Internet in Vietnam, while 73 per cent of Internet users are reported to be under 35 years old.

6. Surborg, "Is It the 'Development of Underdevelopment' All Over Again?", op. cit.

7. "Vietnam", op. cit.

8. Edmund Malesky, "Vietnam in 2013: Single-Party Politics in the Internet Age", *Asian Survey* 54, no. 1 (1 February 2014): 30–38, doi:10.1525/as.2014.54.1.30; Jonathan London, *Politics in Contemporary Vietnam: Party, State, and Authority Relations* (Palgrave Macmillan, 2014); Andrew Wells-Dang, "Political Space in Vietnam: A View from the 'Rice-Roots'", *The Pacific Review* 23, no. 1 (2010): 93–112, doi:10.1080/09512740903398355.

9. Jason Morris-Jung, "The Vietnamese Bauxite Mining Controversy: Towards a More Oppositional Politics", *Journal of Vietnamese Studies* 10, no. 1 (2015): 63–109; Hunter Marston, "Bauxite Mining in Vietnam's Central Highlands: An Arena for Expanding Civil Society?", *Contemporary Southeast Asia: A Journal of International and Strategic Affairs* 34, no. 2 (2012): 173–96; Carlyle A. Thayer, "Political Legitimacy of Vietnam's One Party-State: Challenges and Responses", *Journal of Current Southeast Asian Affairs* 28, no. 4 (14 January 2010): 47–70.

10. Malesky, "Vietnam in 2013", op. cit.

11. The Petition of 72 was also followed up with two other online statements signed by similar though shifting coalitions of individuals, as discussions over the constitutional revisions progressed over 2013. One opposed the constitutional draft approved by the National Assembly in June, while the other provided further recommendations on the Constitution and the Land Law — raising again issues of land loss and expropriation — one month later. Another petition emerged in August to protest new government regulations on Internet use and service providers in Decree 72 as further infringement on constitutionally protected rights of free speech.

12. Edmund Malesky and Jason Morris-Jung, "Vietnam in 2014: Opportunity and Uncertainty in the Wake of the Oil Rig Crisis", *Asian Survey* 55, no. 1 (2015): 165–73.

13. Russell Hiang-Khng Heng, "Civil Society Effectiveness and the Vietnamese State — despite or because of the Lack of Autonomy", in *Civil Society in Southeast Asia*, edited by Lee Hock Guan (Singapore: Institute of Southeast Asian Studies, 2004), pp. 144–66.

14. Dan Slater, "Revolutions, Crackdowns, and Quiescence: Communal Elites and Democratic Mobilization in Southeast Asia", *American Journal of Sociology* 115, no. 1 (1 July 2009): 203–54, doi:10.1086/597796.

15. Ibid., p. 236.

16. Ibid., p. 226.

17. Ibid., p. 206.

18. Ibid., p. 203.

C H I N A

INDIA

BANGLADESH
Dhaka ◙

Bay
of
Bengal

MYANMAR

Naypyitaw ◙

Yangon ●

Hanoi ◙

K
HO

L V
A I
O E
S T
N
A
M

Vientiane ◙

Gulf
of
Tongking

HAINAN

Paracel Islands

THAILAND

Bangkok ◙

CAMBODIA

Phnom Penh ◙

Ho Chi Minh City ●

South China
Sea

Spratly
Islands

Andaman
Islands

Andaman
Sea

Gulf
of
Siam

Nicobar
Islands

Penang

Aceh

Medan ●

Straits of Malacca

Kuala Lumpur ◙

BRUNEI
DARUSSALAM
Bandar Seri Begawan ◙

Kot
Kinab

SARAWAK

S U M A T R A

M A L A Y S I A

SINGAPORE ◙

Riau
Archipelago

Kuching ●

KALIMANTA

Mentawai Islands

INDIAN
OCEAN

I N D O N E S I

Jakarta ◙

J A V A

BA